LEECHES, LOVERS, BEARS, and CHOCOLATE PUDDING

True Tales of One Wacky Family

William Penick

Copyright © William Penick, 2024

Charcoal drawings copyright © 2024 by Lucia Penick

All rights reserved. No part of this book may be used or reproduced without the written consent of the copyright owner.

ISBN 9798869388797

TABLE OF CONTENTS

INTRODUCTION, CONFESSION, AND DEDICATION 1
CAST OF CHARACTERS 5
BEFORE JULIE (1940–1964) 7
   Early Years 7
   Middle Years 10
   Later Years 16
DOWN WITH THE SHIP, SAID HE—HELL NO, SAID SHE 27
BARBARIANS INSIDE THE GATE 33
   Week One 34
   Week Two 35
   Post-Mortem 39
"THE BEST OF ALL POSSIBLE HONEYMOONS"? NOT QUITE! 41
   I. Colorado 42
   II. Las Vegas 47
THE DINNER FROM HELL AND BILL'S SHORT CAREER
   (as told by Julie Penick) 51
THE PERKS OF PREGNANCY 57
   Free Beer 57
   Free A's 59
   Natural Rites 60
   International Sex Symbol 61
LEECHES, LOVERS, BEARS, AND CHOCOLATE PUDDING 69
ON THE ROAD WITH THREE LITTLE BACKSEAT
   ANGELS/BEASTS OF BEDLAM 77
PREDESTINATION AND INNER TUBES 87
OUR OFF-THE-WALL OFFSPRING 91
   The Cursed Waterbed 93
   Hands 95
   The 9-1-1 Filet 96
   Frogs 98
   Teenage Drivers 99
   Unexpurgated 103
   Mama 106
   What Goes Around 109

THE PARENTS-ARE-OUT-OF-TOWN PARTY 113
YOU BURIED YOUR MOTHER WHERE? (as told by Julie Penick)... 119
DON JUAN THE MARMOT 123
OUT AND ABOUT IN THE GREAT OUTDOORS 125
- *Backpacking 125*
- *Hiking 132*
- *Car-Camping 140*
- *Canoeing, Etc. 143*
- *Alpine Skiing 151*
- *Hunting And Fishing 160*
- *Running 165*
- *Piccadilly 169*
- *Baseball, Etc. 170*
- *Callaway Gardens 172*
- *Paragliding 173*
- *Dogsledding 174*
- *Hot-Air Ballooning 175*
- *Dauphin Island 175*
- *Ziplining 176*
- *Rock-Climbing 177*
- *And Lastly, Golf 177*

TEEP AND MR. TEEP 181
STRANGE BEASTLY ENCOUNTERS 189
- *The Master-Builder Mouse 190*
- *The Nearsighted Owl 191*
- *A Bathroom for Wimpy Bighorns 192*
- *Night Of The Bees 194*
- *Bingeing On Berries 195*
- *The Killer Kitten 197*
- *The View From "Charlie's Deck" 199*

IF ONLY HOUSES COULD TALK … 203
SO YOU THINK SHEEP ARE HARMLESS? THINK AGAIN 223
HUMMINGBIRDS AND THE GREAT BEYOND 227

JUST JULIE 235
The Decider.. 235
"Just Little White Lies" 236
Janet's Gang 240
The Comedienne... 243
Automotive Misadventures... 248
Sleepwalking And Celebrities 252
The Bravest Person I Know 254

THE MYSTERIOUS CHARM BRACELETS 261
A VIEW FROM THE PASTURE 281
Travels With Julie 282
Travels Without Julie 305

PREPARING FOR THE IDITAROD (IN MY DREAMS) 311
Lapland (Finland) 311
Northern Minnesota 313
Denali (Alaska) 314
Jackson Hole, Wyoming.. 318

THE COMPASSIONATE SEA LION 321
TRIALS AND TRIBULATIONS 325
ACKNOWLEDGEMENT 365

INTRODUCTION, CONFESSION, AND DEDICATION

Welcome to our madcap world of mayhem and mischief! We are a motley crew of two nominal adults and three nominal children, but deciding who is which may be tricky because our age and maturity are often out of sync.

This collection of stories is primarily about how the five of us fared against the ceaseless curveballs of Random Chance, Mother Nature, Human Nature, and all the other manifestations of Fickle Fate. On one level, it follows the main characters and many others through a wild assortment of adventures, misadventures, and very strange encounters, but on another level, it reveals a variety of human (and animal) minds and emotions at work in an unpredictable world endowed with a notoriously wicked sense of humor. Consequently, you the reader may get more out of the journey by imagining yourself as an actual participant in each unfolding event and gauging how you would have reacted to it. By doing that, we hope you will experience much of what we did in situations ranging from sublime to ridiculous, from tangible to otherworldly, from happy to sad.

It's well known that we often make our own "luck," good and bad, but it's also true that all of us are subject to mysterious factors that are totally beyond our control. You'll find a little of both in the stories that follow. Most of them describe events that actually happened, no matter how implausible some of them may sound. That said, I must confess that Julie and I fabricated a few minor details in the true stories to fill in memory gaps or make an event as real for you the reader as it was for us. For example:

1. When we were canoeing alone in the backwoods of Canada, our legs were not literally "covered in leeches" because there were still a few unoccupied areas of skin, but the phrase conveys our initial reaction to the situation (see "Canoeing" chapter of story entitled "Out and About in the Great Outdoors");

LEECHES, LOVERS, BEARS, AND CHOCOLATE PUDDING

2. The huge "man-eating dog" we encountered on our honeymoon camping trip in the Rockies had probably never eaten a human being, at least not a whole one, but he did look at Julie and me with carnivorous anticipation and was even more terrifying than his master who was still packing the .357 magnum pistol that had allegedly dispatched his wife the day before (all of which resulted in three utterly celibate nights alone on the top of a mountain with an armed killer and his homicidal dog, far different from the romantic interlude we had imagined for our honeymoon)(see "I. Colorado" chapter of story entitled "The Best of All Possible Honeymoons? Not Quite");

3. The "300-pound" snow-tuber who utterly flattened our eight-year-old daughter at a Colorado ski resort may not have weighed quite that much, but to little Ginger, he must have looked like King Kong on an inner tube (see story entitled "Predestination and Inner Tubes");

4. The big, wild bear that my petite, unarmed wife chased a long way into a dense forest after he ate her chocolate pudding may have weighed only 350 pounds instead of 400 as stated in the story (see story entitled "Leeches, Lovers, Bears, and Chocolate Pudding");

5. Will's overflowing waterbed that was on the verge of exploding did not literally fill his entire room, just 75% of it (see "The Cursed Waterbed" chapter of story entitled "Our Off the Wall Offspring"); and

6. We didn't hang around long enough to count the very big bighorn sheep (not the smaller mountain goats) that were crowded into an open hiker's bathroom high in the Rockies to get out of the apocalyptic-looking weather, so they may have numbered only 16 or 18 instead of 20 or so (see "A Bathroom for Wimpy Bighorns" chapter of story entitled "Strange Beastly Encounters").

However, since you may have some doubts about our sanity after reading the paragraph above, I must assure you that there is nothing so very different

INTRODUCTION, CONFESSION, AND DEDICATION

about our little clan, except perhaps for a willingness to take some chances and laugh at ourselves when they go awry, as they often did. Otherwise, we are a perfectly normal family, contrary to the outrageous diagnoses offered up by many of our dearest friends.

Julie, my beloved North Star and co-adventurer for 56 years, died on January 7, 2020, after a long battle with Alzheimer's. Since she inspired this book (and everyone around her) with her wit, grace, charm, wisdom, insight, empathy, courage, energy, compassion, simple complexity, selfless devotion, and total love, it is dedicated to her. And to our awesome children, Casey, Ginger, and Will, who arrived on magic carpets "trailing clouds of glory" and filled our world with beautiful balloons of every color before creating three wonderfully "crazy" families of their own—so the beat goes on.

CAST OF CHARACTERS

The Penicks:
    Bill (b. 8/40) – husband (since 7/64) and father of our brood
    Julie (1942-2020) – wife (since 7/64) and mother of our brood
    Casey (b. 11/65) – our first-born and mother of Emma and Ethan
    Ginger (b. 1/69) – our middle child and mother of Aubrey and Olivia
    Will (b. 2/71) – the "baby brother" and father of Lucia, Pilar, and Isabel
    Mama Dog (1970-1986) – our fourth (and best-behaved) "child"

    Bill and Julie's seven grandchildren:
      Emma and Ethan Hayes
      Aubrey and Olivia Inmon
      Lucia, Pilar, and Isabel Penick

    Nana (1906-1992) – Bill's mother
    Dad (1898-1963) – Bill's father
    Pops (1871-1952) – Bill's grandfather
    Betty (b. 1934) – Bill's sister
    Sue (1935-2023)) – Bill's sister

Affiliated Characters:
    Many friends
    A few adversaries
    Numerous wild animals, friendly and not
    Various guides, instructors, and pilots
    Guardian angels?

BEFORE JULIE (1940–1964)

As hard as it is for me to believe after living with Julie for over 55 glorious years, I did have a life before she entered it. And it was a good life—not as good as it was after she transformed it, but still good.

Early Years

As accidents of birth go, I was blessed. Mrs. Stork delivered me to a happy home filled with love, conversation, books, independence, and hospitality. The only problem for me as a kid was the presence of not one but two older sisters, which by definition is a terrifying challenge for any baby brother, like me and our son Will, but it did teach both of us important survival skills. (It also made me think I was being punished for sins in a previous life.) However, I must admit that Will and I were luckier than most other younger brothers because our big sisters did have some redeeming qualities that *almost* made up for the sibling abuse we suffered as subordinate beings. It's too bad that we weren't older instead of younger brothers—at least we would have been bigger, faster, and maybe smarter than our sisters instead of smaller, slower, and dumber.[*]

Fortunately, I had allies: six other little guys of the same age in the next block of Seventh Street. None of them had older sisters, but they were quick to recognize how Fate had dealt me such an unwinnable hand and therefore stood with me in this epic, existential power struggle against the hordes. And hordes there were, because my sisters' high school sorority (BAG, of all things) held its monthly meetings at our house in a room right beside the big side yard that was our playing field for football and baseball (and my parents' badminton parties), so we were constantly overrun by dozens of older (by five or six years) sisters, my worst nightmare. My brave little gang of allies tried our best to harass and drive them away, but they usually just ignored us, which made us even madder.

---

[*] Like Will, I love my sisters and always have, as they know, which is why I can have a little fun at their expense despite my status as their "little brother" in perpetuity.

LEECHES, LOVERS, BEARS, AND CHOCOLATE PUDDING

We did finally get their attention by lobbing water balloons at them from our roof, but instead of fighting back fairly, they (just like girls) ran to my parents, who banned water balloons and thereby gutted our magnificent Resistance movement. That drove us into short careers of petty crime: stealing our neighbors' magnolias by breaking them off with a long, notched pole and catching them carefully before they hit the ground. We then sold them to motorists on St. Charles Avenue and quickly squandered our ill-gotten gains on sodas and comic books at Moffatt's Pharmacy.

I also had a very special ally inside our house, Pops, my paternal grandfather and best friend for the first 11 years of my life before he died. He was the most patient man I've ever known. Every evening during the baseball season when the New Orleans Pelicans were playing, Pops and I listened to the game on the radio (this was the late 1940s, before anyone had a TV). While Pops sat calmly in his rocking chair, I bounced a tennis ball off the wall and shagged it with my trusty baseball glove, directly under my poor parents' bedroom upstairs. We also listened to football games and boxing matches, as well as *Amos 'n' Andy*, *The Shadow*, and *The Jack Benny Show* on Sunday afternoons. After an evening broadcast, Pops would often take me to the kitchen and fix me a snack of buttered bread and sugar that was very tasty. He also introduced me to alcohol. As a family, we'd sometimes dine at Arnaud's Restaurant in the French Quarter (and even had our own waiter, a pure Cajun with the unlikely name of Chester). Starting around age five, Pops would always give me a sip (or two?) of his wine. By the end of dinner, I was quite tipsy and deliriously happy. On the drive home, I'd watch the streetlights upside down while lying on the shelf behind the back seat and thought they were all moons, which my family found very amusing. It sounds a little like child abuse, but I loved our trips to Arnaud's. (To honor his memory, I took his nickname of "Pops" with our seven grandchildren and only hope I'm half the grandfather he was to me.)

When I was born in 1940, World War II was well underway in Europe. After the United States entered the war a year later and rationing was started, many household items were in short supply. That's the context of my very earliest memory. Somehow I knew my mother had a prized bottle of a favorite cosmetic that was getting low but unfortunately was no longer available to buy. As a helpful three or four-year-old who didn't want his mom to be sad, I decided

BEFORE JULIE

to surprise her by magically magnifying her meager supply of the precious stuff by mixing it with water and, presto, she had a full bottle again. Well, of course, she was surprised but not quite in the way I hoped, as I figured out later (or one of my sisters gleefully told me). Although my mother hid her loss very well, I was terribly embarrassed when I found out what I'd done, which undoubtedly is why it has stuck in my memory so long.

It was probably soon after that fiasco that I suffered my first injury, with lasting effects. While riding barefooted on the handlebars of my sister Betty's bike, I managed to insert my big toe into the spinning spokes of the front wheel. The ensuing cut was not a big deal but there was plenty of blood and I thought my toe was going to fall off. For a long time after that, I thought of bikes as child-eating beasts and never learned to ride one comfortably, even though I was fairly quick to learn other athletic skills.

Besides being quite an athlete herself, Betty maintained a menagerie of very odd animals while I was growing up. The two kinds that "impressed" me the most were the alligators and the skunks. When the 'gators got too big, they were simply deposited into the Audubon Park lagoon, thereby creating a public health hazard for small children who went there to feed the ducks and even for my future wife when she and her fellow members of Janet's Gang romped all over the park. Of the many skunks, one got loose and tried to climb up or down the inside of a three-story downspout but of course got stuck in the middle where no one could unstick him. As sad as it was, the doomed and angry skunk made sure he did not suffer alone.

It was tough enough living in a house with two older sisters, but then my parents sent me at the tender age of four to Miss Aiken's School, which was teeming with scary little girls. And there was a daily dancing class, of all the dumb things, so I had to actually dance with those fearsome creatures and even

LEECHES, LOVERS, BEARS, AND CHOCOLATE PUDDING

come in physical contact with them. That was much more terrifying than my bloody toe and it happened every day! Although the girls outnumbered us from day one, my male classmates gradually and mysteriously disappeared until there were only two of us left standing by the third grade. (My parents should be ashamed.) When recess rolled around, my 20 or so female classmates were instantly transformed into a bloodthirsty mob of whooping savages hell-bent on chasing the two of us to the ends of the earth, a ritual repeated every day. I now have a good idea of what Custer must have felt like at the Little Bighorn. Although I did learn some survival skills that were useful against my sisters, my four years at Miss Aiken's left me with deep-seated fears of "sweet little girls" until I got old enough to realize they did have some redeeming qualities and assets, but I'm still convinced that we men don't have a chance in the ongoing gender wars.

Middle Years

Miss Aiken herself was a dear person and fine educator, but it was a different world altogether when I entered a new school, Newman, in the fourth grade and found, to my great relief, an equal number of boys and girls—and instead of dance classes, normal things like baseball and football. Thanks to Pops, I had become a baseball addict by the time I was eight years old and my favorite team, the Cleveland Indians, won the 1948 World Series, which is also when I started hating their arch-rival, the New York Yankees. (I still hate the Yankees but now root for another arch-rival, the Boston Red Sox, who traded a young prospect named Babe Ruth to the Yankees and never won another World Series for 89 long years after that, until 2004 when they were two outs away from being swept by the Yankees in the playoffs but came back to win four straight games and eventually the title. My earlier love affair with the Cleveland Indians ended quite painfully in 1954 when they finally beat the Yankees for the American League pennant and then lost four straight games to Willie Mays' New York Giant underdogs in the World Series.)

So you can imagine how utterly disgusted I was when my father and our next-door neighbor, Dr. Max Lapham, proudly presented me with a baseball signed by the entire 1951 Yankee team, including legends like Joe DiMaggio,

BEFORE JULIE

Yogi Berra, and Phil Rizzuto. They had obtained the ball from the Yankees' third baseman, Bobby Brown, who was a student during the off-season at Tulane Medical School, where Dr. Lapham was the dean and my father was a visiting professor of surgery. Just a few days later, to show how much I "appreciated" the revolting ball, I almost shot Dr. Lapham with a pellet gun while trying to scare pigeons away from our front porch. Apparently the wayward pellet traveled through Dr. Lapham's open window, missed his head by inches, and broke his bathroom mirror while he was shaving. Despite the suspicious timing, it was an accident, I swear. After banishing the ball to the back of an unused drawer for years, I eventually came to actually appreciate the gift and later gave it to our son Will when he "came out" as another misguided Yankee fan, which I simply cannot explain, unless he was switched in the hospital at birth.

My own career playing the game I loved (and still do) was short and unremarkable—except for one glorious moment I've been re-living for 63 years now. Since Newman did not have a baseball team then, our intramural contests were the big attractions. On this one occasion, I was playing third base, the "hot corner," on our freshmen team against the mighty juniors. They had runners on second and third bases, with none out, when their clean-up batter came up and smashed a scorching line drive over third base that would have scored both runners but for my defensive gem. To the great surprise of everyone, including me, I made a leaping catch of the speeding sphere, stepped on third to put out the lead runner, and then tagged out the other runner who was almost to third when I caught the ball. It was a once-in-a-lifetime event that should have been permanently etched in the memories of all who saw it, especially my teammates. Alas, my fame was fleeting. Exactly none of my senile teammates, who I still see socially, claims to remember THE PLAY, so I'm now a baseball legend only in my own mind. (However, revenge was sweet. At the end of this story is a slightly embellished account of my brilliant feat that was included in our class' 55th reunion handbook of biographical sketches. Since I was the editor and therefore did not have to worry about rebuttals or fact-checkers, I took the opportunity to poke a little fun at my forgetful teammates, especially our pitcher, Billy Mimeles, who still talks to me sometimes but climbed a 14,000-foot mountain in Colorado with me a year after our reunion.)

LEECHES, LOVERS, BEARS, AND CHOCOLATE PUDDING

I also played on a Newman basketball team that was very good, no thanks to me—I was short, slow, and nearsighted, but at least I was the best player (of two) on the third string. (But if only Newman had had a ping-pong team, I would have been a star because I was unbeatable and even now, at age 76, can still lick all those whippersnappers in my family who think I'm over the hill.) My only significant contribution to the team was to provide a secure location for our annual post-season binge following three months of being "in training" (allegedly). Our hideout was my aunt and uncle's weekend home and farm on the Jordan River near Kiln, Mississippi. For some unknown reason, our little gang of 10 or 12 teenage boys had the complete run of the place for three days to "unwind" after every basketball season and we certainly made the most of it. There was of course lots of booze, which was readily available to underage teenagers all over uptown New Orleans. (Drugs, thank goodness, were not an option for us in the mid-1950s.) And cars, since the driving age was 15 back then. And boats to use on the river. And, best of all, we were all alone, without any adult supervision, which sounds like a recipe for disaster, but despite the swagger we were terribly harmless—except to the farm animals, abandoned cars, and a local lass named Gwendolyn.

Our first victims were the hapless chickens, but it quickly became apparent that they were all closet alcoholics. They loved beer as much as we did and greedily consumed all of it that we gave them. Drunk chickens are even funnier than drunk little boys. Watching them try to navigate the ramp up to the henhouse was hilarious. They all survived and always came back for more. Their cousins, the pigs, were far less sociable. All we did was to chase them around their pen in our underwear, usually after a rain when the pigsty was a real cesspool and we were feeling no pain. The object was to catch a pig, which we never did, despite our alleged athleticism. Domestic pigs are clearly faster and smarter than smashed juveniles and probably sober ones as well. Like "creatures from the black lagoon," we emerged from those encounters dripping with goo of the rankest kind from head to toe that required a strong hose or the river to clean off us. Our loving mothers would have been horrified to see us in that condition.

What happened to the abandoned car we found in the woods by Kiln is something else (like my triple play) that my fellow felons have conveniently forgotten all about, so I am confessing on their behalf too, for the sake of their

BEFORE JULIE

supposedly spiritual sides. Whose idea it was to torch that old, rusted-out car without any tires or windows, I cannot recall, although we all gleefully joined in on the fun. Since we were really not hard-core hooligans despite appearances, we did search the car for any sleeping occupants before setting it on fire, but perhaps we overlooked a victim or two because the next morning there were several locals standing around the smoking shell conducting what looked like a wake. Little boys should definitely not play with matches.And now for Gwendolyn. That legendary event was conceived, planned, and executed by one particular classmate who will go unnamed to protect his dubious innocence, so I will simply call him Mr. M. How he acquired the name and address of a girl in Bay St. Louis, Mississippi, we can only guess, but if he was willing to share such priceless information with his buddies who had zero prospects of their own, we were only too happy to accept. So the 10 or so of us actually bathed, put on relatively clean clothes, prayed that Gwendolyn had lots of sisters or friends, steeled our nerves with a couple of quick shots, and headed out with high hopes. To his credit, Mr. M. was the only one of us Don Juans who was brave enough to go to the front door, which unfortunately was opened by Gwendolyn's father instead of our intended prey. Here's the scene spread out before him: a half-drunk teenager on his porch, three others watering his bushes, and several more leering expectantly out of the car windows. And this is when Mr. M. uttered his classic "Can Gwendolyn come out and play?" Wisely, he didn't wait for the father's answer and somehow we made our escape without getting shot. Mr. M. today is widely admired for his athletic feats, his business success, his community service, and his friendly disposition, but it was that one simple question 60 years ago that made him a rock star and legend in his own time.[†]

Did our little gang of teenage reprobates behave any better back in New Orleans? I have to take the Fifth on that, except to say we did spend a lot of free time together and did have access to cars and alcohol, an ominous combination.

[†] Mr. M's long-suffering English teacher, Mrs. Grout, would have been appalled that he used "can" instead of "may" in his timeless question. She taught us (or at least some of us) that the word "can" in that context refers to *ability* and the word "may" refers to *permission*. Since the issue on that fateful evening involved permission and not Gwendolyn's ability to do whatever she did so well as to merit a prominent place in Mr. M's little black book, he clearly used the wrong word.

LEECHES, LOVERS, BEARS, AND CHOCOLATE PUDDING

Despite a legal drinking age of 21, we could get served in many uptown bars at 13 or 14 and had no trouble getting into French Quarter strip shows. (My particular favorite was Lily Christine, "The Cat Girl," who had incredible abs and contorted in amazing ways while climbing down a rope from the ceiling.) High school fraternities and sororities also enabled underage drinking in a big way by organizing frequent wild and wooly "open" parties with plenty of keg beer and other spirits. (There were no longer any high school fraternities or sororities when our three children became teenagers, but two of them followed an honored tradition by hosting an "open" party of their own in our house with 400 "guests" and lots of alcohol while their clueless parents were away, the infamous "Parents-Are-Out-Of-Town Party" that we've painfully described in another story of the same name. That said, I must confess that I prevailed upon my folks, when I had just joined a high school fraternity as a freshman, to allow one of those "open" parties in their large side yard, which quickly filled up with an unbelievable number of intoxicated teenagers, to the great distress of our neighbors and one of our garage walls.) Spring break was an annual orgy of boozing and carousing on the Gulf Coast from Mississippi to Florida, a mandatory rite of passage for any New Orleans teenager who wanted to protect his or her reputation (such as it was), including us.

Despite what you've just read, our Newman gang was relatively benign in the big picture. Our exploits clearly would not have qualified us for admission to the notorious (and all female) Janet's Gang in which my dear wife was a charter member. Even though we marauded and cavorted our way across two states, we never terrorized an entire neighborhood and golf course for years like Julie and her fellow banshees did. (More on Janet's Gang in the story entitled "Just Julie.") And compared to just what our own three somewhat-grown children have confessed to doing at the same age (without counting the other 90% we don't know about), our gang was truly angelic.

My recreational activities, fortunately, were not confined to chasing pigs, corrupting chickens, and ogling strippers. I developed a deep love of the Great Outdoors that has provided me and my family with pleasure galore over many years up to the present day, thanks in large part to a very close friend whose family had a weekend house on a wild river in the woods around Abita Springs, Louisiana. Wardy Moore and I spent many, many weekends and holidays fishing

BEFORE JULIE

the river and hunting the woods from an early age, often with his wonderful father, who taught us how to hunt and handle guns safely, how to fish with a fly-rod, how to call ducks and build a blind, how to pitch a tent, how to clean and dress a squirrel, and much more. For a young boy, it was heaven. At age 12 or so, we frequently hopped on the St. Charles Avenue streetcar to Canal Street and then the St. Claude Avenue bus all the way down to Poydras, the end of the line, to fish in an oxbow lake full of largemouth bass, which we'd haul home in an ice chest on the same bus and streetcar. When we were able to drive, Wardy and I scoured southeast Louisiana for hunting and fishing spots. We also drove every summer up to Grenada, Mississippi, and Jackson, Tennessee, where friends of my parents provided us with food and lodging as well as boats and motors to fish in the nearby lakes.[‡]

Although not outdoor enthusiasts themselves, my parents gave me opportunities to get a good outdoor education. My father took me with him on occasion to a private duck-hunting club on Pecan Island at the edge of the Gulf, with airboats, pirogues, Cajun guides, and lots of waterfowl. Various friends and I would usually hunt local wildlife with our .22 rifles in the evening while the adults played cards and drank toddies. Once, we brought back a possum and a raccoon that the Cajun chef cooked for us—the possum was awful but the raccoon tasted like slightly sweetened chicken and was quite good. I often prevailed upon my dad to take me out skeet-shooting on the Mississippi River levee, not only for the purpose of making myself a better hunter but because I was dating a lovely girl who happened to be the state skeet-shooting champion in her age group, and I badly wanted to impress her. My father and I also rode on a working towboat down the Mississippi from Chicago to New Orleans, a trip

---

[‡] Wardy's enduring impact on my life includes a genuinely happy 55-year-old marriage. Julie and I met in 1963 as a result of Wardy's wedding when I, as his best man, was asked to "please escort" one Julia Lake, a bridesmaid, to a prenuptial party.

LEECHES, LOVERS, BEARS, AND CHOCOLATE PUDDING

that was fascinating to a kid who loved American history and maps.[§] And last but not least, I spent two summers at Camp Mondamin in western North Carolina, where I learned the joys of canoeing, camping, and hiking in mountains.

(All of that wonderful exposure to the Great Outdoors from the Louisiana swamps to the Smoky Mountains as a young boy kindled a lifelong love affair with Mother Nature's domain, especially woods, rivers, and mountains. Julie quickly became as hooked on the outdoors as I was and together we spent much of our marriage canoeing, camping, hiking, fishing, and skiing, sometimes alone and sometimes with our three kids, who as adults have carried on the tradition. See separate story entitled "Out and About in the Great Outdoors.")

Later Years

As the surprised and undeserving winner of a citywide Spanish contest, I got to spend the summer after my Newman graduation in Mexico City attending classes at the local university (I would have preferred a check or car.) But it was an interesting summer in many ways. After living in the Garden District and going to private schools, I had no idea what poverty looked like, until I went to Mexico. On the long walk from my boarding house to the university, I passed blocks and blocks of families living in shanties constructed of random pieces of wood, tin, and cardboard, right in the middle of a rich and beautiful city. It was a shocking picture that no doubt played an important role in making me into the old-fashioned liberal I've been for most of my life.

Two other American summer students lived in the same boarding house I did. Although they were a bit older, we hung out together the whole summer. Betty was from Arkansas and Payton had just graduated from Yale, allegedly. I say that because Betty and I heard rumors that Payton was actually an undercover agent for the CIA, and he was in fact a little mysterious and looked the part of a

---

[§] By the time I was 10 years old, I was addicted to maps and knew every nook and cranny of the United States. Because of that, my parents let me be the sole navigator on a road trip to Boston two years later. Since this predated our interstate highway system, I had a pretty free hand in picking routes that took us right by every Civil War battlefield as well as some pretty seedy areas and cities (since that information is not shown on maps), but my parents bravely persevered.

BEFORE JULIE

le Carré character. He was also a lot of fun. Just ask the middle-aged but attractive woman in a large, chauffeur-driven Bentley who pulled up alongside the three of us and called Payton over to the car. After they chatted a few minutes, he jumped in the backseat with her and utterly disappeared for three days! After a sleep-deprived Payton reappeared, he described how his newfound friend had educated him in the pleasures, etc. of "amor" (sparing Betty some of the more titillating details he shared with me). Young and inexperienced as I was then, I was duly impressed and jealous as hell. Over the course of the summer, Payton disappeared several times into his mentor's den of iniquity and always returned with breathless descriptions of brand-new experiences, etc. Although I believed every word at the time, I wonder if his alleged trysts were a cover for undercover activities of another kind in his alleged role as a CIA agent. Whatever the truth, Payton and his stories were intriguing. The three of us dropped out of school with a week to go and went to Acapulco for a little surf and sand. Although I stayed in touch with Betty after the summer ended, I never heard from Payton again. Betty wrote me later that she understood Payton had died under suspicious circumstances at an early age, which is certainly believable for someone who lived on the edge like he did.

    My real-world education that started in Mexico continued that fall when I entered Williams College in Massachusetts. I wound up with two hard-core Yankee roommates from Long Island, so I naturally had to defend my proud Southern heritage, which I did by hanging a 6 x 4 foot Rebel flag on the wall in our dorm suite. They tolerated it for a while, but one day they showed up with several other Yankee rogues, unceremoniously yanked my flag off the wall, forcibly wrapped me up in it, and carried me horizontally around the freshmen quad while singing "Battle Hymn of the Republic." They all had so much fun that they repeated this outrage a couple of more times, but I and the flag survived and together we achieved a small victory the next year when I joined a fraternity like all my classmates. Mine was filled with Yankee upperclassmen, so another Southern pledge named Pete and I decided we needed to "show the flag" halfway through the initiation period. In the middle of one dark night, without getting caught by our sleeping brothers, we managed to hang my Rebel flag high over the fraternity house yard on a rope between a tree and the roof, for all to see the next morning. Pete and I were of course "punished" to the extent of having to

LEECHES, LOVERS, BEARS, AND CHOCOLATE PUDDING

sing at dinner much more than our fellow pledges, but that was well worth the fun of watching our frustrated brothers struggle to dismantle our masterpiece.

However, by that time, my own attitude towards the Confederate flag and what it stood for was beginning to change dramatically. Until I entered college, it never occurred to me that the flag was symbolic of something evil. There were no African Americans (or Negroes, the prevailing term in the 1950s) at Newman then. The only African Americans in my life growing up were servants in my parents' house. We of course discussed the Civil War in school and at home, but as I recall, there was little if any talk of slavery in the past or segregation in the present. And, although I don't recall my parents ever saying or doing anything unkind to an African American, they did conform silently to a system that classified African Americans as servants and second-class citizens. My favorite book as a small boy was *Little Black Sambo*, which was just one of several popular books in the South that so effectively perpetuated our flagrantly racial stereotyping of African American children. I of course did not realize that until much later because my parents never discussed it with me at the time. They missed another teaching opportunity when they let me fly a small Confederate flag on the car's antenna during our 1953 road trip to Boston, without ever explaining to me how offensive it might be to many people on the way. These are just a few examples to illustrate the fact that I, like most white Southern children in the 1950s, grew up in a moral vacuum that did not require me to think about the question of race or what it meant to the individual African Americans I saw every day. The Rebel flag to me was simply a symbol of the South's gallant struggle against a big, bad bully in the Civil War.

That all changed at Williams. I encountered African American students who were therefore my equals if not betters. I had to answer questions about segregation. My history professors described the horrors of slavery and racism. The civil rights movement was just getting under way. I heard Martin Luther King and Joan Baez speak and sing at Williams about Jim Crow. I finally realized that African- Americans were real people with feelings, issues, abilities, fears, hopes, and rights just like mine. I also came to understand how very convenient for some but terribly unjust for others was the systemic racism in the South and elsewhere. And I learned to view every human being as an individual instead of just one member of a particular group, which I now consider

BEFORE JULIE

fundamentally important in a world so anxious to label and define all of us according to our race, religion, ethnicity, gender, nationality, fraternity or sorority, political party, and other equally superficial criteria.**

In retrospect, that lesson changed my life more profoundly than the academic education I received at a very good college. Julie and I were in New York City with our friend Steve Chaplin when Congress passed the 1964 Civil Rights Act and we all celebrated the historic moment in style. From its inception in the summer of 1966, we worked as volunteers in the Trinity Educational Enrichment Program (TEEP) for low-income, inner-city children, black and white, between 9 and 11 years old. Three years later, Julie and I started taking the TEEP campers in small groups overnight to our weekend house in Covington, Louisiana, to expose them to the woods, rivers, and the outdoors in general, since many of them had never been outside the city or even their neighborhood. Casey was three years old, Ginger was a newborn, and Will was not yet born when we began hosting the TEEP weekends, so all three spent every summer of their childhood eating, swimming, playing, and laughing with African American children and ultimately befriending many of them. (Sadly, after four summers, we had to stop having the TEEP kids sleep overnight in Covington, a hotbed of KKK activity back then, because we started receiving some obvious warnings, like mysterious brush fires in the woods around our house, but we did continue to take them to weekend picnics at public and private campgrounds on the river over there for another 26 years. TEEP just celebrated its 50th anniversary and still includes the Saturday picnics in Covington.) With everything they learned at home, at school (now with African American classmates), and at TEEP outings, Casey, Ginger, and Will grew up to be completely color-blind. One of our very closest friends, Alvin Edinburgh, is an African American and a truly remarkable person who spent 39 years as a public school teacher here and 36 years up to the present time as the Director of TEEP.

** My friend Charles Dew, a revered history professor at Williams, has recently published a wonderfully honest and insightful book, *The Making of a Racist*, about his own personal transition (while a student at Williams in the 1950s) from an "unthinking" or "accidental" racist who grew up in the South (St. Petersburg, Florida) to an outspoken opponent of segregation as the direct successor to slavery. Unfortunately, despite all the legal and institutional progress, the same ongoing process of individual "osmosis" that shaped Charles and me into young racists so long ago is perhaps more subtle but just as sinister today as it was then.

LEECHES, LOVERS, BEARS, AND CHOCOLATE PUDDING

Without that racial education at Williams, I would have missed out on Alvin and TEEP and so many other joys in my life—and, worst of all, our three kids probably would have grown up to be "accidental" racists like me.

The summer after my freshman year furthered my education in a much different way. I spent close to three months as a guest in my dear friend Steve Chaplin's family home in Honolulu, where his father was editor of the morning newspaper. It was an exciting time to be in Hawaii, which was on the verge of becoming a state. The voyage over from Los Angeles was also quite exciting because there were over 100 coeds on board and only three other college-age guys besides Steve and me. If we'd had any sense, we would have hijacked the ship and sailed off to parts unknown. Our arrival in Honolulu was announced in the local newspaper by the headline "Bra Atop Liner's Mast Heralds Coed Invasion." To accommodate as many of these young ladies as possible, I bought the biggest car I could find, a used 1939 Chevrolet, for $75 at the beginning of the summer (and sold it for $50 at the end). Its brakes were a bit erratic but we

BEFORE JULIE

could squeeze upwards of 20 coeds in it, which made up for its other shortcomings. I also got a job making clay Tiki gods for the tourist trade. My boss was a shady character who guaranteed in writing on each figurine that it was "handmade by native labor"—well, I was the "native labor" who "handmade" hundreds of objects each day by popping them in and out of wet molds. When I finished work, I was so covered with dust from head to toe that Mrs. Chaplin usually hosed me off before letting me in the house. But those dousings were nothing compared to the near-death dunkings I suffered while trying to teach myself how to ride a surfboard at Waikiki Beach (and without glasses, so I was blind as a bat). Alas, after several heroic attempts to conquer the waves, I gave up the idea of becoming a surfboard champion like "Rabbit," the coeds' heartthrob and our nemesis. Despite that disappointment, it was a great summer with my dear friend Steve and his wonderful family.

I crossed the other ocean (to Europe) two summers later. There were eight of us altogether: five fraternity brothers from Williams, plus my New Orleans friend Wardy and someone else's brother. Wardy and I went over a couple of weeks before the others in order to see Denmark and Sweden. We spent a hopeful evening at the Tivoli Gardens in Copenhagen but struck out totally with the local girls (perhaps we needed the smooth "Mr. M" to hustle for us), although we did befriend a German medical student named Ulf (derived from "wolf"). Starting the next morning, Wardy as driver and I as passenger toured the Danish countryside on a rented motorcycle with rented fishing gear to see if we had better luck with local fish than local girls. Our luck didn't change, but we did make history of sorts in an out-of-the-way town called Nakskov, where we stayed two days in the local youth hostel. When word got out that we were there, we became instantly famous because Nakskov had not seen an American since the war 16 years earlier. We made the front page of the local paper, with picture, and were wined-and-dined in local homes like celebrities. One of our hosts, Jorgen Hansen, who had a wonderful family with beautiful towheaded children, kept up a correspondence

LEECHES, LOVERS, BEARS, AND CHOCOLATE PUDDING

with me until he died several years later. What I recall of our brief foray into Sweden by motorbike was the grand old sailing vessel that served as the Stockholm youth hostel.

After joining the others in Amsterdam, we drove all over Europe in two rented Citroens. The only time our group split up was when Wardy, I, and Brian King opted to meet Ulf in Berlin instead of driving down the Rhine Valley. Fortunately for us, the Berlin Wall went up (8/13/61) a few weeks after we got there, so the three of us were able to cross into East Berlin, then under Soviet control. What a contrast it was to the wonderful bustle and excitement of West Berlin! Most of the buildings along the main boulevard consisted of presentable facades that concealed dilapidated structures. And the streets were virtually empty, except for a relatively busy grocery store and small circus off the beaten path. Like a fantasy, we watched a so-called parade caravan with some general sitting in an open convertible waving to the adoring crowd—but there was no crowd: we three Americans were the only observers. It was really spooky. We were relieved when we crossed the checkpoint at the Brandenburg Gate back into West Berlin.

Given the choirboys traveling with me and the availability of cheap wine, I'm proud to admit I only got drunk twice in Europe—but my timing was awful. On the way into Italy, we stopped at the Brenner Pass and bought some rotgut chianti at a price that should have made us suspicious. Nevertheless, I curled up in the backseat with my bottle and finished it by the time we arrived in Venice, where I learned to my dismay that we had to park the cars outside the city and lug our heavy, wheel-less suitcases over a mile on foot to our pension (in my condition, it felt like 10 miles uphill). The same thing happened the night we entered Spain from the French Riviera. I was happily passed out in the backseat again when my buddies very roughly shook me awake and dragged me outside, where we were surrounded by Spanish gendarmes with machine guns and blinded by several large spotlights. Since I was the only one in the group who spoke any Spanish, my frantic friends shouted at me to talk us out of getting shot. Hell, I could barely stand up, much less think quickly in Spanish. It was a sobering scenario, but somehow we got across the border and had a wonderful time in Spain. A delightful old gentleman we met in a bar "adopted" us and took us all over Madrid to see hidden treasures, like El Greco ceilings and Goya

BEFORE JULIE

frescoes. We also ran into another fraternity brother in a crowded Madrid nightclub. But it was in the historic city of San Sebastian that we left our mark. When we were unable to find traditional lodging, someone had the bright (and appropriate) idea of spending the night in the local jail. Unfortunately, it was already filled up with other reprobates, but the helpful warden told us we could park overnight in the middle of a well-lit public square and spend the night in the cars safely, so that we did. After a few toddies to help us relax, we slept like logs—only to wake up the next morning encircled by hundreds of parked trucks and dozens of curious people looking through the car windows. It was market day at the public square and we were trapped there for the whole day until the market closed.

Unlike the recent stories about hazing deaths and barbaric rituals, fraternity life at Williams was relatively benign and positive. We were not rushed until our sophomore year and the system was set up so that everyone who wanted a bid got one. I joined a primarily northern fraternity called Psi Upsilon with a good diversity of members from jocks to Phi Beta Kappas, but it was our parties that set us apart. At one of the smaller gatherings on our rooftop deck, I saw the Northern Lights for the first and only time—or at least I think I did, although it could have been wishful thinking triggered by a healthy quantity of beer. We also had a good bowling team that competed in the North Adams leagues. I averaged around 165 and rarely topped 200, but there was the time I started one game with eight straight strikes (meaning I needed only four more strikes for a perfect 300 game). As a crowd gathered to watch history in the making, I became more nervous and drank more beer, so my last few rolls all went astray and I had to settle for a 260 or so.[††]

[††] Julie and I bowled a lot after we got married. It was a Penick tradition to go bowling whenever one of our children brought home a new boyfriend or girlfriend because it was so much more relaxing for everyone. We also bowled often with friends or just by ourselves. After I had one of those rare days and bowled two 200-games with an old alley ball, Julie insisted on buying it for me. She talked (and flirted) the manager into selling her the ball for $5, but before they could close the deal, the manager's wife walked in, took one look at my very pretty agent, and made her pay $25 for the ball. For Christmas that year, Julie got a brand new, psychedelic ball and bag. Both of our bowling balls survived Hurricane Katrina's flood waters, but not so the bags. Three years later, after we moved into the Lambeth House retirement facility, I started a bowling group of residents that lasted about three years.

LEECHES, LOVERS, BEARS, AND CHOCOLATE PUDDING

All of us lived on campus in dormitories as sophomores but then lived in our fraternity houses the last two years, which I thoroughly enjoyed. I had a good roommate named Chuck from Washington, D. C. for both years. We hitchhiked one spring break all the way from northwestern Massachusetts to his parents' home and back again. Hitchhiking was much safer back in 1960 than it is now (and Chuck was a big fellow), but we did meet some strange folks, including one guy with a very bloody face after an apparent fistfight. One of my law school roommates (who became a successful lawyer for 40 years and then a successful sculptor!) and I visited Psi U. during a winter break and had a ball sledding down the long hill outside the house, until I took the skin off both legs and wound up in the school infirmary. Williams banned all fraternities (and went coed) a few years after I graduated, but I still visit and/or correspond with a number of fraternity brothers on a regular basis.

My ulterior motive for including the following adventure is to brag one last time about my ping-pong prowess in order to make up for my admitted failings as a bike rider, surfer, and European Romeo. And to introduce my oldest friend, Charlie Genre. He and I were born two months apart (I'm the older and wiser) and lived two doors away from each other while growing up. Together we lobbed water balloons at my sisters, fought epic battles with vast armies of tin soldiers, stole magnolias, and did all the other stuff little boys do. But most important of all, Charlie and I played thousands of hours of ping-pong on the table in his basement, so he is probably the only person in the whole world who even has a remote chance of beating me at the great game. With that self-serving introduction, let me now turn to our last adventure together before we both entered into the sublime adventure of marriage. After graduating from college, Charlie and I drove up to Ely, Minnesota, near the Canadian border, rented a canoe, tent, and other camping gear, and headed out to the world-famous Boundary Waters of a thousand lakes. Charlie was the cook and I was the navigator, so we spent some of the time lost and/or hungry. He actually did a great job catching and cooking fish, but in the process, he developed a sheer hatred of beavers after they toyed with us fishermen many times by slapping their tails on the water and sounding like a big, hungry fish jumping. (The reader may recall that Julie and I also had some issues with beavers when we canoed the same Boundary Waters a few years later. See story entitled "Leeches, Lovers,

BEFORE JULIE

Bears, and Chocolate Pudding.") Despite a few mishaps, it was a most enjoyable outing.

And then I met Julie in the summer of 1963 at my friend Wardy's wedding and that marked the end of my long adolescence. But I had one more year of bachelorhood before we tied the knot in 1964. I spent that year at the University of Virginia Law School with three classmates in a wonderful rented house on the outskirts of Charlottesville with its own river and valley, gorgeous mountain views, and enough acreage for skeet-shooting. With all of that and a large outdoor patio to boot, our house was the perfect party site, so we four housemates had to give up all plans to study on the weekends, unless it snowed. And the addition of a cute beagle puppy named Mandy Rice-Davies (for the British party girl involved in the Profumo Affair of 1963) was icing on the cake. The setting even inspired me to wax poetic sometimes in my correspondence with Julie, but her poetic efforts were always so much better than mine. It was also during that year that Julie advanced our courtship considerably by convincing me she was the heiress to a sizeable fortune, which turned out to be a slight exaggeration. And which is why we wound up spending our first year of marriage in a lousy basement apartment that was overpriced at $60 per month. For some odd reason, the surface of the yard lined up with the midway point of our few windows, so we could not open them but we did have a spectacular view through the glass panes of ant tracks in the dirt outside. It figured, because our landlords were very strange, as well as nosy, loud, and cheap. We had very little privacy and even less peace and quiet. So I hope you will forgive me if I did, every now and then, think longingly of my previous abode in the Virginia hills.

It's always difficult to give up the freedom and excitement of adolescence but we all have to do it sooner or later (although some of us never succeed). Thanks primarily to Julie, my transition was relatively painless and complete. There are some things that I would change about my life Before Julie, but overall, it was a productive and happy period that helped me raise our own children in a much more complex world and provided me with memories I will always cherish.

LEECHES, LOVERS, BEARS, AND CHOCOLATE PUDDING

ADDENDUM (from Newman Class of 1958 55th Reunion Handbook):

My one Willie Mays moment occurred in a game between our freshman team and the powerful junior team. We were loaded with talent—except for our pitching. Out of misguided sympathy, I was not going to identify our team's weak link as Mr. Mimeles until he attacked my covert golfing skills out of sheer jealousy. Since a walk is always better than a hit, his *best* pitch was a roller that was unhittable. When he did manage to get an airborne pitch anywhere near the plate, the batters hit towering drives to the outfield. As a consequence, there was nothing for us infielders to do. Mr. Johnson at first base had only one put-out the whole game and Mr. Levy, our shortstop, finished his English homework in the field. Our overworked outfielders were so exhausted they had to be relieved by Misses Kennedy, Williams, and Watsky, who did a wonderful job under very trying circumstances.

It was in the third inning that I became a baseball legend, at least in my own mind. Although Mr. Mimeles' pitching was not quite as terrible as usual, we were already losing 18 to 3 when the juniors came to bat again. After feasting on two meatballs from our ever-generous pitcher, they had runners on second and third base with no outs and their clean-up hitter at the plate. Mr. Levy was absorbed in his copy of "Ode on a Grecian Urn," so I had a lot of ground to cover at third base. When Mr. Mimeles' first pitch, his alleged "fastball," finally floated up to the plate at .001 mph, the batter teed off and hit a screaming line drive over third base. With impeccable timing, I dove and somehow speared the speeding sphere, stepped on third to put out that runner, and then tagged out the other, still-incredulous runner from second before he could stop himself.

Thanks to my triple play, it was the only scoreless inning Mr. Mimeles ever pitched in his forgettable career. My defensive gem ignited our offense but we still lost the game 46 to 35. Mr. Mimeles did not register a single strike in the whole game and went 0 for 9 at the plate, but he did manage to lower his E.R.A. (earned run average) as a pitcher to 53 runs a game. By popular demand, he was eventually replaced by Miss Kennedy and our team fortunes improved dramatically. Mr. Levy turned out to be a stellar shortstop but unfortunately his English grade suffered a bit.

DOWN WITH THE SHIP, SAID HE—HELL NO, SAID SHE

As the title suggests, we have spent the last 45 years arguing about what really happened on that fateful day in December of 1963. As a result, neither of us would trust the other to write the story accurately and impartially, so we are presenting it here in two separate voices. But, in order to warn you about our respective spouse's delusions, each of us publicly declares that he or she totally and irrevocably disavows the other's version insofar as it claims to be even slightly truthful and impartial. However, despite the other's shameful attempts to subvert the Truth, the Real Truth of this matter will be obvious to the discerning reader. With that caveat, let us begin.

HE: Dear Reader, this is a true tale of epic heroism (mine) and utter selfishness (hers) in the face of extreme danger created entirely by her. With sincerest modesty, I will describe how I almost sacrificed my life at the altar of love by going down with the ship.

SHE: Dearest Reader, that's baloney. This is a true tale of epic heroism (mine) and utter stupidity (his) in the face of extreme danger created entirely by him (who is my husband today but may not be tomorrow). With genuine modesty, unlike his, I will describe how I lived to love another day by saving myself from the sinking ship and going for help that averted a disaster.

HE: Being December, the duck-hunting season in Louisiana was open. In the course of our six-month-long courtship, Julie had told me that she had been duck-hunting for years (one of several exaggerations I fell for), so I foolishly invited her to go hunting with a good friend of mine and a good friend of hers who were recently married.

SHE: I have never "exaggerated" anything in my whole life. I had never fired a gun before, so I have no idea why Bill thought I was an experienced hunter. I foolishly accepted his invitation to go duck-hunting because I kind of liked him

LEECHES, LOVERS, BEARS, AND CHOCOLATE PUDDING

and thought he had some common sense. And I assumed it would be a pleasant enough outing because my friend Carol was also going. How was I to know that we had to wake up in the middle of the night, wear heavy hip boots that made me look like a pear, go out into cold and wet weather, ride a tipsy little boat through an alligator and moccasin-infested swamp in the dark, walk through soft, glue-like mud and razor-sharp reeds, and then stand very still for hours in freezing-cold water in a cramped, smelly duck blind while millions of mosquitoes attacked me? Duck hunters are nuts!

HE: By the time we got to the duck blind, I had a strong suspicion that Julie was anything but the great hunter she claimed to be. That suspicion became a certainty as soon as I handed her a loaded shotgun and she started brandishing it like a toy water gun. Her first shot at a passing duck (who by then was in the next parish) knocked her off her feet into the water and allegedly "broke" her shoulder. She spent the rest of the morning swatting wildly at mosquitoes and cursing like a sailor, neither of which attracted any wild ducks into our decoys. However, despite the absence of ducks, the rest of us were duly thankful when Julie surrendered her weapon in order to swat mosquitoes with both hands. Everyone was relieved for different reasons when we got back in the boat and started for home, not knowing the real fun was just beginning.

SHE: I have never in my life uttered a single curse word because I'm a lady. That three hours in the duck blind was pure agony. My shoulder was throbbing, my only good ear was still ringing from that one shot, my bottom was wet, my makeup was running, my whole body was freezing, every square centimeter of my face and neck was itching like crazy, and I couldn't go to the bathroom. Duck hunters should be locked up! And I don't even like to eat duck. I don't know what possessed me to accept Bill's ding-bat invitation, so I was very ready to go home when the others finally called it quits. How could things get any worse than they were?

HE: 98% of the boat ride home was uneventful and even a little bit romantic. While our friends operated the outboard motor, Julie and I sat together in the

DOWN WITH THE SHIP

front of the boat holding hands, at least when she wasn't scratching her swollen face or swatting mosquitoes.

SHE: I frankly didn't want anything to do with him at that point, but I allowed him to sit close to me and hold my hand only to get a little warmer.

HE: As we approached the dock, my friend in the back cut off the motor so we could coast in the rest of the way. Unfortunately, when he did that, water started coming in over the bow of the boat, probably because Julie and I shouldn't have been sitting so far forward. Sinking in 10 feet of freezing cold water with our hip boots still on was not a happy prospect, but there was still a good chance of reaching the dock in time to save the boat and ourselves. Julie, however, did not view this as an "all for one, one for all" situation like the rest of us. Accordingly, while I was still seated looking the other way, she stepped on my shoulder, planted a hand on the top of my head, pushed off with all of her might, and launched herself toward the dock. She made it, to my momentary regret. I'm still in awe of the fact that my true love used me as a springboard to her own personal safety without regard to the consequences. Of course, when Julie pushed down on my head and shoulder, she sealed the fate of her three mates in the boat, which immediately sank to the bottom like a lead weight.

SHE: It was not nearly as black-and-white as he makes it sound. At that decisive moment, I realized I had nothing at all invested in Bill. We had gone out a few times and he was kind of cute, but he was also the nutcase who had dragged me out into that God-forsaken swamp with all of its moccasins, alligators, and man-eating mosquitoes, so give me a break. I decided on the spot I didn't even like him anymore. And I was far too young to die, especially in dirty, freezing water wearing all those ugly clothes and boots. My only real concern was my good friend Carol, but I knew she was a strong swimmer and would probably survive even if the guys didn't. So the sensible choice for me was quite obvious. And please don't forget that the execution of my plan was flawless, thanks to some quick thinking and nimble action, even if I say so myself.

LEECHES, LOVERS, BEARS, AND CHOCOLATE PUDDING

HE: The three of us who went down with the boat somehow managed to get out of our hip boots and swim to the surface. The first thing we saw was Julie sitting high and dry on the edge of the dock, swinging her legs like a schoolgirl and asking if there was anything she could do to help. "You've already done enough" was the simultaneous response from all three of us still in the water. We dove back down for the guns but had to pull up the boat and motor with a farmer's truck and chain. We all caught bad colds, except for Julie of course. Luckily enough, I left town for school two days later and didn't have to deal with her for awhile. On that last day, I must confess that I was somewhat pleased to see that her face was still quite red and swollen.

SHE: In the end, I was very glad that my friends and future husband did not drown (they had the keys to our only car), but that bit about sitting on the dock while they did all the work is just too much. I was the one who ran for help and found the farmer. They probably wouldn't have made it without my quick action.

HE: Baloney.

EPILOGUE

HE: Believe it or not, Julie and I were married seven months later, which was another heroic act, given the history above. We never again hunted together but we did discover another form of boating that worked much better for us—whitewater canoeing. We enjoyed canoeing in Arkansas, Georgia (including the Chattooga River of *Deliverance* fame), North Carolina, Canada (see separate story about how Julie dealt with bears and leeches), Mississippi, and Louisiana, generally with a Sierra Club group from New Orleans. In all the time we spent together in a canoe, Julie managed not to sink a single boat by herself, although together we put several large dents in our aluminum canoe, flipped it over a few times, and once, on a rain-swollen river in the Ozarks, wrapped it around a tree into a perfect right angle. However, for the sake of completeness, I must tell you that Julie symbolically "abandoned ship" in a moment of crisis on one other occasion: It was on the Chattooga and we had to run a nasty little shoot of water that was steep, narrow, crooked, and fast. Halfway down was a sharp turn to the

DOWN WITH THE SHIP

left, so I was counting on a good draw-stroke from Julie in the bow at that point. Well, things didn't quite go as planned. As the bow of the canoe was just about to enter the shoot and Julie saw how steep a drop it was, she flung her paddle away, gripped the sides of the canoe with both hands, closed her eyes, and bent over double. It wasn't pretty but we somehow made it through without mishap except for a badly dented canoe.

SHE: He would have to end the story on that negative note. Just like a lawyer to insist on having the last word.

HE: I will admit, however, that if I had been in the bow of that canoe where Julie was, I may have done exactly what she did. And, to her credit, she stayed in the boat this time.

SHE: See what I mean.

THE END!!!

HE: Wait ….

BARBARIANS INSIDE THE GATE

The house-sitters from hell. That's us. Julie and me, albeit with some unwanted help from family and friends. In two weeks' time, we created enough havoc in the Garden District of New Orleans to leave our fair city looking like Atlanta after Sherman's little visit. You think I may be overstating the case against us? Well, read on and decide for yourself.

After tying the knot on July 9, 1964, Julie and I had about two weeks to kill before embarking on our belated honeymoon to Colorado and Las Vegas. As it turned out, those two weeks in New Orleans were just a dress rehearsal for what followed out West. I suspect that the Garden District gods, who witnessed our reign of terror, tipped off their Western colleagues, who were ready and waiting for us with quivers full of "slings and arrows." They could spot us miles away because we looked so guilty because we were so guilty, even my innocent, angelic wife. Our 15-year-old VW Bug whisked us away from the scenes of our crimes as fast as it would go, which was not very fast, to the safety of Colorado, which was not very safe as we soon learned. (See separate story entitled "'The Best of All Possible Honeymoons'? Not quite!")

It feels good to confess at long last, now that the statutes of limitation for vandalism, mayhem, assault, disorderly conduct, disturbing the peace, indecent exposure, harassment, conspiracy, public intoxication, trespassing, larceny, bribery, obscenity, fraud, and open container law have expired. Yep, we packed a lot of criminal activity into a short two weeks. Nothing like starting off a marriage with a little crime wave.

So here are the gory details: Julie and I had no place to live for the first two weeks of our plighted life together, other than my mother's house or her mother's house, which seemed a bit indelicate at best, so my cousin Susan and our friend Knox very generously offered us their beautiful Garden District houses for a week each while they would be out of town and didn't even require us to post a damage bond. Big mistake! To their later regret, we accepted.

LEECHES, LOVERS, BEARS, AND CHOCOLATE PUDDING

Week One

Susan's house came first, lucky for her, because Julie and I didn't hit our stride as a human wrecking crew until the second week. The house survived us quite well, except for a little old glass candlestick that happened to be in the wrong place at the wrong time. No, I didn't batter Julie with it and she didn't hurl it at me. Just the opposite. It was the victim of our enduring love for each other.

We decided to celebrate our one-week anniversary with a sumptuous supper in Susan's elegant dining room. Julie cooked a wonderful dinner and I invested $5 of my meager income in two bottles of Gallo wine. After lighting the candles and turning the lights off, we ate dinner while gazing tenderly into each other's eyes and downing both bottles of wine, at which point it was difficult for me to find Julie, much less her lovely eyes.

We somehow managed to get our dirty dishes into the kitchen sink without dropping any, as best I remember. I assume we were sober enough to blow out the candles, but if so, we did a bad job of it. Then we stumbled towards the bedroom. To her credit, Julie made it (I think) but I didn't. Crawling on all-fours, I made it only as far as one of those old-time floor furnaces, so I spent the night sleeping on a hard metal grill. You would think my loving wife would have figured out that something was wrong when I didn't show up in bed and then come to my rescue, but no such luck. It's likely she did figure out I was in trouble but then decided it was "every man for himself" and went back to sleep. As a result, I slept the whole night on my iron pillow and woke up with an awesome plaid pattern etched on my face, in addition to dislocated bones up and down my body. Lucky for me, it was summer and the floor furnace was off.

We eventually revived enough to notice that one of our dinner candles had burned all the way down and badly cracked the candlestick. It could have been a lot worse, like burning the whole house down and us with it, since our wine-laden bodies would probably have slept through the whole thing. So we thanked our guardian angels (who then took a break just when we needed them). As for the damaged piece, glass candlesticks are a dime a dozen. We'd just replace it or the set with a new one. Good plan, right?

Since Susan had been so nice to us, we didn't want to scrimp and were prepared to pay as much as $50 for a new candlestick or $100 for a set if necessary. And only the best for Susan, so we went for the top of the line at Adler's. I had no credit cards back in 1964 but I had a pocket full of cash ($100) that was more than enough to cover a silly old glass candlestick. I mean, glass is glass. Well, Adler's had a single candlestick that matched the broken one perfectly. How lucky could we get! Looked to me like it might run around $29.95. Even when the salesman said something about "Steuben," I didn't get it and asked him how much it was as I confidently reached for my bundle of cash. That was a big mistake. I thought I heard him say $1,929.95 (at least I got the $29.95 part right). That much for a lousy piece of glass! No way. That was a fortune to me. I was making a measly $200 a month as a summer law clerk. If Julie and I spent none of that on food or gas, we could buy the stupid candlestick in just 10 months and have change left over. On the way home with such good news, I was sorely tempted to invest all of my $100 in more Gallo wine and, with my trusty partner by my side, just sleep through this nightmare, but my "better angels" prevailed, for once. When I recovered from the shock, it dawned on me that we had a new liability policy, which turned out to cover the entire $1,929.95 replacement cost. That, however, marked the end of our good fortune and the beginning of our real criminal careers. Susan got off easy in comparison to what we did the next week to Knox' house.

Week Two

Knox lived just down the street from my childhood home. She had a large backyard with a swimming pool and a long-time housekeeper who came during our stay. Unfortunately, the pool and the housekeeper played leading roles in the coming drama. You will also meet a supporting cast of family and friends who contributed significantly to the destruction of Knox' delightful home, although I must admit that Julie and I were the reluctant stars of the show.

Our first cohort-in-crime was a cute little beagle named Mandy Rice-Davies, after the nubile lass who (with Christine Keeler) brought down the entire British government by playing water polo in the nude with John Profumo, a high-ranking official, which all happened during my second year of law school at the University of Virginia in Charlottesville. My three housemates and I followed the titillating scandal with bated breath, so when we added a beagle puppy to our motley group, we decided to honor Mandy Rice-Davies for her heroic work by naming our new roomie after her. Mandy the beagle wound up in New Orleans that fateful summer because I volunteered to take her home.

But poor Mandy's odyssey was just beginning. About two weeks before our wedding in July, Julie and I were taking her younger brother Bau to practice shooting his new .22 rifle when we were rear-ended at a red light by a pickup truck going at a high rate of speed. The two of us in the front seat escaped with minor injuries, but Bau and Mandy were not so lucky. Bau may well have bled to death from a very deep gash in his head if a passerby, who happened to be a nurse, had not jumped in the back seat and somehow stopped the bleeding. She then disappeared without a trace. We called the local hospitals, put notices in the local newspapers, and tried other ways to find her in order to thank her properly (and at least replace her bloody dress), but we did not succeed. Perhaps she was a real angel.

Mandy too disappeared in all the confusion, but our newspaper notices worked this time and we got her back about the time we were moving into Knox' house. Since it was unfamiliar to Mandy, we decided to make her a comfortable bed in the kitchen with plenty of newspaper on the floor. That turned out to be the first of our many mistakes that week. Mandy had slept in my bed for most of that year in Charlottesville and all of that month in New Orleans before the accident, so she didn't like the idea of sleeping alone and furiously went to work on the ancient kitchen door to get to me. She must have gone at it with tooth and claw all night, because one of the corners was almost sheared off by the next morning. After dealing with Susan's candlestick, I knew exactly what to do: call our friendly liability insurer to pay for a near-perfect matching door that we found after a frantic search. With so much to talk about, we were definitely bonding with our insurance agent, who probably considered getting an unlisted phone number. And my sainted mother agreed to keep Mandy, so things were working out okay. Julie and I were keeping our heads above water, for the time being.

That brief moment of blessed peace lasted about half a day. Oh, the gods must have been rubbing their fat little hands with glee. They were about to stir the pot in the most mischievous way by introducing one Sally P. from Shreveport into our little production. A friend of Julie's older brother, Sally was feared by most everyone in New Orleans, for good reason. Just how she acquired a key to Knox' house is still a mystery, since Julie denied ever giving one to her or anyone. In any event, neither Julie nor I knew that Sally had a key or was going to pay us an unannounced visit in the middle of the night.

It must have been about 3:00 AM when Julie and I heard someone opening the front door and moving around downstairs in the dark. I told Julie to stay in the bedroom and grabbed my only weapon, a tear-gas gun. Dressed only in my Jockey underwear and scared to death, I crept down the unlit stairway to confront the intruder. Halfway down, I detected a movement right in front of me and shot it with my trusty weapon, whereupon the still-unseen intruder screamed bloody murder. Julie must have turned on a light, because I remember standing there in my skivvies in front of Sally, who unfortunately had survived the attack. But the house of course reeked of tear gas. I didn't even bother calling our liability insurer for the third time in five days! We opened every possible window and used a case of air fresheners, which worked fairly well.

She'd done plenty enough for one night, but Sally wasn't through with us quite yet. After Knox' housekeeper arrived the next morning and Sally was still sleeping off her tear-gas hangover, Julie and I left for work with high hopes it would be a better day. Little did we know that the gods had other ideas and had the perfect agent of mayhem (Sally) in a perfect position to carry out their diabolical plot. Which is exactly what happened.

Sally cheerfully told us the bad-news-of-the-day when we got home that afternoon. After waking up and realizing there was someone to do her bidding, she laid out 12 pairs of leather shoes and ordered the "maid" (Knox' housekeeper) to polish them. Not surprisingly, the housekeeper refused, whereupon Sally "fired" her and kicked her out of the house. With Sally, Julie and I were prepared for just about anything except losing Knox' beloved housekeeper and friend of 30 years! Once we had threatened Sally with a slow death-by-dishwasher if she didn't pack her bags and leave the house immediately and permanently, Julie and I jumped in the car and headed to an address somewhere in Central City, since the housekeeper didn't have a phone. We found it at last, but had to beg her to return and promise her that Sally would be long gone. So we dodged another bullet—until the next one, which arrived just three days later.

LEECHES, LOVERS, BEARS, AND CHOCOLATE PUDDING

Julie and I have only ourselves to blame for the next disaster, but we did get a lot of unwanted help from a few dozen freeloading friends of ours. To celebrate almost two whole days without an incident, we decided to throw a weekend pool party in Knox' ample backyard. The weather was perfect and lots of guests showed up. It had all the makings of a great party, until we realized we'd made two little mistakes: I had ordered far too much beer. And Julie had made hundreds of cute little finger sandwiches out of parsley, which is inedible, instead of watercress. But, hey, no big deal. No one would know the difference if we waited long enough to serve the sandwiches until everyone was full of beer. Wrong! When we did finally bring out the sandwiches, everyone was very drunk and very hungry. I have obviously repressed any memory of the next few horrifying minutes because the next thing I do remember is seeing all the half-eaten and uneaten sandwiches floating in the pool and being sucked into the drains, which soon became completely clogged up with parsley sandwiches (could be a good diarrhea remedy) and the pool started overflowing. By the time we figured out how to turn off the pool pump, most of Knox' yard and gardens had disappeared under a lake of water that was also running down her driveway into the street. Our less-than-helpful guests thought it was great fun to splash around like kids and drink our free beer at the same time.

That night, while lying in bed cold sober, I wondered if we had enough liability insurance left, after the candlestick and door, to pay for a new yard and swimming pool. If not, our alternative plan was to flee immediately to Mexico. One of the rare partygoers with a guilty conscience saved the day by hooking us up with someone who came the next day and fixed the pool. Knox' flowers looked a bit waterlogged that morning but perked up after a day of sunshine. So Julie and I were starting to breathe easier and pack for our trip out West the next day when the phone rang. It was not the police, much to our relief, but an old college fraternity brother of mine who was in town and wanted to do the French Quarter. We were lucky to get home at 3:00 AM, four hours before our planned departure for Colorado.

We were deliriously happy to leave New Orleans, the scene of our crime wave. But three weeks later, after a honeymoon from hell out West, we were even happier to return to New Orleans, where we confessed our sins to a most gracious and forgiving Knox and prepared our next journey to Charlottesville for my last year of law school. Julie of course had serious misgivings about spending another year with me after the last five catastrophic weeks, but she bit the bullet and came with me.

Post-Mortem

Now that Julie and I can look back at those first two weeks of connubial bliss with some objectivity after half a century, we're still trying to answer the question why all that bad stuff happened to us, but we've boiled it down to five possibilities:

1. It was punishment for past misbehavior. This is unlikely. Both of us were still pretty innocent and harmless. Other than a few typical teenage pranks and mishaps, we were good citizens with relatively clean records, at least at that point in our lives.

2. The gods of the Garden District were just having a little fun at our expense. Maybe so, if we were talking about the *golf* gods, who are overtly malicious little devils, but not the spirits who took such good care of my widowed mother living alone just a couple of blocks from Knox. Even though I joked about them above, I know they would never do anything as outrageous and undeserved as I've just recounted.

3. It was all Fated to happen. Even the dreaded Fates of ancient Greek mythology could not have dreamed up a one-woman wrecking crew like Sally P., so they can't claim any of the credit.

4. It was just a matter of random chance. That of course explains a lot of things in my humble opinion and might explain one or even two of the calamities that befell us, but not such a continuous string of them. The odds of that happening as it did are about the same as me hitting a golf ball straight, which is about one in a trillion.

LEECHES, LOVERS, BEARS, AND CHOCOLATE PUDDING

5. The utter havoc we created was an "emergent property" of Julie and me. This is the only logical possibility. To explain: The two of us are the sole components of a larger entity that came into existence when we got married. According to the laws of nature, an "emergent property" is a feature of the larger entity but not its component parts. For example, there is nothing about hydrogen or about oxygen to suggest they become water when combined. In our case, the "emergent property" is havoc (or sheer havoc, as some would say). There is nothing about Julie (except maybe her membership in Janet's Gang) or me individually that would suggest we could in combination create so much havoc. But that's what we've been doing for 53 years now, ever since we got married and even before. If you need proof of this, just read all the stories in our family series and you'll be convinced, believe me. And if you combine us with our three children into an even larger entity, the level of havoc rises dramatically.

The only analogy that comes to mind is the DKE fraternity at Tulane. The individual members (the components) are nice, decent guys for the most part, but when they get together in the same place at the same time (the entity), all hell breaks loose. I did not attend Tulane and was not a DKE—I was simply a curious teenager who observed the DKEs in action.

So the mystery is finally solved! It's not our fault, speaking of Julie and me (I'm not as sure about the kids). The impersonal laws of nature were simply acting through us as unwitting agents. Since we were powerless to resist Mother Nature, we're off the hook. No more guilt! We can go on creating havoc with a perfectly clear conscience now. Ain't logic wonderful!

"THE BEST OF ALL POSSIBLE HONEYMOONS"? NOT QUITE!

Gottfried Leibniz (1646–1716) ranks as one of the world's great philosophers. He also invented calculus in his spare time. As a true polymath, Gottfried knew an awful lot about everything—except for one very important subject. He knew absolutely nothing about honeymoons because he never married, further evidence of his great wisdom. [Julie: Give me a break!] This gaping hole in Gottfried's vast knowledge caused him to make a really bone-headed mistake in his grand metaphysical theory of everything, namely, the key conclusion that human beings were fortunate to occupy "the best of all possible worlds."

Poor Gottfried! If only he had jumped just once through that honeymoon hoop, he would have never staked his reputation on such an absurd idea and provided the likes of Voltaire (1694–1778) with such a juicy target. However, at the time it was first published, Gottfried's theory was hailed as brilliant by all the unmarried males of Europe and, far more importantly to the author, by every king with absolute power. On the other hand, those married men who somehow survived the terrors of their own honeymoons were universally hostile to the whole concept. Regretfully, we don't know what women thought of it because they weren't allowed to express opinions back then, which perhaps explains why Gottfried considered his own to be "the best of all possible worlds." [Julie: That was downright crummy. Get a life, Bill.] Moving on, I should also mention that 98% of all math students hated Gottfried for inventing calculus, so the poor guy could have used a good PR agent.

Like Gottfried's theoretical world, the smartass who invented honeymoons concocted an idea that worked much better on paper than in reality. The latest research shows that 98% of all male honeymooners (compared to 10% for women) subsequently develop post-traumatic stress disorder ((PTSD), often accompanied by a homicidal component. [Julie: I bet you got that out of Henry VIII's autobiography, didn't you?] However, by introducing the subject of our honeymoon this way, we don't mean to suggest that honeymoons should be banned entirely (although we do offer some words of advice at the end of our story). Unlike cellphones, fried eggs, and those impossible motel clock-radios,

LEECHES, LOVERS, BEARS, AND CHOCOLATE PUDDING

there is a good side to honeymoons. Most honeymoon survivors who choose to live together outside of an asylum gradually come to realize they can survive *anything* after such a test of their courage. In fact, a typically terrible honeymoon can be the fiery crucible in which the bonds of a really strong marriage are forged.

And that's exactly what happened to Julie and me. After the mistakes and misadventures of our honeymoon, no one would have predicted that our marriage would last another 44 years or even 44 days—yet it did and is still going strong. But we're getting ahead of ourselves, so let's return to the scenes of the crimes back in the summer of 1964.

I must confess up front that I planned the whole honeymoon. And, as usual, it looked great *on paper*. We were going to spend five romantic days camped all alone under the stars on a beautiful mountain in Colorado and then indulge ourselves for two days in decadent Las Vegas. To combine such extreme venues in one trip was positively brilliant, something that Gottfried himself might have thought of on a good day. Alas, I forgot to factor in the slings and arrows of Fate, so things didn't go according to plan—it wasn't even close.

I. Colorado

Actually, Julie must share some of the blame for the disaster in Colorado because she had told me, during our courtship, that she loved hiking and camping in the mountains, meaning she was a veteran. Well, as I found out the hard way, she'd never set foot on a mountain or in a tent. Perhaps I should have checked into her alleged camping credentials, but I had already fallen for another whopper about her alleged hunting experience (see other story about her sinking the boat) and could not believe she would snooker me again so soon. [Julie: But you were so gullible. You even fell for that old one about my imaginary fortune.] I obviously had a lot to learn at the hands of a real master.

In Colorado, thinking Julie was a "veteran" hiker, I foolishly left her to pack our backpacks while I went out for some last-minute supplies. We started

THE BEST OF ALL POSSIBLE HONEYMOONS

off the next day, full of excited anticipation about the adventure ahead. It was a gorgeous August morning in Rocky Mountain National Park and the scenery all around us was spectacular. We hiked uphill for six hours and then pitched our tent in the trees away from the trail. That night we enjoyed a dinner of freeze-dried spaghetti under a very cloudy sky with rapidly dropping temperatures. So far, so good, but things were about to change.

Some of you may be old enough to remember Feenamint gum, a laxative which I think is no longer sold, probably because it either worked not at all or, as in Julie's case, all too well. She'd been chewing the stuff for three days without any results, until 3:00 AM that first night on the trail. By that time, it was pitch-black outside the tent and much, much colder, so when the moment of truth finally came, Julie ventured just two short steps from our tent flap to do her business. What then ensued was a minor explosion, followed by a profound odor that would have killed a skunk. Julie had taken a trowel with her, but because of the cold and darkness, she did a second-rate job of burying the evidence. So we spent the rest of the night trying to sleep (or just survive) two feet away from the putrid product of a three-day Feen-a-mint binge. That's when we should have pulled up stakes and found a good motel, but like the ill-fated Donner Party, we forged on.

Although a serious cold front came through that night and froze the water in our plastic bottles (and a few other items in my pack, as we discovered later), that didn't seem to bother the multitude of flies attracted to our front door by Julie's magnificent gift. We arose at the crack of dawn, packed hurriedly, and started up the mountain again. Then came the snow: a light summer snow that lasted most of the day and made the scenery even more magical. We eventually reached our mountaintop destination and set up camp in a small, primitive shelter with a dirt floor that was open to overnight campers. Aside from Julie's Feen-a-mint-induced diarrhea, everything was perfect: we were all alone on top of the world (13,000 feet), surrounded by majestic, snow-sprinkled peaks, a blue alpine lake just outside, brightly colored wildflowers everywhere, and a nice, warming fire. It was the most romantic of all possible scenes!

Unfortunately, it didn't last very long. As soon as I started unloading my backpack, I discovered that everything in the bottom half was covered with a slimy goo like something out of a B-grade science fiction movie. It turned out to

LEECHES, LOVERS, BEARS, AND CHOCOLATE PUDDING

be an unholy gumbo of "Cover Girl," "Moon Drops," etc., mixed with lots of broken glass (in those days, makeup came only in little *glass* bottles). My lovely bride had brought along an assortment of fine cosmetics for our romantic honeymoon, which was certainly commendable. And neither one of us had anticipated sub-freezing temperatures in August, even high up in the mountains. But she had innocently packed her cosmetics in *my* pack, not hers, so when the glass bottles froze and then shattered the night before, all that goo and glass wound up in my clothes. Believe me, sleeping in long-johns embedded with sticky "Moon Drops" and tiny pieces of sharp glass is pure torture (and also makes for a very chaste honeymoon). Julie's clothes, of course, were pristine by comparison. She had at least six layers of them on to keep warm, which made her virtually impregnable against any romantic advances of mine, although sex was a very low priority for me at the moment.

[Julie: You weren't the only one, buster. In fact, by that point in our alleged honeymoon, I was planning for our alleged marriage to be very short and entirely celibate. I couldn't have been happier about your gooey old clothes. You and Gottfried are a fine pair, with all your bright ideas! This was supposed to be my honeymoon but it had become a nightmare instead. I had diarrhea, the nearest toilet was 10 miles away, it was freezing cold, the food was awful, the roof leaked, sleeping was impossible, and I was married to a lunatic. And I couldn't even call my mother. The whole mess was all your fault, so enough of your griping—you got off easy.]

In retrospect, we now know that was the high point of our outdoor adventure—things were about to get much worse. About the time I finished rehabilitating my poor clothes, in walks another fellow twice our age (we were 24 and 21) with a large pistol strapped on his hip and a gigantic dog at his side. Actually, he was very polite and asked if he could join us in the shelter since it was still snowing outside. After quickly assessing the situation, i.e., the presumably loaded pistol (illegal in a national park), the unfriendly, man-eating dog, the near-terminal, asexual state of my wife, and the fact that help was two days away, I realized our options were quite limited and invited the newcomer to join us. [Julie: That was the last straw for me. I was ready for the guy to shoot us and be done with the whole thing, including my alleged husband in particular.]

THE BEST OF ALL POSSIBLE HONEYMOONS

After the stranger unpacked and Julie finally emerged from her sleeping bag, we all settled down around the fire and introduced ourselves. It was a cozy little scene. The other fellow was friendly and non-threatening, although I can't say the same about his dog Rex, who kept eyeing Julie and me as possible snacks. Just when we were beginning to relax, one of us made the mistake of asking him if he was married. He told us that he had been married up until the day before, when he shot and killed his wife during a heated argument, presumably with the same pistol that still hung by his side. Well, that certainly changed the whole scene a bit. We had never been alone with an armed, self-confessed murderer before and had no clue what to do, but our basic survival instincts kicked in and we both blurted out simultaneously that she must have "had it coming," which seemed to satisfy her widowed husband. For all we knew, she may have been a saint who had been wrongly and prematurely dispatched, but truth (like sex) was a very low priority just then. After condoning his crime, we got along just fine with our newfound friend.

(It may be that our new companion was playing a joke on us or just enjoying some wishful thinking about murdering his wife, but between the gun and the dog, Julie and I were clearly not in any position to demand he produce the alleged *corpus delicti*. Besides, he told his tale with such grisly glee that we suspected he was mentally capable of murder, or more.)

Unfortunately, Rex was not as friendly as his master. He obviously didn't like us, so Julie decided to win him over with a special meal just for him. From our meager selection she chose something called "corn meal mush" that is used for cooking fish in. By itself, or perhaps the way Julie prepared it, corn meal mush looked and tasted awful, but Rex consumed the whole peace offering in five mighty gulps. An hour later, his massive body started reacting violently to the stuff (and I started thinking "better him than me"). Bad as it was going in, it was a hundred times worse coming out the other end. And that it did with sublime regularity, in gaseous, liquid, and semi-solid form, for the next 24 hours. Julie's diarrhea was nothing compared to Rex's. The Feen-a-mint Company could have used some of the stuff in its gum. It appeared at times that Rex might die of dehydration, which would have improved the air quality in our shelter but could have provoked his master to do something we already knew he was capable of, so we prayed to the gods to save him. Rex not only survived but even seemed a

LEECHES, LOVERS, BEARS, AND CHOCOLATE PUDDING

little intimidated by my petite wife who weighed less than he did. (Unfortunately, once Julie discovered the awesome power of corn meal mush, she realized what a potent secret weapon it might be in our marital relationship. Mind you, I have no direct proof, but I seemed to suffer from a bout of diarrhea every time we had an argument after our honeymoon. As a result, whether it was corn meal mush or my own paranoia, I have been conditioned not to argue with my wife, ever. [Julie: I have nothing to say, except that you have indeed become more submissive.])

We spent three nights with our homicidal friend and his mastiff. A small group of fishermen arrived the second day and camped down by the lake, which was of some comfort to us. However, I must admit that neither one of us ever felt like a hostage. Our shelter-mate was always pleasant and even went out of his way to show us where to hike and fish, since this particular spot was an old favorite of his. All three of us knew he would eventually be apprehended because his easily traceable car was parked at the trailhead and that's exactly what happened: Six armed park rangers, who were probably in touch with the fishermen by walkie-talkie, appeared one day while our companion was alone outside the shelter and took him away. He made no effort to resist or escape and bid us a fond farewell. It was frankly a little sad. We'll never know what actually happened because we heard nothing further from him or the authorities and can only hope that things turned out as well as possible for him.

(The fact that the DA's office never contacted us, even though the rangers took our names and addresses, could mean our companion confessed to everything *or* didn't commit any crime in the first place, other than carrying a handgun in a national park. If he had been a murder suspect, there probably would have been a SWAT team instead of park rangers to arrest him. And he didn't try to get away, use us as hostages, resist his arrest, or otherwise act like

THE BEST OF ALL POSSIBLE HONEYMOONS

a desperate man facing capital punishment for murder. So the end-game suggests he had not murdered his wife, but remember that Julie and I didn't have that information during our three anxious nights with him.)

After our friend left, the next two days were glorious. The fishermen moved on, we had this beautiful mountaintop all to ourselves, the weather turned mild, the Feen-a-mint gum finally finished its work, the air smelled sweet again, and we even caught a couple of fish to supplement our freeze-dried food. And, best of all, Julie forgave me for getting her into this mess. [Julie: Not so fast, dear husband. You weren't off the hook yet. I still had a few scores to settle with you at that point.] Which brings me to the second phase of our honeymoon, in Las Vegas, where Julie settled all the remaining scores and then some.

II. Las Vegas

The remainder of our honeymoon consisted of two nights in Las Vegas. After "roughing it" in Colorado, the warm weather, fresh food, soft beds, clean clothes, and other modern conveniences of "civilization" were most welcome. There were also interesting things to see outside of Las Vegas, including Hoover Dam, which is mind-boggling. But the main attraction was of course the gambling—Julie and I had never even seen a casino before this. We fully expected to lose money gambling, so we very carefully set aside the amount needed to cover the four-day drive back home to New Orleans. To our great surprise, the first night of gambling turned out to be extremely profitable. We couldn't lose, Julie at blackjack and me at roulette. My mother, on a pure hunch, had given us a sequence of three numbers to try at roulette and they all came up in the space of 11 total spins. By the end of the evening, we had won over $1,800, which was a fortune to someone who was still in law school and made $200 a month during the summer recess. We celebrated in style with champagne and triple hot fudge sundaes. And talked about the thousands more we were going to win the next night. This gambling business was easy!

When we bounced into the casino that next evening, we must have looked like two puppies, grinning from ear to ear and shaking with anticipation—after all, we were invincible. When we left six hours later, it was a very different picture: we slowly shuffled out like two zombies, with heavy hearts and shattered

LEECHES, LOVERS, BEARS, AND CHOCOLATE PUDDING

dreams—and no money, aside from the $29 hidden in my shoe. Why hidden? Because my sweet and gentle wife, who was a model of true purity (and still is, except for an occasional white lie), had turned into a raving, half-crazed gambling addict. [Julie: That's true. I don't know what happened to me, but I suspect the Feenamint gum had something to do with it.]

Unlike the night before, neither of us could win. We tried everything but kept on losing. After we'd lost all of our previous winnings, it was obviously time to stop. But Julie was convinced her luck was bound to change (famous last words) and went back to the blackjack table again and again. She used every trick in the book from begging to browbeating to coax more money out of me. Having never seen this side of my new bride before, I was utterly defenseless against her wiles and threats. Several times we went toe-to-toe in the middle of the casino, but I always lost the battle (as I did in the future until corn meal mush made me docile). [Julie: That's not true. I let you win some now and then.] So our reserves dwindled steadily. It was only after Julie pleaded on her knees for "just one more dollar" (which of course she promptly lost) that I thought to hide our very last $29 of cash as a last resort. She finally gave up after desperately searching all my empty pockets. There was no champagne or hot fudge that night.

The drive home was deadly. After the back-to-back debacles in Colorado and Las Vegas, we had very little to say to each other. Our meager resources consisted of that $29 (which remained hidden until Las Vegas was miles behind us) and a single Gulf Oil credit card (this was 1964, before credit cards became ubiquitous). Gas was not a problem, but food and lodging were another matter, so we planned to drive straight through except for one night and to eat only one meal a day, plus any chips or cheese crackers we might find at the Gulf stations. To supplement our spartan diet, Julie filled her purse with free crackers and butter at one of the restaurants we visited (an overlooked pad of butter melted in her purse and created a real mess, which in my unspoken opinion was partial retribution for what she did to my backpack).

When it came time to pick one motel on the way home, our choices were quite limited by our financial condition. Some of the motels we looked at were even too scuzzy for the Airline Highway strip in New Orleans favored by Jimmy Swaggart. As we were cruising through one of the seedier neighborhoods, a

THE BEST OF ALL POSSIBLE HONEYMOONS

desperate-looking woman came rushing out to our car shouting that she had "just what you're looking for." What she didn't know was that sex was, once again, the furthest thing from our minds. Nevertheless, Julie was much insulted and waved her wedding ring at the woman to prove she wasn't just a good-time girl. To our regret, we wound up taking a room there, which at only $13.50 was still overpriced. Nothing in the bathroom worked except the sink. The small double bed barely fit in the room. The sheets were grimy. Worst of all, the ancient window air-conditioner hung out over the bed and dripped all night right on our heads. Except for our new head colds the next day, the rest of the trip home was uneventful. We were thankful for even the smallest favors at that point.

After arriving home, we both eventually started laughing about our honeymoon gone awry. One of Julie's Christmas presents for me that year was a new set of unscratchy long johns that served me well for many years. She also gave up gambling and Feenamint gum. We never returned to Las Vegas but we did continue to backpack in the Colorado Rockies for another 40 years, sometimes by ourselves and sometimes with our kids starting when they were 5, 7, and 10, respectively. Julie became a true camping *aficionado*. Aside from a few minor catastrophes, like exploding stoves, flooded rivers, and bad weather (trapped at night in a small tent with metal poles and rising water at 13,000 feet during a severe lightning storm is a religious experience), we enjoyed the Great Outdoors at its best, even without the unique thrill of being all alone with a murderer.

Before closing, as survivors of a decidedly disastrous honeymoon, we feel duty bound to share our hard-earned wisdom with our younger, unmarried readers before it's too late. If and when you decide to take a honeymoon for some reason, please consider the following alternatives:

a) use the honeymoon fund to send your mother-in-law instead of yourselves to some remote spot;
b) have your intended spouse first undergo a thorough psychiatric evaluation;
c) buy "all-risk" honeymoon insurance with big limits;
d) take separate honeymoons apart from each other;
e) take along a chaperone, i.e., mediator, and videotape everything;
f) do any lovemaking before and after the honeymoon, but not during;

LEECHES, LOVERS, BEARS, AND CHOCOLATE PUDDING

g) postpone the honeymoon until your kids are at least semi-responsible (but make sure to lock them out of the house to prevent one of those infamous parents-are-out-of-town parties);

h) pack your own backpack.

THE DINNER FROM HELL AND BILL'S SHORT CAREER
(as told by Julie Penick)

There exists in the greater New Orleans area a facility devoted exclusively to the care, maintenance, and placement of unwanted basset hounds. Each year, for a significant fee, scores of either homicidal or suicidal New Orleanians hand over their basset hounds with almost maniacal glee. They speed away in their automobiles and never look back. Had we known about this wonderful place sooner, Mitchell the basset hound would have been history before he did what he did.

Bill and I had been married for three years and, aside from the occasional glitch (see previous stories), things were working out beautifully. He had recently started working in a local law firm and we had moved into a small "shotgun" cottage in a quiet neighborhood with our two-year old daughter, Casey. A pet for our little girl seemed like the natural next step. If we had done the smart thing and picked out a cute mutt at the local pound, our lives would have remained relatively calm, at least for the time being. But in a momentary lapse of sanity, we decided that Casey "deserved" a pure-bred dog. The choice of a basset hound was inspired by a current TV sitcom about a talking dog (and probably by some significant input from the Devil).

The cuddly little roly-poly pup we brought home and named Mitchell became, seemingly overnight, a huge clumsy beast with an insatiable appetite and a flat brain wave. Worst of all was his determination to "mark" every square inch of our house in the usual fashion. He just wouldn't do his business, No. 1 or No. 2, outside despite our vigorous entreaties. His sole redeeming quality would have been his undying devotion to our daughter had he not knocked her senseless one morning in an overly exuberant display of affection. After that, Casey feared Mitchell with every fiber of her little body. Ultimately we decided that we'd have to find a new home for Mitchell the Marker. At that moment, as we eventually discovered, we had joined the sizeable number of families who were desperately trying to humanely rid themselves of these canine albatrosses.

LEECHES, LOVERS, BEARS, AND CHOCOLATE PUDDING

That was easier said than done, because it was a bear market in basset hounds, so we were stuck with Mitchell for the time being.

Whenever we put Mitchell out in our backyard, he barked by day and bayed at the moon by night. The neighbors naturally complained, but as soon as we brought Mitchell inside, he turned into a highly efficient sprinkler system. So we resigned ourselves to permanent stains on our once-beautiful hardwood floors but were determined to save the brand-new living room rug, which was the only carpeting in the whole house. Ominously enough in retrospect, Mitchell became quite upset that the living room was off-limits to him under all circumstances. The old maxim that "every dog will have his day" had no particular significance for us then, but that was before Bill's boss and his wife came to dinner.

Ever since Bill had started his new job, one of the senior partners, Murphy Moss, had gone out of his way to make Bill feel welcome and comfortable. The Mosses had invited our family to their home on several occasions and of course we felt it was important to reciprocate. Entertaining the boss is one of those rites of passage that many young couples experience and we were no exception. I was especially intimidated by the fact that I was a novice cook on a tight budget planning dinner for a gourmet chef like Betty Moss, but I was determined to put on a good show for the sake of Bill's career. I pored over stacks of cookbooks, compiled a mammoth grocery list that shredded the monthly budget, and polished and scrubbed until everything in the house positively sparkled.

On the evening of our dinner party, Casey went cheerfully off to spend the night with her grandmother, and the Mosses arrived right on schedule. We greeted them at the door and Bill helped Betty off with her lovely, soft cashmere coat with a thick mink collar. Because shotgun houses have a traditional shortage of closet space, he took the coat and laid it carefully in the middle of our bed, well out of Mitchell's reach, he thought. I took drink orders and we all settled down in the living room. As the conversation began to flow, the dinner simmered in the kitchen, and the wedding silver glistened on the dining table, I finally exhaled in silent relief and started to relax when, with impeccable timing, Mitchell appeared at the living room door and started whining to come in and play.

THE DINNER FROM HELL

"What a sweet dog," said Betty. "We have two corgis and love them like our own children." It was an awkward moment. We didn't want to come across as cold and heartless.

"Mitchell's a great dog," Bill lied, "but he's still just a puppy despite his size."

"That's right," I chimed in. "We're still trying to housebreak him and he knows he's not supposed to set foot on the carpet. Don't you, Mitchie?" as I flashed him my sternest look.

Mitchell, as usual, didn't get the message and edged forward hopefully.

"Go play!" Bill barked and Mitchell, feeling crushed and rejected, whimpered tragically and moped down the hall toward the back of the house and our bedroom, the prelude to an act of terrible vengeance.

A half hour later, we sat down to dinner. Betty and Murphy were effusive with their compliments about the display of food on the table. As was customary in our home at that time, we held hands and offered up a brief blessing. (I would have prayed with far greater fervor had I any inkling of what was about to happen.) After pouring the wine and serving the salad, Bill excused himself and headed down the hall to our only bathroom. (Had he experienced some premonition of the impending events?) A few seconds later, the back of the house erupted in sounds that were inhuman and bloodcurdling!

The three of us at the table were starting to get up when an ashen imitation of the man I married lurched into the dining room. His eyes were glazed and blank, his jaw was slack, his face was damp with sweat, and his rumpled shirt was partially untucked. In horror I watched this mindless zombie move jerkily around the table until It halted behind Betty's chair. Then, in a toneless Frankensteinian voice, It uttered those terrible words that I'll never forget: "Mrs. Moss, our dog just ate your coat."

For several seconds, the rest of us were frozen in silence. I remember having a crazy impulse to ask "the thing" what It had planned for an encore. I was also quite sure that my formerly calm and professional husband had been possessed by some alien spirit.

Finally, with her typical compassion and good humor, Betty broke the silence: "Oh, Bill, now don't you worry, dear. This really isn't such a catastrophe. I'm a good seamstress and can mend just about anything." It uttered a negative

LEECHES, LOVERS, BEARS, AND CHOCOLATE PUDDING

"uh-uh" and shook Its head from side to side. The awful truth was dawning on me: this really was my husband and he had experienced something so traumatic that it had driven him insane.

Bill then morphed from zombie to clothing store mannequin. He continued standing motionless and speechless behind Betty's chair, without breathing or blinking. Basic survival instincts came to my rescue and the adrenalin began to flow. "Bill, sit down," I ordered with authority. He moved stiffly to his chair, then stopped. "Sit," I repeated, and he instantly collapsed into the chair like a ragdoll. At least he was capable of obeying.

I turned my attention to Betty: "How fortunate that you're good with a sewing machine. But if you have trouble with the repairs, we'd be more than happy to take the coat to a professional tailor. Isn't that right, sweetheart?"

"Dear God," Bill moaned.

I couldn't resist: "We already said the blessing, dear."

Murphy gallantly picked up the ball and addressed Bill: "So what do you think is going to happen in the Westmeyer case?"

Bill's mouth hung slackly open and I hoped he wasn't going to start drooling. "Bill, eat some salad," I commanded and then replied to Murphy's question: "Bill told me all about that fascinating case and he's betting the motion for summary judgment will be granted."

"Very good thinking, Bill. That was my guess too."

There was a muffled groan from the other end of the table.

Betty: "How's that adorable daughter of yours, Julie? We were hoping to see her tonight."

"Oh, Casey's just great. We're having so much fun with her. She's with her grandmother now. It's wonderful for them to spend time together and Bill and I enjoy the chance to sleep late once in a blue moon. Right, honey?"

Nothing from the other end of the table. My spouse had been struck dumb by the certain knowledge that Mitchell's terrible deed had derailed his legal career after only six months. When Bill gripped his steak knife with murder in his eyes, I knew things were much worse than I thought. Even the Mosses' gallant attempts to save the situation did not help. I desperately offered them coffee but they politely declined and said it was time to go home.

The dreaded moment of truth had arrived.

THE DINNER FROM HELL

In a single file behind my unwilling husband, we all started down the hall to get Betty's coat. Things were eerily quiet until we reached the kitchen door off the hallway. Bill stopped short and stood very still for a moment as though considering some weighty decision. Then he stepped inside the doorway, reached under the kitchen sink, and brought out a large brown grocery bag.

"That bad?" Betty exclaimed in surprise. Bill nodded quickly and resumed the slow, death-like march towards the scene of the crime.

When we reached the bedroom door, Bill's body was gripped by a sudden paralysis, so I moved him gently aside and with mounting terror pushed open the door. Nothing could have prepared us for the magical wonderland we encountered, a fantasy scene both horrible and enchanting. It was snowing Betty's coat! The room was filled with tiny fluffs of floating cashmere and mink, like silent ghosts dancing on the air currents from our overhead fan. Mitchell had somehow managed to get up on the bed for the first time ever and then proceeded to shred Betty's beautiful (and expensive) coat.

I can't recall how long we stood there trying to comprehend the utter devastation before us. When Bill started plucking pieces of coat out of the air and stuffing them, along with a few well-chewed buttons, into the grocery bag, I grabbed his arm and hissed, "Have you lost your mind?" "Yes," he responded miserably. Mercifully, the Mosses came to life: "We do have quite a little mess here, don't we." Betty was obviously stunned but still trying to comfort us. Murphy gently disengaged Bill's clenched fist from the paper bag. "I think you've done your best at gathering the remains. We appreciate the effort," he added with a painful grin.

As we made our way to the front door, the Mosses did everything they could to reassure us that the loss was far from catastrophic, the coat was fully insured, and they had enjoyed a wonderful dinner, all of which Bill responded to with his now-familiar moronic headshake.

After arriving at the door and saying good night, Betty left us with the parting words that would become legend in our family lore: "One day you will laugh about this." "Uh-uh," we both answered simultaneously. We were wrong—and Bill soon became a partner in the firm.

Mitchell also survived to "mark" many other spots in the house because our efforts to sell him at any price and then give him away to any taker came to

LEECHES, LOVERS, BEARS, AND CHOCOLATE PUDDING

naught. At some point, however, we heard about the refuge for unwanted basset hounds and Mitchell was gone the next day, one of the very happiest in our married life. We have celebrated that memorable occasion every year since.

There is a moral to this story for all of my fellow wives: In one very important respect, picking your first dog is not so different from picking your first husband. The correlation between the two has to do with their bathroom habits: make sure they're both trainable in that regard, because you're usually the one who has to clean up their messes. And, believe me, husbands who proudly insist on demonstrating their (alleged) evolutionary superiority by standing up to do their business can be just as messy as a basset hound, even after lots of target practice. Take my own husband, for example. Despite my misgivings after that disastrous dinner party, he has responded to my careful guidance and actually turned out quite well, except for his stand-up accuracy in the bathroom, which is still a work-in-progress 42 years later.

THE PERKS OF PREGNANCY

Of the countless books on the subject of pregnancy, not one talks about it as a golden opportunity to reap unimaginable rewards. What a pity! As a result, most moms-to-be are so focused on the baby or babies in their bellies that they completely overlook the plethora of possible perks that come with pregnancy—but *not* my very savvy wife.

As the proud parents of three perfect products of propitious procreation, Julie and I have experienced the miracle of creating a human life. It is a distinct honor for women to be the ones to compose and carry such a precious cargo in their own bodies. It's also an awesome responsibility and we had some anxious moments during the course of Julie's pregnancies, but they all turned well, in part because my wife gamed the system so perfectly. I know what you're thinking: this sounds just like a guy who never had to deal with morning sickness, unpleasant exams, labor pain, or stretch marks, etc., but please hear me out. I'm not talking about mundane perks like maternity leave or not mowing the lawn. I'm talking about really important stuff like free beer and free grades.

Free Beer

Julie and I were season-ticket holders and loyal fans of the New Orleans Saints for several years at the franchise's outset. Starting with the initial season in 1967, we sat on the hard wooden benches at old Tulane Stadium with several friends and watched in despair as our new football team usually got demolished. We all drained our sorrows in cheap beer on those long Sunday afternoons in a hot, uncovered stadium.

Julie was pregnant with our second (born 1/3/69) and third (born 2/13/71) children throughout the 1968 and 1970 seasons but still managed to attend all of the Saints' home games. Between her enlarged uterus and compressed bladder, the usual mismatch on the field (the Saints were 4–9–1 and 2–11–1 in those two seasons), and the cold beer she drank in moderation, Julie spent a lot of time going to and from the bathroom. Since there wasn't much happening on the field,

LEECHES, LOVERS, BEARS, AND CHOCOLATE PUDDING

her comings and goings were definitely observed by our nearby (mostly male) neighbors, not surprisingly, because Julie was a beautiful woman (and still is at age 69) who absolutely glowed during her pregnancies.

But her effect was not limited to the fans in the stands. In some mysterious way, Julie also galvanized the Saints on the field by just going to the bathroom. It was uncanny and even a little spooky: the few times our team ever scored any points occurred when Julie was in the bathroom. She was the Saints' 12th player.

The causal connection between Julie's bathroom visits and the home team's success did not go unnoticed by the desperate fans around us. After the first couple of home games, they began by asking Julie to wait until the Saints had the ball. When she did go, our new, overly solicitous friends cautioned her to be careful and take her time. Then, in a Eureka moment, some beer-swilling dude behind us suddenly realized that beer and bathrooms were intimately linked and started buying beer for Julie in hopes of triggering her bladder reaction. Other fans picked up the cue and did the same, so we were rolling in suds. I happily drank most of the free beer but that didn't matter to our generous pals, who figured if Julie only took a sip or two out of each beer, that could make all the difference in a close game.

Tennessee Williams was certainly right about "the kindness of strangers." Never in the entire history of the human race was a single individual's bathroom schedule manipulated, monitored, and anticipated so intently by so many observers. Julie's fame spread like wildfire. Toward the end of the season, our section of the stadium erupted in loud cheers whenever Julie left her seat. It was like I was married to a real saint (which she is): Saints' fans, who are a little crazy to begin with, jumped out of her way, reached over to touch her sleeve, and blessed her reverently for just going to the bathroom! Despite their adoration, I was always worried that some extreme fan would lock her in a bathroom stall since she was too big to crawl under or over the door.

Unfortunately, Julie's bladder was not nearly as porous as the Saints' defense and they continued to lose, but because of her offensive contributions, Julie almost won the team's Most Valuable Player award twice.

THE PERKS OF PREGNANCY

Free A's

It's a small jump from Tulane Stadium to a Tulane classroom. Julie had finished two years of college before interrupting her education to help with her very sick father and later to marry me and start a family. In 1968, when Casey was three, Julie decided to resume her studies by taking a night class for credit. She took one or two classes at Tulane, Loyola, and UNO for almost every semester after that, in addition to raising three children and teaching at the JCC Nursery School for 25 years. Julie graduated *cum laude* from Tulane in 1996 in the presence of her very proud family.

When she started that first class in the fall of 1968, Julie was about five months pregnant with our second child, Ginger. She enjoyed the class and did well, but when the date of the final exam was announced, it happened to fall exactly on her due date. She therefore talked to her professor about the conflict, which produced this memorable exchange a month before the exam:

> PROFESSOR: "Well, Mrs. Penick, I can't change my schedule."
> JULIE: "Well, Mr. _____, I can't change my schedule either."
>   (Score 1 for Julie!)

So the impending conflict was not resolved. However, as Julie's belly continued to expand, the professor finally started to realize he might have a serious problem if Julie went into labor in the middle of his exam and he, a music teacher, had to deliver a baby. Julie thought the issue was closed until, out of the blue, he promised her an A in the course if she skipped the exam! Now that's an offer that very few sane students would not jump at with both feet, but he did not know my wife very well. What he'd done by arrogantly refusing her earlier overture was to arouse her fine sense of right and wrong, so she declined his new offer, to his obvious discomfort. He renewed the offer after every ensuing class, with growing urgency in proportion to her growing girth, but her mind was made up. He clearly had no previous experience with very pregnant women of any kind and was mystified by her determination (which he probably called something else).

LEECHES, LOVERS, BEARS, AND CHOCOLATE PUDDING

By the time of the exam, the poor man was a nervous wreck. He could barely remember who wrote Beethoven's Fifth. When the final exam took place, I waited outside the room with the car running in case Julie did go into labor, but that apparently didn't ease the professor's anxiety. Julie said he hovered nearby and came running over whenever she stood up to stretch her legs or even just frowned. She came through it all in good shape, no doubt better than he did, and aced the exam with a real A, the first of many in her subsequent college career.

As fragile as the professor was just then, it probably would have sent him over the edge if we'd told him that Ginger waited another three weeks after his exam to make her entrance into the world.

Natural Rites

And now the action moves from the Tulane campus to a parking lot right next to the busy yard of a Japanese plant nursery.

Julie was near the end of her term and therefore quite large with child, which one I don't remember. The two of us were shopping in Metairie, probably for Christmas, because the stores were very busy. It had been a hectic day fighting the crowds. The store bathrooms were jammed, so Julie's bladder-control was sorely tested.

She met that challenge with extraordinary courage and willpower, until it reached the proverbial tipping point in the late afternoon. We had just parked in a free lot off the main drag when Julie realized it was now or never. Unfortunately, there were no bathrooms in sight. Nor any bushes or trees to hide behind, something Julie had mastered on our camping and canoeing trips. But there were rows of parked cars, which was all the cover she needed.

The only two cars with enough room between them to accommodate my very pregnant wife were right on the end of the first row. Since we didn't see anyone else in the parking lot at that moment, the timing seemed just right—but turned out to be horribly wrong. Just as Julie squatted down between the two cars and proceeded with her business, the end car suddenly started up and quickly drove away. In her haste, Julie had not noticed the driver sitting idly on the far side of the car, probably going over his shopping list, because he didn't notice Julie either.

THE PERKS OF PREGNANCY

The scene created by the departing car was a classic. Hollywood could not have done it better. There was my wife, in all her glory, with skirt up and pants down, merrily watering the asphalt with a mighty torrent. Ten feet away, on the other side of the now-departed car, were several Japanese women tending the plants at the nursery. It was hard to say which of the protagonists was more surprised. Julie's position was pretty well dictated by the insistent demands of her happy bladder, so she could do nothing more than smile and wave until Nature ran its course. That friendly wave made things even more perplexing for an audience that was already puzzled by this bizarre American custom they'd never encountered before.

I could tell Julie was kind of tickled by her exposed situation but the very proper Japanese ladies observing her were definitely not amused. Some of them quickly turned away, some continued staring in disbelief, and some even waved weakly back at Julie. It was a wonderfully ridiculous moment of clashing cultures. I'm sure most of the witnesses left for Japan on the next boat and are still talking about those multi-use parking lots in America.

International Sex Symbol

Julie's perks were not confined to America. We had planned a trip to Europe for the summer of 1965, after I had graduated from law school but before I started my practice, or we started our family. Everything had been arranged when Julie discovered she was pregnant that spring (a family practitioner in Charlottesville initially diagnosed her pregnancy as sciatica). Since the trip fell right in the safest trimester of pregnancy and Julie was in excellent health generally, we decided to go on the trip after getting a green light from her trusted obstetrician and family friend.

London was the first stop. After a day of rest, we boldly struck out for dinner and promptly got lost. As I tried to read a city map under a streetlight, my lovely wife stood there looking positively radiant in the overhead light, which is no doubt why a very handsome English gentleman stopped and offered his help. Then he introduced himself (what else but "George") and invited us to dine with him at "his" nearby restaurant. Although he certainly didn't look like Jack the Ripper, dressed as he was in a suit and carrying the proverbial umbrella, we were

LEECHES, LOVERS, BEARS, AND CHOCOLATE PUDDING

still a little unsure, so he gave us directions to the restaurant and asked us to meet him there if we wanted to. We ultimately decided to accept George's nice invitation and that was the beginning of a rather unforgettable evening.

The restaurant and meal were first-rate. George insisted on picking up the tab. Then he invited us to "his" pub for an after-dinner libation, which turned into several. As the wine and beer flowed and the hour got later, my wife metamorphosed into a walking encyclopedia of "information" about the United States. George was fascinated as Julie reeled off fact after fact about the length and depth of the Mississippi River, the current population of St. Louis, the precise numbers of Catholics and buffalo in America, the military budget of 1963, and sundry other subjects about which she knew absolutely nothing. I don't know if George believed any of the imaginary facts and figures that flowed out of Julie's mouth all evening, but I must say that she sounded very certain and convincing. It was intriguing. And it was something she never did before or after that night, so I doubt the wine could be the only explanation. I briefly thought about calling an exorcist, except that her personality remained just as sweet as ever.

Whatever happened to Julie, George loved it and kept buying drinks (far better stuff than Saints' beer). We sampled three or four of his favorite pubs, took a private tour of London after dark in his car, and even watched the Queen Mother leaving Buckingham Palace. Our generous host dropped us off at our hotel about six hours after we met him. Julie and I slept late the next morning and woke up with mild hangovers, which could have been much worse. Once back at home, we corresponded with George, an innkeeper, for several years.

George was not the only Brit who treated us wonderfully. I remember in particular a London bobby who teased us amiably when we asked him for directions. Unfortunately, that kind of friendly hospitality disappeared when we left England for France. Although I don't remember any specific problems in Paris, our first stop, everyone we encountered there seemed to lack any kind of warmth or interest, unlike the British. The highlight of that visit was running into several of Julie's New Orleans friends while admiring the Eiffel Tower. There was, however, a very unpleasant incident at a countryside inn east of Paris where we had stopped late and asked for a room. After first telling us she had one, the innkeeper changed her story when she found out we were Americans, even

THE PERKS OF PREGNANCY

though Julie was obviously pregnant and tired. Granted, this was the time of The Ugly American, but we didn't fit that picture.

We were therefore quite happy to leave France behind and enter Switzerland. With the help of our New Orleans doctor, we had scheduled an appointment with a Geneva obstetrician named Paul Primavesi ("spring" in English). He determined Julie was doing fine and weighed "13 stones," which apparently was a bit more than the ideal, so his only advice was "Don't eata too much."

From Geneva we went to Morcote, a very small Swiss town on beautiful Lake Lugano near the Italian border and spent a leisurely week there. Julie woke up the sleepy town by going to a lakeside beach and showing off her svelte figure in a form-fitting, pea-green maternity bathing suit with a large orange dragon on the front (how could I forget it). The reaction of the local male population was instantaneous. Whenever Julie floated belly-up on her raft, several young studs would leave their bikini-clad, even svelter girlfriends (I happen to remember them too) and come over to gawk at my sexy wife. It's true that pregnant women in Europe rarely appear in public (we saw two the whole time), much less in bathing suits, but the male attention Julie received on that beach was more than mere curiosity. She had become a sex goddess, with child! Needless to say, Julie spent as much time as possible on the beach with her adoring fans, to the obvious displeasure of their abandoned girlfriends, who clearly needed consoling that I was gallantly ready to provide if my rather unfair wife had not shot me one of those knowing looks that all husbands understand—and obey, without question.

In addition to the local beach population, we explored the surrounding hills and danced away three nights under moonlight on a lakeside pavilion. We almost triggered an international incident when we unknowingly crossed the Italian border in a rowboat and incurred a frantic warning through loudspeaker. Morcote was Julie's favorite stop that summer, for obvious reasons, and I enjoyed it too despite feeling so sorry for those poor, lonely girlfriends, so we returned 35 years later and found the town to be pretty much as it was, minus the girls.

On the way to Venice, we spent one night in the city of Verona, a World Heritage Site, and enjoyed *Aida* in a Roman amphitheater under a cloudless sky. Much of the audience held lighted candles, which enhanced the wonder of the entire evening. There was plenty of action on stage, with horses, cattle, and even elephants during the Grand March. It was a sensational performance in a spectacular setting.

Venice was beautiful but seemed a bit anticlimactic after Verona, despite one very energetic gondolier with a fine tenor voice. And a funny incident: While we were browsing in a china shop, another American tourist came in and started admiring the Napoleon brandy glasses with the large "N" on them. When the saleslady explained what the "N" signified, our fellow American responded thus: "Napoleon, nuts. These are for Naomi, who don't know nuthin' about Napoleon anyway." Which reminds me of another American classic that a friend of ours overheard in the Sistine Chapel: "Jesus, Louise, look at dem ceilings!"

Then to Florence, our second-to-last stop that turned out to be our last one because young Casey had had it with the traveling and raised a ruckus in Julie's belly. Our first full day there happened to fall on my birthday. Julie discovered she didn't have any clean underwear, so she borrowed one of my Jockey shorts, which fit just fine. After a couple of hours of sightseeing, Julie started bleeding, not heavily but enough to scare us. We rushed to the nearest hospital, only to find out it offered no obstetrical services but would have a doctor examine Julie. Even before he pulled down her underwear, the poor doctor looked quite confused, which is when we both remembered she was wearing male underpants with a fly in the front. He reassured us as best he could in Italian and referred us to an OB hospital across town.

You gotta love the Italians, if not their hospitals. It would have been a real challenge for us to find the other hospital driving on our own through Florence's tangled streets, but then a very nice lady spotted our obvious difficulty and offered her assistance. With her leading the way in her own car, we reached the other hospital in good time—and were sorry we did.

Julie did get checked in quickly, but it was all downhill after that. The waiting room was a mess. There were half a dozen empty beer bottles on the floor. The windows were open and the flies were plentiful. I was already disgusted when Julie came rushing out of the examination room, visibly angry and upset. What happened in there was barbaric. She had been placed on one of two parallel beds a mere six feet apart. On the other bed was a woman giving birth! There was no drape between the beds, so Julie had a ringside seat, not that she wanted it. After delivering the baby, the doctor turned around to examine Julie, without changing his bloody gloves or washing his hands. My wise and wonderful 22-year-old wife told him "Don't touch me," jumped off the bed, and ran out the room. We left the hospital without stopping.

Things improved after that, thanks again to the warm and caring nature of Italians. Back at the *pensione* (a small family-run hotel) where we were staying, we called Julie's New Orleans OB, who advised her to rest in bed for several days and then come straight home. The three magnificent sisters who ran the *pensione* spent the next week pampering Julie like she was Queen of the Nile. Although her feet never touched the ground, she was bathed, fed, changed, and fussed over with genuine TLC. One of the sisters kept patting her abundant stomach and proudly proclaiming "*ocho bambinos*." They apparently knew exactly what to do for Julie and did it happily, from what Julie told me.

My information is secondhand because our hosts gently shooed me outside every day after a big breakfast. I was allowed to sleep there (on a couch), take a shower, and visit Julie briefly (always with a chaperone), but then I had to hit the road so Julie could rest (my thoroughly spoiled wife never once protested my banishment). So I walked the streets of Florence for nine hours a day, seeing all the sights and dining on street-vendor pizza, but you'll hear no complaints from me about those saintly sisters because they probably saved Casey's life and possibly Julie's too. After seven days of royal treatment, Julie was well enough to drive to Rome and fly to New Orleans.

She did very well back home, despite a major hurricane not long after we arrived. We even managed a fishing trip just before the storm (the weather was beautiful) and Julie caught a goodly bunch of fish because it was still "too tiring" for her to pilot the boat or do anything else other than handle a rod and reel. I of course had to clean "her" fish. When Hurricane Betsy did hit New Orleans two days later, it knocked out the power to our refrigerator, so we quickly sent out a "free beer" message to our Pavlovian friends who flocked over for a backyard barbeque with fish cooked on a Coleman stove and beer cooled by a block of ice from the Dixie Ice House (with a line three blocks long).

Going back to the night of the hurricane, a now legendary monster, it sounded like all the windows in our tiny apartment were going to blow in, so I got not a wink of sleep. Did my loving wife stay up and worry with me? Not

LEECHES, LOVERS, BEARS, AND CHOCOLATE PUDDING

even for a moment. She went right to bed and slept soundly all night (another privilege of pregnancy?), just like she did the following summer in the Canadian woods with a hungry bear outside our tent (see separate story). "What, me worry?"

But we survived Hurricane Betsy and Julie delivered a beautiful, healthy baby in November. We thought about naming our new daughter after one of those heroic sisters in Florence but couldn't choose between them, so she wound up as "Katherine" shortened to "Casey." Or sometimes "Scoot," which is another story. And Julie 46 years later is just as sexy as she was on that Swiss beach in her dragon bathing suit—and definitely svelter.

* * * * *

Alas, just when you could really use one of those perks, like desperately needing a dime or quarter to get into a pay toilet, pregnancy sometimes doesn't deliver the goods. And it might even make a bad situation worse, as Julie found out the hard way.

Julie was about four months pregnant with our first child when her best friend Murray came to visit us in Charlottesville, Virginia, where I was in my third year of law school. After a very nice visit, we drove her back to the airport in Washington, D. C. We were running late and worried about Murray missing her flight, so we couldn't make any bathroom stops. As a result, Julie was in serious distress by the time I dropped them off at the airport. While Murray raced to her gate, Julie raced to the nearest bathroom, only to find it had pay toilets and she had no change. Her only option was to slide under the door, if she could fit. It didn't help matters that we'd gone out to dinner the night before and she'd consumed, in addition to a full meal, *four* large hot fudge sundaes, each consisting of three scoops of ice cream, lots of homemade fudge sauce, and the usual nuts, cherries, and whipped cream. (Eating for two? It looked like she was eating for very happy triplets.) Getting her expanded belly under the toilet door took some pushing and pulling, but she finally made it in the nick of time, so it all worked out.

Or so we thought. The initial drive home, which included another bathroom stop an hour outside of Charlottesville, seemed thankfully routine until

THE PERKS OF PREGNANCY

we turned down our street and Julie started looking for her purse, which was not *in* the car, so we turned around and drove back to the last stop. I waited in the car while Julie went inside and then came out empty-handed. But on leaving the store, she spotted her purse sitting on the roof of the car, right where she'd apparently left it when we stopped there the first time. It had not budged during two hours of fast highway driving because it was a bean-bag purse and was filled with all the usual junk that women carry around with them. And maybe because the god of pregnancy perks wanted to atone for being asleep in that airport bathroom.

LEECHES, LOVERS, BEARS, AND CHOCOLATE PUDDING

How would you like to be married to a certified leech-plucking bear-chasing woman? Even those fearsome 400-pounders with the big teeth and sharp claws are no match for my 100-pound, 5-foot wife. And if they aren't, how much of a chance do you think I, at a mere 175 pounds, have against her?

The word is obviously out among the bear population of North America: don't mess with Julie! And none has since that fateful day in the summer of 1967, even though we hiked and camped in bear country many times after that. But actually the leeches came before the bear, so I'd better start at the beginning.

Before plighting my troth on another fateful day 46 years ago (as of yesterday), my very dear friend Charlie and I spent two adventurous weeks canoeing through the Boundary Waters Canoe Area of northern Minnesota and Ontario, Canada. He "cooked" and I "navigated." Needless to say, we spent most of the time hungry and lost—but we still managed to have a great time in a pristine neck of the woods. And the bears kept their distance, thanks no doubt to the sublime malodor of Charlie's culinary disasters.

So when it came time to plan a summer vacation with Julie a few years later, another trip to the Boundary Waters sounded perfect. Even though our previous track record together in the Great Outdoors was anything but stellar (see stories about the duck-hunting trip and our ill-fated honeymoon), I assumed we had used up all of our vacation bad luck (wrong). And if two stumblebums like me and Charlie could survive for two weeks in the North Woods, Julie and I could survive for a week or so. She was, after all, a good cook (too good, as it turned out) and I had finally learned to read a map (wrong again). We planned and prepared so meticulously that nothing could go awry this time.

After renting our canoe and other gear in Ely, Minnesota, we took a seaplane across the Canadian border about 35 miles back into the Quetico Provincial Park. There was nothing but woods and water as far as we could see. No roads, billboards, buildings, power lines, motorboats, or other detritus of civilization, at least on the Canadian side where we'd spend most of our time. It was a truly unspoiled wilderness. The pilot dropped us off in the middle of a

LEECHES, LOVERS, BEARS, AND CHOCOLATE PUDDING

shimmering lake and went on his way. Julie and I sat very still in our canoe for several minutes, savoring the absolute solitude, the unfamiliar silence, the perfectly clear water, and the wildlife returning to the lake. Then we picked up our paddles and headed for the outlet river running south.

That's when Lady Luck abandoned us again. Our river route no longer existed! The entrance to the river was blocked by a huge beaver dam, which reduced the flow of water downstream to a mere trickle. Of the hundreds of full-flowing rivers and streams in the area, the beavers of course picked ours to dam. I say "ours" because it was the *only* way to go by water on our chosen route back to Ely. We therefore had no choice but to follow the course of the semi-dry riverbed to the next body of water and hope the beavers did not get there first. (We found out later we could and should have made a hole in the beaver dam and waited for the river to fill up enough to float our canoe.) Since there was nowhere near enough water to do that then, we had to drag the canoe and the heavy gear through five miles of very soft and slippery muck that was filled with horrors we never imagined. Dressed in our once-clean tennis shoes and long pants, we sank a foot or two in the muck every time we took a step. Walking the muck while pulling a sizeable load was bad enough, but then our legs started itching all over for some unknown reason.

Enter the leeches. Hordes of them. An inspection of our legs revealed they were covered by leeches happily sucking our very tired blood. Bogart's and Hepburn's brief encounter with a mere handful of them critters in *The African Queen* was a cake-walk compared to our situation at that moment: not only did we have dozens of leeches already embedded in our legs, we still had miles to go through leech-infested muck. And John Wayne was nowhere in sight. Julie and I were all alone in a vast wilderness, surrounded by hungry little cannibals eager to devour us, bit by bit. It was certainly not where we expected to be at this point in our vacation. Our only choices were to panic or pluck, so we plucked, pulling the slimy, squishy things out of our skin one by one. Julie was a rock, plucking away without a single complaint. At long last, we were free of leeches and ready to move on, but knowing what awaited us there, it took some willpower to step back into that muck.

We dragged the canoe for another hour or so before stopping to pull off leeches again. It's not something I'm really proud of, but by the fourth stop, we

LEECHES, LOVERS, BEARS, AND CHOCOLATE PUDDING

had become pretty damn good pluckers out of sheer desperation. During one of those stops, we were treated to the awesome, close-up sight of a bull moose with an enormous rack of horns. He ambled out of the woods and stopped to feed in the riverbed only a stone's throw from us. They are magnificent creatures, but they can be unpredictably bad-tempered and, at half a ton, quite dangerous. We had nowhere to run or hide, so we just remained very still and very quiet in the canoe, not even moving to scratch our itching legs. Had he charged us, he would have easily finished what the leeches started, but fortunately he was in a good mood and left us alone. He fed contentedly for about 15 minutes and then sauntered back into the forest. It's still a special memory for us both. How anyone can kill such a majestic animal for a mere trophy is beyond me. Having said that, however, I must confess to you that I feel quite the opposite about beavers after what they put us through that day. They're even worse than those devilish sheep (see sheep story).

After several hours of pulling and plucking, we finally reached a floatable river as the sun was going down. Exhausted to the bone, we found a spot and put up the tent in record time, pulled off the last few leeches (so we thought), hung the food pack in a tree, crawled into our sleeping bags, and went sound asleep without any dinner.

The next morning was a whole new ballgame. Aside from the numerous welts on our legs, we felt rested and ready to take on the world (but not a bear). It was a beautiful day. The river was deep and fast. The only problem was that it was flowing in the wrong direction, according to my reading of the map. I read that darn thing every which-a-way and it never turned out right. The possibility of my being wrong was of course ridiculous, so either the mapmakers got it backwards or the river reversed itself. Despite Julie's pleas to my alleged common sense, my stubbornness (she called it something else) prevailed and we aimed our canoe upstream. Paddling against the strong current got us nowhere fast, so we decided to go with the flow, wherever it might take us. You'll never guess what happened next. After paddling for a couple of hours, we wound up right where we were supposed to be! I naturally had to eat a little crow dished up with relish by my loving wife. But all was forgiven when we took a very cold dip in the crystal-clear water that did wonders for body and spirit.

LEECHES, LOVERS, BEARS, AND CHOCOLATE PUDDING

We covered several miles that day without another hitch. No more beavers or leeches, thank goodness. Canoeing in exquisite country like that is definitely the best way to experience it. And we didn't have to share it with anybody else until we crossed the American border six days later. Except for the pleasant sound of water running over rocks and the occasional call of a loon or duck, the silence was total. While paddling across lakes, we were often accompanied by a variety of wild ducks who played with us by swimming alongside the canoe and then diving under it to the other side. It was a remarkable exhibition of trust and goodwill. The same applies to the chipmunks who approached us for handouts of GORP (good ole raisins and peanuts) and other goodies.

Amidst all of this beauty and bonding, however, we encountered two unwanted guests who brought us back to earth. The first was the fattest, happiest leech you could ever imagine. He was nestled in the protective arch of Julie's foot and therefore went unnoticed for two days. After slurping her blood nonstop for that long, he was a grotesque blimp of a leech on the verge of exploding. It was a bit dicey getting him off, since he couldn't be burned off or pulled out like the others, but we finally succeeded with rubbing alcohol and recycled Julie's precious blood by feeding him to the fish. But, as they say, he died happy.

The other uninvited guest was a good bit bigger and scarier. Julie and I had set up camp beside a small gem-like lake and had enjoyed an early dinner, to be followed by a dessert of chocolate pudding. While the freshly cooked pudding cooled, I went out fishing in the canoe and Julie watched the sunset from the water's edge. Enter a large black bear, lured by the irresistible smell of chocolate. When I first saw him, he was shamelessly devouring our dessert like Winnie-the-Pooh with a honey pot. Even though he was only about 30-35 feet behind her, Julie did not see or hear him enter our campsite. Fortunately for her, Winnie's only interest was the pot of chocolate pudding and our still-open pack of food for the next several days. I yelled at Julie that there was a bear in the camp and to "let him have it." That particular choice of words was most unfortunate. I meant for her to stay put until I came with the canoe and let the bear have whatever he wanted, but she thought I wanted her to go after him. And that's exactly what she did. Following the advice of a ranger to make noise if we encountered a bear, Julie grabbed two aluminum plates, banged them together,

LEECHES, LOVERS, BEARS, AND CHOCOLATE PUDDING

and shouted loudly as she charged right at the startled bear. By that time, Winnie had finished the pudding and started in on our food pack. I can only imagine what he thought when he saw my very angry but diminutive wife running towards him. He could have swatted her like a fly—but he'd obviously been conditioned by his own wife to run like hell from any aggravated female,

Charcoal drawing by Lucia Penick

whether big or little, so he ran like hell but with our food pack in his mouth and Julie in hot pursuit. It was a chase scene out of the Keystone Kops if it had not been so real. First came Winnie, then Julie, and then me, still yelling stupidly at Julie to "let him have it" and Julie yelling "I am" over her shoulder at me. The chase finally ended at a small clearing, where Winnie had dropped the food pack in the very center and retreated to the far side to watch over it. When I caught up with Julie, she and the bear were glowering at each other across the clearing. Neither one was willing to budge, one way or the other. The standoff ended a few minutes later when Winnie ambled off with one last knowing growl.

LEECHES, LOVERS, BEARS, AND CHOCOLATE PUDDING

We quickly retrieved the near-empty pack and double-timed it back to the campsite. The chocolate pudding pot looked like it had been scoured with a Brillo pad—Winnie hadn't left a smidgen. We considered moving our campsite in case he returned that night looking for more easy food, as I figured he would, but it was getting dark and too late to do that. So we hung the food pack in a tree, scrambled into the tent, zipped the tent door and flap tight, and checked our weapons, which consisted of one machete and one tear-gas pen, just enough to irritate an attacking bear. At least there would be two of us fighting together against one of him—or so I thought until Julie crawled into her sleeping back and calmly fell asleep. When I gently tried to wake her up to fight beside me, she actually growled at me just like Winnie, who by comparison seemed the lesser threat at that moment. It was going to be a very long and lonely night in that tent.

And so it was, the perfect Hollywood setting for the climax of a horror movie: The two of us trapped inside a tiny tent in the middle of nowhere, stalked by an angry bear. The moonless night black as pitch. The eerie silence broken only by the chilling call of a loon. The scene was all set for Winnie to make his grand entrance and bring the curtain down. Well, fortunately for us, he forgot his lines. He did in fact return to the scene of his crime—although I could not see him through the zipped-up tent and certainly wasn't about to poke my head outside, he did come close enough to hear his breathing and twigs snapping under his paws. But he left the tent alone, no doubt because he knew my fearless and ferocious waif of a wife was inside it and he didn't want to tangle with her again. So I must begrudgingly admit that it was Julie who saved the day, even though she slept peacefully through the whole scene while I stood guard over her, for what that was worth. The happy ending also proved that (1) Winnie was a gentleman after all; and (2) Julie asleep was still more intimidating than I was awake.

(At the end of the trip, we learned that some bears don't seem to mind a little noise, contrary to what that ranger had told us at the beginning. While we were out in the woods, another bear apparently chased a park ranger up a tree and mauled his foot badly. It's a good thing that our Winnie followed the rules.)

We had no more trouble after that (and of course no more chocolate pudding either), except for one little detail: we didn't have nearly enough food

LEECHES, LOVERS, BEARS, AND CHOCOLATE PUDDING

left to get us home. But we did have spinning rods and the fishing was good, so we were able to supplement our meager food supply with lots of grilled fish. The walleyed pike were particularly tasty. However, a steady diet of mostly fish for breakfast, lunch, and dinner gets pretty old after four days. By the time we crossed back over the American border, we were both craving anything edible but fish. That's where the lovers came into the story. Imagine Burt Lancaster and Deborah Kerr in that famous scene on the beach in *From Here to Eternity*. Then add (1) a large picnic basket, and (2) Julie entering the scene with a lean and hungry look. Although Burt and Deborah had not the slightest interest in food at the moment, I was still reluctant to interrupt their amorous exploits, but not my intrepid wife. While I sat sheepishly in the canoe, Julie marched right up to the startled and still-entwined couple, told them we'd been starving for days after a bear stole all our food, and demanded something from the picnic basket. You can surely imagine their response, which I cannot repeat here, but she came away with two sandwiches and an apple that we devoured like animals after leaving our frustrated benefactors in peace. That sandwich could have been raw possum tongue for all I know, but it sure tasted good.

Thus ended another overly stimulating encounter with Mother Nature. Our chewed-up legs and feet eventually healed. We adjusted quickly to civilization again, especially the plentiful food. We returned happily to our two-year-old daughter in New Orleans. And the trip inspired us to take up canoeing as a favorite form of family recreation and teach our children the glory of paddling down a beautiful river. But my best memories from our sojourn in Quetico are of Julie's courage and composure under fire. In addition to the usual rigors of living outdoors, she took on the leeches, the bear, "starvation," and the hostile lovers without ever flinching. I always knew she was someone special, but that trip revealed a new and wonderful side of Julie that's one of many reasons why she's such an extraordinary wife, mother, teacher, friend, and person. There's another adversary now (Alzheimer's) that's even tougher than those leeches and bear, but she's battling it with the same courage and composure as before. As Julie herself said so often to others, "you go, girl!"

ON THE ROAD WITH THREE LITTLE BACKSEAT ANGELS/BEASTS OF BEDLAM

It's the ultimate test of parenthood: driving young kids cross-country on a family vacation without murdering, maiming, or misplacing them. Julie and I have always loved our kids dearly (except maybe for a few days here and there), so we had no idea that such a trip brings out the hidden beast in even the sweetest child, as our own kids proved many times over. Although we somehow managed to pass the test, just barely, we subsequently learned the odds were against us. According to the latest statistics, the failure rate is a dismal 78.4% of all Americans who undertake such a perilous journey. The stats are even worse in China despite the fact that parents there only have to contend with one child. Of the 21.6% who pass the test here, most of us suffer some kind of serious emotional damage and wind up in anger management classes.

And yet this insanity persists as a rite of passage for young parents. It could be easily stopped if all of us wounded "veterans" would simply advise our own grown children not to make the same mistake, but the majority of us would rather avenge ourselves on them by remaining silent. And yet, beyond the slim chance that our now-adult kids will read this, Julie and I feel a duty to warn all the other clueless parents out there, so here are our suggestions to save the country from this scourge:

1) fund research to clone Stepford copies of real children;
2) establish a Parentcare program, like Medicare, but for parents of abusive children;
3) charge interstate tolls every 100 miles for each passenger under age 11;
4) design cars with soundproof cages in the backseat, with optional airholes;
5) exempt parents from any criminal liability for harming or abandoning young children on long driving trips;
6) hire a driver, preferably a Navy SEAL or Green Beret, to take the kids while you take the train;

LEECHES, LOVERS, BEARS, AND CHOCOLATE PUDDING

7) require parents to first undergo counseling before taking a driving vacation with young children;
8) formulate strong (and appropriately safe) sedatives for children;
9) hypnotize young children to obey all parental commands in a car (a possible alternative is to brainwash them as in *The Manchurian Candidate*, but that might be too radical for some faint-hearted parents).

Now the sordid facts. As painful as it is to remember those dark days in the summer of 1976, we hope it'll provide us some cathartic relief to finally reveal our worst Freudian fantasies.

To celebrate America's Bicentennial Year, everyone with a car set out that summer to see the country. We too thought it was a good idea. Casey was 10, Ginger 7, and Will 5, so it seemed the right time to introduce them to the majestic beauty of the Colorado mountains. Having already backpacked in the Rockies, Julie and I were ready to share our own wonderful experiences there with the kids. Driving would provide the perfect opportunity for the whole family to bond together during the three-day trip to Colorado. How naïve we were! Instead of bonding, we came unstuck.

The first day on the road was not so bad. We had a big Chevy wagon that was filled with games, comic books, coloring books, treats, and other bribes that occupied them for awhile. (This trip took place before there were any iPods or electronic games, which may have made a big difference, although we're pretty sure the kids would have still found ways to torment us.) Unfortunately, the novelty of all the goodies lasted just one day. Then the Age of War and Woe began. No amount of bribes and threats could stop the deafening din of complaints from the backseat:

"Are we there yet?"
10 minutes later: "When are we gonna get there?" (crying)
"I need to go tee-tee."
"Me too. I'm gonna wet my pants." (crying)
30 minutes later: "I left my teddy in the bathroom." (crying)
"Stop it."
"You started it."
"Mommy, she hit me." (crying)

ON THE ROAD WITH THREE LITTLE BACKSEAT ANGELS

"I'm hungry."
Mommy: "How about a snack?"
"I hate those." (crying)
"I wet my pants." (crying) (crying in front seat too)
Etc., ad nauseam.

The constant clamor drove us nuts, but the infrequent lulls were no better because we knew the kids were hatching some kind of plot, like the calm before the storm. Or flashing "HELP!" and "SAVE US!" signs to passing motorists. And then there was Casey's portable tape recorder, a good idea gone wrong. As we found out later, she took it into bathroom stalls and secretly taped the candid conversations of strangers. She did the same thing to us in the car as Julie and I quietly discussed ways to make the children shut up or just disappear. When we eventually realized our gleeful ruminations about de-populating the backseat had been recorded and could be used as evidence against us in a triple-murder trial, it made us lower our sights in favor of more subtle solutions. With the benefit of hindsight, it's now clear that we were all saved by a Radio Shack tape recorder.

In an effort to pacify the restless rabble without exterminating them, Julie and I bought sandwiches and found a scenic spot on the side of the road for a nice family picnic, but alas, the Fates had other plans for us. As soon as we spread out the food, hundreds of flies appeared out of nowhere and a Texas wind blew dust into our sandwiches and eyes, so we fled without eating. Well-fed children are bad enough, but hungry children are terrifying. Julie and I considered binding and gagging them but figured someone would report us to the police and the seat cover in the back would probably be ruined. Instead, we just stopped driving earlier in the afternoon so we could start drinking sooner. That helped some until one morning, while waiting in a long line for breakfast, when our seven-year-old asked us in a loud voice "Do you need beer in the morning too?" and 30 people turned our way with looks of horror and disgust. We cut back on the alcohol but then became even more homicidal as the backseat mayhem intensified. By the end of the third day, if a certain grizzly bear (coming later) had been handy, we probably would've fed the children to him.

It didn't help the situation that millions of other saps like us were traversing the country that summer. The motels and especially the bars were jammed. All the parents with young children wore the same dazed, defeated

LEECHES, LOVERS, BEARS, AND CHOCOLATE PUDDING

look. In one city, the last motel with a vacancy was a seedy joint that rented rooms by the hour, if you know what I mean. The sheets looked half-washed, so the kids slept on towels, and the TV had nothing but porn, so we kept the kids out late. That we were not alone was the only consolation: it was amusing the next morning to watch all the other shame-faced parents trying to sneak out to their expensive cars without being seen. In another suburban motel of slightly higher quality, we awoke at 4:00 AM to the soothing sound of many basketballs being dribbled up and down the hallway outside our room. It seems we were located next door to a Mexican high school basketball team that was departing early. We spent the next night in the historic town of Central City (now a gambling center), but the old hotel didn't have a TV set, so our deprived children spent an hour at the window watching a neighbor's TV across the narrow street, without any sound! (We put our only TV in the attic when we got home.)

Once we parked the car at the trailhead and started hiking, things got much better, which proves that cars + kids are a devil's brew. The hike we'd picked was about four miles long, with a gentle incline, beautiful wildflowers, great views, and a rushing trailside stream, ending at the lower of two alpine lakes. Julie and I carried most of the camping gear, but Casey, our 10-year-old, toted her own sleeping bag, mat, and clothes, plus some of the food. Ginger and Will also helped by hauling their own change of clothes in fanny-packs strapped around their waists. Unfortunately, after initially charging up the trail, they both ran out of gas in about five minutes, so Casey took their fanny-packs the rest of the way while Julie and I lugged the tired hikers. Although we had tried to acclimate them to the higher altitudes of Colorado, hiking uphill at 10,000–11,000 feet is a challenge for young children, especially flatlanders like ours. But they did their best and we finally made it to the top, which was definitely worth the effort.

The setting was spectacular! The crystal-clear water of the small alpine lake sparkled in the bright sunlight. Trout swam lazily near the shoreline. There was a full-bodied waterfall flowing from the upper lake to its lower companion. The thick aspen and fir forest we'd hiked through did not reach the lake, which was above timberline, so there was ample clearing for a campsite. The Columbine and other wildflowers were out in abundance. And we had all of this to ourselves—except for the local inhabitants. We were greeted by the high-pitched squeaks of unseen pikas and marmots that live in tunnels in the rocks and are intensely reclusive (except for one very weird marmot that lusted after Julie on a later hike, the subject of another story). Chipmunks, on the other hand, are anything but shy. As we set up camp, they scurried from rock to rock, looking us over and hoping for a tasty handout. With all this company, we never got lonely.

We decided to set up camp on a flat area near the point where the outflowing stream left the lake. Like a Siren's Song, the stream beckoned the kids to cool their weary feet in its shallow, babbling water that was also incredibly cold because it came primarily from melted snow. After possibly 10 seconds of wading, they leapt out of the water yelling bloody murder and dancing around like banshees. Julie and I reluctantly rose to the occasion and warmed their frozen feet on our bare tummies. Then we put up the two tents side by side, unrolled the sleeping bags and mats, and set up the "kitchen," which consisted of one ornery gas stove the size of a soup can and one pot. Dinner, and all other meals for four days, consisted of freeze-dried packages of beef and chicken, summer sausage, sliced cheese, peanut butter in a tube, pita bread, and GORP spiced up with M&M's. Even the chipmunks wouldn't touch the freeze-dried stuff, but they loved the GORP, minus the raisins. The stream supplied our drinking water, although we had to treat it chemically for giardia and other animal-borne organisms.

Following a less-than-gourmet dinner, we put the kids to bed while there was still some daylight. Julie, an extraordinary mother and pre-K teacher with a deep love and understanding of young children in general, was also a consummate storyteller. She could mesmerize children with stories she usually made up on the spot, a talent she put to good use that and every night on the mountain. The three kids were not scared, because they'd done a lot of overnight camping in southern Louisiana and Mississippi, but they were very wound up, so Julie had to work her magic to settle them down. While she did that, I re-packed the backpacks and tied them closed as tightly as possible to keep out the nosy, gluttonous chipmunks. (Aside from the lack of space, backpacks containing food are a no-no inside a tent because of bears, even though Colorado black bears are very shy—unlike a certain wayward and much more dangerous grizzly that enters our story later.)

LEECHES, LOVERS, BEARS, AND CHOCOLATE PUDDING

The next three days were wonderful. We left the campsite in place and took day hikes to the waterfall, the upper lake, and nearby peaks. Ginger had a touch of altitude sickness, so we named the waterfall "Virginia Falls" in her honor. We showed the kids how to fly-fish but managed to catch only one brown trout that we cooked in tinfoil over an open fire. After several meals of freeze-dried food, the kids attacked that poor little fish like cannibals at a barbeque. We did catch another fish, by hand, no less—a good-sized rainbow trout that had trapped itself in the shallows of a stream. Some serious soul-searching resulted in the unanimous decision that it would be unfair to eat him under the circumstances, so we gently freed him from his bind and watched him go his merry way. We also made friends with the chipmunks, who would do anything for food. Soon they were climbing all over us, which the kids loved.

Leaving that idyllic spot was sad but unavoidable because we'd brought only four days of food—and the kids were starting to agitate for "real" food. So, after hiking out and packing the car, we stopped at the first fast-food place we saw. Little did we realize just how badly our five sweaty, unbathed bodies stank after several days of primitive living. As soon as we walked through the door, heads turned and then headed to the exits. Totally unconcerned, the kids gorged themselves on burgers, fries, shakes, cokes, and sundry other kinds of "real" food. They were completely transfixed. And, to be honest, that "real" food tasted pretty good to the parents too.

Before heading home, we stopped at Mesa Verde, the site in southwest Colorado where ancient cliff-dwellers lived from 600 to 1300 AD and then abruptly vanished into thin air. The buildings they left behind are truly spectacular, well-preserved, and surprisingly accessible. Unfortunately, on the short drive there, the bad car-karma had again transformed our kids into three Mr. Hydes, only worse. Julie and I therefore raced through the magnificent ruins, with teeth gritted. Although we considered a number of options from ritual sacrifice to semi-spontaneous cave-ins, we decided to do the humane thing (proof that we do have consciences, however tiny) and just abandon the kids in hopes that some nice tourist would take care of them, since they were all cute, on the surface at least. The plan was to send them to the gift shop with lots of money, then dash to the car and make our getaway. But the kids obviously sensed something was up (maybe the money gave us away) and never let us out of their sight (but kept the money). Drat! Foiled again! Julie and I were clearly outmatched.

Whereupon, we had one of our rare brainstorms—something actually constructive, no less. Once we herded the little fiends back into the car, we pulled out a book and it changed everything. *The Book of the Dun Cow* is a gripping tale of Good versus Evil that pits a heroic rooster and a ridiculous dog against two invincible serpents from the underworld. The backseat became silent and still as soon as we started reading. The kids were hooked. Casey was old enough to be spellbound, Will was still young enough to be scared witless (as he told us later) but interested, and Ginger was somewhere in between. Peace at last! The book was long enough to get us back to New Orleans, so Julie and I quietly celebrated our good fortune.

A bit prematurely, as luck would have it. The day following the Mesa Verde fiasco, our long-suffering Chevy broke down on a lonely road in the middle of a Navajo Indian reservation west of Albuquerque. After seeing no other cars for an hour, we were all a little desperate. Finally, a vehicle appeared in the distance. It turned out to be an old beat-up, graffiti-adorned van with four young pot-smoking hippies, which was not that unusual back in 1976, but I would have preferred anything else. Even though Julie and I had agreed we should all stick together under any circumstances, here was a real dilemma: whether to (a) expose her and the children to a possible danger inside the van or (b) pass up the only opportunity we might have for a long time. So, with dusk fast approaching, I split the difference. Against my better judgment and my wife's frantic pleas, I hopped in the van and left my family behind on the roadside, one of the hardest things I've ever had to do. But my hippie hosts could not have been nicer. They dropped me off at the first service station and I returned joyfully to my brave little clan in a tow truck, which the kids thought was pretty cool. A new water-pump was installed and we hit the road again.

Our last stop before heading home was Carlsbad Caverns in southern New Mexico. We spent the night there and then exacted a small but sweet measure of revenge by waking up the unhappy kids at 4:00 AM. All for a good reason, of course: the famous, once-a-year Bat Breakfast, featuring millions of bats returning to their home in the caverns through a single, small hole in the ground. Their velocity and accuracy were amazing. Once they reached a point

LEECHES, LOVERS, BEARS, AND CHOCOLATE PUDDING

directly above the portal, they made a sharp right-angle turn and dove hundreds of feet straight down at top speed. They never missed, despite their blindness and the size of the target. And they never collided with one another, despite the countless number of bats speeding through the crowded opening at the same time. It was an incredible sight that even our young kids appreciated. After a tasty outdoor breakfast, we toured the caverns themselves, which were equally spectacular.

The long drive home through Texas was actually pretty good. The highlight was a stirring rendition of "Hansel and Gretel," starring Casey and Ginger as the title characters and Will as the Wicked Witch, in a sneak preview of his future career as actor and screenwriter. The kids' choice of this particular tale was a bit unsettling for us because it's about young children abandoned by their bad parents. Sound familiar? Yes, indeed, proving once again that kids are smarter than you think. And very creative. Will, decked out by the girls in a dress, bonnet, high heels, necklace, and a long cigarette holder, stole the show. A born ham, he threw himself into the role and clearly relished the chance to chase his older sisters around. We were in stitches. It was so good that a horse poked his head through an open motel window to watch, I kid you not.

So the vacation ended on a very happy high note, thanks to the genius of our brilliant, talented, extraordinary, wonderfully wacky offspring, who are still driving us crazy 36 years later. This story is dedicated to them, with love from Mom and Dad.

But wait, you say, that's all fine and dandy, but what about the grizzly bear? Well, he didn't show up until we got back to New Orleans—not in the flesh, fortunately, but in the local newspaper. There was this picture of a hospital patient in bandages from head to toe, who was being prosecuted under the

ON THE ROAD WITH THREE LITTLE BACKSEAT ANGELS

Endangered Species Act for killing a grizzly that happened to be chewing him to pieces before he stopped it with a hand-held arrow to the bear's throat. Then we discovered, to our horror, that the same thing or worse could have happened to us! According to the report, the bear's attack occurred in Colorado at the very time we were camped out there and only a short distance away. Unlike their much smaller cousins, grizzly bears are huge, ferocious carnivores that weigh up to 900 pounds, twice as much as all of us put together, and run as fast as 40 miles an hour. But everyone knew that Colorado was completely free of grizzlies because they had all retreated up to Wyoming and points even further north, so the reporter must have identified the wrong kind of bear, right? Just to be sure, I called the nearest ranger station in Colorado and learned, to my dismay, that they still had the carcass and it was definitely a grizzly. Julie and I thanked the bear gods profusely and made a solemn vow to mend our ways, which has been much harder to do than we ever imagined—just ask the kids.

* * * * *

Let's see how that first long road trip with our kids stacks up against other experiences and possibilities. For example, poor Julie had to drive carpool once or twice a week for years with not just three but a car full of whining, crying, screaming, fighting, biting, or otherwise misbehaving kids. What she did (with her usual grace and patience) for so long makes our cross-country trek seem like a walk in the park by comparison.

We also have to consider what our trip would have been like without roaches. Yes, roaches. Specifically, the dozens if not hundreds of them that lived quietly in The Great White, the big Chevy station wagon that took us out to Colorado and back. (It was a super car that survived many trips out West in summer and winter as well as a number of remote mountain roads that would have destroyed a lesser vehicle.) Before realizing how much help those six-legged squatters could be with the kids, we had an exterminator spray the car, twice, but that didn't phase them. On that 1976 trip, they were much better behaved than their fellow passengers in the back seat because they appeared only at night and politely vanished into the chassis as soon as an interior light came on—try as we did on several extreme occasions, we never could make the kids

LEECHES, LOVERS, BEARS, AND CHOCOLATE PUDDING

vanish like that. They also cleaned up after our messy kids had littered the backseat with countless crumbs and half-eaten food. Our little allies also served another good purpose: the only threat that had any effect on the kids' behavior was that of having to sleep one night in the car with the roaches. Julie and I of course would never have done that to them, but maybe an hour if they were really bad. In any event, we never had to carry out the threat.

That brings me to technology. What happened to us on that first road trip out West is unlikely to happen today because of all the video games, musical devices, cellphones, and other modern marvels available to entertain (distract?) children of any age. As a result, the backseat bedlam we encountered back then has now been replaced by total silence, as we've seen with our grandchildren. We find the same tech gap if we go back in time instead of forward. In 1953, when I was 12 or so, I drove with my parents and sister from New Orleans to Boston. The only entertainment technology then was the car radio, but there was not much on it of any interest to me. Nor did we have any air-conditioning, so we drove across the whole country twice with the windows open. And without any interstate highways or fast-food restaurants yet, the drive took forever. I had good reason to scream bloody murder the whole time, but luckily for them and me, my parents made good use of my interest in maps and history by letting me pick the route, so I spent most of the time poring over road maps looking for Civil War battlefields to visit, i.e., I never got bored. Julie and I should have followed their good example, but at least we had tape and CD players, better radio choices, an air-conditioned car, good highways, and fast-food outlets. If our 1976 venture had taken place in the tech-void Dark Ages of 1953, all five of us would probably be in a nut house right now.

With that perspective, maybe Julie and I should count our blessings that the trip turned out as well as it did. And it certainly did, especially if we regard the driving portion as a learning experience for all five of us, as it apparently was, because our future road trips with all or some of the kids were nothing like that first one.

PREDESTINATION AND INNER TUBES

It was the ultimate unguided missile: a 300-pound man on a large inner tube plunging pell-mell down a snow-covered hill. And the target? Unfortunately, our eight-year-old daughter Ginger, all 60 pounds of her alone at the bottom of the hill like a lamb before the slaughter.

Needless to say, the setting was another of those idyllic family vacations, this one in Colorado. We should have stuck to downhill skiing (which does eliminate most 300-pounders and does provide some steering capability), but we decided to spend a day snow-tubing with the kids. Julie of course, with her uncanny nose for impending disaster, picked this day to catch an alleged cold and stay home. But, hey, snow-tubing is a "safe, simple, fun-filled activity for the whole family," so what's to worry about? It's just like tubing down a river, except that a tube going downhill on snow moves much faster and cannot be steered or stopped, especially if bearing a very large person.

It was a blast—we had a great time sliding and tumbling all over a long, wide hill. We even got pretty good at riding the bizarre tow system that literally dragged us up the hill upside down and backwards on our tubes, but it sure beat walking up a slippery slope. Anyway, things went very well—until the final run of the day. Ginger decided to sit it out and wait for us at the bottom. When Casey, Will, and I reached the top, we were all alone except for a very rotund gentleman. Since the sight of a good 300-pound man riding an inner tube is quite unusual and interesting, we stopped to watch his descent before starting our own. Far down the hill, Ginger looked like a fragile doll.

When the other tuber reached the halfway point, Ginger sauntered casually to one side in order to give him more room at the bottom. Then the darnedest thing happened: as she moved off to one side, the descending tube gradually turned in the same direction. When she turned around and headed in the opposite direction, the tube likewise changed course again. This seemed a bit strange but nothing to worry about since the tuber still had a long way to go and Ginger had at least 100 yards of running room at the bottom (she could run from side to side but not away from the hill because of a fence). However, despite the long odds, Ginger started moving a bit faster, just in case.

This amazing tango became more and more intense—every time she moved to the left or to the right, the tube veered in the same direction, just like a homing torpedo. Ginger must have felt like she was being pursued by a gigantic Pac-Man come to life. As the gap between them closed, both Ginger and Pac-Man reacted in frantic (but understandable) ways. He of course could not stop or steer his tube, so he simply waved his arms wildly as if that would make Ginger disappear. Thankfully, he did not bail out of the tube, which given his size and speed would have created a more dangerous missile at best or started an avalanche at worst. As Pac-Man bore down on her, Ginger ran faster and faster, back and forth, reminiscent of the revolving bear in those electronic target-shooting games.

Let's now freeze the two protagonists and focus for a moment on those onlookers at the top of the hill. Being Ginger's father and siblings, we had a very personal interest in the action below. We of course were rooting for Ginger's salvation (except perhaps Casey, who had to share a bedroom with her), but there was absolutely nothing we could do to stop the speeding Pac-Man or otherwise save her. Ginger's fate was in her own hands and she was clearly working hard to save herself. In fact, we were amazed that Ginger, who disdained any form of exercise as a child, could run so fast and turn so quickly on her little short legs. Not that Ginger ever looked like any kind of ball, but watching her run back and forth over and over again reminded me of a good ping-pong match. Meanwhile, Pac-Man, who was now yelling and waving like crazy, must have realized at last that his rubber chariot was possessed by some kind of evil inner-tube spirit bent on squashing little Ginger. Despite the potential danger, we knew of course that the odds of a collision were still infinitesimal. Which explains why we were more amused than anxious at this point—after all, the scene unfolding before us was truly a masterpiece of slap-stick comedy. As shameful as it sounds now, I could not stop imagining Ginger in a two-dimensional format, much like the old cartoon coyote who always got flattened by the roadrunner.

Anyway, all three of us at the top were utterly transfixed, torn between feelings of hilarity and horror as things rushed towards a climax. Ginger had just made her twelfth (and last) U-turn and run a good quarter mile in all at top speed

PREDESTINATION AND INNER TUBES

in her heroic effort to elude Pac-Man and the relentless killer tube. But she simply could not shake them—on they came, twisting and turning and hurtling down the slope towards their innocent prey. Ginger, her trademark dimple now replaced by a look of grim determination, was straining mightily for one last ounce of speed. There was still ample time and room for a near-miss. But the moment of truth finally did arrive—it was a direct hit, against all odds, as if that clumsy, clueless piece of rubber had been guided to the pre-arranged target by some unseen hand of Fate. Surprisingly, the collision generated no sound whatsoever. On impact, Ginger went up, not down, which was lucky. Her limp body, spinning slowly and silently as it rose higher and higher, looked like a ragdoll. It was an awful sight. She remained airborne for at least three full revolutions in the thin Colorado air.

When we reached her, Ginger was lying there very still and spread-eagle like a delicate little snow angel. Miraculously, there was no blood and no broken bones. Although quite stunned and frightened, she would recover fully after consuming the biggest hot fudge sundae I ever saw. On the other hand, Pac-Man's prognosis was much more in doubt—when we left him, he was still inconsolable and threatening to kill his inner tube, which at the time seemed like a pretty good idea.

As a consequence of this near disaster, I was demoted still again but in the gentlest possible way. Whenever I proposed to take the kids on an outing after that, Julie dropped everything (including a Paul Newman movie on the tube) and went with us as a bodyguard to her brood. It reminded me of a previous demotion after I *accidentally* pinned one of those old-fashioned diapers to our firstborn's leg. That was the last dirty diaper I ever had to change (I swear it was an accident), but as a consolation prize, Julie appointed me the chief custodian of the dirty diaper *bag*.

OUR OFF-THE-WALL OFFSPRING

The long-awaited moment has arrived! After covering up for our dear children all these years, it's time to tell the truth (or at least as much of it as we know, which is only about 10% of all the bad stuff they did, according to Will—our ignorance is definitely bliss). The forthcoming disclosures will be quite cathartic for Julie and me, but hopefully they will serve as a warning for young couples who are thinking about starting a family (if you do, you may survive after all is said and done, but be prepared for the unexpected, the illogical, the outrageous, the unexplainable, and everything in between).

Our three (sometimes) human children, Casey, Ginger, and Will, somehow avoided juvenile detention, eventually grew up (about time!), and turned out surprisingly well, considering what they had wrought in their extended adolescence. Our canine, quasi-human child, Mama, passed on to her well-deserved reward after helping us parent the others for 15 years, starting around the time Will was born.

Before getting to the painful Truth, I want to make sure you understand that Julie and I were good parents to our progeny, as a few examples will demonstrate:

LEECHES, LOVERS, BEARS, AND CHOCOLATE PUDDING

1) We didn't set them adrift in a canoe on the Tangipahoa River like Baby Moses (we wanted to keep our canoe);
2) We didn't abandon them at Mesa Verde when they disobeyed for the umpteenth time and got lost (Julie got cold feet halfway to the car);
3) We didn't feed them to the nearby grizzly bear in a remote Colorado wilderness (we believed in being kind to the local wildlife);
4) We didn't send them across the New Mexico desert for help when our car broke down in the middle of nowhere (we needed to use them to hitch a ride);
5) We didn't send them "up the river" for a few years whenever they broke the law (they had too much on us);
6) We didn't ship them off to Greenland as teenagers to study polar bears, which was always my favorite solution (Greenland already had enough problems of its own);
7) We didn't lock them in the basement (we didn't have one);
8) We didn't allow them to play with loaded guns (we worried about Mama getting hurt);
9) We didn't administer any kind of well-deserved physical punishment (Julie cried all day after gently spanking two-year-old Casey once);
10) We didn't emancipate them legally at age 10 (we couldn't afford to move to Texas, where anything goes); and
11) We didn't exchange them for three house-broken turtles (Mama was afraid of turtles).

Those are some of our more benign fantasies inspired by The Children, or at least the human ones (assuming for the sake of argument that teenagers are human). They finally grew up to be model citizens and parents only because Julie and I exercised amazing self-control during their "formative" years from ages 1 to 30. Despite the daily provocations that would have justified a triple filicide in any court of law, we just gritted our teeth, predicted incorrectly that things would get better, and drank a lot.

The saga of surviving our children should start with the most outrageous of their many exploits, the notorious parents-are-out-of-town extravaganza, but

OUR OFF-THE-WALL OFFSPRING

that has already been memorialized in a separate story, so we have to start elsewhere.

The Cursed Waterbed

When he was about 12, Will somehow prevailed upon us to get him a waterbed. That was one of the stupidest things we ever did, among many. We should have known that Will was a con man, even then, but he was so cute and cherubic—and smooth as silk. His beloved pillowcase said it all: pictures of sharks with the words "TRUST ME," which he picked out himself.

His waterbed was a living beast, a work of the devil, a two-ton water-bomb lurking on the second floor of our house. For Julie and me, it was fear and loathing at first sight. The Thing "belched" at us whenever we dared enter Will's room. We slept with one eye open, knowing it was slithering down the hallway to crush or drown us. How do you stop a rogue waterbed on the loose? Shoot it? Use a flamethrower? Too much collateral damage.

So The Thing survived, laying in wait for the perfect opportunity to destroy us all, which young Will created soon enough. After giving us his solemn oath that he would change the water regularly, he never got around to it for five long years. As a result, the water started to look and act like a witch's brew, bubbling and changing shape mysteriously. It even became too much for Will (or The Thing planted the idea in his head), so he decided one day to change the water, while I was at work. After draining The Thing without incident via a hose out the window, he then hooked the hose to a faucet outside and turned on the water. So far, so good, but stay tuned.

While it was slowly refilling, Will got involved in some other interesting project and promptly forgot all about The Thing. By the time he remembered and rushed back to his room, it had metamorphosed into The Hulk of all waterbeds. It was several times its normal size and filled most of Will's room from floor to ceiling. The seams were stretched so much that they were leaking enough water to flood the room and run down the walls of the dining room underneath it. The Thing was ready to explode and take out most of the neighborhood. Will's woeful cry for help (and the water in her dining room) brought Julie running. They tried unsuccessfully to disconnect the hose upstairs

LEECHES, LOVERS, BEARS, AND CHOCOLATE PUDDING

before turning off the water outside and draining the swollen bed. Throughout this first-class calamity, Will kept urging Julie "Don't tell Dad."

Well, their cover-up worked for a few days. By the time I got home from the office, the walls had been wiped dry and the water on the floor mopped up. Julie, Will, and now Ginger (Casey was away at school) met me at the front door and offered me drinks, massages, foot rubs, and anything else I wanted, which should have set off all sorts of alarms, but I wasn't about to miss such an opportunity. They quickly herded me through the dining room to my recliner in the den, chattering constantly to distract me from any telltale signs of a disaster. It was a carefully coordinated conspiracy worthy of the CIA, but I was also pampered as never before or since. It was a few days later that one of them fessed up once they figured the house was going to survive after all.

Will went away to school in Connecticut soon after that (no, it was not a form of punishment) and left us with his battered waterbed. So it sat there, ominously, year after year until Ginger decided the time had come to kill it while Will was still away. She and Julie and I were the willing but nervous executioners. But the damn thing wouldn't go quietly to its just reward. When we hooked up the hose to drain it, nothing happened, probably because the water was now the consistency of lava. An electric suction pump to draw out the water only made things worse. We had to re-route the hose and extension down the front steps in order to plug the pump into an electrical outlet. As soon as we turned it on, all hell broke loose. Water came spewing out of all the connections and out of the pump itself, which happened to be in my hand and connected to 110 volts of electricity, so I thought The Thing upstairs had finally done me in, but I somehow managed to survive. To finish the job, we had nothing left to try but old-fashioned buckets. Armed with small kitchen buckets, the three of us took turns filling them up while someone stood on the waterbed to force out the water and then quickly emptying them in the nearest toilet, which miraculously flushed automatically with each dumping (did you know they did that? we didn't). After a couple of hours of this, The Thing was dead, once and for all. We were exhausted and half the house was a mess, but we had won a glorious victory over the forces of evil.

OUR OFF-THE-WALL OFFSPRING

And now we wait with gleeful anticipation: When Will's three wonderful daughters turn 10, they will each receive a shiny new waterbed as a birthday present from Nana (Julie) and Pops (me). Revenge will be sweet! We can't wait.

Hands

When she was four or five, Casey got into a tussle with one of those old-fashioned clipboards that ensnared her like a wild animal trap. She apparently was putting her index finger in the round hole of the metal clip when it got stuck and started to swell. It looked pretty bad when we first saw it. Julie and I tried soap and water but that didn't help and Casey was too uncomfortable to try anything else. The only other option was the ER at Ochsner, so we actually flipped a coin to see who would take her, as shameful as that was. I lost and Julie got to stay home with Ginger.

Not surprisingly, Casey's bizarre predicament turned quite a few heads in the ER. To Ochsner's credit, the nurses were very sympathetic toward Casey (unlike their attitude toward me, the negligent father) and a young doctor appeared quickly. Since Casey's painfully swollen finger was not coming out of that hole any other way, the doctor used a large metal cutter from the Maintenance Department to carefully snip off the clip, which my brave daughter watched but I couldn't. After a big lollipop for Casey and one last disapproving look for me, we headed home with the gutted clipboard that we kept for many years to remind us to check out the kids' toys for hidden dangers.

Not long after Casey's ordeal, Ginger cut her thumb badly on a sharp metal piece inside a child's kaleidoscope that she had taken apart unbeknownst to us. Thankfully, it was Julie's turn to take the latest abused child of ours to the ER, but I did go fuss with the toy store about selling dangerous toys.

Typical of our youngest child, Will had two hand mishaps that were even more bizarre. One involved locking his fingers in a car door. If you think about that for just a moment, you'll wonder how anyone could do something so ..., so addlepated, especially a smart, sober young man of 16 who went on to win the top citizenship awards at his prep school and summer camp. Well, he did. And he was alone. And it was nighttime. But, hey, no big deal—all he had to do was fetch the car keys from his pocket and unlock the car door. Only one thing could

LEECHES, LOVERS, BEARS, AND CHOCOLATE PUDDING

go wrong with such a foolproof plan and of course it did: he dropped the car keys on the ground just out of his reach even after stretching as far as he could. Now it was a big deal. Cursing didn't help but maybe praying did by bringing his sister to rescue him. Luckily for Will, this took place in front of our house and Ginger happened to see his predicament through a window. Knowing how Ginger now uses her cellphone camera to record people in funny situations (like Julie stuck in a deep snowbank while skiing), Will was also lucky there were no cellphones then to publicize his embarrassing plight on Facebook. However, we can be sure that Ginger drove a hard bargain and extracted several concessions from Will before she finally agreed to unlock the car door.

The next episode occurred during one of our early drives out West with the kids. Will was too young at that time to be called addlepated, but I certainly wasn't. You be the judge of what happened. It was a historic moment: for the first time in his young life, Will was going into the little boys' room with Daddy instead of the little girls' room with Mommy, to wash his hands before lunch at a roadside restaurant. He dashed through the bathroom door, anxious to show me he was up to the challenge, and by the time I caught up, he was already washing his hands—in the urinal, using the deodorizer bar as soap! Being a germ-phobic fanatic, I could imagine billions of slimy little critters crawling up his arms and thought briefly about amputating them at the elbows. Instead, I grabbed Will (avoiding his hands, of course), dragged him over to the sink, and incinerated all those bugs in hot water. He, poor thing, had no idea what was going on and voiced his displeasure loudly, so I spent the next month in everyone's doghouse, as I probably deserved. And while I was in that doghouse (for not the first or last time), it dawned on me why this had occurred: since little girls' bathrooms don't have urinals, little boys don't have any way to learn about them with their mommies before they graduate to the big boys' bathrooms with urinals and other cool stuff.

The 9-1-1 Filet

It was a perfect evening. Julie and I were dining at the legendary Antoine's Restaurant in the French Quarter with clients of my law firm, which therefore would pick up the tab. Tomorrow was Sunday and a day off, as much as that was possible in that phase of our lives. Our three young children were at home with their favorite babysitter. I had just finished my first bite of a delicious filet mignon and put the second in my mouth with taste buds aglow. Julie was enjoying her usual soft-shell crab. The wine was also superb. A second bottle had just been opened. That's when the phone call came.

The worried waiter told us there was an emergency call from our babysitter. This was long before cellphones, so I took the call in some office while I was still chewing my delicious filet. The babysitter told me she thought our seven-year-old daughter Ginger was having an attack of appendicitis and she had called 911 for an ambulance. It sounded really bad. I gulped down my half-chewed filet, rushed back to our table, gathered up Julie, looked longingly but quickly at my uneaten steak, apologized to the clients, and rushed out of the restaurant.

As luck would have it, a police car was just then cruising slowly in front of Antoine's, so I flagged it down instead of taking the extra time to get our car out of a busy parking garage two blocks away, since our daughter's life was on the line. The two policemen could not have been nicer. After hearing our sad tale, they told us to jump in the back seat (which was a cage for arrested suspects) and they'd get us home as fast as possible. Despite her tight and abundant dress, my graceful wife slipped into the back seat without a hitch, but I turned it into a failed circus trick and managed to catch my best suit pants on some metal object and rip them all the way down one side. No matter—Ginger's life was all that counted.

Off we went, with lights blazing and siren blaring. Although we made it home in record time, it seemed like an eternity to Julie and me because we didn't know if our dear little daughter was dead or alive. It didn't help our fast-vanishing peace of mind that a fire engine and an ambulance with flashing lights were parked in front of our house. And the whole street was crowded with anxious-looking neighbors. We jumped out of the car and raced into the house with pounding hearts and one pair of flapping trousers.

And there was Ginger, still alive and sitting comfortably in a chair with her legs crossed, grinning ambiguously, and eating a big bowl of ice cream, which reminded me of my uneaten filet before a flood of relief took over. The

LEECHES, LOVERS, BEARS, AND CHOCOLATE PUDDING

babysitter explained that Ginger had been doubled over in pain clutching her stomach but then had a "miraculous" recovery after she'd called us and 911. We assured her she did absolutely the right thing and used her many times after that to babysit the kids. The paramedics had checked out Ginger and told us she was fine. But the happiest person of all was young Will, then five, not because his sister was going to live but because he got to wear a fireman's hat and a policeman's hat. For some time after that, Will kept talking about how much fun Ginger's "tummy ache" was.

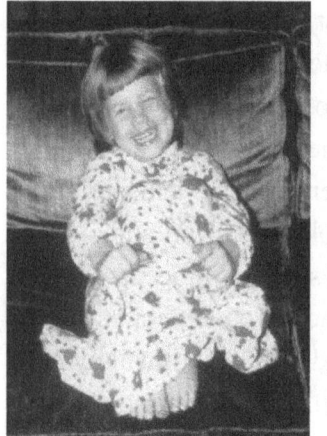

So everything worked out well, except for my uneaten filet and unsalvageable pants. We didn't lose our abandoned clients, who told me later they finished off that second bottle of wine, ordered a third, and had a grand time after we left. Julie and I returned to Antoine's later by ourselves and ordered the same dinners, which we finished this time. When she got older, Ginger came to love good filets, so she can fully appreciate what I gave up to rush home to her aid, which of course I don't let her forget. Since we didn't get a bill for any of the emergency services rendered that night, we did commend our two wonderful chauffeurs to their chief. And, best of all, Ginger's appendix is still intact 42 years later, probably because of the ice cream cure.

Frogs

There are two kinds of frogs: real and imaginary. Casey's frog was imaginary but ferocious; Ginger's was real but gentle.

Casey was strong-willed when she came out of the womb. She had somehow mastered the word "no" during gestation and it comprised 98% of her verbal output for the first five years of her life until she figured out that the word "maybe" opened up all sorts of good negotiating possibilities. There was only one person who wouldn't take "no" from Casey and that was Odelise, my mother-in-law's housekeeper and our sometimes babysitter. She was a force to be reckoned with. Odelise resolved a dispute with one of her neighbors by bashing her over the head with a brick in a pillowcase. Fortunately, the victim

OUR OFF-THE-WALL OFFSPRING

survived but sued Odelise for her injuries. Pascal Calogero, who later became Chief Justice of the Louisiana Supreme Court, represented the plaintiff and I defended Odelise as a favor since she was uninsured. We settled the case on the morning of trial. It's no wonder that Casey was terrified of Odelise—we all were. Odelise was the only one of us who found a way to get Casey out of the tub after a bath instead of playing in the water for half an hour. She did it by inventing a fearsome frog that lived in the bathtub drain and was ready to come out and devour Casey if she didn't get out of the tub quickly. It worked like a charm. Casey never again lingered in a bathtub until she went away to college.

Ginger's frog really did live in a drain, which is how our young daughter became the only known frog-caller in the entire recorded history of the world. Needless to say, Julie and I are quite proud of creating such a unique and important talent. We had no idea that Ginger was a frog-caller until we moved into a new house in 1971 when she was going on three. In the open passageway between the kitchen and playroom was a small covered drain and in the drainpipe lived a frog that no doubt had been a charming prince who ran afoul of a bad witch. Unfortunately, the drain cover was cemented into place, so Ginger could not kiss the frog and change him back to a prince. But she obviously did enchant the poor fellow because he always came right up to the drain cover whenever she called. And then they "talked," as well as a young child and an old frog could. It always made Ginger a little sad because she couldn't free him, but he surely appreciated the attention from a kind soul who understood his plight. Julie and I never saw him except when he was "talking" with Ginger. On those occasions, he looked happier than any other frog we've ever seen.

Teenage Drivers

Let me start with a relatively honest disclaimer: neither Julie nor I attained perfection as teenage drivers. Julie wrecked her mother's shiny new Christmas present before it was a day old. I sideswiped a parked car while trying to drive and impress my date at the same time. And I'm sure there were a few other inconsequential mishaps lost in the fog of time. So it is with humility, sympathy, and understanding that I recount the driving adventures of our teenage children (in retrospect, it really would have been cheaper to buy them all horses).

LEECHES, LOVERS, BEARS, AND CHOCOLATE PUDDING

Casey, our first teenage marauder, actually gave us a sneak preview of her later driving "skills" when she was only 13 months old. That's when we first introduced our young daughter to the joys of camping (with a bunch of Sierra Club friends in a Mississippi state park). We had a sleeping bag and pad for Casey but had to borrow a tent, which turned out to be an old one without a floor. You can imagine the panic when Julie and I woke up that first morning and realized that Casey's sleeping bag was empty. We found her about four feet outside the tent, still sound asleep inside her padded pajama suit, with the top of her head resting against the trunk of a small tree. She had apparently, in her sleep, squirmed or "scooted" her way out of her sleeping bag and under the side of the tent until she ran into that fortuitously placed tree. That's how Casey acquired the additional nickname of "Scoot" for scooter.

Some 14 years later, Casey picked up where she left off on that camping trip by starting her driving career with a bang—actually, six of them, in the space of just two months after getting her license. The only difference this time was the fact it was other cars instead of trees that stopped her forward progress. All or most of her victims were rear-ended, including three passengers in a taxi (two ambulance-chasers arrived on that scene within minutes). Casey eventually learned where the brake pedal was and what it was for, thank goodness!

Ginger was more selective. She foiled the escape of a nice old lady from a nearby nursing home by nailing her in a crosswalk. To complicate things, Ginger was driving the borrowed car of a friend who had promised her mom not to let anyone else (like Ginger in particular?) drive it. Will followed suit by ramming another little old lady who allegedly ran a stop sign. Fortunately, their prey all survived without serious injury and the children eventually became careful drivers, not that it did us any good because by then they had their own insurance, but at least the world is a little bit safer now.

Will wins the prize for the scariest escapade. Being a teenage (16) driver doing 107 miles per hour through a notorious speed trap in the middle of the day is probably not the smartest thing he ever did. He and his good friend Scott were driving through Slidell, Louisiana, on their way home from a Mississippi beach when our old Volvo lit up every police radar screen for miles around. Fortunately, Will was cold sober. And Scott was sound asleep at the time and therefore not complicit in Will's crime spree, so the police let him drive the car home. The distress call from Slidell came in the middle of a deposition I was taking. It was the only time my incredible secretary Maria ever interrupted a deposition, but I was still inclined to refuse the call when she made it very clear that "you really need to take this call!" When I told the other three attorneys and witness exactly why I had to postpone the deposition and leave immediately, they were very understanding, perhaps because they had teenage sons of their own.

Since I was obviously angry, Julie and Ginger insisted on going to Slidell with me, probably to stop me from killing Will. Ginger kept asking me to promise that I would spare her brother, which I wasn't about to do, until I saw how smart the Slidell police were. They had placed Will on a stool all by himself in the middle of a large, busy room where everyone knew what he had done. By the time we got there an hour later, young Will had been quite embarrassed and humbled. Nevertheless, when he saw how mad I was, he almost volunteered to remain in custody instead of going home with me to a dire fate, but the girls guaranteed his safety, so he finally agreed to leave, albeit reluctantly. Will and I eventually appeared before a friendly judge, I vouched for his good "heart," we paid a reasonable fine, and Will swore up and down that he would henceforth drive responsibly. And (as far as I know) he has kept that promise, so things turned out much better than they could have.

While Will holds the family speed record, Ginger holds the family record for distance. And for stealth—but we nabbed her anyway. During the summer before she left for college, she made plans to spend a couple of weeks by herself in Breckenridge, Colorado. It was going to be a quiet time of self-discovery and preparation in a beautiful setting. However, love, in the form of her steady boyfriend Edward back home, soon trumped all that cerebral stuff. What she did, without telling us, was drive to New Orleans, pick up Edward, and drive him back to Breckenridge, all in just a few days. It was an audacious plan that was executed perfectly in utter secrecy—except for one minor detail: gasoline. Every time Ginger stopped for gas, it showed up on our Texaco bill. And since we had driven that same route many times before, it was easy to plot her course back and forth across four states. But by the time we got the bill and figured what was going on, she was back in Breckenridge, so Julie and I decided to "save" our secret information until the perfect opportunity. Which arrived a few years later

LEECHES, LOVERS, BEARS, AND CHOCOLATE PUDDING

while Ginger was gushing to friends about her two idyllic weeks of peace and quiet in Breckenridge. That's when we sprang the trap. It was a priceless "gotcha!" moment that proved, once again, that Parents are not quite as dumb as their Children think.

Since Ginger and Will got into so much trouble while driving separately, you would assume that Julie and I, being sensible parents, would never let them take a long road trip together without any adult supervision. Right? Wrong! We must have been out of our minds—they were still teenagers, 19 and 17. But off they went in our trusty old Volvo to see the "key ceremony" at Camp Cheley in Colorado where Will had won the citizenship key the previous summer. In the middle of Nowhere, tumbleweed country between Dallas and Amarillo, the car started falling apart. The first thing to go was the air-conditioning and it was hot as hell, but there was no one around to see them, so they peeled off their clothes and drove on in their underwear. Then the engine fell out of the car! (I know what you're thinking. I swear, we had the Volvo fully checked and serviced right before their trip.) So there they were: practically naked, without cell phones back then, in an engine-less car on a forsaken highway in West Texas. They needed a miracle and luckily they got one. They were able to coast to the next exit and there was Bob's "Volvo" dealership, in the middle of Nowhere.

The coasting car finally came to a stop right in front of Bob's service window, where Ginger and Will emerged in their skivvies. Bob was a little hesitant at first but eventually agreed to do what he could. He retrieved the engine from the highway and somehow rebuilt it over the next two days. Our intrepid pioneers spent that time in the only motel within miles. It was obviously designed for short-term stays lasting a couple of hours at most instead of a couple of days: there was nothing on the TV but porn and the free continental breakfast consisted only of cold refried beans. But Bob saved the day and sent them on their way with a working vehicle.

The return trip to New Orleans was not quite as exciting but still memorable, at least from Will's perspective. Since Ginger was the navigator, poor Will was pretty much at her mercy. The plan was to drive straight through without stopping overnight. When they were in Nowhere again, i.e., West Texas, and it was Will's turn to drive (it was also getting dark), Ginger told him to wake her up when they reached a certain town about two hours away. Well, Ginger slept for 10 hours and they never did reach the designated town. After driving that long at night and watching for wildlife on the highway, Will was a basket case. Ginger had to pry his fingers off the steering wheel. He could not stand up straight or close his eyes. Ten minutes after Ginger started driving again and Will had just gone to sleep, she got her first (allegedly) ticket for speeding and was so rattled that she couldn't drive, so poor, exhausted Will had to wake up and drive for another hour, an eternity to him. They somehow survived and made it the rest of the way home without incident.

Unexpurgated

All three of our teenagers led X-rated, expurgated lives, but Will is the obvious star of this section. Not because of his irrepressible wild oats or his creatively illicit enterprises or his underage exuberances or his multiple definitions of truth—no, he's the star because of simple Filth. Although he has finally changed his ways (thank you, Sienna), young Will flourished in his own black hole of filth. You've already heard about the fetid fluid he slept on. But his waterbed was probably the cleanest part of his room. Despite Julie's best efforts to pick them up, his dirty clothes and wet towels were everywhere all the time. Even when he was supposed to set a good example for the other students after becoming Head Prefect at The Gunnery, he still hung his unwashed clothes and towels outside of his dorm window to air out and get rain-washed. On our first visit, Julie and I could spot and smell his room halfway across the campus.

We should have known what was coming and prepared better because Will as a toddler loved to waddle after garbage trucks and then cried when he couldn't catch them. But his filth fetish actually started even earlier. Soon after his birth, Will was given two knitted baby blankets and it was love at first sight. Thus began the saga of "bankie" (for "blanket") and "uzzer-one bankie" (for "other-one blanket")—even though they were identical white blankets with small pink roses on them, Will somehow knew which was which. They went everywhere with him, rain or shine. He wouldn't let them out of his sight, even to wash them. As a result, they remained totally "pristine" for over 22 years, until he got out of college, by which time they were in shreds, smelled like rotten eggs, and looked like Dijon mustard. It was all very sweet while Will was young

LEECHES, LOVERS, BEARS, AND CHOCOLATE PUDDING

but then became a little creepy as he got older. When we accidentally left "bankie" and "uzzer-one bankie" behind in a Georgia motel, Will was inconsolable for three weeks until he found (or probably smelled) them wrapped up under the Christmas tree, thanks to a kind-hearted motel maid.

Unlike Linus in *Peanuts*, Will never did outgrow his two blankets, which finally disappeared from his life with an ex-girlfriend in New York City. Ironically, Will played the character Linus in a staged production of *Peanuts* at The Gunnery and of course used "bankie" and "uzzer-one bankie" as Linus' security blankets on stage. As Julie and I watched him sing to, dance with, and passionately caress his beloved blankets, we knew he wasn't acting at all—we'd seen him do the very same things at home many times.

(Incidentally, when we left "bankie" and "uzzer-one bankie" in that Georgia motel, we were on our way home from Disney World and had a new passenger in our little car, namely, a human-size Winnie-the-Pooh teddy bear we'd bought there for the kids. During a drive through Lion Country Safari near Atlanta, we discovered the car was almost out of gas, so we had to turn off the A/C and roll down the windows [it was a hot summer day]. That was a little scary with all the wild beasts around us, but the only ones who gave us any trouble were the ostriches, who smelled the kids' popcorn and made a beeline for it. Before we knew it, the car was surrounded by ostriches poking their long necks through the open windows looking for snacks. But three-year-old Will thought they were after the smelly blankets in his lap and bravely shielded them with his own little body against their hard beaks. Such is love. And our young Horatius at the bridge.)

Sadly enough, even heroes sometimes lapse, given the right temptation. For Will, it was phone sex. You may think that phone sex is pretty mild stuff now, but back in 1981 it was the only game in town for two curious 10-year-old boys. Will and his neighbor James somehow crammed $900 of phone sex into only one month before we got our unduly large monthly phone bill and realized what had happened. Like millions of other unsuspecting boys and girls, Will and James had no idea that such good, clean fun was not free for everyone. They learned a good lesson, albeit an expensive one.

The next Will-and-filth story is based on hearsay testimony and no personal knowledge, thank goodness! It also involves an act of outright terrorism that undoubtedly traumatized a great many innocent bystanders. During the summer after Will graduated from The Gunnery, he and three classmates took a long bike trip through Europe. Other than the usual mishaps like lost passports and wrong turns, things went well—until about eight days before their flight home. At that point, they realized they were out of time, money, and clean clothes. They were much further away from their departure airport in England than they should have been. And since they were broke, they couldn't afford a hotel with a good bath. Nor did they have the time or money to wash clothes. So they rode like the wind in the summer heat and worked up a good sweat each day; slept in sheep fields at night; and never once changed their rancid clothes in eight days! Unfortunately for everyone else on board their flight home, they made the plane, just barely. It must have seemed like a Viking invasion to the other passengers. Can you imagine sitting for seven hours next to one of these creatures with their record levels of BO, utterly grimy clothes, and probably an array of happy fleas? But no one fainted, as far as we know, and the plane landed safely, although it then had to be fumigated. Will was met at the New York airport by his current girlfriend, who reportedly smelled the gang before she saw them.

Garbage trucks, "bankie" and "uzzer-one bankie," phone sex, barbarians on a plane, and a toxic waterbed—Will's long association with Filth was a bit excessive, even for a normal, unclean teenage boy. But I'm happy to report he turned a corner since those dark days, thanks primarily to his wonderful wife Sienna, who somehow introduced him to the merits of soap.

By comparison to their baby brother, our daughters were relatively sanitary. Casey's moment came during a long weekend trip to the Grand Hotel near Mobile with the two grandmothers and stepfather, who were supposed to babysit our 1½ year-old child so Julie and I could relax. Well, as soon as we arrived, the three elders disappeared and had a fine time. Young Casey didn't like the situation any more than we did and showed her displeasure by having a large, clandestine bowel movement in our hotel closet. By the time we returned to the room several hours later and discovered her deposit, the smell was overpowering. We were moved and the reeking room aired out for several days.

Ginger's fetish as a toddler was the blue liquid toilet bowl cleaner that was a staple in every house back then. As soon as we turned our heads, she would

LEECHES, LOVERS, BEARS, AND CHOCOLATE PUDDING

shuffle to the nearest toilet, immerse her face in the blue johnny water, and drink thirstily. Other than a permanently bluish tint to her tongue, we haven't noticed any other consequences of her early addiction. A little later, when Ginger was about two, Julie dressed her up as a princess for a Mardi Gras parade but forgot to put on her diapers. Our bottomless daughter was a big hit sitting on the top of a ladder in her short, windblown skirt just a few rows away from the passing floats. We thought it was so nice that the riders kept pointing at Ginger and showering her with beads. Only when we got home and started to change her did we realize why she had attracted so much attention. And luckily for the parade watchers standing nearby, she didn't empty her bladder or bowel on them.

(If you find the word "fart" offensive, you may want to skip this paragraph, but it is a funny story. A month or so after Hurricane Katrina, as Julie and I were waiting in Denver for Ginger to have her second child, we were poking around a toy store when we found the ideal gift for Ginger's husband John, who has a perfectly wicked sense of humor. It was called a "Fart Machine" and it consisted of a small wireless speaker and a remote control. Well, about three weeks after Olivia was born, we held a family meeting to discuss what to do with our flooded house in New Orleans. Olivia came in a baby carrier and slept the whole time, but halfway through the meeting, the unmistakable sound of passing gas erupted from her carrier on the floor next to Ginger. John had hidden the speaker in Olivia's blankets and then triggered it with the remote control under the table. The only one who didn't know about the Fart Machine was Casey, who found it hysterically funny that such a small baby could generate such a large sound. About five minutes after she stopped laughing and the meeting had resumed, it happened again and Casey almost fell off her chair. Two or three more well-timed eruptions rendered Casey virtually helpless, so we took pity and finally told her the truth. Which is not the end of story, because in this family of ours, no prank goes unpunished and this one was no exception, as you'll hear in a minute.)

Mama

Our fourth child was a truly noble beast in every way: elegant, loyal, spiritual, intelligent, proud, loving, intuitive, profound, forgiving, humble, unselfish, and

OUR OFF-THE-WALL OFFSPRING

wise beyond belief. And much better behaved than her young human counterparts. Mama, for instance, didn't poop in closets. Or drink from toilets. And she was much cleaner in mind and body than The Filthy One.

Shortly after moving into a new house on Bellaire Drive with three children five and under (and being burglarized a month later), we found a young lovely dog in our backyard. She was very pregnant and terribly sick from living on the street. The kids immediately adopted the poor thing and named her "Mama." Unfortunately, the vet could not save any of the puppies but did nurse her back to health. And so began our 15-year love affair with Mama.

It was like finding a perfect diamond in the rough. I have no doubt that Mama had royal canine blood from the first domestic dogs in Mongolia. When she got excited, while playing with the kids, for example, she literally "roared" like The Lion King. Coming from a 20-pound dog, it shocked us at first but we soon recognized it as her "happy sound." And when Casey (an expert paddler) took her kayaking on the Bowie River near Hattiesburg, Mama was a bit nervous until Casey got out and left her alone in the cockpit. Sitting there calmly in the kayak while Casey towed it in the shallow water, Mama looked just as regal as Cleopatra on her barge in the Nile. It was the same thing when she rode in a car. Instead of poking her head out of a window like most dogs, she sat up very straight and still on the back seat, surveying the scene, like the famous picture of Washington crossing the Delaware.

Everyone in the family treated her like a princess, which she accepted graciously. Whenever we stopped for ice cream on a road trip with the kids, Mama got hers too, served in a spoon by one of us (her favorite flavor was vanilla). My sister Sue cooked her scrambled eggs every time she babysat the children overnight. The Covington picnics that Julie and I hosted over 30 summers for 9- to 11-year- old inner-city kids (as part of TEEP, the Trinity Educational Enrichment Program) turned out to be a festive bonanza for Mama. Besides all the attention she got from the young campers, she especially enjoyed all the barbequed hotdogs that were slipped to her or dropped "accidentally" for her benefit. Mama also won the hearts of our Bellaire Drive neighbors, who always rewarded her with a bone or snack whenever she showed up on their doorsteps, as she often did. She was a universally beloved citizen of the

LEECHES, LOVERS, BEARS, AND CHOCOLATE PUDDING

neighborhood because she was "so polite," as one of her benefactors described her.

The one time that Mama was not polite got me into trouble with a burly taxi driver. My elderly mother was about to get into a cab in front of our house when Mama jumped in first, so I yelled "Mama, get out of the cab." The driver, who had not seen what happened, was appalled and scolded me for treating my mother so badly. He was not altogether mollified by my explanation that I was addressing a dog.

Mama loved the frequent camping trips we took as a family and she usually slept in one of the kids' tents, even when they were teenagers and brought friends with them. The one thing she didn't like about camping was the swimming. She enjoyed playing along the riverbank and sticking her nose in the sand for some reason, but she wouldn't go in the water, even when the children invited her in to play. As a result, one of us always wound up carrying Mama across the shallow rivers to the other side or to a wonderful island in the Bowie River outside of Hattiesburg, Mississippi, where we camped dozens of times on some good friends' undeveloped property. It was there that she encountered numerous turtles she carefully avoided by pretending they didn't exist.

On a number of occasions, we also rented beachfront cottages in Dauphin Island in the Gulf of Mexico near Mobile Bay. Mama romped all over the beaches but never set foot in the water. During one of those outings, she was anxious to get outside and ran pell-mell through a sliding glass door that was open but obviously didn't notice the sliding screen was closed. She hit the screen door at top speed and stretched it to the limit before it sprang back like a slingshot and threw poor, startled (but unhurt) Mama halfway across the room. It was a funny moment that reminds me of another similar incident at home. Before the dreaded waterbed (which Mama knew was evil because it made her seasick), she usually slept in the bed with Will (and his "bankie" and "uzzer-one bankie"). Once, just as he reached down to lift her up, she jumped for the bed and they cracked heads, hard and loud enough for us to hear in another room. When we checked, both Mama and Will were quite dazed from the collision, but eventually recovered.

It's hard to understand how anyone could harm such a smart and lovable animal. But Mama had been abused, according to our vet, and then turned out into the street before wandering half-dead into our backyard, a lucky day for all of us. She often whimpered in her sleep, a likely residual of the cruelty she had suffered. Thankfully, she survived to become a remarkable addition to our family for some 15 years. Mama was very protective of the children when they were young. She was incredibly intuitive about so many things, like knowing what to do before we told her, that Julie and I began to think she could read our minds. She had beautiful eyes that reminded me of my beloved grandfather Pops for some reason. Mama also had good taste in music: she liked classical, especially Beethoven. And when I was riding the bus to work, she would meet me every afternoon, running semi-sideways down the street in her unusual gait.

Mama died of leukemia in 1986. The night before we took her to the vet for a shot to end her suffering, Julie and I slept on the floor with her. Letting her go was one of the hardest things we ever did—we bawled like babies. We buried her in the backyard and made her a tombstone, which is now on our porch at Lambeth House. Rest in peace, Mama.

What Goes Around ...

Don't get me wrong: Casey, Ginger, and Will were (and still are) great children who now have seven wonderful kids of their own. But they drove us flat-out crazy at times, just as kids are supposed to do, although ours was (and still is) a happy and blessed family. Julie and I love our children dearly for the few things they got wrong and the many, many more things they got right.

For example, when they were about 16, 13, and 11 (Casey had her driver's license), they took us totally by surprise and "kidnapped" us on Christmas Day. After we'd opened the presents, eaten brunch, and awaited the usual afternoon guests for drinks, snacks, and bourre (a Cajun poker game), they told us that the plans had changed and all the guests canceled. Julie and I were then blindfolded, hustled into the car, and driven to the old Cornstalk Hotel in the French Quarter, where the kids had stowed a suitcase full of clean clothes and an awesome array of champagne, wine, and other goodies, as well as the keys to our other car parked outside. It was a well-planned conspiracy that they carried out perfectly. Julie and I had a fabulous time roaming the Quarter, having a leisurely dinner, and seeing a good movie ("Dune") that Ginger and Will were

LEECHES, LOVERS, BEARS, AND CHOCOLATE PUDDING

also attending, unbeknownst to us (they recognized Julie's cough). That was just one of a huge number of joyful memories provided by our children.

On the other hand, they were all quite proficient at creating untimely mischief and mayhem that kept their poor, beleaguered parents on their toes 24/7, so a little harmless revenge is perfectly justified, don't you think? Enter Brian the Brain, a true work of the devil. What a warped mind it must have taken to design such a wicked plaything for children! Brian was a spooky-looking plastic head filled with electronics that allowed him to think, speak, and respond very realistically on his own. And if you turned him off, he could automatically turn himself back on. Brian therefore was the ideal Trojan Horse for getting even with our adult children, so we gave one each to Casey's and Ginger's young kids (Will was spared only because he didn't have any kids then—but he does now and Christmas is right around the corner, ho ho).

Casey's lasted a week before she had to get it out of her house and gave it to an unsuspecting friend, who gave it away in turn (I understand Brian takes an average of just 9.5 days to wear out his welcome in any one household). Ginger simply turned it off after a few days, buried it deep in their bedroom closet, and forgot all about it—which made Brian very, very unhappy. He bided his time for a month, waiting patiently for the perfect opportunity to strike back. Ginger's husband John created that opportunity by stumbling half-asleep into the closet in the middle of a dark night. The stage was set: everyone else was asleep, the house was silent, and the closet was pitch-black, when he suddenly heard a strange, bodiless voice from somewhere close by: "Aubrey [their son], is that you?" John jumped a foot, as I certainly would have in that situation. Anyway, John survived but Brian did not—he was gone the next day.

But in our family, it's a matter of honor to have the last word by pulling off the last prank, so no one can ever relax for very long. After Brian the Brain, I knew my time would come sooner or later and it did last April (2015) during our annual family ski reunion in Breckenridge. Unfortunately, Will was collateral damage. We were the benighted butts of the latest round of jokes. Although I have no doubt that Casey, Ginger, and John wanted some revenge for Brian, they left it up to our granddaughter Emma to administer the coup de grace, which she did with great aplomb. She and her boyfriend announced over dinner at a fondue restaurant that they had become engaged on the lift going up

OUR OFF-THE-WALL OFFSPRING

Peak 9. Will and I fell for it hook, line, and sinker, but we should have known better because Emma turns into her notorious grandmother on April Fools' Day, which it was. Exactly one year earlier, she and Casey (remember that Fart Machine joke?) had fooled John, who is not at all gullible, into believing Emma had skied out of control through a children's ski class and broken the instructor's rib. Will and I were shocked because Emma had just turned 18 and picked a college. He, the father of three young girls, kept giving her fatherly advice about working things out with her mother (whose head was on the table, no doubt to hide her laughter). As the oldest alleged adult at the table, I made a most solemn toast, which is when all the other conspirators finally lost it and cracked up.

That's the way things stand as I write this. But there will be another round, hopefully soon, to settle scores with the other motley members of our wonderful family. And then still more rounds after that, ad infinitum. Shame on us if it ever stops. We have great fun together, laughing at and with each other.

THE PARENTS-ARE-OUT-OF-TOWN PARTY

It is one of the most insidious conspiracies of all time. It's an underground movement of epidemic proportions, one that is starting to destabilize our entire society. Little is known about it because of their code of secrecy and our lack of vigilance. The few experts on the subject think it's caused by some kind of brain virus that affects only American teenagers. But a virus cannot explain a syndrome that is so universal and deep-seated in our children. Every red-blooded American teenager experiences this irresistible impulse sooner or later, no matter how pious or pure he or she used to be. Therefore, it must be genetic—some diabolical little gene that lies dormant for exactly 14 years and then attacks the still-undeveloped teenage brain. It's a genetic time-bomb of the worst kind, probably planted by the Communists during the Cold War to create generational warfare in America. There is nothing we parents can do to stop it, except perhaps to (1) support genetic engineering; (2) temporarily banish all teenagers to Greenland; or (3) form neighborhood watch groups modeled after the Spanish Inquisition.

Julie and I are two of the lucky ones—we survived a monster "parents-are-out-of-town party" with a minimum of mental scar tissue. Notice that the emphasis here is on psychological, not physical, damage. That's because teenagers are real masters of the cover-up—compared to them, Nixon was a novice. As wild and destructive as these parties usually are, the perpetrators and their friends, like ants repairing an anthill, always swarm over the crime scene afterwards and eliminate all traces of their barbaric behavior. Consequently, the parents/victims usually return to a pristine house—and a world that will never be quite the same.

The first thing you notice is a subtle change in your teenage son or daughter (or both, as in our case). It starts with the eyes. They shine a little brighter (so proud of pulling such a fast one and getting away with it). They dart around furtively (searching for any clues that were overlooked). And they even look a bit sad (just a smidgen of pity for the poor dumb parents). And, wow, the kids are being so solicitous—maybe they really are glad to see you, but no, that's

LEECHES, LOVERS, BEARS, AND CHOCOLATE PUDDING

too out of character for any teenager, so you start to worry some more. There is of course nothing you can put your finger on, only a slight tingling of that sixth sense. This in turn is exacerbated when you notice that your neighbors are also acting funny. The absence of the customary wave, the averted eyes, the crossing over to the other side of the street, the whispering together, the persistent lack of time to stop and chat—these are the tell-tale signs of some recent and mysterious change in your relationship. By this time, your confusion is verging on paranoia, but still there's no reason to suspect your children, who after all are model citizens. What finally puts you over the psychological edge is the behavior of the children's friends and, even worse, your own friends. Those few who were *not at the party* of course heard about it, so all of them wear the same smug and knowing look, especially around you, just to make sure you know they know something you don't. You sometimes detect a glimmer of sympathy in the adult friends, but the basic message you receive is still the same: you are dimwits of the first degree. Surrounded by children, neighbors, and friends all acting so strangely, is it any wonder that you come to believe you've finally lost touch with reality?

In our case, Julie and I probably escaped permanent psychological damage because we learned the truth relatively early. It was a combination of luck and good Soviet-style interrogation techniques. This particular party was so massive that it was hard to keep secret. Our young covert operators almost succeeded, but they left behind one little clue: a few days after our return from vacation, we discovered one of our houseplants in a closed cabinet (all the others were back where we left them). Unable to find any logical explanation for putting a plant in such a sunless place, we asked our children, Ginger and Will, who had been house-sitting while we were away. That produced the big break in the case: their answers did not jibe. (If there had been only one perpetrator instead of two, we would have never broken the case open.) We were then able to play one off against the other and eventually extracted their confessions, albeit under serious distress. Fortunately, it was not necessary to break out the rack or even the thumbscrews, but we did have to mix a little terror into the proceedings. Our kids hated to do the laundry, so the traditional punishment in our family was laundry duty, usually just a few days' worth for a routine offense. Because we suspected a much more serious breach in this case, we started with a month of

THE PARENTS-ARE-OUT-OF-TOWN PARTY

laundry duty and then gradually increased the pressure by upping the ante. Boy, did they sweat, but to our amazement, they didn't cave in until we reached the 10-year level! Ironically, they wound up escaping the full sentence by going away to school (where they washed their clothes maybe once a month), but at least they did confess all the gory details.

Before describing the party itself, let us give you some background information about Ginger and Will. They were then 17 and 15 respectively, old enough to house-sit for a week while Julie and I were away. Even though teenagers, they were really good kids. Ginger was an honor student and had recently been picked as a peer support group leader in school. Will was president of his class and had just won the top citizenship award at his summer camp in Colorado. Their friends were very nice. Both Ginger and Will were level-headed, well-behaved, polite, and responsible. We were proud of them. They were *not* the kind of kids who would do anything behind our backs, at least nothing really bad. (Well, as it turned out, this secret plan of theirs was hatched only 30 minutes after they learned we were leaving town.)

So we left on our trip, confident in the knowledge that our nice little house was in good hands. "Sure, it's okay to have a few friends over to barbeque or watch movies" were our parting words. "A *few* friends" certainly does not mean 400 people, especially in a house that might hold 50 max. Now Ginger and Will didn't have anywhere near that many friends or even acquaintances between them, so how they reached that number is most interesting. Typically, they were worried that no one would come to their party. To make sure that didn't happen, they naturally went to the other extreme. In a big way. Like all teenagers planning a covert operation, they were inspired. Their written invitations came right out and declared it to be a "PARENTS-ARE-OUT-OF-TOWN PARTY." It was simple, yet brilliant and daring. But they didn't stop there (that PAOOTP gene was now red hot). To guarantee it reached the widest possible audience, they added the fateful message "BRING SOME FRIENDS," which in teenage code means "pass this around—there's plenty of beer." At that point, they crossed the Rubicon. Their only hope was a postal strike.

Alas, the mail got through. As our intrepid hosts learned later, many of their invitations (now highly valued by collectors) wound up posted on telephone poles all over the city. And people came in droves, over 400 in all, drawn like

LEECHES, LOVERS, BEARS, AND CHOCOLATE PUDDING

swarming locusts by that siren song of free booze and no chaperones. Not just teenagers, which would have been bad enough, but a good number of adults as well, who were anything but a restraining influence. Apparently everyone there had a great time—all except Ginger and Will. They later admitted, somewhat sheepishly, that they knew only a small percentage of their "guests" and were totally unprepared for such a crowd. (That may be so, but luckily they were prepared with enough beer to keep 400 friends and freeloaders happy for six hours on a hot summer night; otherwise, our poor old house would have been torn down brick by brick.) Things eventually got so out of control that Will himself called the police and pretended to be an angry neighbor, but his gamble was doomed from the start. New Orleans, after all, is called the "Big Easy" for good reason, including the fact that the police haven't shut down a single party in the city since 1882. And besides, there were probably a few off-duty cops in our house at the time, enjoying all the free beer.

So the beat went on. One unknown "guest," a late-blooming Woodstock wannabe, set out to redecorate our bourgeois house by writing "PEACE AND LOVE" with a black Magic Marker on every wall. Armed with a bottle of Windex (the real cleaning came later), Ginger and Will spent a frantic hour following her trail until she was finally nabbed in the act. They confiscated her array of writing utensils and sent her far away in a cab. Undaunted, she returned later with a brand-new supply of Magic Markers, intent on spreading her message of salvation among such a large group of barbarians who clearly needed saving. But this time she was intercepted early and banished for good. At another point, Will went up to his room to escape the chaos below, but instead found four strangers dismantling his stereo. Thinking him just another party crasher, they brazenly offered him a share of the loot. He managed to save the stereo but lost what little peace of mind he had left. These two incidents no doubt represent just the tip of the iceberg. All in all, it was a very, very long night for the two beleaguered hosts (perhaps longer for Will than Ginger, who gave up trying to keep the lid on things and just "went with the flow" like a good party girl—something she did not confess until the statute of limitations had expired).

We remained out of town for several days after the party, happy in our ignorance, so they had ample time to recover, both physically and mentally, and to clean up the bodies and other debris. Thus, when we did come back, the house

THE PARENTS-ARE-OUT-OF-TOWN PARTY

was spotless and the kids were cheerful and solicitous. Perhaps a little too solicitous—they even volunteered to meet us at the airport and carry our bags! That's definitely not normal behavior for any teenager. Once inside the house, they followed us around step by step, like soldiers marching, Will behind Bill and Ginger behind me—we thought nothing of it at the time, but we now know they were looking over our shoulders to make sure there wasn't anything suspicious from our viewpoints. The vinyl floor in our kitchen did seem a bit sticky, but Will (always so creative) assured us it was "only the humidity." With the benefit of hindsight, it's clear we missed these clues, but we were too travel weary to notice anything amiss. It was also lucky for them that we didn't go into the backyard until much later, because one or more of the "guests" had obviously mashed in one side of a metal bike shed (which they missed during the clean-up)—when I confronted him with this, Will told me with a perfectly straight face (he was born to be an actor) that a large bird (like maybe a pterodactyl or just a California condor off course in Louisiana?) must have crashed into the shed at high speed (then gotten up and flown away, leaving no blood or carcass?). It was typical Will: sheer genius and a lot of hutzpah. My homicidal rage turned into helpless laughter and Will escaped yet again. He did earn another year of laundry duty, but he begged his mother for mercy and got it (as usual).

Have these painful memories faded with the passage of time? Sadly, no. Even now, about once a month, we encounter an old friend of Ginger's or Will's who insists on telling us in great detail what an unforgettable party it was—and they all talk about it with a look of pure rapture, like it was akin to a religious experience. So the party lives on as a bright, shining memory in hundreds of minds. And we have become ikons as "THE PARENTS" in the title of this historic event (which, in local lore, is second in importance only to the Saints' one division title). Since the party is our only claim to fame, we grin and bear it stoically. Which is the same way we deal with those adult friends of ours who were at the party but never confessed their involvement. They even wear that same smug and knowing look after all these years. So busy gloating at getting away with it, they fail to realize that there were other "parents-are-out-of-town parties," some of them closer to home than they would like to know. And, believe me, they were all good parties.

LEECHES, LOVERS, BEARS, AND CHOCOLATE PUDDING

Will and Ginger are now successful young adults. We love them dearly. Unfortunately, they live where we have no jurisdiction to enforce their unfinished sentences. But it's not over yet. One fine day, Will and Ginger will have teenage children of their own—children who will surely inherit a powerful PAOOTP gene (especially if our prayers are answered). The rest is inevitable. We hope to attend all of our grandchildren's PAOOTP parties and enjoy ourselves thoroughly. Who knows—with our valuable experience, we may even get to help them with the covert planning. Ah, revenge will be sweet!

YOU BURIED YOUR MOTHER WHERE? (as told by Julie Penick)

My dear, sweet Mama died in the late summer of 1988. She had leukemia, so Bill and I and the kids were prepared but it was still a shock when the end finally came. I spent the rest of the summer virtually overcome by grief. But then something happened that changed everything.

It was bright and early on my first day back at school where I taught four- and five-year-olds. On the way in, I fell into step with another teacher who had been on staff just one year and knew me only casually at the time.

"How was your summer?" Susan asked me cheerfully.

"Pretty bad," I answered. "Mama died."

"Oh, I'm so sorry. Had she been sick?"

"She was quite old and then developed leukemia but was doing fairly well until five or six weeks ago when she started going downhill fast, which was tough on all of us." I was surprised how comforting it felt to unload my feelings, even to a relative stranger, and Susan was obviously touched that I was sharing such a personal experience with her.

"Worst of all, our son Will, who was Mama's favorite, was away at summer camp for another two weeks and might not make it home in time to say goodbye. Mama's doctor was a friend, so we talked to him about the situation and he came up with the idea of a blood transfusion, which did in fact keep her alive until Will came home."

Because Susan was beginning to look a little shocked, I hurried on with my story. "Her last night alive was really tough. Bill and I spent the whole night talking to her and stroking her hair to convey our love." Susan turned slightly pale.

"The next morning, we brought her to the doctor and he said there was nothing more he could do, so he gave her a shot to put her out of her misery." As I recall, Susan stopped breathing at that point.

"Then we took her body home, wrapped it in a brand-new blanket for the occasion, said our tearful goodbyes, and buried her in our flower garden instead of some cold cemetery."

LEECHES, LOVERS, BEARS, AND CHOCOLATE PUDDING

Susan was aghast. Her mouth was wide open and she was struggling to say something but nothing came out. When I finally realized how many wires we'd crossed, I started laughing hysterically and blurted out "But, Susan, Mama was a dog!" before realizing my statement could be interpreted in two very different ways. Susan of course drew the unintended inference, i.e., "my mother was a bitch, so we dispatched the old girl and buried the evidence," so now she was utterly horrified. From her standpoint, I had just confessed the motive for our dirty deed.

Susan started walking away rapidly, no doubt looking for a phone to call the police, before I caught up with her and explained that Mama was a four-legged dog, not my mother (who, by the way, was buried in a real cemetery). I still feel bad that I unknowingly traumatized her, but she recovered and we became good friends.

That funny encounter did wonders for my whole frame of mind. Ever since Mama died, I'd been grief-stricken like the rest of my family. That night I told them what happened at school and we all had a good laugh. From that moment on, we were able to put Mama's death behind us and focus instead on the many wonderful years we had with her.

Mama entered our lives the very same day that Bill and I moved into a new house with two young daughters and a six-week-old son. When she showed up in our new backyard that day, Casey and Ginger were ecstatic and promptly named her "Mama" because she was very pregnant and gave birth a few days later to eight cute but sickly puppies that did not survive. Mama was a midsize mutt, although a beautiful one with striking eyes, who had been living on the street and was not in great shape, but she responded to some good veterinary care and lived to a ripe old age, happily enough for us.

Given her uncanny intelligence and sweet personality, Mama quickly became a much-loved member of our family and the neighborhood in general. Even though Bill does not believe in reincarnation, he had the distinct feeling there was some kind of connection between Mama and his beloved grandfather who died many years before. We took her everywhere with us, including the beach and the woods, which her beagle half preferred. She loved scrambled eggs, pancakes, cheese (especially Gouda), and ice cream, but her favorite snack was a barbequed hotdog "under the table" from one of the Irish Channel kids on our

YOU BURIED YOUR MOTHER WHERE?

summer picnics to Covington—over the course of her 15 summers with us, Mama probably consumed close to 500 of them, which may explain her long life. Almost all of our neighbors were utterly charmed by Mama and always seemed to have a supply of bones on hand for her. Whenever Will as a toddler would lose his diaper, Mama would immediately bring it to us; and when he was old enough to have a real bed, she slept in it with him, although she drew the line at the waterbed he got as a teenager. One of the most endearing things about Mama was her "roar," literally like a lion, that was her way of expressing herself during a particularly happy moment.

Mama, you were quite a lady. Rest in peace.

DON JUAN THE MARMOT

Julie and I have encountered many different kinds of wild animals during all of our time in the Great Outdoors, but the weirdest by far was the marmot we met on a hike in the Rockies.

Marmots are cute, furry rodents that weigh around 10–12 pounds. Those in the Rockies live in tunnels and hibernate in the winter. Our own sightings have been few and fleeting because marmots are notoriously shy and stay far away from humans. However, there's always one exception in every crowd and that's the one who fell madly in love with Julie and couldn't take his paws off her.

It was a beautiful summer day in the Colorado mountains. We were hiking a new trail when we stopped in a clearing to drink some water and enjoy the view. One of the nicest things about hiking in the mountains is the solitude, but this time we had some unexpected company in the form of a smallish marmot that ambled out of the rocks, chattering excitedly as if he'd just won the lottery. I'm using the masculine "he" because it soon became very obvious he was every bit a male. And oh so dashing, with his well-groomed hair, sensuous nose, unshaved whiskers, perfect teeth, perfumed smell, svelte body, rakish grin, come-hither look, and foreign-sounding accent to his chatter.

Ignoring me completely, he marched right up to Julie, sniffed her in a gesture of friendship, and gazed up at her with big, soft eyes. We were intrigued and a little flattered to see a marmot up so close and personal, until he got a bit too personal by thrusting his head up Julie's pants-leg and then trying to wedge his entire body inside, which of course was impossible even though she was wearing loose-fitting pants that flared at the bottom. Luckily, Julie was also wearing long, thick woolen hiking socks, so she didn't get scratched, but it was still unnerving for her to have a wild animal trying to get in her pants.

LEECHES, LOVERS, BEARS, AND CHOCOLATE PUDDING

Julie jumped away and shook him loose, but he was clearly in love and not about to give up so easily on his amorous quest, although his persistence was never threatening to either one of us. In fact, after several futile attempts to crawl up her pants, we were both laughing hysterically by the time Julie's unrequited lover finally gave up and sulked away, frustrated and forlorn. I must confess, however, that I was a bit hurt (and also relieved) that he showed no interest whatsoever in me.

No one, of course, can fault his choice of Julie with all of her grace, beauty, and sex appeal. I've always known that she is a remarkable woman who, without even trying, can charm the likes of Paul McCartney (true—see separate story entitled "Just Julie"), but who would have guessed she'd have the same effect on a wild marmot! However, after giving this question a great deal of very serious thought, I've come up with the only plausible explanation: the legendary Don Juan did not go to Hell as alleged in all the literature about him but was reincarnated as a hypersexed marmot in a remote corner of Colorado (so the accent I heard must have been Spanish).

One can easily imagine the shock when Juan first realized his new reality and took a look at his potential mates. By the same token, the female marmots in the area must have been even more traumatized when this rank upstart with an outsized libido began pursuing them in unseemly and indelicate ways, which explains why they all fled to the next county, leaving our frustrated friend in a state of deep clinical depression, without any Masters or Johnson around to counsel him. Although he made his own bed, so to speak, it's a real tragedy but it does help us to understand why he fell so hard at his first sight of my lovely wife.

We never returned to that particular trail, but succumbing to the chance for a bit of innocent mischief, we recommended the same hike to a couple of female friends without warning them of the cute little pervert lurking there. Unfortunately, it didn't occur to us then that a prolonged monastic lifestyle might eventually transform Juan the harmlessly horny marmot into a crazed libidinous monster. And, oddly enough, we've never heard from those friends again, so who knows what strange things may have happened to them in those deep, dark, mysterious woods?

OUT AND ABOUT IN THE GREAT OUTDOORS

I was lucky. After our disastrous outdoor honeymoon, Julie had every reason in the world to bid farewell forever to the Great Outdoors—but she didn't. Despite leeches, bears, ticks, mosquitoes, redbugs, tarantulas, freeze-dried food, ornery stoves, wet clothing, cold nights, heavy backpacks, exhausting hikes, unprivate bathrooms, lightning strikes, blistered feet, flooded rivers, overturned canoes, ski-lift fiascos, skiing collisions, a mild fear of heights, and many other tests of her resolve, my intrepid and determined wife stuck with it and soon came to love camping, hiking, backpacking, canoeing, downhill skiing, and jogging as much as I did. And she mastered all of them. As a result of our common interest, the Great Outdoors in one form or another became our primary destination for weekends and vacations.

Backpacking

As used here, the term "backpacking" refers to overnight trips of several days sleeping in a tent high up on a mountainside, as distinguished from "hiking," which refers to walking trips in the woods or mountains that begin and end on the same day. Other than with our children and their friends, Julie and I usually hiked and backpacked by ourselves. Because the Colorado Rockies are so vast and beautiful, we did all of our backpacking and most of our hiking there.

You will recall that our first backpacking trip together was rudely interrupted by an intruder bearing the very weapon he had allegedly used to dispatch his wife just hours earlier (see "'The Best of All Possible Honeymoons'? Not Quite!"), so you may be surprised to learn that we were dumb enough to even consider the possibility of (1) taking another backpacking trip; (2) all alone in the same isolated mountains; (3) without a machine gun or two to protect ourselves. Well, it took us a few years to get up the nerve to try it again, but given the daunting alternative of staying home with three fearsome children, we did go back and this time got hooked for good. Why was backpacking in the Colorado Rockies so addictive? Since you asked, please bear

LEECHES, LOVERS, BEARS, AND CHOCOLATE PUDDING

with me for a minute or two while I wax a little poetic about the wonders of backpacking, which left us both with many of our most enduring memories.

[INTERLUDE: Backpacking in the mountains is a truly sublime experience. Not so much the hike up, which can be grueling, as the sequel, the reward at the end of the trail. It's always amazed Julie and me that we could live for a week quite comfortably and quite alone under the stars with no electricity, no hot water, no toilet, no car, no phone, no stores, just what we could carry on our own backs. (Julie, who was surprisingly strong for a petite woman, always insisted on taking a fair share of the load.) Considering the size and weight of the essentials like tent, sleeping bags, foam mats or air mattresses, first aid kit, toilet paper, aluminum pot, cups, and spoons, detergent, stove and gas, water bottles, food, and the backpacks themselves, there's not much room left over for personal

OUT AND ABOUT IN THE GREAT OUTDOORS

items: maybe one change of clothes per person, one book, one small flashlight for reading in the tent, and exactly four ounces of brandy. Believe me, every ounce can make a big difference on a long, strenuous hike to a destination 3,000–4,000 feet uphill, so we usually squeezed out half the toothpaste, carefully measured the cooking gas, chose the lightest clothes and food, and inevitably wound up weighing our filled packs at home and jettisoning stuff before getting it right. Once we had lugged all that weight up the mountain and pitched our tent, that was our permanent home for the duration of the trip, but from there, we ventured out every day with just water, lunch, and raincoats to explore all the nearby lakes, rivers, and peaks.

Was the payoff worth it all? You bet! Julie and I usually camped at 12,000 feet or higher, always by an alpine lake with a supply of running water. Rarely did we ever encounter another living (human) soul. The solitude was exquisite. There were no rules, other than packing out your trash and leaving everything cleaner than before, doing your bathroom business well away from the water and burying your waste, and just enjoying Nature at her very, very best. The combination of mountains, water, forests, flowers, and wildlife was jaw-dropping awesome. We saw bighorn sheep, mountain goats, moose, deer, and eagles—but no bears, even though they're out there, and no snakes, because they prefer much lower elevations. Colorado has 54 peaks over 14,000 feet high (called "fourteeners"), so there's always a stunning vista in every direction. Contrary to what most people think, mountains are alive, in the sense that they change colors during the course of a day, from flat gray to bright yellow to blood red (no kidding—we have photos to prove it). There's nothing like sitting beside a quiet alpine lake with a sip or two of brandy and watching the setting sun paint different colors on the nearby peaks and reflecting waters. The mountains also change their shapes constantly, depending on one's viewpoint. And there are beautiful little flowers growing in every mountainside nook and cranny, which is amazing that anything so delicate can survive way up there on virtually no soil under such extreme weather conditions.

The nights, too, are magnificent because of two things unknown to city dwellers: the absolutely total silence (aside from any wind in the trees or the hoot of an owl) and the equally total darkness (aside from any moonlight). It's cold and lonely outside the tent when nature calls nocturnally, but the price is right

LEECHES, LOVERS, BEARS, AND CHOCOLATE PUDDING

just to see the stars on a clear night. Of course, some nights above timberline in a small tent with metal poles can be really fearsome in the middle of a major thunderstorm, with nowhere to hide. But that's just another way of communing with Nature, which is what it's all about. END OF INTERLUDE]

Julie and I took a number of backpacking trips all over Colorado on our own before (and after) the kids were old enough to join us. We actually didn't know that much about the art of backpacking when we started, so the early trips were like journeys into the unknown for us but also great learning experiences. We got much better at choosing equipment, loading packs, selecting trails and campsites, and just existing all alone for several days in a gorgeous but sometimes hostile environment without any comforts or protections of home. One of the first things we learned the hard way was how terrible freeze-dried food tastes (at least back in the 1960s and 1970s) and how we could supplement it with cheese, peanut butter, and other items that didn't require refrigeration (although there were usually patches of snow near our campsites even in late summer). We also brought fishing gear and caught trout from the alpine lakes that we cooked on open fires in tinfoil, which was much lighter than a metal pan.

Our favorite food supplement by far was GORP (good old raisins and peanuts), with some M&M's added for flavor. The kids and their friends ate gallons of the stuff. But the biggest fans of GORP were the ever-present chipmunks wherever we camped in the mountains. They loved the peanuts and M&M's but not so much the raisins. Chipmunks are very cute, very shy, and forever hungry—their appetites always trumped their timidity. Whenever Julie and I scattered some GORP on the ground, chipmunks would suddenly materialize out of nowhere and quickly grab a goodie or two before dashing back to the rocks with their prizes. After we resided in one spot for several days, the local chippies got to know us and became much friendlier, eating out of our hands and sometimes even crawling on us.

I have two particular chipmunk stories to share with you. The first is of Julie sitting against a rock trying to read a book while three or four chipmunks scrambled all over her looking for handouts, sometimes inside her shirt. And then there was "Greedy," so named because he was noticeably bigger than the other chipmunks and was a true glutton. Since he obviously didn't want to share

OUT AND ABOUT IN THE GREAT OUTDOORS

any morsel with his colleagues, he stuffed his mouth with GORP until his cheeks were puffed out like a cartoon character, but that didn't stop him from trying to fit in one more peanut, which caused another to pop out the other side of his mouth. He was either a wonderful comic or a very determined chipmunk, because he did that for a good 15 minutes while Julie and I almost wet our pants laughing so hard. But he got even with us that night, when we made the mistake of leaving out the GORP in a sealed, clear plastic bottle that was placed in a metal cooking pot. Well, some hungry chipmunk, presumably Greedy, worked all night on getting into that bottle of goodies and made a racket doing so (we stayed in the tent in case it was a larger animal, but the numerous tiny teeth marks we found all over the plastic bottle the next morning told us who had ruined our sleep). Apparently chipmunks become nocturnal dynamos whenever there's food around, like in our packs, which we always left outside our little tent for reasons of space and safety, so we learned the hard way to seal the packs tightly to keep the little devils out.

We started taking the kids with us on backpacking ventures when Casey was 10, Ginger was 7, and Will was 5. That first trip with them (and the nearby grizzly bear that wasn't supposed to be there) is the subject of another story, "On the Road with Three Little Backseat Angels/Beasts of Bedlam." We were lucky that they were all comfortable in tents from the previous car-camping we did as a family (discussed later) and never had a serious problem with the high Colorado altitudes. The same, unfortunately, is not true of their New Orleans friends who started coming with us around age 12. None of them had ever slept in a tent anywhere before, much less at 12,000 feet, so some of them did suffer a little altitude sickness but always recovered quickly and wound up having a ball, which was fun for us too. Ginger's guest of the same name came with us twice and now hikes and camps often with her own family in Vermont.

LEECHES, LOVERS, BEARS, AND CHOCOLATE PUDDING

The one thing that our kids and their guests never did adjust to was the ubiquitous freeze-dried food that tasted like cardboard, so they always insisted that we stop at the first fast-food restaurant we saw on the drive home. After wearing the same sweaty, filthy clothes for such a long time without ever bathing or even washing up, you can imagine what five or more of us smelled like to our poor fellow diners! Most of them finished up and left in a hurry. It was very funny to watch the other patrons but also our own starving kids as they voraciously consumed vast quantities of "fresh" food like burgers, shakes, and especially fries (with lots of ketchup).

A couple of notable post-backpacking occasions with the kids are worth mentioning. You can imagine how wonderfully decadent it felt to sleep in a real bed after spending a week in a clammy sleeping bag on the ground. Well, while sleeping soundly on motel beds during our first night back "in civilization," we all were rudely awakened at 3:00 AM by loud talking and the sound of many basketballs being dribbled right outside our door. It was a Mexican boys' high school team checking out (and dribbling up and down the hall in the process). A long night, to say the least. After two other backpacking trips, we took the kids (and a friend of Casey's on one of them) to the Old West town of Central City, Colorado, with its many saloons (including one with the famous painting of "The Face on the Barroom Floor") and now casinos. Once we stayed in an old hotel with no TVs in the rooms, which was a problem for our kids who were already addicted at ages 10, 7, and 5. They improvised by staring transfixed out of an open window at a TV screen across the narrow street, even though they couldn't hear any sound! Other than that semi-crisis, Central City was good fun for the whole family.

OUT AND ABOUT IN THE GREAT OUTDOORS

During our many backpacking trips, there were only two close calls. On that initial venture after our honeymoon debacle, Julie woke up early the first morning to explore our new home at over 13,000 feet while I slept in. She was so enchanted that she started singing and dancing around like Julie Andrews in *The Sound of Music* until she almost stepped backwards into a small unmarked but very deep mining shaft, which she may not have survived. It turned out to be one of several similar shafts dating back to the 1880s when the heavy equipment used to dig them was hauled in by horses. We encountered old, rusted mining equipment high up in the mountains on other trips but not any more of those treacherous shafts, thank goodness.

On our very last backpack, after the kids had grown up and left the nest, Julie and I returned to a beautiful spot we had enjoyed 20 years before. It started off well enough. We found a shorter trail to our destination and had the whole alpine lake to ourselves. Then the weather turned bad, always a risk in the mountains. After a night of constant rain and lightning, everything was soaked. I was ready to ride out the storm but my sainted wife wisely decided it was time to get out of there while we still could. So we did, only to discover that our nice trail up was now a dangerous minefield. Besides the ongoing rain and lightning, the rocks were slippery, the muddy trail was hard to follow, and worst of all, a couple of small streams we had crossed easily going up were now raging torrents. We had to search for crossings that were narrow enough to throw our packs across instead of trying to cross with all that weight on our backs. Even then, the water was too strong for us to cross safely, had we not found overhanging trees to hold onto and large boulders to brace against. Since the only alternative was to wait until the water levels went down, which could have taken a couple of days, we had to risk it and somehow managed to get across both streams, but it was very, very dicey, to say the least. As she proved many times, Julie is one tough cookie.

Ginger in particular has carried on the family tradition of backpacking and hiking. After she married John, they spent several months camping in a tent along the four edges of our country. They also hiked all the way into and out of the Grand Canyon with heavy packs on their backs, which was no mean feat, believe me. Since their later move to Denver (where Julie and I almost settled), they have hiked and camped all over the Rockies with their two kids. And now that they have experienced the pride and pleasure of climbing one of Colorado's many "fourteeners," the sky's the limit.

Hiking

Our hiking activities were also centered in the Rocky Mountains of Colorado. There were many wonderful day hikes around Breckenridge (which is near the Continental Divide), where we spent a lot of vacation time after buying a condo there in 1981.* The McCullough Gulch Trail was Julie's favorite because it followed a lovely river with cascades and rock shelves where she could eat lunch, read a book, or take a nap right next to the falling water. But every hiking trail was unique and interesting in its own way in the form of abundant wildflowers, shapely aspen trees, century-old log cabin remnants, rivers and waterfalls, and always an alpine lake or two at the end with awesome vistas.

But much of our hiking efforts in Colorado was devoted to climbing as many of its "fourteeners" as we could. That took us all over the state because most of the fourteeners required technical skills we didn't have, so we had to settle for the less or moderately difficult peaks. That may sound like a walk in the park, but the so-called easier ones we climbed were plenty challenging enough for us flatlanders. Walking up and then down 3,000 or 4,000 feet in relatively thin air with two quarts of water each was physically demanding. Often

---

* The plan was to sell the condo in 3–4 years while the real estate market out there was booming and use the enormous profits to pay for the kids' college educations. Well, the market crashed, dramatically, just six months later. The resale value of our heavily mortgaged condo plunged 50% before we knew what hit us, so we had no choice but to ride it out. Scary as that was, it was also a blessing because our family and friends made good use of the condo. Though it took 15 years for prices to recover, they're now healthy and we're still enjoying Breckenridge.

OUT AND ABOUT IN THE GREAT OUTDOORS

we had to cross fast-running streams, walk along high, narrow ridges on slippery snow or shifting scree (small, loose rocks), retrace our steps to find the trail again, and literally run down mountains to avoid being caught at the summit during the usual afternoon lightning storm. On two fourteeners, Mount Yale and Quandary Peak, we tried to beat an incoming storm to the top and got to within a mere 200 yards of our goal before we had to give up the quest. When the hair on our necks started tingling from the electrified air, we knew it was time to find cover in the trees 1,000 feet below us and did so as fast as we could in our heavy boots. (We did go back later and summit both peaks.)

Julie and I wound up climbing 16 of Colorado's fourteeners. They included two in one day (Grays Peak and Torreys Peak) and three in one day (Mount Lincoln, Mount Bross, and Mount Democrat) that were conveniently connected by "saddles" or ridges between them. When we were descending Mount Democrat, Julie found a long vertical vein of unmelted snow and decided to slide down it for fun. I hiked down to the bottom to catch her in case she got going too fast and couldn't stop herself. Sitting on her poncho, she slid all the way down without mishap, hollering joyously the whole time. Since she was still

going at a good clip at the bottom of the snowbank, I did have to literally tackle her before she slid off onto the rocks and we both wound up rolling around in the snow, laughing our heads off. After that little adventure, whenever Julie

LEECHES, LOVERS, BEARS, AND CHOCOLATE PUDDING

found a good thick vein of snow for sliding, that's what she did, with me as her backstop at the bottom. It's too bad she never had a chance to try ziplining, which is something like the sliding she loved.

One of our easiest fourteeners was the highest of them all, Mount Elbert, at 14,439 feet. It was a clear day and the scenery in all directions was stupendous, including the large cross-shaped veins of snow at the top of the nearby and aptly named Mount of the Holy Cross. As Julie and I were eating our lunch and celebrating our conquest on the small summit, we were joined by a young man who played a royal trick on us. One minute he was standing by the snowbank that encircled the top and the next he was falling backwards over it and presumably down the mountain. With pounding hearts, we rushed over to the edge, only to find him grinning up at us from the safety of a sturdy snow basin just under the lip. He'd obviously practiced this stunt on other unsuspecting souls, but we all had a good laugh.

We did encounter snow on the trail a few times high up, even in late summer, but nothing that gave us any trouble. On one occasion, however, we actually hiked all day in calf-high snow and it was wonderful. We'd had to cancel our summer trip out West, so we went back to Breckenridge in October for our annual mountain fix. Despite a freak snowstorm the night before, we strapped on our good boots and waterproof pants and headed to a pretty, gentle area near Boreas Pass. We had the whole place to ourselves, except for a number of tracks in the snow left by the local wildlife. The plan was to hike around for an hour or two and then go back to town for lunch, but it was all so pristine and peaceful that we kept hiking for six hours. By the time we stopped at 4:00 in the afternoon, we were both starving. Luckily, one of our favorite restaurants in town took pity on us and let us in well before opening time, sat us by a roaring fire, and brought us steaming bowls of freshly made chicken stew. We each had three helpings, with a couple of beers to wash it down. That clearly was one of the very best meals we've ever enjoyed, anywhere.

Unlike most of our hiking in Colorado, we took some nice, easy hikes in the scenic areas around Colorado Springs while staying at The Broadmoor, a legendary mountainside resort opened in 1918. Julie and I celebrated four of our July wedding anniversaries in the 1990s at The Broadmoor. It was totally decadent—but oh so wonderful (and the first of many signs that we were getting

OUT AND ABOUT IN THE GREAT OUTDOORS

old). There was the landmark lake, beaucoup bars and restaurants, an excellent art gallery on-site, and three championship golf courses (where we watched an unknown but pretty, young Swedish golfer named Annika Sorenstam practicing for the U. S. Women's Open, which she won on her way to becoming the best female golfer in the world). The famous Cheyenne Mountain Zoo overlooked the golf courses. The old part of Colorado Springs, including a large model town with moving inhabitants, was most interesting. On a few occasions, we stirred long enough to drive out to the nearby Pikes Peak and Garden of the Gods and even hiked around a bit if we weren't too tired from our indolent lifestyle at The Broadmoor.

Besides Colorado, Julie and I also hiked in the Swiss Alps, the Canadian Rockies, the Smoky Mountains, the White Mountains of New Hampshire, the Taconic and Berkshire Mountains of western Massachusetts, Norway, Ireland (including the highest mountain there), and Scotland (where our conquest of the tallest mountain was foiled halfway up by a sudden summer snowstorm). In October of 1987, we also did the Grand Canyon, down and up, on foot instead of the back of a mule, which looked very uncomfortable and precarious. The walk down from the South Rim through all the different geologic strata with the Colorado River gleaming below us was mind-boggling. That includes the well-named "century plant," a single stalk that slowly grows upward for about 100 years before it finally blooms just once and then dies. And the ravens that fly upside down with the same grace as right side up. There were also the bats that came out just after sunset and buzzed Julie's hair, much to her distress.

We stayed in the Canyon for three nights in one of the three private Phantom Ranch cabins, with a wild turkey on the roof and some deer around most of the time. During the day, we explored along the river and hiked part of the way up to the North Rim. After a particularly hard and dusty hike, we raced to the commissary for a cold beer and got there at 3:58 PM, two minutes before it shut down to prepare for dinner. When we ordered four beers, the attendant reminded us the doors closed at 4:00 sharp and we couldn't take anything out with us, so to his astonishment we finished two beers each in about 90 seconds. My petite wife finished hers before I did mine—I was very impressed, as was the attendant. It would have made a great beer ad. (As mentioned already, Ginger and John hiked in and out of the Grand Canyon a few years after we did, but unlike us, they carried heavy backpacks and camped on the river. At a midway point on their hike out, my exhausted daughter called me at the office and begged me, only half-joking, to send a helicopter because she wasn't going to make it. They eventually did, on their own.)

After running the New York City Marathon together in 1997, Will and I teamed up again in 2004 in a father-son effort to climb another "fourteener," Mount Shasta, a quietly active volcano in northern California. But we planned this as a winter hike in snow and Mother Nature obliged us royally—even though it was April, there was still 15 feet of snow on the mountain from four late snowstorms. We practiced how to stop a fall with an ice axe and then spent one night in a tent on snow at 8,200 feet. Unhappily enough, we didn't get much sleep because there were four of us crammed into a two-person tent, so we all stepped on each other's heads and faces, etc., in the dark whenever we had to do our business outside. The guides woke us up at 1:00 AM, gave us an hour to eat breakfast and put on our crampons, headlights, and other gear, and then started eight of us up Avalanche Gulch (not a reassuring name) at 2:00 sharp. Hiking in the dark and snow with crampons for the first time was a struggle for me, but I managed to keep up for over four hours and made it to about 10,500 feet of elevation. At that point, the slope became much steeper and the guide instructed us to "rope up" by hooking the carabiner on our belts to a common rope in order to stop anyone from sliding and falling down the mountain. Along with another guy even older than me, I decided to turn back instead of killing myself or someone else. Escorted by an exquisite sunrise in front of us, we walked back to our tents and immediately crashed for several hours.

OUT AND ABOUT IN THE GREAT OUTDOORS

Will and four others made it all the way to the top around noon after a climb he described as "the hardest thing I've ever done." His "roped-up" group had traversed back and forth across that one long slope because it was so steep, which required them to change directions at the end of each traverse by balancing on one foot in slippery snow at a precipitous angle while stepping over the safety rope with the other, since they could not unhook themselves from the rope for any reason, such as calls of nature (the group included men and women). After the slope came a rough, jagged ridge that took them to the summit. We have a wonderful photo of our heroic son standing proudly at the top of the world with his arms outstretched and holding his ice axe. We also have a picture of the very moving note of dedication to me that he left in a notebook there, which I will always cherish, although I probably didn't deserve it after causing him to hike down and up an extra quarter mile looking for a water bottle I thought I'd left behind. What took 10 trying hours to climb up took only two hours to come down because Will, like his mother would have done, slid most of the way on his fanny in the snow, using his ice axe as a brake. I was of course disappointed

LEECHES, LOVERS, BEARS, AND CHOCOLATE PUDDING

about not reaching the summit, but it was still an extraordinary experience for me and the happiest of endings in the form of Will's success. (Will married Sienna about three months later, another happy event, and I subsequently took Julie to Mount Shasta to show her what he had done.)

Between Hurricane Katrina and her Alzheimer's diagnosis in 2006, Julie and I did no more hiking together, except for a few familiar trails around Williamstown, Massachusetts. After she moved into the nursing care unit of Lambeth House in 2011, it was another four years before I tried hiking again, starting with the circuit around Mont Blanc that meandered through three countries, France, Italy, and Switzerland, which turned out to be really more than I could chew. The trails, unlike ours, were fairly primitive and littered with boulders of all shapes and sizes that were difficult to navigate. The trek was far too challenging for anyone my age who hadn't done any serious mountain hiking in over 10 years and I had quite a few close escapes and several raw and bloody toes to prove it, but the scenery was worth all the trouble: ice-blue glaciers, waterfalls, lakes, wildflowers, alpine chalets, and of course Mont Blanc, the tallest mountain in Europe. Our group usually ate a lunch of local cheeses and meats in farmhouses and slept in simple mountain lodges. At one stop, as the only single in the group, I had to stay in a co-ed dorm room with bunk beds. My only roommates that night were eight young Japanese women, so I slept with one of my trekking poles to protect my virginity. Fortunately (or unfortunately?), nothing happened.

In 2017, I took a Road Scholar trip to Nepal, which included six days of low-level hiking in the Himalayas up to 8,400 feet. We weren't close enough to see Mount Everest but did get a good, long look at the famous Annapurna. Instead of trails, we hiked mostly on crooked, primitive steps cut into the rock generations ago, which made things a little tricky when it was wet. And instead of heaters in our bedrooms for the cold nights, we had old-fashioned hot-water bottles in our beds and plenty of blankets, but after several local beers sitting around an open fire before dinner, we usually slept like babies. The last three days of the trip were spent in southern Nepal, which is all jungle with elephants, rhinos, crocodiles, tigers, wild hogs, and other assorted denizens. Riding on top of elephants afforded us the opportunity to get up close and personal to the wild rhinos because they could not see us way up there. Bathing with the elephants

OUT AND ABOUT IN THE GREAT OUTDOORS

was also a hoot. First, they would lay down in the river and we would rub them with rough sponges. If we missed a leg, they'd let us know by raising it out of the water. They would then return the favor by showering us with trunks full of water while we straddled their necks and held onto a safety rope for dear life.

But it was in good old Colorado where I discovered the hard way that my aging body was quite different at 65 and 75. When I tried tackling the "fourteeners" again in 2015 after ten years of relative inactivity, the results were very mixed. With a high school classmate, Billy Mimeles, I managed, barely, to summit Mount Bross, one of the three fourteeners Julie and I did in one day when we were much younger. I climbed another old friend, Mount Sherman, by myself the following summer just to prove to myself I could do it. And in 2017, with Ginger and her entire family, I tried a fourteener, Grays Peak, that Julie and I had climbed easily in our heyday. After reaching the 14,000 foot mark with only 278 feet more to the summit (where I could see Ginger and John waving me on), my infuriated mind and body finally screamed "enough!" Although the hike up was excruciating, the walk down was even worse. As happened on Mount Bross and Mount Sherman as well, but never before that, I was quite dizzy and had trouble maintaining my balance (thank goodness for trekking poles to keep me upright). That convinced me I'd done my last fourteener, but there was good news too: Ginger (at age 48) and John had bagged their first fourteener and their kids, Aubrey (14) and Olivia (11), had come very close on their initial attempt. Two new generations take up the challenge!

On the hike up Grays Peak, I had one scary moment that the irrepressible Olivia turned into a very funny memory. After stopping to rest and drink some water, I reached down for something and lost my balance, thanks in part to the shifting weight of water in the camelback pack on my back. Luckily, another man caught my arm before I tumbled down the incline. Olivia was right behind me and saw the whole thing. This is how she described the incident later to her

LEECHES, LOVERS, BEARS, AND CHOCOLATE PUDDING

mom with a perfectly straight face: "When the teachers ask us next month what we did over the summer vacation, I'll tell them I watched my grandfather fall off the side of a big mountain." I'm still laughing at the wonderful joke. Thank you, Livy.

I plan to continue hiking (and just completed a relatively easy but wonderful hike in the Alps between Munich and Salzburg with a great group of 17 from Country Walkers in June of 2019), but will now settle for viewing the "big mountains" instead of climbing them.

Car-Camping

This is where our family's love affair with the Great Outdoors started. Casey, our firstborn, was only 13 months old when we went camping in December with several friends in a Mississippi state park. We did have sleeping bags, including a little one for Casey, but we had to borrow a tent to fit us all in. The tent was old but worked fine, except for the absence of a sewn-in floor that all modern tents have, which I'll come back to in a minute. Sitting around a nice fire with the usual supply of spirits that first night, the group listened to election returns on a radio and celebrated loudly when Moon Landrieu won the runoff for mayor of New Orleans. One of our friends took a great photo of Casey standing by the fire with her ragdoll on a bench behind her. After a good night's sleep, Julie and I woke up to find Casey's sleeping bag empty. We rushed outside in a panic and found her sound asleep in her PJs on the chilly ground just outside the tent. While still asleep, she had apparently wormed her way out of the sleeping bag and then under the walls of the tent, which earned her the nickname "Scooter" that she still answers to 52 years later. And of course we immediately bought our own tent with a sewn-in floor.

OUT AND ABOUT IN THE GREAT OUTDOORS

That was the first of many such outings, usually with the kids but sometimes by ourselves. After a New Orleans chapter of the Sierra Club was opened by our friend who took that photo of Casey (and who later became president of the national Sierra Club and then a powerful spokesman for conservation in Washington, D. C.), our camping (and canoeing) group expanded and scheduled outdoor events on a regular basis. Our favorite destination was a beautiful parcel of wooded, unimproved land along the Bowie River just outside of Hattiesburg, Mississippi. One of the owners' young sons christened it "Nopotopia" (translated from his youthful language as "no pot to pee in") because there was no toilet, so they eventually installed one (without any housing) in the middle of the forest (it was dubbed "the throne"). We often camped there with the usual group of friends, which always involved late-night revelries around a warm campfire after the kids had been tucked into their sleeping bags. In an effort to top the roast suckling pig, sides of beef, and other exotic goodies we sometimes feasted on, one happy member of the group tried to "cook" a plastic Igloo ice chest in the nightly campfire, but it quietly exploded, which was the end of that experiment.

During one of those weekend trips to Nopotopia, Julie and I decided to camp somewhat apart from the main group, so we pitched our two tents (one for the kids) out in a field away from the river. The kids at that point were probably 7, 4, and 2. After settling them in their tent, along with our beloved dog Mama, Julie and I opted to sleep outside our tent because it was such a crystal-clear night. Well, that didn't last. We slept like logs until a cow woke Julie up at around 3:00 AM by licking her face. At that point, the skies opened up and it started pouring. With our now-soaked sleeping bags, we got inside the tent and then went to check on the kids and Mama. Fortunately, their tent was right next to ours. Mama was awake but all three of the kiddies were still asleep in their warm, dry sleeping bags on top of air mattresses that were now floating on about an inch of rainwater in their tent. It would have made a terrific picture. We carried the kids in their sleeping bags to our tent, which by now was pretty wet, muddy, crowded, and generally disgusting, but the little ones never woke up and we all managed to survive what we heard the next day was a nearby tornado.

LEECHES, LOVERS, BEARS, AND CHOCOLATE PUDDING

The six of us, including Mama, loved Nopotopia for many different reasons, especially the beachfront and the river itself. Since the other side of the Bowie across from us was also heavily wooded and totally unimproved, our spot was very private except for an occasional canoe. Bathing therefore was a no-brainer, despite the absence of a bathtub or shower. The fast-running water was fairly cold but clear and invigorating, so it was hard to keep our three little piscine critters out of it. (Mama was a different matter, although she loved the sandy beach.) We have great photos of Julie, in her bikini, bathing our nude brood in the river. Wonderful memories indeed, for all of us. Those au naturel baths continued until the kids got old enough to worry about other people showing up.

OUT AND ABOUT IN THE GREAT OUTDOORS

Nopotopia was also the launch site of many a tubing trip down the Bowie to a bridge four or five miles downstream. There was always an extra inner tube to carry the ice chest full of cold beer for the adults and soft drinks for the kids. When Casey acquired her used single kayak, she would sometimes join us tubers on the river. On one occasion, she tried putting Mama in the kayak with her, but that didn't last very long—Mama got so nervous with all that water around her that Casey had to get out of the kayak and hold onto the side while Mama floated all alone in her royal barge, like Cleopatra. She really did seem to relax and enjoy the ride once she had the kayak all to herself.

And then there was the time Julie and I spent the night in a tree. It was similar to car-camping in that we drove in rather than hike in, but otherwise it was nothing like sleeping on the ground. Our arboreal home was some 30 feet up in the air, built around a tall spruce tree in southwestern Oregon. It was the highest of 16 units in an amazing treehouse motel designed and operated by a 1960s hippie-architect. Every treehouse was different. One that was built close to the ground had doors too small to fit anyone but young children. To get to our treehouse, we had to climb two tiers of ladders and cross two hanging bridges. Luggage was hoisted up on a pulley system. Inside was toilet, wash basin, electric heater, canvas flaps for windows, and great views. We could hear wolves howling in the distance but slept well despite that. The next morning, we showered in a communal bathroom, ate a hearty breakfast, met the owner himself, and hit the road feeling utterly refreshed.

Canoeing, Etc.

I've taken three long overnight canoe trips in Canada. One was with my friend Charlie Genre before I was married, one with Julie, and one just recently with a Road Scholar group. The first two are the subject of another story, "Leeches, Lovers, Bears, and Chocolate Pudding." The third will be discussed near the end

LEECHES, LOVERS, BEARS, AND CHOCOLATE PUDDING

of this section. All the rest of our canoeing activities took place in the South, specifically Louisiana, Mississippi, Arkansas, Georgia, and North Carolina.

After I finished law school at the University of Virginia and we moved back to New Orleans, Julie and I started canoeing on weekends with the same group of friends we camped with. We usually canoed as a team, with Julie in the bow and me in the stern. She learned very quickly and soon became really good at spotting hazards ahead of us and steering the bow around them on short notice. And she taught me a good lesson on those occasions when she had to stay behind with one of the children and I went canoeing without her, albeit "reluctantly." Unlike the fine California wine she brought along with her, she always sent me out alone with the very worst wine I've ever tasted, A&P Rose, at 39 cents a gallon! That eventually put a stop to my solo trips.

Those weekend canoe trips were memorable. There were many fine, fast-moving rivers with good sandbars for camping in Louisiana north of Lake Pontchartrain and in southern Mississippi, all within an hour's drive of New Orleans. So on Friday afternoon, Julie and I would throw our canoe on the top of the car (the neighbors could not believe how strong my small wife was) and then meet the rest of the group at our starting point on the chosen river, enjoy a communal dinner with them, consume a large quantity of alcohol around a fire as we solved all the problems in the world, and finally sleep it off in our tents (assuming that we could make it back to our tents, which sometimes didn't happen). Surprisingly, there were very few hangovers the next morning, probably because of the clean, fresh air we slept in. After striking our tents, eating a good breakfast, and tying our gear (and trash) into the canoe, we headed down the river. We'd stop for lunch and again for the night on a sandbar big enough to accommodate us all (10 or 12 canoes was not unusual). Saturday night was a repeat of the first night. The Sunday paddle was usually a little shorter than Saturday's in order to give us time to drive home and get unpacked.

As you can imagine, there were many funny incidents on those outings, but the funniest that I recall involved a jeep in the river, not a canoe. On a beautiful stretch of Black Creek in Mississippi, our flotilla of about six boats came upon a young couple sitting in street clothes in an old-fashioned, open-top jeep parked on a sandbar. As we approached, the boy behind the wheel decided to show off just how cool (or stupid) he was to his passenger and maybe us too

OUT AND ABOUT IN THE GREAT OUTDOORS

by suddenly heading across the river in his jeep. Unfortunately, it didn't get there but died instead in some three feet of water, above the girl's waist. Without saying a word but deciding telepathically that the boy didn't deserve our help (and probably just wanted us gone), we quietly floated by them as the girl screamed bloody murder at him and he looked for a place to hide. It was truly surrealistic.

We enjoyed many such trips by ourselves until the kids got old enough to join us. That involved a bit more work and equipment but it was well worth it all for them and us. When they were still little, they'd ride on our gear in the middle of the canoe, which made it a bit tippier and caused us to turn over a couple of times in shallow water. Other than those surprise dunkings, our kids enjoyed themselves, especially if other young kids were along as well. For Casey's eighth birthday, she invited her friends over to paint the sides of our canoe and they responded with highly creative efforts. Julie and I had the coolest canoe in New Orleans until it met its untimely end on the Mulberry River in the Ozarks many years later, which we'll get to in a minute.

Once we had honed our skills on the local rivers, our adventurous little group was ready for the big time, i.e., some real whitewater in Arkansas, Georgia, and North Carolina. Between the Chattooga, Nantahala, Buffalo, and

LEECHES, LOVERS, BEARS, AND CHOCOLATE PUDDING

other wild and scenic rivers, we enjoyed much more than our fair share of thrills and spills but somehow survived without a scratch, although there were some close calls. On an earlier trip without Julie to that same Mulberry River in the Ozarks that almost killed Julie and me later, my new bowman and I had to negotiate a steep and narrow chute of whitewater that ran directly into a rock wall at the bottom and made a 90-degree left turn under a head-high tree growing out horizontally from the left bank. With luck, some help from the river gods, and inches to spare, we made it without overturning or even hitting the rock wall or tree. And we saved the MD 20/20 (Mogen David aka Mad Dog 20/20) that was happily consumed that night on a sandbar.

On another Ozark waterway, the Ouachita River, after a first day full of rain and lightning (which is scary in an aluminum canoe on water), Julie and I decided to paddle on to the get-out spot where our car was parked instead of camping overnight with the group. Once we got there, threw the canoe on top of our station wagon, and started to dream of hot showers, the car wouldn't start, so we opened another bottle of wine and prayed to the river gods again. They must have taken pity on us, for a few minutes later, another member of our group showed up and drove us into town in his car. To set the upcoming scene, it was late Sunday, the Fourth of July, and still raining, so the chances of finding someone to start our car were very slim. But the town was Mount Ida, Arkansas, which supposedly served as a model for the fictional town of Mayberry in *The Andy Griffith Show*, and the people there lived up to their image in the TV show. This wonderful man left his Sunday dinner, drove us to the river in his own repair truck, worked on our car for an hour in the rain and darkness until it started, and then asked us apologetically if $10 was too much for all of his help! We gave him $40 and blessed the Mount Idas of this world.

Aside from that adventure in Canada where Julie earned her bear-chasing stripes, our favorite canoe trip involved the Chattooga River, made famous by the movie *Deliverance*. Twelve of us drove up to northern Georgia together in a big van (and must have towed our canoes, but I can't remember). We ran Stage 3 of the river, which was full of rapids but not as difficult as Stage 4 where the movie was filmed and several canoeists have drowned. At one point on our journey, all of the river's flow was funneled by a protruding rock ledge into one narrow, steep, and crooked chute of fast, boiling water. Some in our group chose

OUT AND ABOUT IN THE GREAT OUTDOORS

to portage their canoes around the chute, but the rest of us ran it, one at a time. Although it looked bad enough from the back of the canoe where I sat, it must have looked much worse from Julie's perspective in the front. As soon as our canoe went over the front edge, Julie chucked her paddle and dove for cover in the bottom of the boat. Enter the river gods again. We bounced around a lot going down the chute and put some good dents in our canoe but somehow made it in one piece to the nice, calm pool below, where we all celebrated with cold beers.

Our celebration was interrupted by a truly frightening sight: a couple (plus a young child) who obviously knew nothing about paddling a canoe that was headed straight for that dangerous chute we'd just run. We all stood on the ledge and yelled at them to go ashore and portage around it, but they didn't understand or couldn't overcome the force of the water pushing them towards the chute. We could see that they were terrified and had no idea what to do. Their canoe was totally out of control and wound up pinned sideways to the flow on two rocks halfway down the chute, where they would have been stranded for some time if we hadn't been there to throw them ropes and help them out of the canoe onto the ledge. We then dislodged their canoe with some effort and watched with mixed feelings as they headed on, hopefully a little wiser. Unfortunately, on our various whitewater outings, we encountered others like them who had no business being anywhere near water like that.

And now for the really sad part: after mastering the Chattooga and saving three lives, we were all starving. Why? Because a good friend who had

LEECHES, LOVERS, BEARS, AND CHOCOLATE PUDDING

volunteered to supply lunch that day forgot to bring the cold cuts, so we had nothing to eat but mustard sandwiches. However, our friend was just getting warmed up. To make up for her grievous error, on the drive home she snuck into a field of ripe corn to steal some for the rest of us, who of course encouraged her to do so. She disappeared for five minutes and then reappeared at the business end of a large shotgun held by the irate farmer. He apparently didn't buy her story about going to the bathroom, just because she had an armful of his corn, but he let her go with a warning about never coming back, which he didn't need to worry about. We missed the fresh (and free) corn but had a good laugh on the way home.

Our least favorite trip, which illustrates the serious dangers of whitewater canoeing, was our last one, again on the Mulberry River. There were just three boats from New Orleans on this outing. Heavy rains in the Ozarks had flooded the Mulberry well over its banks, which not only increased the speed and force of the water but also made it harder for us to "read" the river without the usual landmarks (now underwater) to guide us. However, after driving 14 hours to get there, we all decided to give it a go. The first three hours on the racing river were exhilarating, the best ride I can remember. After a quick lunch, our good fortune ran out. While trying to find the right channel, Julie and I managed to lodge our canoe against a tree on a now-submerged island in the middle of the river. It was shallow enough for us to stand up, but the force of the water bent our aluminum canoe into a right angle around the tree. And the channels on both sides of the island were too deep and fast for us to cross to dry land on our own, so we were stuck there.

Luckily, our fellow boaters (including Mike Osborne and his wife) came back on foot for us and brought a lot of rope with them. They threw us two ropes that we tied to the tree to use as "guide rails" on either side to help us cross the channel. I went first to test the plan, which seemed good in theory, but as soon as I took my first step off the island, the great force of the water swept my feet out from under me and rapidly carried me downriver. I wound up in a grove of willow trees in only three feet of water but could not stand up because the water was so strong. Even with my life jacket on, it kept pushing me back underwater whenever I popped up. I was totally helpless and started thinking I was going to drown (in waist-deep water, no less!). Finally, after four or five ups and downs, the river popped me up near a tree and I grabbed onto it for dear life. From there I pulled myself from tree to tree until I reached the shore.

That still left Julie by herself on the island. As I found out later, my brave and sainted wife also thought I was going to drown in the willows and was ready to jump in to save me when I popped up for good. Since the "guide rail" ropes were obviously not enough in the strong current, our friends threw Julie another rope to tie around her waist, which probably saved her life. Like me, she was knocked off her feet and swept downriver, but this time we reeled her into shore like a fish (or mermaid) with that third line around her waist. Julie and I both were pretty shook up but safe, thanks to the Osbornes and the other couple—they were great! I don't remember how we got out of there, since our trusty canoe was now a deformed derelict in the middle of the river, but we somehow made it to a motel and headed home the next morning, a little wiser, very humbled, and profoundly grateful to our noble rescuers. After all of that excitement, it was an easy decision for us to give up canoeing for good.

To our regret and embarrassment, Julie and I broke our no-more-canoeing oath just once many years later. At a weekend house party across Lake Pontchartrain, the agenda included a nice, leisurely canoe outing on a nice, easy river, since most of the group had never canoed before. Julie and I were selected to carry everyone's booze in our canoe because we were the "experts." Yeah, right! I can still hear the river gods laughing about that one. Not surprisingly for this group, they piled enough beer, wine, and whiskey in our canoe to sink a barge. Then off they went, leaving us to bring up the rear. Well, we showed them—our overloaded canoe turned over within 30 seconds of pushing off. All that wonderful booze went overboard, but not to worry, since the water there was so shallow that we were sure to find most of the stuff, right? Wrong again. Ten of us spent a good hour walking barefoot up and down the river, hoping to feel bottles with our feet. We found exactly one bottle—of tonic water. To see so many thirsty New Orleanians without any spirits to drink is a sad, sad sight. But as time goes on, the more I think that Julie and I were used by some higher spirit to save the group from itself—or simply play a bad joke on us all.

Tubing was a good substitute for canoeing in late summer when outside temperatures were still high and water levels in our Louisiana and Mississippi rivers were generally lower. It also required less gear and planning because it

LEECHES, LOVERS, BEARS, AND CHOCOLATE PUDDING

was a one-day instead of an overnight outing. Most important of all, however, was the fact that we could carry as much cold beer as we could in a canoe, by wedging large ice chests in extra inner tubes and tethering them to our tubes. Julie and I tubed with our fellow canoeists and other friends on many of the free-flowing, sandy-bottom rivers within easy driving distance of New Orleans.

We also enjoyed two tubing adventures on the Comal River in New Braunfels, Texas, with old friends who had moved from New Orleans. Both outings started with some of their special, homemade margaritas for the stated purpose of making us more seaworthy. The spring-fed river was ideal for tubing: crystal-clear water around 2–3 feet deep, a soft, clay-lined bottom, no obstacles to dodge, and both banks lined with a municipal water park. After a delightful hour's ride, we would wind up at our friends' house on the river (with more margaritas). Sadly, their beautiful house was totally lost after a freak, catastrophic rainstorm turned this short (two miles long), shallow, gentle river into a raging 30-foot-high wall of water that destroyed everything in its path. Our friends had a half-hour notice to get out of the house before it was knocked off its pilings and swept downstream. Happily, their brand-new house in the same location survived another similar "100-year flood" just three years later.

Our rafting experience consists of just two trips. Early in our marriage, Julie and I met another New Orleans couple in Big Bend National Park in Texas on the Rio Grande. There we encountered our first tarantula, sitting defiantly in the middle of a desolate road. Julie and I got out of the car to examine this rather large, fearsome-looking creature from what we thought was a safe distance, until it jumped a good eight feet in one mighty leap, which sent us scrambling for cover. After that, we hooked up with our friends and hiked with them all over the beautiful canyons and rock formations by the Rio Grande. We also ventured out into the famous river in an inflatable plastic raft we'd bought for the trip, but the water level was very high, so we stayed near the shore (unlike our later insanity on the Mulberry). When we were a good bit older, Julie and I rode a large commercial raft down the Arkansas River in Colorado. That was fun and scenic (and very cold, as I remember), but unlike paddling your own canoe, we just sat there and relied on a guide to steer the raft.

In 2016, after Julie got sick, I joined a six-day Road Scholar canoe trip down the Yukon River in northwestern Canada near Alaska. It was glorious. The

OUT AND ABOUT IN THE GREAT OUTDOORS

Yukon Territory is a true wilderness, with miles of permafrost and many more moose, bears (grizzly and black), wolves, and eagles than people. Our small group of about 10 paddled some 30 miles a day and then camped at night on one of the many sandbars along the river, after first checking it out for animal tracks (specifically for moose, which are territorial and even more dangerous than grizzlies, according to the locals). We slept in individual tents and used the woods as a bathroom, always careful to bag our waste and burn it in the nightly campfire. We also had to sing or whistle loudly whenever we went into the thick forests in order not to surprise a moose or bear. I took exactly one bath that lasted all of 10 seconds in the fast and freezing water. Sitting around the campfire after dinner and hearing stories and poems about the area's colorful history (including Julie's favorite, "The Cremation of Sam McGee") was delightful. The trip ended in the famous town of Dawson, center of the Klondike Gold Rush of 1898, with lots of hot water, good food, and dancing ladies. It was definitely a better ending to our canoeing adventures than the two previous trips.

Of our three children, Casey is the one who enjoyed a real love of paddling, but her chosen craft was a kayak instead of canoe. She became an excellent kayaker at age 14 after two weeks of intensive instruction at the Nantahala Outdoor Center in North Carolina and got her own used kayak two years later. During her teenage summers, she worked at our local Canoe and Trail Shop and even led some of its canoeing and kayaking trips (as she did later on whitewater rivers in North Carolina after moving there). Despite her training and skill, Casey was excluded from her high school class canoeing trip for boys only, until she complained all the way up to the headmaster and then wound up teaching most of her male classmates how to paddle. Her son Ethan became an avid kayaker himself while attending summer camp at Mondamin in North Carolina (where I also spent two blissful summers as a youth).

Alpine Skiing

Alpine, or downhill, skiing (as distinguished from cross-country skiing on relatively flat terrain) is a sublime and exhilarating experience, especially for those of us like Julie and me who live where there's no snow or mountains. There are many reasons why it's so special: The unmatched beauty of snow-covered peaks all around you. The fresh and invigorating air. The relative silence. The grace and good cheer of the strangers you meet on the lifts or slopes. But most of all, it's the terror and the thrill of flying down a mountain on nothing but two thin strips of laminated wood that are diabolically designed to go faster than you want to. Julie and I never came close to matching our son Will's top downhill speed of 56 miles per hour while on The Gunnery ski team in Connecticut (his mother almost fainted when he proudly told her that). We probably hit 20 miles per hour on a good day, which is pretty slow for a car, but it feels a lot different and a lot faster when you're all alone and unprotected on a steep snow-covered slope. It's just you and the mountain. And that's what makes alpine skiing both thrilling and terrifying.

Accidents and injuries do occur on the slopes, but Julie and I were lucky in that regard. I fractured two ribs on an escape road for beginners, of all things, and Julie cracked her sacrum (tailbone) when she slipped carrying her skis in a parking lot. There were, however, a few close calls, which was not so unusual for the two of us. On two separate occasions, I was skiing too fast when I "caught an edge" while turning, went airborne, did a half forward flip, and landed directly on the top of my head. In addition to escaping injury to my head or neck, I provided some comic moments for the other family members who witnessed my unplanned acrobatics. A few years later, after Julie's Alzheimer's had been diagnosed but she was still able to ski, I was leading her carefully down a run with our daughter Ginger trailing behind her, when I slowed down and turned around to see how Julie was doing. That's when Julie, who had been skiing right behind me and couldn't stop or swerve in time, hit me like an NFL linebacker. We both went flying. The next thing I remember is lying sprawled in the snow seeing stars as Ginger leaned over me with a terrified look on her face. Poor Julie didn't fare any better, but we both recovered after a few minutes and got down the mountain safely (and slowly).

Our uneven history of skiing together began four decades before that, during our first year of marriage. We were living in Charlottesville, Virginia, where I was in my third year of law school and Julie was teaching pre-K kids. During our winter break, we visited my alma mater in Massachusetts and then went to a nearby resort in Vermont to learn how to ski. Although I learned nothing useful from it, I had "skied" exactly one day in college with some alleged

OUT AND ABOUT IN THE GREAT OUTDOORS

friends who tricked me into riding a lift with them to the top of a mountain where they laughingly abandoned me to my own devices, which didn't exist. I don't remember how I got down the mountain but it was certainly ugly and traumatic. Despite that, my dear wife, who never lacked for courage, foolishly trusted me enough to take on this new and strange experience, which I'm sure she quickly regretted, not for the last time.

Looking back, it was destined to be a disaster from the get-go. Having no ski clothes, we dressed in cotton blue jeans that soon became soaked in the snow and miserably uncomfortable on our frozen legs. Then the fun really began when we had to get on a chairlift (a continually moving set of chairs hanging from a cable) to go up the mountain the first time. We got in the right position to sit down in the lift chair when it arrived behind us, but we both sat down too soon. The result was a first-class Penick debacle: We were both half in and half out when the chair scooped us up, gained altitude, and headed up the mountain. I managed to somehow pull myself into the chair but Julie spent the whole trip with her bottom half out of the chair and holding onto me for dear life as she dangled 100 feet or so above the ground. To make a bad situation even worse, one of her skis had come off and was hanging from her boot by the safety strap. Since we had no exit strategy for getting off the lift at the top, we were much relieved when the lift operators finally stopped it at that point and helped us off.

But then we had to get down the mountain on our own. Looking down from the top, it seemed impossible for novices like us, but we had no choice. I advised Julie to ski across the run because it was the easiest way down, but she fell down after some 30 feet, so I went to her "rescue." Just like Tarzan, right? Well, as I skied toward Julie and got closer, I realized I didn't know how to stop or turn. My aim, however and unfortunately, was perfect. While yelling to warn Julie, I skied right over her prone body before wiping out big time. As pitiful as it was, we both laughed our heads off before returning to the very delicate problem of getting ourselves down the mountain in one piece. Somehow we did and even decided to take another run, which of course required us to get on the same lift again.

When he spotted us waiting in line, the lift operator looked like he'd seen two ghosts and was ready to quit on the spot rather than deal with us again, but we managed to get fully in the chair this time, to his utter surprise. After a few

LEECHES, LOVERS, BEARS, AND CHOCOLATE PUDDING

more runs and many more falls, Julie and I were exhausted, battered, soaked, and frozen. Julie was first in the shower but jumped out screaming bloody murder after just a few seconds when the very hot water hit her very cold body. But things returned to normal (whatever that word means for the two of us) after a few hot toddies and some heartfelt hallelujahs that we'd planned only one day of skiing.

Julie continued to have a love-hate relationship with chairlifts ever since that first disastrous matchup, but also because she did not like heights and was therefore uncomfortable sitting in a moving wooden chair dangling from a single cable way up in the air. But she is one very courageous gal, so she did it because chairlifts were a necessary part of the alpine skiing she learned to love. Sometimes we encountered signs warning us not to jump from the lift when the ground was 100 or 200 feet below us, which Julie thought was hilarious. That is, until she herself jumped from a moving lift chair. Luckily, it was only two feet off the ground. She was riding up with Will when they passed a closed midway get-off station, which must have triggered some kind of subconscious reaction in Julie that made her jump out of the chair. As she lay in the snow looking up at Will still in the moving chair, she yelled up at him to "go on without me" (a movie line?), to which he replied rather ungallantly "don't worry, I will" as his chair gained altitude. He watched as his mother was roughly yanked to her feet by a ski patroller who thought she was a teenager showing off until he realized she was a middle-aged woman and became very apologetic.

At the end of that same trip, after the weather had turned brutally cold and windy, I was riding the chair behind Julie and Will when they, to allegedly keep warm, broke out in a full-throated rendition of "You Are My Sunshine," which did in fact warm up the world around them momentarily and distract us from our misery. It was also a good example of something really funny or unusual happening whenever Julie and Will rode a chairlift together.

OUT AND ABOUT IN THE GREAT OUTDOORS

Following our Vermont debacle, Julie and I licked our psychic wounds for three or four years before mustering the nerve to try skiing again. We had the right clothes and wisely took lessons this time. Taos, New Mexico, just north of Santa Fe, is where we finally learned to ski for real. We picked Taos because of the price, but it turned out to be a first-rate ski resort with great snow. We enjoyed it so much that we returned the next year. That second trip to Taos turned out to be quite memorable, for two reasons.

After spending a lot of the previous year canoeing and camping with our good friend Pete and his girlfriend (and future wife) Jerri, she decided to join us in Taos and try out skiing. As luck would have it, one of our young kids came down with chickenpox just before the trip and Julie decided to postpone her departure but urged Jerri and me to go on as planned ("go on without me" again?). So for the first two nights in Taos, I was accompanied to dinner in the lodge by a young, attractive blonde woman named Jerri. Unfortunately, Jerri injured her knee on the last run of our first day skiing and had to fly back to New Orleans the next day for medical care, which happened to be the same day that Julie flew in. After dropping Jerri off and picking Julie up at the same airport, I showed up at the Taos lodge that night with another young and attractive woman named Julie on my arm. I was the envy of every other male in the lodge. Besides the knowing winks and thumbs-up, one of them even asked me "what happened to the blonde?" My undeserved fame as a serious stud lasted exactly two days until I was knocked off my pedestal in the worst kind of way.

Whatever his ulterior motive was, our ski instructor told me I had learned enough to involve entering the weekly Nastar race, so I foolishly signed up. Stupid, stupid, stupid! The Nastar involves skiing as fast as possible in and out of slalom poles (or gates) placed in a line down a steep mountain slope. Naturally it was a cold and windy day. Julie was in the crowd watching from the sidelines. To my utter horror, I quickly realized this was a race for professional skiers as my fellow racers sprang out of the starting gate and flew through the slalom poles at top speed. I should have withdrawn but didn't for some crazy reason. Since I did not throw up out of terror, my only hope was that the electronic starting gate would malfunction and not open for me. Alas, it did and I gently headed downhill, straight into the first pole, fell down, got up and crashed into the second pole, fell down, got up, and did the same thing two more times. At that

LEECHES, LOVERS, BEARS, AND CHOCOLATE PUDDING

rate, with about 30 or so more poles to go, I figured it would take me another two days to finish the course, if I even survived that long. So I held up my ski poles in utter defeat and skied off to the sidelines looking for some much-needed TLC from my loving wife. Alas yet again, she had other plans, namely, to avoid any public association with her klutzy husband. Instead of rushing out and throwing her arms around me, she tried to hide at first and then relented and claimed me as hers for all to see. (Had our roles been reversed, I'm not sure I would have claimed me.) I never went near a Nastar after that fiasco.[†]

A few years later, my sneaky wife cajoled me into entering another slalom race (at a private party) because the two of us would be competing head-to-head and she wanted to beat me, so how could I possibly refuse her challenge to my manhood? I should have known better. This time, there were two sets of just 12 poles placed side by side about 15 feet apart. At the midway point, we were both skiing hard but were neck and neck. Then Julie made a very wide turn around her pole (probably deliberately, the little devil) that put her directly in my path. To avoid a collision, I had to veer sharply off the track and out of the race. Julie finished and, despite my official complaint, won a medal that she proudly (and smugly, at least around me) wore for the rest of the trip.

As dangerous as it was to ski with Julie, it was much more so to ski with our teenage son, whose off-key motto was "Trust Me." (To commemorate that and our suckerhood as parents, Julie bought him a pillowcase with a bunch of sharks and his motto all over it. Ironically, he used it on his equally infamous waterbed that he had talked us into buying for him, thereby rubbing salt in our wounds.) Will was a good skier and loved skiing the so-called "back bowls" where the real pros skied because of the length, steepness, and moguls (or bumps). Whenever he needed some comic relief, he would taunt me enough to go with him, to my later regret. Standing at the top of a back bowl and looking down all the treacherous terrain between me and survival, I was always reminded of my Nastar fiasco. The results on the back bowls were about the same, with

---

[†] But Will did. When he was about seven, he ran a kids' Nastar and crossed the finish line in a record time, as announced over the loudspeaker. On review, the officials noticed that Will, in all innocence, had skied straight down *between* the poles instead of *around* each one. His record time was therefore canceled, but believe me, his Nastar run at that tender age was a whole lot prettier than mine was.

young Will at the bottom urging me to hurry up and me praying for some kind of divine rescue. He did the same thing to a friend and law partner who failed to heed my warning about skiing with Will. I ran across Darryl two hours later lying on a snowbank and gasping for breath. "He (Will) tried to kill me" was all he could say. I knew exactly what he meant.

But I'm happy to report that Will got his comeuppance when he and his college roommate Gabriel Macht (now a TV star) went out to Breckenridge and hooked up with a good friend's daughter-in-law, who happened to be a ski instructor. Well, after hearing the boys brag about their skiing skills, she tested them on some very challenging back bowls until they were begging for mercy. Thank you, Sue. Will switched from skiing to snowboarding soon after that.

All of our kids became very good alpine skiers. After one trip to a ski resort in North Carolina when they were still pretty young, we took them out to ski in Colorado every year (and once in Utah) and wound up buying a condo in Breckenridge that we've enjoyed in the winter and summer for 38 years now. Our annual ski trip with the kids usually occurred during Mardi Gras week when their schools were closed. Eventually we discovered how to save a good bit of money by swapping our house (and car) in New Orleans at a peak time for a ski condo (and car) somewhere in Colorado. That worked like a charm for eight years in a row and gave us the chance to try many different ski areas. It also worked well for our beloved dog Mama, who got to stay home and be pampered by our guests instead of spending a week in a kennel. Julie of course can no longer ski but the other four of us are still skiing or snowboarding. As are our grandchildren except for the youngest two, who will start this year (2019).

LEECHES, LOVERS, BEARS, AND CHOCOLATE PUDDING

Before moving on, let me just say a quick word about Breckenridge itself. When our friends Diane and Charlie found $89 roundtrip tickets to Denver (plus free lodging to boot), Julie and I jumped at the chance of going with them to Breckenridge to house-hunt a possible retreat location for the medical staff of Ochsner Clinic, which included Charlie. We'd never been to Breckenridge before and quickly fell in love with its 1850s' charm and authenticity, unlike the "pop-up" ski resorts of Vail, Keystone, and Copper Mountain that surround it. We also met two lovely locals, Vern and Betty Johnson, a realtor (and ex-FBI agent) and a ski instructor respectively, who became good friends of ours after we made Breckenridge our second home the following year with Vern's help.

The Johnsons lived in an extraordinary seven-story house built some time ago up the side of a mountain, with its own ski jump. One of the smaller stories, only four feet high, was obviously designed as a unique private space for young

OUT AND ABOUT IN THE GREAT OUTDOORS

children only. Julie and I went with them one January evening to listen to the Pablo Casals Trio perform on one of the ski mountains. With the sun setting dramatically behind them, they played a Schubert trio and one by Dvorak called *Dumky,* which refers to Slavic folk music that alternates between sad and happy passages, as the piece did in a beautiful way. Julie, who had not listened to much chamber music before that, was absolutely blown away by the *Dumky* (plus the gorgeous sunset) and has since then listened to it countless times at home, which always reminds us of the Johnsons. Vern died many years ago but Betty, one of the most gracious ladies I've ever known, died only last year (2018) at age 96.

Despite our limited skiing skills, none of ever suffered any injury—until last year, 2021. After surviving a case of Covid and then eight months of "cabin fever" the year before, I planned to spend a week skiing in Park City, Utah, where Will would join me mid-week. Unfortunately, in the first hour on the slopes, I partially tore a ligament in my left knee, which put an end to any more skiing that trip, but Will and I had a good visit. Back in New Orleans, I had two months of physical therapy that was completely successful in terms of being able to ski again.

So I went out to Breckenridge in March of this year to test my left knee, which worked fine—and of course wound up injuring my right knee even worse, but this time it was at the end of the trip on the very last run. I had been skiing with my son-in-law John and grandson Aubrey, then a freshman in college. They are both excellent skiers (Aubrey skied all 21 lifts spread out over five mountains in one day!) but I somehow managed to keep up until we were three minutes from the condo on an easy trail, when I "caught an edge" in melting snow and did a split. Unable to stand on my right leg, I rode a mountain litter to the nearby clinic, where a complete tear of my ACL (anterior cruciate ligament) was diagnosed. The first orthopedic surgeon I saw in New Orleans confirmed the diagnosis but said I was too old (81) for that type of surgery, so I looked around for another surgeon and even considered surgery in Colorado if necessary. Lo and behold, I found a wonderful surgeon at the Ochsner Sports Medicine Clinic who was willing to operate because the MRI showed very little arthritis in my knee. He did his job so well that I had zero post-operative pain and almost a full range of motion in that knee only four days after the surgery. Casey came down from North Carolina for the surgery and stayed a week, which probably saved

LEECHES, LOVERS, BEARS, AND CHOCOLATE PUDDING

my sanity because of a non-functioning bladder that required catheterization for a month. I'm now completing five months of physical therapy in preparation for a hiking trip in Patagonia next month. Things look good but all my fingers are crossed.

Hunting And Fishing

All of the hunting and fishing I did growing up, most of it with my friend Wardy, is described in another story (see story entitled "Before Julie"). The same is true of my ill-fated first (and last) hunting trip with Julie, who sent her future husband down with the ship while saving herself (see story entitled "Down with the Ship, Said He—Hell No, Said She") and our wacky canoe trip in Canada when fishing kept us alive for five days after a bear ate our food supplies before my petite but ferocious wife chased it away (see story entitled "Leeches, Lovers, Bears, and Chocolate Pudding").

Along with some other friends, Wardy and I continued to hunt ducks for a few years after we were both married. Julie, perhaps as a form of redemption for sinking our boat, encouraged the hunting and learned how to clean, gut, and then cook a mean duck. About eight of us leased a block of marshland down by Lafitte, Louisiana, and built (and rebuilt every year) a number of duck blinds out of the local rozo cane. On one particular trip, while hunting with a friend and law partner, we stayed longer than usual and didn't notice how much the water level in our pond had dropped from an outgoing tide. As a result, there was not enough water to float our pirogue when we finally left and the muddy bottom was too soft to support our weight if we tried to walk, so all we could do was to slide in the mud on our knees while pushing the pirogue until we reached deeper water, which took us well over a very sloppy and exhausting hour. Thank goodness for hip boots!

But most of my post-marital hunting involved the Pinfeathers Club (so named for a duck's immature feathers) with its ramshackle bunkhouse on a river in Pointe-a-la-Hache, right in the middle of the famous duck-hunting marshes of southern Louisiana near the Gulf of Mexico. The 12 or so members included several good friends and fellow lawyers. In addition to providing our own pirogues and decoys, we annually built the duck blinds in the nearby marshes we leased for hunting. There was always a good bourre game (a kind of Cajun poker mixed with bridge) with lots of beer the night before every morning hunt. Then we'd wake up around 3:30 AM, eat a quick breakfast, pack our pirogue, pushpole over the shallow water to our assigned blind, put out our decoys, and be in the blind ready to hunt before the sun came up. I never saw a moccasin or alligator, but they were out there (you could hear them splashing ominously in the dark), along with thousands of hungry mosquitoes, but the sights, sounds, and even smells of a marsh morning with the sun rising and ducks flying everywhere were truly spectacular, at least before the shooting started. The actual hunting was usually over in a couple of hours.

I started taking Will hunting with me at Pinfeathers when he was about 10 years old. He enjoyed the hunting part, but he really loved the bourre games because he'd quickly pocket the winnings and hit up his old man when he lost— I'm still trying to figure out how he pulled that one off. Will never was a morning person, so getting him up at 3:30 AM on a cold morning was challenging. Even after that, it took him a couple of hours to reach a minimal functioning level. Once we were in the pirogue, it was his job in the front to show me where to go by keeping a light shined on the shoreline. When the light beam slowly drifted away from his target, I knew he was falling asleep and had to wake him up to get my bearings again. His first duck, a beautiful greenhead mallard, was mounted and hung over his notorious waterbed, which was kind of fitting. During a trip to Pinfeathers without me, the boys (…being boys) "initiated" Will into the sacred rite of eating duck hearts and livers.

One of our most memorable hunting weekends together involved no hunting. After driving down to Pointe-a-la-Hache, we turned right around and came back to New Orleans because we learned the temperature the next morning was supposed to be near 0 degrees and it would have been even colder in a duck blind. There was just one problem: we couldn't go home. Julie had already planned an overnight "hen party" with several of her friends, so Will and I dared not go anywhere close to the house. Instead, we checked into a Metairie motel, had a deliciously unhealthy dinner, and saw the newly opened movie *The Terminator* with lots of popcorn for dessert. It was all very decadent, but fun.

Although my interest in duck hunting had already begun to wane after Will left for school in Connecticut, it was a pair of spoonbill ducks that put me

LEECHES, LOVERS, BEARS, AND CHOCOLATE PUDDING

over the tipping point. Ducks usually mate for life, so I assume the two of them were an old married couple not unlike Julie and I a few years later. I was alone in the blind when they started circling over the pond and decoys. They were obviously tempted but also wary of something and therefore just kept circling, so I finally took a very long shot and hit one that dropped dead into the pond. The other wouldn't leave its mate behind and continued to circle over the pond for another 10 minutes at least. It was still within possible range of my 12 gauge shotgun, but I didn't have the heart to shoot at a duck that had already suffered a grievous loss. That's when I finally decided to quit hunting.

The Pinfeathers Club had a couple of power boats that we sometimes used in summer to fish for speckled trout and redfish on the edge of the Gulf. On one such trip, I hooked a furious 10-pound redfish but it was poor Julie who had the intimidating job of netting and wrestling it into the boat. She then cooked the big fellow perfectly and created several delicious redfish dinners for us and my mother. Two weeks after that, I took a good friend, Jim Petersen, to the same spot where the redfish lived (and dolphins played nearby). He landed another big red and we also caught a number of specks before disaster struck: our 90-horsepower motor would not start and we were a long way away from the clubhouse. We eventually managed to get back to Pinfeathers on a 3-horsepower spare motor, but what was a 30-minute trip going out became a 4-to-5-hour trip going back. Although we were never in any danger and it really was quite peaceful chugging along at the speed of a fast turtle, we had no cellphones back then to call our wives and there was no one around to help us. Jim and I didn't get back to Pinfeathers (and a phone) until it was dark, by which time Julie and Betsy were frantic. Julie had called another Pinfeathers member who had called the president of Plaquemines Parish (where we were), who in turn had provided a helicopter to look for us. It was just about to lift off from Audubon Park with our friend on board when I finally got in touch with Julie. It was quite an adventure, surely more so for our wives. For the life of me, I don't remember what happened to all the fish we caught.

I should've known something like that would happen, given our history of fishing catastrophes that started two days before Hurricane Betsy hit New Orleans in October of 1965. Julie was about seven months pregnant with Casey. The two and a half of us rented a boat and motor on Pearl River, the boundary

OUT AND ABOUT IN THE GREAT OUTDOORS

line between Louisiana and Mississippi. It's a freshwater river that runs into the Gulf of Mexico. Even with the approaching storm, it was a beautiful day. After finding a nice, quiet spot to try our luck, Julie announced she was too pregnant to do anything but fish, so I ran the motor, baited Her Majesty's hook, and removed the fish she caught. And she did catch fish! 16 in all, half of them largemouth bass (a freshwater fish) and the other half speckled trout (a saltwater fish), each in the very same spot with the very same kind of bait in no more than an hour's time. She caught a fish on almost every cast. Apparently the storm in the Gulf had not only made the fish ravenous but had also pushed enough saltwater up into the river to bring the specks with it. I fileted the fish and put them in our freezer, which of course died two days later when the hurricane hit us and all the power went out. Faced with the loss of both fish and beer, we had a true brainstorm in the form of an old-fashioned fish fry after the storm had passed on. Two dozen friends enjoyed fresh fish cooked on Coleman stoves and lots of still-cold beer to wash it down. It was a grand success. The power came back on two weeks later and Casey arrived a little early in November.

Our next fishing expedition was a disaster from beginning to end. The year after Hurricane Betsy, Julie and I joined a deep-sea fishing venture with four other friends. The three girls had each brought a large picnic basket filled with food and drink. Unfortunately, the boat we'd reserved was well past its prime and barely seaworthy in a very rough Gulf several miles from shore on that particular day. Two of the girls (including Julie) and one of the guys (not me) got terribly seasick (as did the boat captain!) and spent much of the time throwing up over the side or vying for the only toilet on board. In the middle of a serious bowel movement, a big swell rocked the boat and caused the other sick girl (who will remain nameless) to slide off the toilet seat and across the deck on her bottom, while actively discharging her colonic contents on the floor. The good news is that she didn't pick up any splinters. As that was happening below deck, the healthy three of us were having a great time on deck stuffing our faces with goodies from the picnic baskets. The only fish anyone caught was a shark, but at least we made it back to shore safely.

Julie and I did take the kids on a few fishing excursions around New Orleans or Dauphin Island, Alabama (which is covered in more detail in the later section on "Dauphin Island"). On one of those outings, Ginger (then about 10)

LEECHES, LOVERS, BEARS, AND CHOCOLATE PUDDING

hooked what was probably a large stingray, which stripped the line off her reel so fast that she got scared and threw the whole rig overboard. We also fished with the kids on some of our backpacking trips in Colorado and have some funny photos of them learning to cast. After a hiatus of many years, I took up fly-fishing again post-retirement during our summer stays in Williamstown, Massachusetts. Following a successful debut with a terrific fishing guide from Orvis (which has its incredible world headquarters just up the road from Williamstown), I made the mistake of taking Julie along on the next trip two weeks later somewhere in Vermont. You can guess who caught the biggest fish (an 18-inch rainbow trout, no less!) and then bragged about it to our friends for weeks. I went back again with other friends but never again invited Julie (or caught a big rainbow like hers).

OUT AND ABOUT IN THE GREAT OUTDOORS

Running

"Running" may be a slight exaggeration as a description of what Julie and I did for so many years in Colorado and Massachusetts as well as New Orleans, but we did get a lot of good exercise and fresh air in the process. More important, our children followed our example. All of them ran the Crescent City Classic (6.2 miles) with us more than once, as I recall. Ginger later ran a half-marathon in Phoenix with her husband John. But it's Will who has "gone the extra mile" in a big way. At the ripe old age of 48, he runs 10 to 15 miles in the Hollywood Hills like it's a walk in the park, has run several marathons, and is now training for a triathlon! It all started when he ran his first race (the 5-mile Turkey Day Race) at age 10 and sprinted to the finish line while Julie and I were just happy to finish.

For me, the obvious high point of my undistinguished "running" career was finishing the New York City Marathon with Will in 1997, when I was 57. It was the first of many marathons for him and the last of one for me. I of course trained religiously for a whole year for the November race. That was probably harder on Julie than me, because she usually followed me on her creaky old bike during my training sessions, carrying my water and energy bars and generally encouraging me. Because of the summer heat and humidity in New Orleans, we often started before sunrise and traversed the cart paths of the City Park Golf Course. Amazingly enough, we encountered a few crazier-than-normal golfers practicing in the near-dark. On one memorable occasion, while going over a high overpass, Julie was struggling to keep up with me on her pitiful bike when a car full of happy teenagers saw the situation and called out to Julie "you're losing him, lady." If looks could kill, they would've all died on the spot. On another

LEECHES, LOVERS, BEARS, AND CHOCOLATE PUDDING

occasion, during a long training run of 20 miles in Williamstown, we stopped halfway to listen to the news of Princess Diana's death.

After all of that, the big day finally arrived. Julie and Ginger joined us in the Big Apple to cheer us on or, more likely, pick up the pieces. Unfortunately, the excitement started the night before the marathon, when Will cut open his foot at home and Ginger left her professional notebook and schedule in a taxicab. Will was still able to run with a stitched-up foot and Ginger's notebook was returned the next morning by the thoughtful passenger who followed us in the cab (after she had called out to John in Denver to locate Ginger in New York City).

On race day, Will and I were two of 33,000 real or would-be jocks jammed into a corner of Staten Island for three hours before the 9:00 AM start because the island was closed to traffic much too early. Most of that time was spent waiting in a long line for one of the too few porta-potties, since everyone was hydrating like mad and challenging their poor bladders (and self-control). Finally the race started, but with so many runners and the funnel effect at the starting line, it took us over 10 minutes to just get there. Soon after, we reached the Verrazano Bridge that connects Staten Island and Brooklyn. The view down to the water was really spectacular, but that didn't quite explain why both sides of this very long bridge were literally lined with hundreds of runners who were stopped there instead of running. Then we realized what they were doing: they were all peeing off a bridge that seemed a mile up in the air, fulfilling an urge that was certainly understandable. Men and women alike, standing or squatting side by side, without batting an eye. So Will and I honored this wonderful tradition and joined them at the rail, after waiting a short time for openings at the world's biggest urinal! That was a hoot.

Brooklyn was next and that too was a hoot. Despite a steady drizzle, a good many neighborhood residents turned out to watch the runners go by. Mothers with babies often held out the child's hand for us to touch as we ran by, for good luck or whatever. The ethnic makeup of the onlookers changed every few blocks because the neighborhoods in Brooklyn are so diverse. There was also a good number of bands. It was all very festive, which was really uplifting for both of us. The light rain, which continued for most of the race, also helped by cooling us down on an unusually warm day for that time of year.

OUT AND ABOUT IN THE GREAT OUTDOORS

Then, after running through a corner of Queens, we crossed into Manhattan over the Queensboro Bridge. It would, of course, start to lightning as soon as we set foot on the old metal span, so Will and I maintained a record pace (for us) in getting across and out of harm's way. Julie and Ginger were waiting for us as we turned north on First Avenue and we still had plenty of energy at that point to stop and give them big (wet) hugs. Shortly after that, we were passed by a true running legend, Grete Waitz of Norway, who won the New York City Marathon nine times between 1978 and 1988. This time, she was pushing a legless racer in a wheelchair, an awesome example for all of us. There were far fewer onlookers in Manhattan and it was harder to find a "bathroom," which usually consisted of nothing more than a bush or fence in Brooklyn.

We followed First Avenue all the way to the Bronx, where we spent only ten minutes before heading south again on Manhattan's Fifth Avenue. That took us through Harlem with its savory scents of cooking food (I remember the fried chicken in particular), which was seriously tempting to two guys who hadn't eaten in seven hours and were starving, but we somehow resisted the urge to throw in the towel and gorge ourselves, even though we were both pretty tired at that point in the race. Fortunately, when the route veered into Central Park, there were many onlookers with trays of snacks for the runners, which was a timely boost. At around Mile 23, we passed Julie and Ginger again but were too exhausted to do anything but wave feebly. I distinctly remember that's about when Will and I started setting goals of running to the next light pole before deciding whether or not to go on.

Those blessed light poles finally got us to the finish line in Central Park, 26.2 miles from the Staten Island start. Our official time was 5 hours and 8 minutes (only 3 hours behind the winner!), but when you subtract the 10 minutes or so it took us to reach the starting line, we finished in under 5 hours (every little minute counts after running that far). I'm also proud to say that we finished in the top 29,000 runners. Being a loving parent, I of course let my son finish a step ahead of me so his name would appear before mine in the newspaper, but please don't tell him that. The girls met us with cold beer and donuts as we'd previously requested, but we were too beat to take more than a sip and bite or two. Will and I were in pretty bad shape. In addition to his stitched-up foot and a huge blister on the other foot (amazing that he ran the whole race with two painful feet), we were drenched by a combination of sweat and rainwater, which chilled us to the bone after we stopped running. I remember feeling like I was in some kind of trance.

Luckily, the girls and I were staying in our friends the Genres' nearby apartment and didn't have far to walk, but poor Will couldn't find a cab and had to ride the subway back to his apartment at Battery Park on the southern tip of Manhattan. When he got on the subway still wearing his marathon number, everyone stood up and offered him their seats, which he recalls was "overwhelming emotionally" and is still an "incredible memory" for him today. Bedtime couldn't come soon enough for me, but the serious leg cramps started the minute I lay down and kept me up most of the night. The next day as

OUT AND ABOUT IN THE GREAT OUTDOORS

previously arranged (talk of poor planning), Julie and I visited a friend on the 5th floor of a walk-up, which was like pouring salt in a wound.

However, despite all the aches and pains, running that marathon with Will was one of the great experiences of my life and has left me with a wonderful memory that I've cherished now for 22 years.

Piccadilly

Piccadilly is the nickname of a small parcel of land we had on the Bogue Falaya River in Covington, Louisiana, an hour's drive over the Lake Pontchartrain Causeway from our home in New Orleans. Julie and I (and our friendly bank) purchased Piccadilly in 1967 when Casey was barely walking and still our only child (Ginger was born in 1969 and Will in 1971). It consisted of eight wooded acres along a private stretch of a shallow, sandy-bottom river that was perfect for young children to play in. In addition, there was a small, concrete-block house with three bedrooms, one bathroom, and, best of all, a large screen porch that looked out on a thick forest of very large pine trees. There was also a second, one-room bunkhouse with a half-bath that we made good use of later (see below). Piccadilly turned out to be a perfect weekend getaway for us and a good place to introduce our kids and others to the Great Outdoors. When Mama entered our lives in 1971, she loved the place as much as we did.

For some strange reason, despite my well-proven shortage of building skills, I decided we needed a real, in-the-ground barbeque pit just off the screen porch and thus spent several weekends of hard labor building one of concrete blocks. Well, like most swimming pools, my masterpiece was rarely used and my great sacrifice of "blood, sweat, and tears" never appreciated. On the other hand, we used the woods and river constantly. The kids, when they were still young, never got tired of playing in the water and sand. Mama was not a water dog but enjoyed playing around the water's edge and digging in the sand. We also spent time exploring the woods all around us. Three of our most popular investments were an ice-cream churn, a hammock, and a ping-pong table for the porch. After finishing a busy day, making s'mores over an open fire and putting the kids to bed, Julie and I would unwind on the porch with glasses of wine and watch the lightning bugs (fireflies) come out. Piccadilly was a paradise. Before the kids became teenagers, we as a family spent at least one or two weekends a month over there.

For five years starting in the summer of 1969 (when Casey was 3½ years old and Ginger was only 6 months old), Piccadilly hosted groups of African American inner-city children between ages 9 and 11 who were enrolled in the Trinity Educational Enrichment Program (TEEP) in New Orleans. (See story herein entitled "TEEP and Mr. TEEP".) They spent most of Saturday and Sunday playing in the river or woods, ate four meals with us, and spent Saturday night on mattresses in the smaller bunkhouse. Those four to six weekends every summer were exceedingly joyful and educational for our entire family as well as the young TEEP campers. Unfortunately, for reasons explained in the separate story, we had to change those overnight Piccadilly visits to a day-long swimming picnic at a public park in Covington and then at a private campground in nearby Folsom, but those TEEP picnics are still going strong today (2024), although Julie and I retired from hosting them in 1999 after 30 years of doing so.

Even without the TEEP campers, Piccadilly was enjoyed for many more years by the two of us and many friends as well as our children and their friends. A few years after our kids all went away to school, we finally sold it to a nice couple (and paid off the mortgage) but retained a lot of happy memories.

Baseball, Etc.

It may be a stretch to include baseball (and some football) games in even a broad definition of the Great Outdoors, but keep in mind that all except one of the many games we attended were played in *outdoor, uncovered* stadiums, so we were communing in a way with the good and bad sides of Mother Nature as we ate our peanuts and drank our beer while sitting worthlessly on our duffs.

OUT AND ABOUT IN THE GREAT OUTDOORS

With that behind us (no pun intended), let us tell you how much Julie and I enjoyed those baseball games all over the country. We watched Major League games in Boston (as proud members of the Red Sox Nation), New York City (as proud members of the I-Hate-the-Yankees Nation), Chicago, Atlanta, Denver, San Francisco, Washington, D. C., and Houston (the only covered stadium). We saw great players who were later voted into the Baseball Hall of Fame (which we visited twice in Cooperstown, New York, a two-hour drive from Williamstown, Massachusetts). New Orleans has a top-level minor league team formerly called the Zephyrs and now the Baby Cakes of all things (taken from the "baby" in our Mardi Gras "king" cakes!).

Julie and I attended several Zephyrs' games and found their hotdogs to be very good, which was an important component of any basement game for my wife. She never touched a hotdog in the real world, but as soon as she entered a baseball stadium, she always made a beeline to the nearest food counter, ordered the biggest hotdog offered, promptly buried it in three or four inches of relish and other condiments, and then consumed the resulting god-awful mess with great pleasure. It mattered not to her whether the particular dogs were good or bad, as long as she got her annual hotdog fix. And besides, by the time she'd finished loading on all the relish and other stuff, the hotdogs were irrelevant anyway.

Our most vivid baseball memory, by far, involved a game in the old Candlestick Park of San Francisco. Since it was the middle of the summer (which means "hot!" to us New Orleanians) and a nice day to boot, we dressed lightly for the early-evening event. Bad mistake! On the bus going directly to the stadium were people with heavy coats, ski parkas, and even sleeping bags. They obviously knew something we didn't, but hey, we were used to extreme temperatures and were pretty hardy in those days. What we soon learned is that Candlestick was located on a peninsula notorious for its brutally cold and windy weather even in summer (which is why it was torn down just a few years later). We spent three hours on the verge of full-body frostbite. We gave up our reserved seats near the field for warmer seats under the distant overhang. And instead of the customary beer, we guzzled hot chocolate. (If only we could have bought blankets....) It happened to be the first big league game of a budding star who had just been brought up from a minor league team in the warm South.

LEECHES, LOVERS, BEARS, AND CHOCOLATE PUDDING

When asked later why he muffed three easy fly balls in centerfield, he answered "Man, I was freezing out there." Amen to that!

Julie's love affair with stadium hotdogs began in 1966 with the advent of the New Orleans Saints pro football team. Along with four other couples, we bought a block of season tickets and sat on the hard wooden bench-style seats of old Tulane Stadium watching the Saints lose game after game. Despite that, those afternoon outings with good friends were really fun. We could drink a lot of beer in those days and that actually helped the Saints, who seemed to score only when Julie was away in the bathroom, so we and other nearby fans encouraged her drinking to support the team (see more on this in another story, "The Perks of Pregnancy"). We finally gave up our seats after six frustrating seasons, but we did see the Saints' Tom Dempsey kick an impossible 63-yard field goal in the final second to win a game and set a record that stood for many years before it was tied and later broken by a measly one yard in the much thinner air of Denver, which therefore shouldn't count.

Three years later, Julie and I were back in Tulane Stadium when the Green Wave football team beat its arch-rival, LSU, for the first time in 24 games, which moved many Tulane alums to tears as the game ended.

I still miss those baseball games with Julie and watching her vain but creative efforts to eat her unmanageable hotdog conglomerations without spilling any.

Callaway Gardens

Callaway Gardens is a very large outdoor resort in the Appalachian foothills of western Georgia. It is well-known for its beautiful woods and lakes, many hiking and biking trails, and good fishing, but its most popular attraction is the Florida State University circus that operates there as a summer camp for kids.

Julie and I took our kids to Callaway Gardens for a week three summers in a row. They loved it and we did too, primarily because they were in the circus camp from 9:00 AM to 3:00 PM every day and we had those six blissful hours all to ourselves without any children within miles, i.e., something for everybody. Casey was old enough to work out on the trapeze bars with the teachers/performers, but I can't recall if Ginger or Will got to try that. In any

OUT AND ABOUT IN THE GREAT OUTDOORS

event, the circus camp was by far the high point of those summer expeditions for all three children. Their camp counselors also performed for the rest of us, as did some amazing waterskiing professionals.

We lodged in our own private cabin in a wooded area with other cabins occupied by similar families with children of the same ages, so ours had a lot of playmates and made some friends. Except for eating and sleeping, we were all outside hiking, swimming, or fishing most of the time when the kids were not in camp. There was also an interesting vegetable patch and a busy butterfly garden to enjoy. And, with a name like Callaway, it won't surprise you to know the resort featured a world-class golf course, but thankfully enough, that was long before Julie and I started playing golf, which we've since learned is a surefire way to ruin a good vacation. While the kids were in camp, the two of us vagabonds sometimes visited a few of the historical sites in the area, the best of which was President Franklin Roosevelt's Little White House in Warm Springs, Georgia, where he died in 1945.

Paragliding

I've paraglided twice and I'd do it again without hesitation if the opportunity ever presented itself. The first time happened in Chamonix, France, during the free day in 2015 before our group started the hike around Mont Blanc (described in the "Hiking" section above). After riding two funiculars up to a point way above the city, I got a quick lesson about paragliding. Although my role was to simply sit in a lawn chair hanging from a large, elongated parachute and enjoy the view, I in my inimitable way managed to crash the whole apparatus on takeoff. With the guide or pilot sitting directly behind me, we were supposed to run as fast as we could down a gentle slope until the air currents caught the parachute and lifted us up in the air (unlike parasailing, which requires one to jump off a high cliff, which is not for me). Sounds simple, right? Well, yours truly ran a little ways and then leapt high into the air, in a spastic imitation of Superman, but alas it was too early and the whole rig with us in it came crashing down to the ground. After the pilot had repaired his outfit and sternly reviewed his instructions with me, we tried it again.

This time, I ran down the slope like crazy until my feet were off the ground and away we went. What a ride that was! Chamonix is surrounded by exquisite mountains and two ancient glaciers that almost reach the town itself, so the scenic beauty all around us was breathtaking. Although we were quite a distance up from the ground, I had no qualms about my safety because it was clear from the start that the pilot knew what he was doing and had absolute control of our airborne taxi's direction and elevation. After circling the town for 30 minutes, he landed us very gently in a soccer field. Armchair sightseeing at its very best!

I paraglided again on that Country Walkers hike in the Alps between Munich and Salzburg (June 2019). My pilot this time was a young woman from California who was living in Germany. I remember that it seemed very windy (the pilot said that was normal) and our rig rocked a good bit, but it was a nice ride and the scenery again was gorgeous. Best of all, I didn't crash the rig this time.

Dogsledding

Julie would have loved everything about dogsledding, including the dogs, the scenery, and the physical challenge, but unfortunately we never tried it before she got sick. My first three dogsledding trips since then, in Finnish Lapland, northern Minnesota, and central Alaska near Denali, are the subject of a separate story (see story entitled "Preparing for the Iditarod (In My Dreams)"). I enjoyed another short dogsledding venture in Wyoming with Road Scholar in February of 2020, just before the pandemic reached us, but this time we were not allowed

OUT AND ABOUT IN THE GREAT OUTDOORS

to drive the sleds ourselves. Hopefully there will be other dogsledding trips in my future.

Hot-Air Ballooning

Julie and I did have a chance to try this once with two of her closest high school friends who were visiting us one summer in Williamstown, Massachusetts. That particular adventure, which started in Vermont and ended in New Hampshire, is described in another story (see story entitled "Just Julie").

Dauphin Island

As people who loved the mountains, Julie and I did not care much for beaches, with one very big exception. Dauphin Island is located in the Gulf of Mexico near Mobile Bay off the southern tip of the Alabama mainland, about a two-hour drive from New Orleans. It's a long, narrow island with miles of sandy beaches facing out into the Gulf. Best of all, it is a non-resort, which is exactly why we loved it so. Its two restaurants and one grocery store are well past their prime. There are lots of midsized cottages there, but no nightlife and very little in the way of other attractions besides a primitive golf course, a walking park in the woods, and an old Confederate fort. Unlike the gaudy beaches all along Florida's nearby panhandle, Dauphin Island is the perfect escape for people interested in communing quietly with nature or a good book.

We rented beachfront cottages there numerous times

over many years, with the kids when they were younger and then by ourselves after they had all left for school. Mama of course went every time during her long 15 years with us and she loved it as much as the rest of us, especially since she would get her own ice cream treat on the drives over and back. With the kids, we spent lots of time in the water or on the beach and occasionally went fishing with them. When Ginger was about 10 and Will about 8, her favorite activity was lying lazily on a raft as her little brother pushed it from behind, like Cleopatra commanding one of her slaves. If we were by ourselves, Julie and I sometimes played golf at the local course or took a ferry across Mobile Bay and played one of the better courses on that side. Usually, however, we just relaxed by walking up and down the beach, jogging along the one road, or just reading on the cottage deck in the fresh air.

Ziplining

The only time I tried ziplining was just outside of Denver in the late winter of 2017 when there was not enough snow to ski, so Ginger and her family took me on another kind of adventure. There were about 15 towers with cables strung between them. We rode in individual chairs attached to the cables and wore heavy padded gloves to lightly grip the cable to slow us down as we approached the downhill tower. Despite doing that, I usually came in too fast and had to be grabbed by the attendant at each tower. The distance between the last two towers was the longest of all and, instead of the usual one, there were two cables side by side that could be used for racing. Aubrey, our 14-year-old grandson, challenged me to a duel and I agreed against my better judgment (for what that's worth). Well, even though the little rascal was a veteran zipliner, he still jumped the gun at the start, which he vehemently denies to this day. He therefore started five feet ahead of me and that was his winning margin. Although my official protest was summarily rejected without a proper hearing, I felt good about just keeping up with him after the disputed start. The next race will be different.

OUT AND ABOUT IN THE GREAT OUTDOORS

Rock-Climbing

Our granddaughter Emma was about eight years old when she started practicing on rock-climbing walls and got to be pretty good at it, from what I could tell. On the other hand, there's not much of a future in it when one starts at age 67, as I did. Rock-climbing was not on my bucket list, so let me tell you how it came about. A contemporary and friend of ours in Williamstown won a rock-climbing outing for two at auction. As he looked around for someone to go with him, he discovered there were not many other guys our age who were both interested and fit enough to try this out, which is why I got invited to join him.

Our little group consisted of two middle-aged women in addition to David and me, plus the instructor who was a former Navy SEAL close to my age. The destination was a popular rock wall somewhere in Massachusetts. We attempted to ascend the wall one by one after being attached to the belay rope that was manned by the instructor at the top of the wall. The younger woman went first and made it to the top following a really athletic leap sideways to grab a key handhold. I went second and did not reach the top, but came pretty close. It was harder than I expected. Going straight up was not so bad, but I had trouble when I had to reach far to the side for a handhold or foothold, especially when that required me to literally jump sideways as the first climber did. I stopped when I was unable to advance further up the wall and then rappelled down using the belay rope. My friend went next and did reach the top, but the second woman failed after a truly valiant effort that moved everyone there. I now have a greater appreciation of those kids and others working so hard to climb those practice walls.

And Lastly, Golf

I'm a little embarrassed to admit that I even play this truly fiendish game (or try to). The *only* positive things about golf are (1) being outside with good friends (unless it rains and you're not Irish); (2) the lucky few golf balls, obviously handpicked for salvation by some higher power, that don't wind up in the water soon after I remove them from the box; and (3) the proverbial 19th hole. Julie

LEECHES, LOVERS, BEARS, AND CHOCOLATE PUDDING

and I must have been plum crazy to take up this stupid game when we were both in our 50s and supposedly wise enough to know better.

But there were some memorable moments, along with many more unforgettable moments. I have very fond memories of Julie and I playing the Eastover Golf Course on Sunday afternoons in the fall when all the other local golfers were watching the Saints' game, so we usually had the whole course all to ourselves and then topped that off with a nice dinner out, often at the lakeside Ground Pati with its unshelled peanuts. And I had a hole-in-one on the par-3 fourth hole of Audubon Golf Course in the summer of 2020 during the pandemic. I did not see my shot after I hit it, but according to my playing partner, it landed a foot past the hole and spun backwards into the cup. Just like the pros do it, right? Don't forget "luck" and "random chance." One quasi-perfect shot in 30 years of playing this stupid game is not much to brag about, but I'll take it. And besides his incomprehensible love of the New York Yankees, it's something else I take great pleasure in crowing over with my son Will, who's a much better golfer than I am but does not have a hole-in-one. However, acting purely out of magnanimous love for my child, I have offered many times to show him how to get a hole-in-one but he has always huffily refused my generosity for reasons I just can't understand.

And then there was The Crow. I used to admire crows for their intelligence until it wiped out (literally) my one chance at a little glory. It was two years ago, 2019, on the nearby Audubon Golf Course. I was obviously possessed by the ghost of Bobby Jones because I finished the front nine holes in 32 strokes, one over par, compared to my usual 40 to 44 at that time. Everything I hit went in the hole (except for a simple two-foot putt that would have given me a par 31). "Luck" and "random chance" were working overtime. While walking back to our cart with my golfing partner after parring the difficult par-5 ninth hole and thinking this was a small miracle, I spotted The Crow standing on the top of the cart's steering wheel looking for food, which is not unusual. He flew off as we approached. I slid into the driver's seat, grabbed the pencil to record our scores, and then looked at the score sheet—and went into immediate shock. It was literally covered, entirely, in runny crow poop. My soon-to-be-famous score card that I was going to frame and hang on the wall. The Crow had picked that particular time and place to have a record bout of diarrhea. "Random

OUT AND ABOUT IN THE GREAT OUTDOORS

chance"? No, I don't think so—not even "random chance" could have arranged such a precise juxtaposition of so many circumstances. But surely, you ask, the poor little crow didn't intend any harm, right? Absolutely wrong! How do I possibly know that? Because the *top* of the steering wheel, where he stood to do his business, is tilted away from the driver, so if he had been standing on the top of the steering wheel facing towards the driver's seat (as he would have done if looking for food), his poop would have easily missed the scorecard in the middle of the steering wheel. The fact that he scored a bullseye on the scorecard means that he was facing *forward* when he let loose, so it's plain as day he was *aiming* for the scorecard. Anyway, I grabbed my golf towel and frantically wiped off the poop, but with the poop came the pencil scores for the first eight holes. The score card was not only putrid but also empty. My historic round no longer existed. I immediately started planning ways to extinguish the entire crow population on Earth, which explains why I finished the back nine holes at *22* over par. All I can do now is to remember: for one shining moment, I played like a pro—until The Crow from Hell intervened.

* * * * * *

As the preceding memories demonstrate, our family has made good use of Mother Nature's largesse. Although she can of course be very fickle and downright heartless, she has also bestowed on all of us a natural world of wonder that is a matchless gift. The Great Outdoors is truly amazing in every respect. It's there for everybody to admire, understand, and enjoy, but in doing so, we need to respect and preserve it. We now know that it's not indestructible and that we humans have the power to destroy it. The possibility of losing all or part of that irreplaceable gift is a terrifying prospect for anyone who thinks about it and especially for those of us who have spent so much quality time in the Great Outdoors.

TEEP AND MR. TEEP

The Trinity Educational Enrichment Program, usually shortened to TEEP, is a six-week summer program in New Orleans for about 100 inner-city children ages 9 through 11 that offers them courses in math, science, language arts, music, and art, plus guest speakers and a variety of field trips, to enhance their traditional education. It is supported financially by Trinity Episcopal Church and numerous private donors. The long-serving Director of TEEP is Alvin Edinburgh, affectionately known as "Mr. Alvin" by his many students and "Mr. TEEP" by his countless friends and fans all over the City.

TEEP has been a remarkable success since it was started 54 years ago in 1966. The idea originated with a local lawyer and church parishioner, Tom Jordan, who donated and raised money to create a memorial for his recently deceased daughter, and Reverend Tom Shaw, who was the Headmaster of Trinity Episcopal School that was associated with the church. Since the beginning, TEEP has served close to 5,000 students. Many of them went on to successful careers and several even returned to TEEP as teenage aides or actual teachers years after "graduating" from the Program.

Julie and I volunteered as drivers and chaperones on field trips during TEEP's first three years. Sometime in early 1969, while having dinner at the Hong Kong Restaurant on the lakefront and enjoying a nice bottle of wine, we started talking about getting more involved in TEEP. That led to the idea of inviting the TEEP campers in small groups over to our little house (named "Piccadilly") in Covington for the weekend. It was only an hour's drive from New Orleans. Although the main house was quite small and basic, it did have a big screen porch, was situated on eight acres of woodland fronting on the Bogue Falaya River (a shallow stream with sandy beaches that was perfect for the TEEP campers), and best of all, had a separate bunkhouse-style building with no furniture but its own bathroom and just big enough for 10–15 mattresses on the floor.

The first of the Covington field trips happened that summer of 1969. As I recall, there was a total of 60 campers that year, so we had 10 different

LEECHES, LOVERS, BEARS, AND CHOCOLATE PUDDING

TEEP'ers per weekend for the six weeks of the program. They were driven over by aides or other chaperones on Saturday morning and then back home on Sunday afternoon. Julie and I brought our three-year old daughter Casey and her six-month old sister Ginger. We stayed very busy the whole time, but the weekends were incredibly successful and fun for everyone, including our children, who got lots of attention.

We spent most of the time in the river with inner tubes we'd bought for all the campers. Many of them had never seen a river before, other than the Mississippi, and thought it was a strange kind of swimming pool. They also had trouble understanding the idea of a current and why their tubes floated away when they left them in the water. Julie became an expert at building sandcastles with them or burying them in the sand. I tried to teach them swimming or dragged chains of occupied tubes up and down the river. They also used little plastic boats to slide down the slippery riverbanks into the water, which was thrilling for them. When not in the river, we took them hiking through the woods or sometimes played Capture the Flag. After supper, which usually consisted of hot dogs or hamburgers, we would build a small fire in the driveway, toast marshmallows, and make s'mores. That was very popular, not surprisingly. All of the campers seemed to enjoy playing with our young children, but one in particular, a large, athletic youngster named David W., stood out because of how gentle and intuitive he was with them. We had a one-day reunion in Covington with 10 selected campers at the end of the summer and handed out signed Saints footballs to them, which were happily received.

TEEP AND MR. TEEP

That first summer was also our introduction to the amazing Randall family. The parents, a postal worker and a devoted mother, raised 10 incredible children. All but Tony, the oldest, were TEEP campers (he was already too old when TEEP started). The next oldest, Gerriette, was a camper that summer and a talented Capture the Flag player. After that came Cedric, Eric, and twins named Romaine and Ramona, the four we remembered best, and their younger siblings. Eric came back as a teenage aide and for many summers after that as a volunteer. His sister Romaine is now the Assistant Director of TEEP and a full-time teacher at Newman High School.

Those TEEP weekends (and picnics later) served as a good lesson in race relations for our own kids (Will was born in February of 1971) because almost all of the TEEP campers, aides, and staff were African American. As a result primarily of that experience, all three of them grew up to be completely color-blind. As a good example of that, when Will was about 8 or 9, he invited a classmate of his to spend the night in our New Orleans house after telling Julie and me everything possible to know about his friend, but he never once mentioned that he was African American because that was irrelevant to Will. We were very proud parents. After our kids moved away from New Orleans, they sometimes came back with husbands or girlfriends to enjoy another picnic with the TEEP'ers.

But there was a terrible downside. Back in the 1960s and 1970s, St. Tammany Parish (where the TEEP weekends and picnics were and still are held) was reputed to be a Ku Klux Klan (KKK) hotbed. After our first two summers of our TEEP guests, it was obvious that local people were talking about the "black" children in "their" river. Julie and I started getting questions from neighbors we knew and strange looks from others in stores there. But it was two mysterious brush fires on the property that really got our attention. At that point, considering the potential danger to the TEEP'ers and our own kids, we decided in 1974 to end the overnights at Piccadilly but still offer the TEEP campers an opportunity to experience wild rivers and woods. The final decision was to change the outings to a full-day picnic and move them to the Bogue Falaya State Park in Covington proper, where there were many wide beaches and a wider river that was still shallow enough for the campers to enjoy safely.

LEECHES, LOVERS, BEARS, AND CHOCOLATE PUDDING

And it was there that Alvin entered the picture—and our lives. He had been hired by the then-Director, Laverne Thornburg, as a creative drama teacher. When she retired in 1976, the TEEP Board followed her recommendation and selected Alvin to be the next director. It was the perfect choice for all the TEEP campers, the TEEP staff, Trinity Episcopal Church, the Irish Channel community, the City in general, and anyone having any connection with TEEP, including the entire Penick family.

What Alvin brought to TEEP as director was 39 years as a public school teacher in New Orleans, personal insight into the challenges facing 9- to 11-year-old inner-city children, a total commitment to the idea of TEEP, an awesome work ethic, a sincere and selfless humility, a great sense of humor, and a very, very big heart. Not surprisingly, he loves his job and has given it 100% of all he has to offer. As observers of Alvin's work over so many years, Julie, who was a teacher herself, and I marveled over the fact that Alvin treated each of his individual campers with both love and respect, which endeared him to all of them, many of whom remained in touch with Alvin for decades after graduating from TEEP. He instilled in his students the five core values of TEEP: Respect, Responsibility, Reciprocity, Restraint, and Redemption. In addition to enriching the lives of his young campers, Alvin promoted TEEP widely, assembled great staff, provided a wonderful example to his many teenage aides, and generally expanded connections between the black and white communities of New Orleans. Under Alvin's leadership, TEEP has become a program that is admired and emulated throughout the country.

The weekend outings for TEEP campers were continued after Alvin took over the Program. When the Bogue Falaya State Park was closed because of upstream runoff problems, we found the Land-O-Pines Family Campground in Covington, which turned out to be a wonderful discovery and the site of our picnics for the last 40 or so years. It's a commercial campground, but the back of the property includes a long frontage on another branch of the Bogue Falaya River and many large beaches just perfect for the TEEP youngsters as swimming and picnic areas. The management, now headed by Leanne Everhardt and by her parents before that, has been incredibly supportive of TEEP since the very beginning. The TEEP campers of course love the clear water and sandy beaches, as they have reported enthusiastically ever since we started picnicking there.

TEEP AND MR. TEEP

From the start, Alvin threw himself into these weekend outings with the same energy and devotion he brings to TEEP in general. He never missed one of the scheduled picnics and often brought his young granddaughter Kelly. He also encouraged parents of the TEEP campers to join us and many of them did, to everyone's delight. By the time we started having the picnics at Land-O-Pines, TEEP had grown in size to about 100 campers per summer, so we had some 25 of them every weekend, plus the aides, teachers, volunteers, and some parents. Eric Randall was a regular. Needless to say, the picnics were always nonstop but also loads of fun, not only for the campers but the adults too.

When they arrived on Saturday morning in a bus and various cars, we headed straight for the river. Since the spring-fed water was much colder than the campers were used to, it was always a challenge to get them into the river for the first time, but once they got in, it was even harder to get them out. When we found a nice, unoccupied beach with a good log or two to sit on (more on this later), we staked our claim. While walking up and down the river, we often passed white bathers sitting on the beach but, surprisingly enough, we never noticed any adverse reactions to our mixed group.

As usual, Julie did a steady business of burying campers in the sand (always with a flower poking up) and teaching them how to build sandcastles. Alvin and I, along with the aides, spent most of our time in the water with the campers, teaching them to swim, playing tag and other water games with them, and pulling chains of them on inner tubes up and down the river—at least at the beginning. As Alvin and I got older, we spent more and more time sitting together on one of those nice logs watching the campers entertain themselves and solving all the problems of the world, which of course earned us the dubious

LEECHES, LOVERS, BEARS, AND CHOCOLATE PUDDING

nickname of "bumps on the log" from the likes of Julie and Eric. Eventually Julie became another "bump on the log" when she started joining us. Larry Nevil, the art teacher for many years who later became a well-known painter and teacher in France and Japan, loved the picnics because he (and I sometimes) would find large pockets of clay in the riverbank that he would take home in plastic bags of 50 pounds or more to use in his classes.

Will's favorite water sport when still little was to play "king of the hill" on a large tree trunk that had conveniently fallen across one of the deeper holes in the river. His perennial opponent—and victim—was Cedric Randall, a former camper and then a long-time aide. Despite being at least four times Will's size, Cedric always lost these epic battles with our own little "David" in the most dramatic fashion, howling in agony as he fell mortally wounded into the water. Will, of course, loved it—and so did we.

We broke for lunch in the middle of the day at the original get-in site near where the cars were parked. "Cooking" for some 40 people was always challenging. The "entrée" was hotdogs on an open grill most of the time, accompanied by Kool-Aid and a good assortment of cookies donated by TEEP's many friends. By that time, of course, I had become a pro at turning out perfectly grilled hotdogs on demand every time. Since Alvin was anxious to learn my grilling secrets and was so good at everything else he did, I agreed to teach him. He was an eager student and quick learner who ultimately produced a very tasty hotdog, but as good as it was, it never quite achieved the perfection of my own, which has been the subject of an ongoing debate between us for years now. Thanks again to Cedric Randall, I hold the record for cooking the most hotdogs (11, no less) consumed by one person (and he survived), which occurred before Alvin joined TEEP. No one came close to that timeless record after Alvin took over the cooking duties, except maybe our dog Mama, who ate whatever was dropped "accidentally" by the campers, but Mama was never very picky about her hotdogs (or ice cream).

After lunch, everyone went back into the water for another two or three hours. Actually, the campers couldn't get enough of the water once they realized how much fun it was. There was always a lot of moaning when it was time to leave. The adults, on the other hand, were usually exhausted, but it was a good kind of exhaustion that came with a wonderful feeling of brotherhood and time well spent.

Alvin's leadership of TEEP over more than four decades is now legendary among his graduated students, his fellow teachers, and the hundreds of others who actively support the Program. In recognition of what he has contributed to the lives of so many youngsters in New Orleans and to the city itself, I secretly nominated Alvin to be an official Torchbearer of the Olympic Torch Relay for the 2002 Winter Olympics in Salt Lake City, Utah. Not surprisingly, he was not only selected but also featured with an interview and picture in the Olympic newsletter. And he carried the Torch through most of our French Quarter to cheering crowds that included Julie and me. It was a well-deserved honor for a truly remarkable man and educator.

1999 was our last year of hosting the TEEP outings to Covington after 30 wonderful years of doing so. That's when Julie and I started spending our summers in Williamstown, Massachusetts. However, I'm very glad to report that the picnics have continued to happen up to the present time of 2024, with two years off because of the Covid pandemic, and that Alvin at the ripe old age of 90 is still leading TEEP with the same professionalism and gusto he has for almost 50 years. And he continues to be a very close friend of our whole family, including our children. Julie and I met him for dinner on a regular basis, spent time with him in Williamstown and Breckenridge, Colorado, and even ran a few road races with him before Julie's Alzheimer's. After that, Alvin and I visited Italy five years ago and have continued to dine together about every six weeks up to the present. Reprising our earlier roles as "bumps on the log," we keep solving the world's problems over and over again in hopes that someone somewhere will finally listen to us.

STRANGE BEASTLY ENCOUNTERS

The title may be a bit exaggerated, but there were some near-misses. Julie and I and the children have never had a life-threatening encounter with a wild animal (except maybe for that Canadian bear who was definitely in more danger than Julie), even though we have (a) hiked and camped in wild places with bears, cougars, moose, and wolves; (b) canoed, hunted, fished, and pirogued in rivers and swamps with alligators and water moccasins; and (c) bathed with wild elephants in crocodile-infested rivers. We did take precautions, like black pepper spray in bear country, a very loud bike horn to scare off any cougars, and checking for snakes and scorpions in sleeping bags, but our good fortune was probably due more to luck (and Julie's well-deserved reputation as a bear-chaser) than anything else. Whatever, none of us ever suffered any kind of animal-inflicted injury, except for one very angry little lizard that clamped down on Julie's finger and wouldn't let go for anything.

But we did have the luck or misfortune, take your pick, to have any number of really bizarre encounters with members of the animal and insect worlds. Some of these critters have been featured in other stories, including the following:

1. evil sheep (see "So You Think Sheep are Harmless? Think Again");
2. bears, moose, and leeches (see "Leeches, Lovers, Bears, and Chocolate Pudding");
3. oversexed marmots (see "Don Juan the Marmot");
4. man-eating dogs (see "'The Best of All Possible Honeymoons'? Not Quite!");
5. talking hummingbirds (see "Hummingbirds and the Great Beyond");
6. caring sea lions (see "The Compassionate Sea Lion");
7. career-wrecking pets (see "The Dinner from Hell and Bill's Short Career");
8. wonderful huskies (see "Preparing for the Iditarod (in My Dreams)"); and last but not least, the most terrifying of all wild beasts,

LEECHES, LOVERS, BEARS, AND CHOCOLATE PUDDING

9. our three kids (see "On the Road with Three Little Backseat Angels/Beasts of Bedlam," "The Parents-Are-Out-Of-Town Party," and "Our Off-the-Wall Offsprint").

The Master-Builder Mouse

As we all know by now, our standard-model mouse comes in all levels of intelligence, just like its human cousins. Unfortunately, Julie and I unwittingly played host for nearly a year to a genius-level mouse who almost burned down our house on Bellaire Drive. In a former life, our brilliant little boarder probably designed the Pyramids.

It all happened right under our noses in the busiest part of the house, our kitchen. The first thing we noticed was a small puddle of water coming from under the refrigerator. After checking for leaks inside the fridge and finding none, we forgot about it—until another puddle appeared a couple of months later. This time we called a repairman, who checked the back of the refrigerator and found a tiny hole in the plastic water line to the icemaker. It was just big enough to release a few drops of water a day without affecting the icemaker. Stuff like that happens, so we replaced the water line and assumed the problem was fixed.

Until another puddle developed a few months later. This time the repairman suspected foul play after finding a similar hole in the new water line. But, other than the mysterious hole, there was nothing amiss in the general area that might provide a clue. Finally, in frustration, the repairman lifted the top of our gas stove that was separated from the fridge by an 18-inch-wide countertop.

And there it was! In the small open space under the stovetop was an elegant nest made out of paper napkins that our furry friend had chewed into little fluffs and placed carefully around the opening. His furniture and bedding came from a basket of paper napkins on the counter near the stove. Since he never left any paper shreds or other evidence of his activities in the area, he must have dragged one whole napkin at a time through the opening in the back of the stove and then shredded it under cover of the stovetop. Although that open gap was literally stuffed with fluffs of paper, the culprit was savvy enough not to place them too close to the gas pilot lights or burners. And his droppings were neatly confined to one far corner of his homestead. He used the same uncanny precision in making holes in the two water lines that were just big enough to provide water on demand without setting off any alarms. The little devil was either very smart or very thoughtful or both. In any event, he left us nary a clue of his very busy life in our kitchen until we stumbled across his well-hidden nest.

Our diminutive Frank Lloyd Wright had created a palatial estate fit for the highest order of rodent royalty. There was a ready supply of clean water nearby for drinking or bathing. There was a fully furnished home with featherbeds and plenty of privacy. There was fire to provide heat and light for general body comfort, heating up leftovers, and reading his miniature blueprints. And there were usually enough crumbs and other tasty items around the kitchen to keep him fat and happy. No telling what our guest would have done next in the way of home-improvement if we had not interrupted his idyllic existence so rudely.

It was a little sad to do so after seeing how much he'd accomplished, but the risk of a fire was too high to leave him be. He had somehow managed to cram enough paper in that little space under the stovetop to start a major fire if accidentally ignited by the gas flames. We therefore had no choice but to remove all the paper (and the napkin basket), seal the back of the stove, and replace the plastic water tube with a metal line. We never did catch the critter and assume that he set up house elsewhere in our humble abode and lived happily ever after.

The Nearsighted Owl

Fortunately, I've been mistaken for a tasty forest treat only once in my life, but that one time was definitely a vivid experience. It's also a little embarrassing to think I looked like a rabbit, mole, or opossum (did I have a beard then? perhaps I needed a haircut). The only logical explanation is that my assailant, a very large owl, must have been very nearsighted.

There I was, still half-asleep that early morning, washing a dish at the kitchen sink in front of a large picture window in our Williamstown, Massachusetts house, which is located next to some thick woods. When the owl took off from its perch in a tree, I noticed because of its movement and size. As it flew directly towards the house and got larger and larger, it was an incredible sight to behold. Thinking that the owl would do what many other birds did and accelerate over the house at the last minute, I just stood there enjoying the show, even though this gigantic carnivore was coming right at me. But instead of elevating over the house, it hit the picture window head-on at full speed directly in front of my head, only two feet away. Just before impact, I dropped the plate, which broke, and jumped back from the sink because I wasn't sure the glass would hold, but fortunately it did. The owl crumpled and fell but somehow managed to right itself and fly off, albeit a little wobbly, leaving a good amount of its blood and brain matter on the window.

If not for that wonderful window, I could have enjoyed 15 minutes of fame as the first full-grown human to be eaten by an owl. It was definitely a close encounter of a strange kind: the margin of safety was a mere two feet and a thin piece of glass. I can't imagine myself as a culinary delicacy even for a carnivore, so I have to assume my would-be devourer was drawn to me by intense hunger and awful eyesight. I do wish the owl well despite the attack, but I did become a little wary about walking outside in the early morning after that.

A Bathroom for Wimpy Bighorns

Bighorn sheep are those majestic animals with the large curved horns that live on mountaintops all over western North America. Since they can endure the harshest winter weather at high elevations, you would expect them to be incredibly tough and hardy. Well, I can assure you they don't like bad weather any more than we do.

Mount Evans, halfway between Denver and Breckenridge, is one of Colorado's 54 so-called "fourteeners" because it rises over 14,000 feet. Besides Pike's Peak, it's the only fourteener with a road all the way to the top. After climbing a few of the other fourteeners, Julie and I decided to tackle Mount Evans next. The plan was to park at a public bathroom for hikers at about 11,000 feet elevation and then hike up the side of the mountain to the summit some 3,000 feet above us.

And so, we woke up early one morning, drove the hour or so from Breckenridge to Mount Evans, and arrived at our destination around 8:00 AM, which would give us four hours or so to make the ascent, eat our packed lunch, and be well off the summit before the usual afternoon thunderstorms rolled in. But the best-laid plans sometimes go awry. By the time we reached our starting point, that public bathroom, the weather had turned decidedly foul. It was in fact the very rawest day I have ever experienced, even worse than skiing in 4 degrees F or dogsledding in Lapland during a winter snowstorm. There was no rain or snow, but given the ominous darkness, a temperature near freezing, and a savage wind that made it feel 30 degrees colder, it was brutal, even a bit apocalyptic. For something so extreme to happen in the middle of summer, some kind of freak barometric singularity must have occurred.

While I waited snugly in the car, Julie walked quickly over to the concrete outhouse to relieve herself but just as quickly returned, with a dazed and goofy smile on her face. When she told me the bathroom was full of bighorn sheep, I guessed she meant mountain goats and went over to see for myself. Sure enough, both bathrooms, with their doorless entrances, were filled with bighorn sheep, which are much bigger and stronger than mountain goats There were probably 20 or so of them, sheltering from the weather outside and looking a little embarrassed to be there. I would assume they, like other animals and fish can do, detected the severe drop in barometric pressure and wisely sought any cover they could find.

We should have followed their good example and headed home, but since we were already there, Julie and I decided to see how far up the mountain we could get. However, given such a strong wind and the absence of any trail, we couldn't risk bushwhacking our way over large boulders and loose rocks as planned, so we tried hiking up the road. Even that was impossible. The wind was so strong and cold on our faces that we had to walk backwards into it. After 15 minutes of very hard going that gained us a mere 100 feet or so, we threw in the towel.

We did return the following summer and this time, aided by much kinder weather, did manage to scramble our way to the summit from that fateful bathroom. It happened that we emerged somewhat bedraggled from the rocks right under a viewing overhang and startled a number of tourists gazing at the sights. Nice as it was to add another notch to our "belt" of conquered fourteeners, our most vivid memory of Mount Evans will always be those bighorn sheep huddled together inside the bathroom on that dreadful day. Since they are very shy about humans and agile enough to keep far away from them, it was a rare opportunity indeed for us to encounter these beautiful animals so up close.

Night Of The Bees

What's not to like about honeybees? They're loyal, brave, smart, and industrious; they pollinate crops and flowers; they create beauty, music, and honey; they're incredible architects; and they usually mind their own business. But—they are really terrible houseguests, especially in very large numbers. Because of our own shameful record, Julie and I know all about terrible houseguests (see story entitled "Barbarians Inside the Gate").

It's certainly true that timing is everything. Had the invasion occurred at any other time, it would have been a minor irritation at worst and may have had a happier ending, but it happened two days before our daughter Ginger's large, formal wedding, i.e., during the height of the customary prenuptial meltdown. Full of bridesmaids from out of town, our house was literally humming with activity, in more ways than we ever could have imagined.

Starting a few days before that, we had noticed a faint hum in the powder room off our den, which was command-central for the wedding. With all the last-minute things to do, we had ignored the hum, until a few bee bodies appeared in the ceiling light fixture. The situation became a bit more ominous when several live bees joined the wedding party and the humming got much louder. By Thursday night before the Saturday wedding, we knew we had a serious problem that wouldn't wait.

We had no idea what to do, so we were overjoyed to find three "beekeepers" listed in the yellow pages. Our joy turned to panic when the first two told me they were booked up for the next three weeks. Luckily, the third, no doubt in response to the hysteria in my voice, promised to come right out, even though it was 10:00 at night. When I met him at the front door, he was dressed from head to toe in full battle gear, which brought home to me with a shock just how bad a problem we had.

After listening to the powder room ceiling with a stethoscope, our knight in shining armor simply whistled at the size of the hive in the space between our two floors. He then found and plugged the entrance hole outside, which looked no bigger than a quarter inch in diameter, but still big enough for thousands of bees to pass in and out of. How they found such a tiny opening says volumes about their scouting and communication skills. Unfortunately, the only way to resolve the problem quickly was to poison the bees through a small hole he cut in the ceiling. The resulting howl of the trapped bees was terrible to hear. The beekeeper returned the next day, cut a sizeable piece out of the ceiling, and extracted a beautiful foot-long honeycomb and enough bee bodies to fill one quarter of a tall kitchen trash bag. Sad as it was to destroy so many bees and their magnificent hive, Ginger's wedding trumped everything at that moment.

Things improved dramatically after that little crisis. The wedding was beautiful and the reception was enjoyed by the hundreds of guests. It was a perfect evening, although the allegedly "private" post-reception party attended by many dozens added considerably to my hangover and tab, which included the large bowl of $3 per-head shrimp ordered by our other daughter, Casey.

Ginger and John just celebrated their 18th anniversary while we just finished paying off the wedding/reception bill. And, to their everlasting glory, the bee gods obviously acquitted us of mass murder on grounds of self-defense (or perhaps temporary insanity) and blessed the marriage and wonderful family that ensued (except for a couple of distinctly unblessed dogs). Ever since that fateful Night of the Bees, Julie and I have bestowed tender, loving care on each and every bee we've found in our house, car, tent, or bonnet, out of gratitude for the bee gods' mercy (and fear of their wrath in the event of a second offense). As a gesture of atonement, I've designed a contraption to safely and humanely remove bees (and other critters) from unwanted places and promised to donate all the unlikely profits to IBRA, which is the International Bee Research Association for those of you who may not be familiar with it.

Bingeing On Berries

Ever heard of a "drunk tank" for birds? Well, they actually exist in some places because birds, like humans, sometimes get very drunk from eating fermented berries, like those beautiful red holly berries that adorn so many homes at Christmas. Regretfully, Julie and I didn't know this when we planted a holly tree in our backyard in New Orleans. It was the right size, it was attractive, and it didn't require much upkeep. And it seemed so perfectly harmless until we found out otherwise.

After gracing our yard for several years, the tree suddenly changed into a lethal trap for foolish fowl. It happened one peaceful afternoon while Julie and I were home alone and reading in our den that looks out on the backyard. The first unusual thing we noticed was an increased level of bird chatter outside. The holly tree was almost completely covered by busy birds. As we watched, the yard itself started filling up with excited birds flying in from all directions. It was quite fascinating at first, but then it became more and more eerie, like those scenes in the old Hitchcock movie *The Birds*.

When the first bird crashed loudly into one of the den windows, we realized we had a problem. Other birds then followed the first into the long row of windows facing the backyard. We had no idea what to do. It would have been suicidal to go outside with hundreds of crazy birds flying every which way, so we were literally prisoners inside our own house. The only thing we could do was to open all the roll-out windows in the line of fire, but that would have exposed the flimsy screens to the feathered missiles. Luckily, the sun was going down and the birds started leaving. They were all gone by the time it was dark. When we finally felt safe enough to go outside, there were well over a dozen dead or dying birds on the ground under the windows. Not knowing what else to do, we grabbed all the duct tape we could find and put it all over the targeted windows, just like we New Orleanians do in preparing for a hurricane. We also draped long strips of tape down from the gutter above the windows in hopes of diverting the birds away from them.

The next day started with an early phone call from our neighbors across the yard who thought maybe we had joined some kind of duct-tape cult. Then the birds returned and their kamikaze attacks on our poor windows resumed. All the tape seemed to make little difference. Julie and I spent another stressful day trapped in our house by a large airborne army of little leering lunatics. But it was all over by 3:00. The birds disappeared as suddenly as they had arrived. We cautiously went outside to take stock and found 18 dead or dying birds this time. And the holly tree, which had been loaded with ripe, red berries just two days before, had been stripped clean of every single berry.

STRANGE BEASTLY ENCOUNTERS

It took a little research to clear up the mystery. Those beautiful little berries, while toxic to us, are irresistible to certain kinds of birds, like robins and jays, if they become fermented. That's what attracted all those birds. And that's why they were flying so blindly out of control—they were drunk on fermented berry juice. It was an avian orgy. A two-day bacchanal of birds in our backyard that made "Animal House" look like a tea party.

But we survived and the tree did too. We briefly considered cutting it down to save the neighborhood birds and our den windows, but decided instead to put it on probation in hopes that this was a one-time offense. And that it was. Our leniency was rewarded and we never had another orgy like that one.

The Killer Kitten

Of all the dangerous creatures I've been exposed to in their natural habitats, including moose, grizzlies, black bear, elk, lynx, foxes, wolves, coyotes, bighorn sheep, mountain goats, ibexes, rhinoceroses, elephants, sharks, barracuda, sea lions, eagles, moccasins, alligators, and tarantula, none of them ever tried to attack or hurt me except for that nearsighted owl. Julie, my fearless, bear-chasing bodyguard, deserves much of the credit for her role in keeping most of those critters away from us (she was absent when the owl attacked). However, the most vicious animal I ever encountered was not a wild beast but a half-grown domestic cat that even Julie could not intimidate. Smudge was a born killer.

You ask how I can possibly judge a cute little kitten so harshly? Well, I speak from very personal knowledge. I was the intended victim. Not just once, not just twice, but three different times. And, oh so sneaky. Smudge intended to smother me while I slept and make it look like I died in my sleep from natural causes, i.e., he left no telltale marks on me. How did he do this? By stealthily draping his furry body over my nose and mouth so that I couldn't breathe. He didn't lie down next to my head or on my chest as a sign of affection, but always over my breathing portals. Three times I woke up in the middle of the night gasping for breath and found this blasted thing across my face. When I pushed him away, he didn't go willingly. And he never did anything to endanger Julie. But we did find him one day in our infant daughter's bassinet and that's when

LEECHES, LOVERS, BEARS, AND CHOCOLATE PUDDING

we banished him from the house. I was relieved, thinking his Reign of Terror had come to an end. Little did I know.

We then lived in a small house on Audubon Street. Like all "shotgun" houses in New Orleans, it was squeezed in between two other houses, with maybe five feet of clearance on either side. Our backyards were separated by low chain-link fences. One set of neighbors, a physician and a professor, had a noisy bulldog named Stonewall whose barking discouraged our oldest daughter from playing in the backyard. Other than that, we enjoyed a wonderful relationship with those neighbors.

One night Julie and I were awakened by loud noises coming from inside our neighbors' house just a few feet from our heads. We assumed it was another typical late-night party and thought nothing of it. At least until the next morning, when one of the neighbors called to ask how Smudge was. We looked outside and saw Smudge licking his paws like nothing unusual happened. The neighbor then told us what actually did happen the night before.

The racket we heard was the result of dog chasing cat through their house, just like the old cartoons. Apparently when they opened their back door to let Stonewall out for a bathroom break, Smudge slipped in and Stonewall gave chase. In the ensuing mayhem, vases, pictures, plates, and tables were knocked over. To his regret, Stonewall finally cornered Smudge and moved in for the kill before the neighbors could stop him. It was short but not sweet. Despite the great difference in their sizes, Smudge ripped Stonewall's two ears almost off and his snout wide open, without suffering any injury himself.

After two weeks in the hospital and surgical repairs of his ears and nose, the heavily bandaged Stonewall that returned to Audubon Street was nothing like his former self. He eventually recovered from the physical injuries but not the psychological ones. He never barked again and had to be encouraged to leave the house. If Smudge was anywhere nearby, Stonewall cowered by the back door. The neighbors had every reason to be very angry with us for keeping a killer cat around, but they didn't blame us for anything and couldn't have been nicer.

We quickly decided that Smudge must go, hopefully far away, but he didn't go quietly. Shortly after he destroyed Stonewall, he somehow wedged himself between the screen and glass of our bedroom window and could not get out. The noise of his claws frantically scratching the windowpane was awful, although I must confess that it sounded like music to my spiteful ears. I was quite ready to leave him there indefinitely, but Julie insisted I save him, even though it was the middle of the night, freezing cold, and raining hard. So Smudge lived to see another day and continue his destruction. One of my distant cousins agreed to take him to her farm far away from New Orleans. I only hope she didn't have any dogs or chickens or other potential victims for Smudge to assault.

The View From "Charlie's Deck"

The subject deck is a second-story structure that looks out over a fairly large backyard surrounded by woods, mountains, and a horse farm in the bucolic college community of Williamstown, Massachusetts. To escape the long, hot, hurricane-prone summers and falls of southern Louisiana, Julie and I spent most of those two seasons in the cooler, calmer, and colorful climes of New England since retiring in 1998, including three entire years there after our New Orleans home was destroyed by Hurricane Katrina in 2005.

Julie and I, along with our kids and grandkids as well as numerous friends visiting from New Orleans and elsewhere, could often be found on that deck, especially in the early morning or late afternoon. We would talk, read, listen to music, admire the vibrant fall colors, or just quietly watch the abundant animal life in, above, and around our yard. In addition to the horses feeding, frolicking, and flirting with each other in the pasture next door, many forms of wildlife paraded past our elevated viewing stand. The deer, sometimes with their young, were frequent callers in the morning. As were the coyotes who crossed our yard on their way home in the woods from their nocturnal hunting ventures. A few of them actually laid down in the grass and peered up at us on the deck for several minutes at a time, which was a little creepy because they are predators and (unlike fox) are slinky, sinister-looking critters. We sometimes heard them howling at night in the adjacent woods to celebrate a kill. On one occasion, we woke up to find two beautiful mink sunning themselves in our yard. Early mornings in the late fall or early winter often featured a noisy flock or two of migratory geese barely high enough to clear the roof of our house—a real sound and light show. On their annual trek from Canada to the Gulf of Mexico,

LEECHES, LOVERS, BEARS, AND CHOCOLATE PUDDING

hundreds of them spent the night in a large, safe pond just two miles north of us, so they were still getting airborne by the time they reached our house the next morning.

It was a different story in the afternoon. No deer or coyotes or geese. There were usually a couple of wary rabbits nibbling grass and an occasional fox crossing the yard. It was also fun to watch small birds (jays?) attack the much larger crows that strayed too close to their treetop nests. But the bats were the most entertaining of all. In the last half hour before nightfall, there was just enough light for us to see a host of very agile bats twisting and diving while feeding on mosquitoes and other bugs (which is probably why we never had a mosquito problem). Those lovely little fireflies commenced their deadly mating/feeding rituals at about the same time. They signaled their amorous intentions by flashing their lights (twice by the males, once by the females), but the resulting tryst never quite satisfied the female, who then ate her mate for dessert. As predators, the female fireflies made the coyotes look like choirboys.

The background music for this spectacular afternoon tableaux was provided by a chorus of lusty bullfrogs that lived in a marshy area next to our yard. When Charlie and Diane, our very dear friends from New Orleans, visited us for the first time and slept downstairs with their windows open to enjoy all that cool, clean New England air, Charlie told us the next morning he didn't sleep much because of the roaring dragon in our yard. He was much relieved to find out it was just the bullfrogs and eventually came to appreciate them. (During their many subsequent visits to Williamstown, Charlie spent so much time on that deck every morning with his coffee and newspaper that we wound up naming it "Charlie's Deck" in his honor, with a plaque to prove it.)

Of all the good memories from Charlie's Deck, three animal-related incidents stand out because they were so funny:

a) Besides the 20 or so horses they boarded, our neighbors maintained a kennel of beagles, which sometimes got loose and roamed through the nearby woods. Beagles are hounds known for their tracking skills, but what we observed that afternoon was not very reassuring. They bay when tracking other animals, so we knew the baying beagles on the wooded ridge were hot on the trail of something. Soon a beautiful red fox emerged from the same woods, sat down in the middle of our backyard, looked up at us for a moment, scratched an ear, and then casually loped off in the other direction. He was obviously not worried about the hounds finding or catching him, for good reason. As soon as he disappeared, two beagles burst into the yard with their busy noses to the ground. They did track the fox's scent to the spot where he'd sat and scratched, but that's as close as they got. After circling the spot several times, they took off running and baying in two completely opposite directions, neither of which was anywhere near the route taken by their target. If the fox was watching, he must have been laughing his head off, just as we were. A few minutes later, our neighbors ran into the yard, looking for their dogs. When they asked us which way they went, we pointed in the two opposite directions like the Alice in Wonderland character, which made them laugh too.

b) On another occasion, while a young deer was alone in the yard happily munching something, a domestic cat walked in, which immediately piqued the deer's curiosity. It ambled over for a closer look at this unknown creature and got within three feet before the cat moved away a few feet. When the deer followed, the cat moved again, but could not shake the deer. This scene repeated itself a few more times before the cat, now clearly annoyed by this invasion of his privacy, tried to lose his antagonist by going around the house to our front yard, but it didn't work. We were so intrigued that we followed the chase from inside the house. Sure enough, the deer followed the cat around the house and continued its slow-motion pursuit until the frustrated cat gave up and ran back home.

Young deer are not only beautifully delicate but extremely curious. I can remember at least three occasions when Julie and I were approached by young deer while hiking in Colorado or Massachusetts. They never came close enough to touch but did venture pretty near, like 10 feet away. They were not at all shy about standing there very still for a minute or two gazing directly at us with their soft, radiant eyes, trying to figure out what we were or perhaps looking for new friends. Unfortunately, we'll never know what they were thinking, but it's enough to know they were

LEECHES, LOVERS, BEARS, AND CHOCOLATE PUDDING

thinking hard about us. The wonder of such close encounters with the wild side of Nature is vividly captured in Mary Oliver's poem "Five A.M. in the Pinewoods" about a similar experience with a young deer and "the world that is ours, or could be.

c) A couple of years later, two young deer twins bounded out of the woods into our yard, followed slowly by their mother. It was obvious she was exhausted and they were bursting with energy. As soon as she caught up to them, they raced off in totally opposite directions and disappeared. Instead of giving chase, the mama just stood there for a few seconds with her head down and then glanced up at us with the most pitiable look on her face. As recovering parents ourselves, Julie and I could figure out what she was thinking—"What have I gotten myself into?" or perhaps "Now's my chance to escape while they're not looking"—and wished her luck either way.

* * * * *

What's next? Who knows. Maybe Bigfoot or Bessie, the Loch Ness Monster. Julie and I have visited their homes in California and Scotland but never crossed paths with either one. Or maybe it'll be some little green (and hopefully friendly) beast from outer space. Whatever, we'll be ready.

IF ONLY HOUSES COULD TALK …

It survived 34 years (1971–2005) of the Penick Five (or Six, if you include Mama), who were 31, 28, 5, 2, and ¼ years old when we moved in. It even survived the legendary Parents-Are-Out-Of-Town Party as well as an invasion by 100,000 bees on the eve of Ginger's wedding and the explosion of Will's overfilled waterbed (all separate stories). But it didn't survive Hurricane Katrina, although it took the heroic house another 13 years to give up the ghost completely. 378 Bellaire Drive in New Orleans was a noble beast that served us extraordinarily well. May it rest in peace.

In the seven years before moving there, Julie and I had earned straight Fs in all three house management courses we attempted. With the first two houses that we borrowed from friends right after getting married, we repaid their trust and generosity by unintentionally trashing each abode in the one week we occupied it (the subject of another sad story). Our third victim was the first house we owned, but before that adventure was a nine-month stop in Charlottesville, Virginia, while I finished law school there.

Surrounded by the beautiful Blue Ridge Mountains, Julie and I lived half-underground like moles in a basement apartment that was tiny, noisy, damp, and spartan but blessedly cheap at $60 a month. The windows were very weird: most of them were traditional double-hung windows that were half-above and half-below the ground, so we could readily see the insect tunnels in the dirt but had to stand on a chair to see the grass. Since the lower half was in direct contact with the soil, there was no way to open the windows. Why anyone would design such a contraption is a mystery.

Unbeknownst to our landlords, we soon turned their backyard into a burial ground for squirrels, which I know sounds like some kind of cult ritual, so let me explain. Julie worked as an assistant teacher at a private, one-room school. Besides running the best pre-K in town, the owner/teacher considered squirrel meat a culinary delicacy (along with wild mushrooms, one of which accidentally killed her husband), so she trapped, skinned, cooked, and ate squirrels on a regular basis. Unfortunately, she sent many of her skinless victims home with

LEECHES, LOVERS, BEARS, AND CHOCOLATE PUDDING

Julie for us to enjoy as a high-protein meal, but all of them were immediately buried in our backyard, with all the appropriate rites.

We both have fond memories of that strange little apartment during our first year of marriage, including Julie's pregnancy which she celebrated by somehow consuming *four* huge hot fudge sundaes (*three* scoops each) after a fancy meal out. But I must tell you that our marital bliss was rudely interrupted on two memorable occasions. The first involved an unusually fierce argument over something I can no longer remember (although I suspect it was her mother). Before rushing furiously out of the apartment, Julie made a point of slamming shut the bedroom door with not one but two hands (she's quite strong), which probably would have shattered all of those underground windows and precipitated a massive cave-in of the backyard. But instead of a deafening crash, there was nothing (soon followed by my frustrated wife's anguished scream). What saved the day was one of my dirty socks that had wedged itself between the door and doorjamb and thereby thwarted Julie's malicious intent (which again makes me think of guardian angels). It took the landlord and me two hours to find Julie sitting and stewing still in a public park. She and I eventually made up and lived happily ever after ….

…Until I did something really dumb. Julie insisted that she was a "lady" and therefore did not snore, so I recorded her snoring one night on an old-fashioned reel-to-reel tape deck—then put the tape away for future unveiling and promptly forgot about it. Sometime later, we had a few friends over for dinner (including a Williams classmate and then University of Virginia medical student who went on to become a renowned cardiac surgeon and CEO of a major medical institution) and I put on one of my self-made tapes of soft background music. Well, you can guess what happened: Midway through dinner, the quiet music changed abruptly into the distinctive (and truly "unladylike") snorting of someone snoring. If looks could kill, I would have died on the spot with my head in the soup. I'm surprised Julie didn't dump the bowl of ice-cream dessert in my lap. The guests of course laughed loudly at the comic scene, which made it even harder for me to convince Julie I hadn't planned the whole thing. So much for my guardian angel when I needed some divine intervention in the worst kind of way. After numerous apologies on my knees, I survived, but it was a close thing. The tape did not survive.

IF ONLY HOUSES COULD TALK …

Our next stop was a two-story apartment, all above ground, on Walmsley Avenue in New Orleans for one year. That was our home when Hurricane Betsy struck the city in September of 1965 and, after all the power went out, we served numerous friends with beer and fish (cooked over Coleman stoves) that Julie and I had caught (and cleaned) only two days earlier on the Pearl River between Louisiana and Mississippi. Waiting in line at an icehouse downtown for one big block of ice became a bi-weekly ritual. Our daughter Casey was born about two months later. Like all brand-new parents, we didn't have a clue but gradually learned from countless trials and errors. In those pre-Velcro days of long ago, diaper pins were works of the devil, especially in my nervous, inept hands. As you've already guessed, I did pin Casey to her diaper (so sorry, Casey—it was an accident) but only once because Julie never let me change another diaper until Velcro showed up, which ended my happy retirement from diaper-changing.

In 1966, we splurged and with help from a friendly bank bought a cute little shotgun house at 332 Audubon Street in a heretofore quiet Uptown neighborhood. We had to control our house-wrecking instincts with this one because of the financial hook we were on and the need to set a good example for our young daughter (followed soon by two siblings). Nevertheless, that is where our Baskervilles Bassett hound gleefully marked all the wooden floors many times over and then ate my boss's wife's cashmere coat (a separate story); where our "rescue" cat demolished our next-door neighbors' dog (another story); where one sweet little canary cannibalized the other on the morning of my first jury trial; where "Mr. Stein" became a legend in Uptown pest control by nabbing 47 well-fed rodents that had feasted for months on all the unwanted baby food that our little daughter Casey had cunningly deposited behind a sofa without our knowledge; where even Mr. Stein could do nothing with the army of roaches that made their home in our car with its never-ending supply of food dropped by the kids; and where an unfixed leaky toilet finally fell through the rotten bathroom floor.

But to be fair, we do have some wonderful memories of our five years on Audubon Street, such as watching the first moon landing in 1969 with our two young, half-asleep daughters, meeting new friends while Julie was picking peas on the front steps, having a great Halloween costume party, and playing countless games of "Diplomacy" with friends that activated the ruthless, double-

LEECHES, LOVERS, BEARS, AND CHOCOLATE PUDDING

crossing gene in all of us, much to Julie's displeasure when she was the innocent victim of my treachery (which the game required to win). And the idea of weekends with the TEEP campers at our Covington house was conceived over a nice bottle of wine at the wonderful Hong Kong Restaurant during this time. It was an idea that gave us and our children lots of joy and wisdom over the next 31 years. Despite the usual growing pains, we have many great memories associated with Audubon Street. However, if houses could talk, I'm sure that one would have cheered loudly when we finally departed in 1971, but at least the neighborhood rats and roaches were sorry to see us go.

We were still living there on Audubon Street when a college classmate arrived in New Orleans for one night before shipping out the next morning to Vietnam as a medical officer. That was indeed a night to remember (or forget)! As requested, we fixed him up with one of Julie's friends as a date. Big mistake! He was already three sheets to the wind when we picked him up, which is not so surprising for someone on the verge of going to war. Our visitor had heard tales of Pat O'Brien's in the French Quarter and wanted to see it, not that he was seeing anything well at the moment. Another big mistake! There he quickly consumed three of its famous Hurricanes, a rather large rum drink, and passed out on the table, to his date's utter relief. Unfortunately, on her way to the bathroom (perhaps to escape through a window), she banged her head into a heavy metal tray wielded by a waiter and fell to the ground with a two-inch, horn-like hickey in the middle of her forehead. After rousing my doctor friend from his nap, he literally snapped to attention and proceeded to examine the victim in a pseudo-professional manner but then declared he had to conduct a full-body examination on her to make sure she was okay, at which point I forcibly marched him back to our table where he immediately resumed his nap. The ride home was touch and go at times, but Julie's friend somehow survived her date (only to enter a convent the next day) and he survived the war. He, Julie, and I have laughed about that evening many times, including one occasion with his mother and sister, who thoroughly enjoyed hearing about his antics. (This version has been cleaned up a little to protect the reputations of innocent and guilty alike.)

IF ONLY HOUSES COULD TALK ...

Typical of us, our arrival on Bellaire Drive was totally auspicious. A month after we moved in, the house was burglarized in the middle of the day, during the one hour per week that it was empty while Julie took the kids to swimming lessons. And since the burglars came in through a hidden window in the back of the house, we suspect it was some kind of inside job involving our moving company and possibly a local lookout, which was a little disturbing (although it turned out to be one of the safest neighborhoods in New Orleans, especially for young children). The burglars took a bunch of silver wedding presents that we didn't have much use for anyway and then hid them in a container of dirty diapers, which is what really hurt. Thankfully, that was the last of our security problems, but I must confess that Julie and I sometimes joked when short of cash that what we needed was another burglary and the resulting insurance benefits. What made the house even more secure after that episode was the semi-miraculous appearance in our backyard of a very pregnant, very hungry, and very sick mutt who was named "Mama" by the kids and quickly became our fourth child. We weren't able to save her puppies but Mama enriched all of our lives for another 15 years.

Since that house is where we raised our children, Casey, Ginger, and Will, let's start with their babysitters. My personal favorite, for all the wrong reasons, was a very attractive, over-developed 15-year-old who lived nearby. Because of her unusual endowments, Julie and I started calling her "Big Boobs" between ourselves, but unfortunately Casey, who was then four, must have overheard us. And you, dear reader, can guess what happened next. "Big Boobs is here" is how our young daughter announced in a very loud voice that our babysitter had arrived at the front door. Red faces all around. I wisely left through the back door and let Julie handle the delicate situation, as I did many

LEECHES, LOVERS, BEARS, AND CHOCOLATE PUDDING

times after that as well. Julie must have done a good job, as she always did, because Big Boobs continued to sit for us and even volunteered one weekend to help with the TEEP kids in Covington (which I happen to remember because of the bikini she wore while we were swimming with the campers in the Little Bogue Falaya River).

There were other memorable babysitters, including a good friend's secretary who made an indelible impression on our half-grown children on the one occasion she took care of them. As the kids reported to us after that fateful weekend, the over-enthusiastic babysitter took them to the lakefront to create some kind of an Indian scene with headdresses, drums, chants, dancing, and such. All was good until she started an Indian campfire to dance around and somehow caught her hair on fire (she was wearing a large hat when we arrived home). The kids of course loved that part of the outing, especially the babysitter's authentic "chanting" and "dancing" as her hair burned.[*]

Will's personal "favorite" of our various babysitters was Mrs. Sterling, who usually came whenever Julie and I were out of town for a few days or more. He always expressed his keen excitement at the prospect of seeing Mrs. Sterling again by threatening to run away or kill her but not with love. Poor Mrs. Sterling! All she did to enrage young Will was to feed him pot pies, endlessly. According to his possibly suspect version, that's all she ever fed them, for breakfast, lunch, and dinner. And worst of all, she made him eat the whole damn thing before he could leave the table. From his perspective as a 5- or 10-year-old, that was "cruel and unusual punishment" of the highest degree. It's like the movie *The Manchurian Candidate*: if I just say her name, Will blinks a couple of times and then turns into this wild-eyed terrorist. He also accused Mrs. Sterling of putting

---

[*] Her fire-safety skills were no worse than those of her boss, Harry C. On one Fourth of July weekend that our young family spent in Arkansas with his family, Harry started a potentially dangerous but short-lived fire in the nearby woods with his fireworks display. In his thank-you note, our five-year-old son said he loved Harry's forest fire best of all. This was the same weekend that his daughters and ours unknowingly flushed some kind of potting clay down the toilet of Harry's country house and destroyed the whole system. It was also so hot that Harry loaded up his pickup with blocks of ice from the local icehouse and dumped them in the pool to cool off the water, to no avail.

IF ONLY HOUSES COULD TALK ...

half-chewed gum behind her ears, which I know is untrue because she stuck it instead on the underside of every table in our house, as we discovered years later.

However, the very worst of our babysitters by far was none other than yours truly. Only twice did Julie leave me alone with one or more of our young children and each time turned into a disaster. The first time, she left me with just Will while she took the girls to visit my mother and sister in Maryland. Will, then three or so, promptly dived head-first off a couch into a coffee table and made a bloody mess of his lip, which required a few stitches as I recall. My grade as a babysitter was D. A few days later, Julie and I were watching *Jaws* in a theater when we suddenly remembered Casey and Ginger were going to swim in the Atlantic Ocean the next day. We couldn't get to a phone fast enough to call my mother and tell her not to take them anywhere near water of any kind. Sometime later, when Julie left me with all three, I thought it would be fun to try go-carting with them. Will, who was only five or so, rode in my lap but Casey and Ginger had their own carts. Well, Will and I rear-ended Ginger when she stopped suddenly and both of them wound up with bloody noses and cut lips. To make it up to them, I planned our menu accordingly. Since my culinary skills are limited to opening cereal boxes on a good day, we had every breakfast at Dunkin' Donuts and every other meal at a friendly Taco Tico, which rewarded us with free glasses every time we showed up. By the time Julie came home, the house was overrun with Taco Tico stuff, so she carefully checked the kids (but not me) for scurvy. Babysitting for me usually meant spending time in the proverbial doghouse.

Speaking of that doghouse, the longest period I resided there was a month but I probably deserved more (Julie thankfully was a forgiving sort). It was the Friday before Christmas, so we had planned to take our young kids (maybe 5, 7, and 10) to the Festival of Lights and Carols at Trinity Church at 7:00 PM. Unfortunately, my law firm, Lemle & Kelleher, had its Christmas luncheon at Antoine's Restaurant the same day, but I would still have plenty of time to get home and change for the Festival, right? Yes, on paper, but the facts on the ground indicated otherwise. After a long and enjoyable lunch, some of us retired to the Napoleon House with Harry Kelleher, one of the senior partners, to extend our celebration just a bit longer. Mr. Kelleher not only bought us drinks but then signed an open credit card voucher before he left. As dinner time approached,

LEECHES, LOVERS, BEARS, AND CHOCOLATE PUDDING

our crowd had dwindled down to just two of us, me and a new lawyer my age named John Reynolds. By 1:00 AM and several rounds of free drinks, after the two of us had solved all the issues in the whole world, I suddenly remembered the Festival. Instead of taking a cab home, as I should have done, I walked the eight blocks or so back to my parked car without getting mugged and somehow found my way home without a major mishap or DUI ticket (this is about when I started seriously thinking about guardian angels). Julie, poor soul, was so frantic that she hugged me when I stumbled through the front door instead of attacking me with a meat cleaver. My well-deserved punishment was doing the laundry for the next month.

I associate the following episode with the house because of a photo of Casey as a four-year-old ballerina standing by the front door on her way to a recital. Julie's mother and stepfather, who adored Casey, went with us. Well, Casey stole the show, even though her little group numbered about 12 youngsters, including her friend Becky Hotstream. After about five minutes of artistic mayhem and bumping into each other, they headed offstage behind the curtain—except for Casey. She walked right up to the edge of the stage and looked intently for us in the audience. She also ignored a teacher calling for her

IF ONLY HOUSES COULD TALK ...

to come back to the curtain. The audience loved it. Daisy and Erwin almost fell out their seats laughing so hard. Casey held her ground for several minutes until a teacher came out and took her hand. The show went on with some older groups, but Casey's performance was clearly the high point of the night for everyone there.

Julie liked a good party herself and was a great hostess. She was particularly known for her afternoon bouree parties on Christmas Day that went on for long hours, sometimes six or seven. Bouree is a Cajun poker game that looks innocent enough (10 or 25 cent antes, with no betting or raising like regular poker) but it can be dangerous because the pot can grow quite large very quickly. To prevent any really serious losses, we always put a limit of $5 or $10 on the pot. Despite that, lightning did sometimes strike. The most memorable occasion involved my mother, who took her card games seriously and was an uncanny bridge player, and Casey's new boyfriend Eddie, who fancied himself to be an excellent poker player. Well, after two hours (with other players too), Eddie had lost about $200 mostly to my mother. When Casey sometime later took her grandmother aside and asked her to return the money to Eddie, who apparently was in shock, my mother refused, which ended Casey's new romance a week later. That episode was unique, though—usually the players won or lost no more than $10 or $20 total. Our kids and their friends loved to play because they kept their winnings and hit their parents up to cover their losses. The bouree game was just a small part of the larger party with drinks, food, and a lot of fun. After one of the better parties, our friend Harry (the same one) passed out and woke up on the floor the next morning to find (a) our three little kids sitting on him while watching TV cartoons; and (b) a note from his wife to walk across the Lake Pontchartrain Causeway (24 miles) and meet her in Covington if he ever wanted her to speak to him again.

There were other memorable gatherings at Bellaire Drive aside from the utter calamity known as "The Parents-Are-Out-Of-Town Party," the sad subject of its own story. Casey's seventh or eighth birthday party consisted of having her friends over to paint the aluminum canoe we kept in the backyard. It was a mess but very successful. And we had the finest-looking canoe on any Louisiana river for years after that. Jumping ahead to Casey's freshman year at Kenyon College in Ohio, Julie sent her, as requested, some unshelled crawfish and a case

LEECHES, LOVERS, BEARS, AND CHOCOLATE PUDDING

of Dixie Beer in long-neck bottles. Since it was illegal to send any alcoholic beverages through the mail, Julie had to fudge a bit in describing the contents to the postal clerk. As luck would have it, i.e., "timing is everything," this occurred shortly before we were to host a dinner at our house for a cabinet member of the Portuguese government who was visiting New Orleans. (Steve Chaplin, a close friend, was then serving in Portugal as a diplomatic officer and asked us to entertain the Portuguese official, a friend of his.) Shortly before the dinner and shortly after Julie had mailed that clandestine package, she received a call from the FBI. Before the caller could explain why he was calling, Julie's guilty conscience kicked in and she began "confessing" to her illegal-beer crime and pleading for mercy, to the utter consternation of the FBI agent, who was calling as a security precaution about our distinguished dinner guest. Well, Julie did not go to jail, Casey and her friends enjoyed the crawfish and beer, and our dinner turned out very well.

    That wonderful house was also the site of a memorable first meeting of a future mother-in-law (Julie) and her future son-in-law (John Inmon) when Ginger brought him home from Atlanta to meet us. They arrived by car in the middle of the night after Julie and I were asleep, so nothing happened until the next morning. Since Julie and John both get up early, their encounter was unexpected and unfortunately unwitnessed but etched in Penick history since then. After surprising each other in the kitchen and briefly identifying themselves, this is what transpired:

    Julie: "I smell like a wino because I spilled some wine on myself while recycling just now."

    John: "I didn't know that winos recycled."

    And from that classic moment on (after Julie stopped laughing), she and John were fast friends who shared a wonderfully wicked sense of humor that became legendary in our family.

    Bowling was high on our agenda for getting to know John, as it was for the countless boyfriends and girlfriends that passed through our humble abode. Instead of the standard interrogation of a very nervous contender for one kid's affections, bowling was a good way to relax everyone and show each other our real selves. And we always had a good time. John turned out to be a pretty good bowler (which may perhaps have played some part in winning Ginger's heart),

IF ONLY HOUSES COULD TALK ...

but there were others at the other extreme, like Casey's wonderful long-term boyfriend in high school, the inimitable Rodolfo, whom we all loved, even Mama. After trying him unsuccessfully at bowling, we tried him on the ski slopes of Breckenridge, Colorado, as Casey's guest. Well, it was an athletic disaster but a great social success, mainly because of Rodolfo's upbeat attitude about everything. On one memorable occasion, he skied into a "snow hole" near the base of a tree and found himself buried in snow up to his chest. Since he was helpless to free himself, all five of us Penicks went to work on extricating him. It took us a good half an hour of digging, pushing, pulling, twisting, turning, and yanking poor Rodolfo, who spent the whole time laughing at his plight and our efforts. He made it fun. Even after he and Casey broke up, Rodolfo kept in touch with the family and brought us a huge wheel of cheese every Christmas for years. All of us have very fond memories of the young man who had emigrated with his parents from Cuba at a young age, who was always polite and dressed like a preppie, and who brightened every occasion with his charm and humor.

Unfortunately, Rodolfo was not around to cheer us up when we added another bedroom and made other structural changes to the house in 1978. Casey was 12, Ginger 9, and Will 7 at the time. Julie and I were old enough to know better. At the end of the eight-month ordeal, we were crazy—and broke. Our contractor, Wallace, a very nice man and good contractor when sober, would disappear for weeks at a time. His "precision" painter was virtually blind, so his work on our trim was a bit erratic but interesting. One of his A/C sub-contractors, whom we called "John Travolta" because he was constantly combing his long,

LEECHES, LOVERS, BEARS, AND CHOCOLATE PUDDING

black hair, accidentally released Freon from a condenser and almost killed our beautiful cypress tree. Wallace's efforts to seal the house from weather and whatever were less than effective. At a high school reunion, Julie and I invited friends over to "swim in our kitchen" after a heavy rain. Julie was taking a bath upstairs when a strange dog came in and started lapping water from her tub. For a couple of weeks, all five of us had to sleep in one king bed with a rack full of clothes hanging over us. However, our kids loved Wallace because he took them for rides in his truck. And the work finally did get done, thanks primarily to Wallace's gifted carpenter who took over the job at the end. He brought his wife by the house a few months later to show her the beautiful mantelpiece and wall-to-wall bookcase he had fashioned for us.

With its new addition, the house served us well and survived the rampages of three rambunctious teenagers, including the infamous Parents-Are-Out-of-Town Party of 1987 with its 400 invited and (mostly) uninvited guests. It also survived a rare hailstorm in 2000 with baseball-sized hailstones that broke most of the windows on the north side and damaged the roof. The hoods and tops of our two cars parked outside took a beating as well, but that generated some cash and a good story for Julie and me. We weren't planning on making insurance claims on the cars (since they worked fine and that's all that mattered to us) until I read about a quick drive-through claims service, so I decided to try it. After a 15-minute inspection without any paperwork, the adjusters rated the quality of my car's outside paint before the damage as "excellent" and handed me a check for $7,800. Just like that! Easiest money I ever made. When Julie heard about it, she couldn't wait to take her car in, which she did first thing the next day, with decidedly different results. The adjusters kept her waiting two hours and then gave her a long form to take home and fill out, without any check. They inspected her car again and decided to pay her only $2,400 for the same damage as mine on the basis that the pre-storm condition of her paint was only "fair." Julie was furious. Whereas I had not washed my car even once, Julie washed hers every two weeks and was rightly proud of its nice glow, so the difference in our paint condition grades stuck in her craw big time. She claimed gender discrimination (seriously) and accused me of being part of the conspiracy (half-seriously). That's probably when she started calling me a "mcap" (mostly joking), short for "male chauvinist asshole pig."

IF ONLY HOUSES COULD TALK …

Our kitchen was the scene of a funny event around the same time. We were sitting at the counter enjoying a bottle of wine with our good friends, Diane and Charlie Genre, and I was singing the praises of a Japanese magnetized cream called Nikken for healing the painful bone spur in my heel without the surgery recommended by an orthopedic specialist. Charlie, a very fine pathologist, guffawed in disbelief while I defended my claim. After some 10 minutes, Diane quietly asked him if that new mattress pad had helped his aching back and he answered yes, although the connection to my magical cream was unclear. Then she announced to Charlie that the mattress pad was also a Nikken magnetized product and she had been representing Nikken online for two years, obviously unknown to him. His jaw must have dropped a foot. We all had a good laugh. And Charlie himself started using the same Nikken cream shortly after that.

The wonderful old house on Bellaire Drive finally met its match when Hurricane Katrina devastated New Orleans in late August of 2005. Eighty percent of the below-sea-level city was flooded by water pouring through broken levees alongside the many overwhelmed drainage canals. Our house had five feet of very dirty water in it. Julie and I were fortunate to be in Williamstown, MA, when it happened but did not get back into the house until late November. When we arrived initially, all of the furniture, rugs, flooring, appliances, etc. from our first floor were stacked in the front yard, a mind-boggling introduction to the shocking end of our home of 34 happy years. Except for that bookcase mentioned previously, a contractor-friend had stripped the ground floor down to the studs and slab. As requested, he had given us time to save some of the books before taking out that wall. In about two hours of painfully going through hundreds of beloved books, we selected about 50 to keep.

But we were lucky in two important respects. Our blessed next-door neighbors (who were allowed back into the city early because he was a contractor) broke into the house and removed all the paintings, prints, and photographs on the wall to a dryer place. If they had been left in a very wet house without any power, they all would have been destroyed by dampness and/or mold. Instead, we were able to save and restore most of them. The other lucky event involved a 150-year-old French farm table (the only piece of our furniture to survive the floodwater). All of our family photos albums were on it when Katrina hit. The water in the house was a good bit higher than the table, but

LEECHES, LOVERS, BEARS, AND CHOCOLATE PUDDING

happily enough, it floated. And did so somehow without tipping one way or the other, unlike heavy refrigerators that invariably tipped over onto their sides in the flood waters. As a result, all the albums but one on that table were saved. (I'm attaching a letter that we wrote at year's end to our friends around the country who supported us through the ordeal.) Since the house was uninhabitable without major work, Julie and I lived in Williamstown until 2008 when we moved into Lambeth House in New Orleans after collecting the limits of our flood insurance policy on the house and selling it "as is" to the same next-door neighbors at a marked discount. The unrepaired house was demolished in 2018.

Living year-round in the Williamstown house, which we had acquired in 2000 and used previously as a summer/fall residence, was a new and exciting experience for us, although we missed our home and friends in New Orleans. From the back deck, we looked out over a neighboring horse farm to the distant mountains with their lush forests and splendid fall colors. Julie and I often hiked up 2,000 feet or so to Pine Cobble, near the Appalachian Trail, where we could see our little house and the whole town while picking wild blueberries and having lunch. (We also enjoyed our four hikes to the top of Mount Greylock, the tallest mountain in Massachusetts at 3,500 feet.) Two sides of our property bordered on dedicated "conservation land," so we were surrounded by maple, birch, spruce, and many other trees, which explains "The Tree House" nickname. Since our bedroom was only 30 feet from the forest's edge, our front and backyards hosted deer (sometime with fawns), bears (likewise with cubs), foxes, rabbits, chipmunks, minks, coyotes, woodchucks, and possum, not to mention the airborne critters like owls (including one that tried to eat me—a separate story), migrating geese, hawks, hummingbirds (including the one that brought us a message by flying a unique infinity pattern—another separate story), bats, lightning bugs, and a small, totally yellow bird I cannot find in the *Peterson Field Guide of Eastern Birds*. We started off with a bevy of local friends from my four years there at Williams College and made several new friends, including two New Orleans couples who relocated to Williamstown after Hurricane Katrina.

One of those couples, Steve and Laura Dankner, became very close friends of ours. Steve, a Juilliard graduate, is a gifted composer who had several symphonies and other works performed by the Louisiana Philharmonic Orchestra and also taught at Loyola University and NOCCA for young aspiring

IF ONLY HOUSES COULD TALK …

musicians. In 2007, he dedicated his 9th String Quartet to Julie and had it performed in the auditorium of the Clark Art Museum, followed by a reception we hosted with our three children and some grandchildren. (In 2021, shortly before this was written, Steve dedicated his 25th String Quartet to Julie's memory and had it recorded by the Martinu String Quartet in Prague.) Both pieces are exquisite. During those three years in Williamstown, Julie and I also enjoyed concerts at nearby Tanglewood (usually on blankets or in chairs on The Lawn outside the covered seats) and in New York City by great visiting orchestras from Europe and Russia. For the latter, we'd hop on the train near Albany, ride for two and a half hours along the bank of the Hudson River, exit at Penn Station, visit a museum or other site, grab a dinner, enjoy the concert and then a piece of deli cheesecake, spend the night in a nearby hotel, and ride the train back the next day.

We made about a dozen trips to NYC like that and enjoyed every minute. On another occasion, we spent a wonderful weekend (which included two Broadway plays) there with an old Williams friend and his wife who came in from Philadelphia. (They now live in Baton Rouge, Louisiana.) At a dinner we hosted for incoming freshmen, Julie and I met a young student from China named Ran Bi and became good friends. When she graduated four years later, her parents came over from China and stayed at our house for three days. They did not speak a word of English but were delightful. Ran is back in China but still in touch. Robb and Charles Dew also became close friends. He was a long-time history professor at Williams and she was an author who won the National Book Award for her first novel. I researched and wrote my own book, *Beyond Faith: Our Role in Transforming God*, mostly in Williamstown, but unlike Robb's, it had to be self-published and didn't win anything.

With its separate downstairs apartment, The Tree House was perfect for visits by friends and family from New Orleans and elsewhere, including Washington, D.C., St. Paul, MN, Kansas City, Los Angeles, Denver, Chapel Hill, NC, Houston, Easton, MD, and various other places. Starting in 2000, our good friends Steve and Carol Chaplin from Washington spent a week with us every summer for 10 straight years. The Genres from New Orleans, mentioned previously, were a close second in time spent with us in Williamstown. Because Charlie loved reading, gazing, and napping on our deck, it was named "Charlie's

LEECHES, LOVERS, BEARS, AND CHOCOLATE PUDDING

Deck" in his honor and has a sign to prove it. During the COVID-19 pandemic summer of 2020, our granddaughter Emma and her dog Dexter spent a month at the house by themselves. Williamstown, located in the very northwestern corner of Massachusetts close to Vermont and upstate New York, is so alluring to visitors because of its scenic beauty (tourists from all over the world come to see the fall colors), its friendly people, and its many nearby cultural attractions such as Tanglewood, The Clark, Williamstown Theatre Festival and two others, Massachusetts Museum of Contemporary Art, Jacobs Pillow, Norman Rockwell Museum, Hancock Shaker Village, and the homes of famous authors like Melville, Hawthorne, Dickinson, and Wharton, as well as a number of historical churches, cemeteries, and battlefields.

    Speaking of friendly people, of the 23 nights I've been in Williamstown this trip (June 2021), I've been out to dinner with friends 18 times. New England is also the only region I've seen with a number of unmanned roadside stands that sell local produce and rely on the honesty of their customers to leave the right amount of money in open cigar boxes! But the very best "kindness of strangers" story involves our little house there. It was January of 2004. Julie and I were at home in New Orleans when we got a phone call from someone named Mary at West Oil Company of neighboring North Adams, Massachusetts, which provided the oil for our furnace in Williamstown. She told us that one of its tanker-truck drivers just discovered our oil tank was still full after a month of very cold weather up there and recommended we have someone check as soon as possible to see if our furnace was working. We immediately called a good friend and contractor with a key to our house and he rushed over to find that the automatic furnace was in fact not working and the temperature in the house was close to freezing. He quickly got the furnace running again and the house survived. From what he reported to us later, the water in our baseboard heating pipes would have frozen within the next few hours and then the pipes would have burst soon after that, flooding the house and ruining the entire interior, as had happened to three or four other uninhabited houses like ours. So our house was essentially saved by a timely long-distance phone call from a complete stranger who just happened to be a very kind, caring, and thoughtful person. The next time we were in Williamstown, Julie and I stopped by West Oil and brought

IF ONLY HOUSES COULD TALK ...

Mary a big box of candy with our sincere thanks. She is special to us but also quite typical of the folks we have met in New England.

The long-range plans for our second home in Williamstown were somewhat dashed when Julie's Alzheimer's was diagnosed in December 2006. She was 64. After Hurricane Katrina, we remained in Massachusetts until we moved back to New Orleans and into a long-term care facility named Lambeth House in the spring of 2008, but we returned to Williamstown for several weeks that summer and again in 2009 and 2010. By the spring of 2011, Julie needed more care than I could provide and therefore moved into Lambeth House's Nursing Care unit where I could spend precious time with her every day until she died there on January 7, 2020, two months before the pandemic reached New Orleans.

There are two related memories from Lambeth House that I've recounted to many friends. When Barack Obama was inaugurated in January of 2009 as our first African American president, Julie and I were still relatively unknown to the other residents and were maybe two of just four liberals living there. After being inspired by his inaugural address, we went down to lunch in the Lambeth House dining room and sat by ourselves, surrounded by the long faces of our fellow residents. The African American head waitress named Vanessa asked us what we wanted to drink (meaning coffee, tea, or juice, since Lambeth House had no liquor license) and I (in typical smart-aleck fashion) replied that we'd like champagne to celebrate this awesome occasion. Vanessa turned around without saying a word and marched into the kitchen. I thought I might have somehow insulted her. Just the opposite—a minute later, she came out of the kitchen with two full champagne glasses on a tray and a big smile on her face. The surprised looks on the other residents' faces were hilarious. When I asked Vanessa where she got the champagne, she said "Never mind" with another smile. Obviously the kitchen staff were celebrating just like we were. After we finished our champagne, Vanessa brought us two more glasses, to the chagrin of all the other jealous diners. Julie and I became instant celebrities, of a sort. But the story gets even better. The morning after Obama was re-elected four years later, Vanessa showed up at Julie's new room in Nursing Care with two glasses of champagne. She did it all on her own—we were totally surprised. The fact that she could remember the earlier occasion after four years was amazing and

LEECHES, LOVERS, BEARS, AND CHOCOLATE PUDDING

deeply touching to us both. And, since our three kids were in town, Vanessa invited all of us to the kitchen before the dining room opened to celebrate with more champagne. It was a memorable celebration. I will never forget her kindness and generosity.

Although Julie's inevitable decline was very painful for the whole family, there were many other happy memories from Lambeth House and will hopefully be many more. It was there that we met Erna Deiglmayr, a spry 96-year-old, who at the time was still walking the two blocks every Tuesday to the farmer's market and carrying home a bag full of fresh produce in her arms. A native of Antwerp, Belgium, she had been very active in the Resistance during the Nazi occupation of her country from 1940 to 1944. Her untold story was so compelling that I and an assistant wrote a 52-page account of her six years in Belgium during World War II and her seven years as a United Nations officer working with the countless refugees in Germany after the war. That story is now on file at the World War II Museum in New Orleans and its counterpart in Belgium. When she was 99, Erna was interviewed live on-camera for two hours at the New Orleans museum and clearly outlasted her much-younger interviewer. She died at age 101.

In my 13 years so far at Lambeth House, I've met dozens of really fine and interesting people and shared many good times with them. The Friday afternoon Happy Hour of free wine, beer, and cocktails is always a fun and well-attended occasion. Recently it was the scene of a best-shirt contest in honor of a fellow resident and good friend who died two years before. When he did, his family donated all 150 of his high-quality, brightly patterned shirts to the other residents who had always admired them. Those were the shirts judged at that Happy Hour. I also have good memories of our bowling league. In 2019, two of us started a literary journal for resident authors only and its fourth issue of 68 pages is due out this month. Like Erna, many of the residents have some very interesting stories to tell. Another resident and I hope to lead a small group of residents to Ireland next year, which should produce a lot of bawdy and possibly intellectual material for the journal. I also associate Lambeth House with the only two accomplishments of my long, undistinguished golfing career at the beautiful Audubon Park Golf Course only two blocks away. One was my only hole-in-one, made during the 2020 pandemic. The other was a front nine that I

IF ONLY HOUSES COULD TALK ...

played at an unbelievable (for me) one over par, compared to 22 over par for the back nine! Why the difference? A damn crow (and I used to like crows). As I was parring the par-5 ninth hole, that blasted crow sat on the steering wheel of our golf cart (not that unusual) and emptied his bloody bowels on the score card just below—the same score card I was going to proudly frame, but when I frantically tried to wipe off his dripping doo-doo, my beautiful penciled score came off too. And that's why I reverted to my usual unskilled play on the back nine.

Despite all the happy memories, Lambeth House, like any home, produced its share of unhappy memories. COVID-19 hit Lambeth House like a hurricane in March of 2020 and devastated everyone. Within two weeks, 54 residents (including me) tested positive and were quarantined. My case was relatively mild but many others were not so lucky. Thirty-three residents and one employee died. I lost several good friends during that one tragic month. The saddest memory, of course, was Julie's death two months before the pandemic. All three children were there at Julie's bedside when she died. Two days later, we had a beautiful "celebration" of Julie's life in the auditorium there that was attended by many of our friends from inside and outside the facility and by our entire family from all over the country, including grandchildren and spouses. Julie would have been very moved by the tributes from family and friends, all of which were totally deserved by a most extraordinary woman, wife, mother, grandmother, teacher, and friend.

As I finish this story on Will's used laptop at my desk in Williamstown on July 4, 2021 (having just marched with friends in the local Independence Day parade), I am packing to head home to New Orleans tomorrow, sad to leave a place that played such an important part in my life with Julie and our kids but happy to return to a place that played an even longer and more important part in our lives. Although they are as different as night and day, they are both "home" to me and a lifetime of vivid memories.

SO YOU THINK SHEEP ARE HARMLESS? THINK AGAIN

Until a recent trip to Norway with Julie, I believed, like everyone else, that sheep were cute, dumb, innocent animals that people ate or wore. Let me assure you that sheep are neither cute nor dumb nor innocent. They are in fact cloven-hooved terrorists who tried to kill me.

Our story opens at the end of a beautiful hike in the mountains of Norway. Driving home on the long private road to the trailhead, happily remembering the fantastic waterfalls and snow-capped peaks, we came to the fence that separated someone's sheep from the outside world (and, as we now know, protected the outside world from those sheep). I was driving, so Julie got out to open the gate. We were totally alone, except for a mother sheep (whom we'll call Griselda) and her two babies. It was a bucolic setting, with woods, wildflowers, and those adorable sheep. Griselda peacefully nibbled grass some distance from the gate, seemingly oblivious to anything or anyone around her. But as Julie approached the gate, Griselda became as focused and still as a bird dog pointing a quail. The sudden look of malevolent intensity in her normally glazed eyes was quite shocking. As I watched this transformation from the car, it slowly dawned on me that our perfect day was about to end. Julie missed all of this because she was gazing in the other direction at Griselda's two little lambs, who had obviously been directed to line up where they would draw attention away from the wily old mastermind herself—she had used her own children as decoys! Griselda did not move a muscle until the gate was almost fully open. I shouted at Julie to shut the gate, but she was focused on the little decoys and did not hear me until it was too late. By that time, Griselda had shot through the gate in a burst of incredible speed. But then she stopped only a few feet beyond the fence (this is what finally persuaded me that we were vastly overmatched) and literally taunted Julie to come get her. And that's exactly what Julie started to do, instead of closing the gate first to keep the lambs in. As soon as she turned her back to go after Griselda, the youngsters, who knew exactly when and what to do, made their move and were through the gate in a flash.

LEECHES, LOVERS, BEARS, AND CHOCOLATE PUDDING

It was one of the most premeditated acts of pure treachery ever perpetrated in Norway, even among the trolls. Griselda and her duplicitous little accomplices had obviously designed and practiced this gambit with great care. All they needed was a couple of human bumpkins like us to come along. When we did, they executed the plan flawlessly—the moronic mask worn by Griselda to hide the evil intent within, the strategic positioning of the three conspirators, the irresistible gamboling of those cute little devils, and the precise timing of their respective moves were truly brilliant.

The multiple escapes left us in a very unpleasant situation. What we knew at the time was definitely not encouraging: (1) we had been victimized by three lousy sheep, of all things; (2) sheep are much smarter and faster than they look; (3) the escapees now had at least 20 square miles of unfenced terrain to run wild in; (4) they had no intention of cooperating with us; (5) we had no idea how to herd sheep; and (6) Norwegians don't look kindly on people, especially foreigners, who let their sheep loose. My most fervent prayers to Odin for a sheepdog or two went unanswered. The option of "leaving the scene" was sorely tempting (and would have been the wisest choice, in retrospect) but we decided to do the right thing, especially since the farmer may have taken down our license plate number.

However, what really galvanized me into action was the unmistakable fact that the grinning sheep, even the little ones, were challenging us. Thus it became a test of wills and brains between sheep and man—I assumed that an average human was still smarter than a brilliant sheep, but just then I wasn't too sure. Luckily, I must have been a shepherd in some former life because I knew instinctively what had to be done: get on the other side of the sheep and chase them back through the gate. Simple enough, except that my quarries were now trotting rapidly away from the fence, so I had to circle around them by running up a rather steep hill—all I needed after a strenuous hike. It was not pretty, but I did succeed in outflanking them. I soon realized, however, that one very tired sixty-year-old man on foot cannot possibly corral three very nimble sheep inside a gigantic semicircle. As soon as I got close, they broke formation on cue and ran off in three different directions. After chasing them for an hour without any progress, I was out of gas and obviously outclassed. It was hopeless.

SO YOU THINK SHEEP ARE HARMLESS?

And, oh, how very messy! When Griselda finally ran into a small shed, I thought she was trapped and plunged in after her, with homicidal intent. Unfortunately, the thrilling anticipation of slowly dismembering Griselda part by part was my undoing, for I simply ignored the fact that my olfactory nerves were screaming at me to stop. Instead, I raced headlong into the shed, only to realize too late it was a pigsty and I was shin-deep in pig poop. My first thought was of my beloved hiking boots that had served me so well in the Rockies and the Alps—what an ignominious end! I would avenge them by nailing Griselda's black heart to a tree, but alas, she was gone, out of a back door I hadn't seen in my haste. Life seemed totally unfair at that moment.

As I emerged from the muck bellowing like a wounded Creature from the Black Lagoon, utterly defeated and reeking of pig doo-doo, I was comforted by the expectation of my dear wife wrapping her arms around me, patting me on the head, and whispering that everything would be okay. No such luck. There she still stood by the gate, holding her nose and laughing her head off at the same time. For a brief (but ecstatic!) moment, I seriously thought about ending 36 wonderful years of marriage by strangling Julie and burying her body in the pig poop. Her hysterical laughter is a bitter, bitter memory even now. Obviously she never considered the possibility that sheep rustlers are lynched in Norway.

Just then, as I was deciding whether to execute Julie or Griselda first (I was favoring Julie because she was catchable), the gods took pity on me. Another hiker came out of the forest like Prince Valiant himself and saw (smelled it too) that I was having a bad-hair day. As soon as he started to help me (Julie was still doubled-over laughing), Griselda demurely led her two little terrorists-in-training back through the gate as if they were the most harmless, angelic creatures on Earth—it was a bravura performance obviously intended to make me look bad one last time. And when we finally drove away from that Norwegian Amityville, the vicious old witch couldn't resist twisting the knife a bit more by flashing me her most triumphant grin. On the way home, still chuckling over my own less-than-sublime performance, Julie mused about mounting a "Free Willy" campaign for all the sheep in Norway. Even though it was a bad joke (I think), the mere thought of millions of those sinister creatures on the loose was more terrifying to me than any Hitchcockian nightmare.

LEECHES, LOVERS, BEARS, AND CHOCOLATE PUDDING

Despite a newfound respect for sheep in general, I have made a solemn vow to save the world by consuming as much lamb and wool as I possibly can. And the choice of Julie's anniversary charm that year was fairly obvious: a little sheepdog, in recognition of my new role in our ongoing marriage.

Postscript

I never expected my vow to "save the world" by eating lamb to be taken seriously by anyone, but apparently someone (or something) did. At a recent dinner, an innocent-looking but obviously programmed-to-kill piece of lamb (of course) intentionally lodged itself in the narrowest point of my throat and refused to budge until someone used the Heimlich maneuver on me as I gasped for breath. So it seems that the epic battle started in Norway is not yet finished. I must remain vigilant.

HUMMINGBIRDS AND THE GREAT BEYOND

It lasted no more than 30 seconds, but it was one of the most unforgettable (and puzzling) sights we've ever seen. Nine years later, we're still wondering what the message was. And who sent it. Julie and I are convinced that a hummingbird tried to tell us something by flying a *perfect* infinity pattern, over and over again, for our benefit alone. It sounds preposterous, but bear with us until you've read the whole story.

On a beautiful July morning in Williamstown, Massachusetts, Julie and I were standing at our kitchen window watching a hummingbird drink at a nearby feeder. We were at the far end of a 10-foot-wide window so as not to disturb him. After feeding (the feeder was still half-full), he flew directly to the window right in front of us, looked straight at us from four feet away, and hovered there at eye level for a few seconds as if to make sure we were watching. (This by itself was not that unusual: several times before, while the feeder was down for cleaning and filling, other hummingbirds—or perhaps the same one, since hummingbirds are notoriously territorial—hovered in front of us to complain about the missing feeder.) What happened this time, however, was altogether different.

Instead of flying away after hovering, he immediately started flying a pattern in the shape of the well-known infinity symbol. It was easy for us to follow because he was so close and flying at a relatively slow speed. Each of his *eight* circuits was a perfect infinity sign, about three feet wide and two feet high. The shape, size, speed, and location of each circuit was exactly the same every time. And his entire course was seamless: he never flipped over to right himself, so half his route was flown right side up and the other half upside down. After this amazing show, he pointedly hovered again in front of us ("So, did you get it?") and then flew off, leaving us both a little stunned.

LEECHES, LOVERS, BEARS, AND CHOCOLATE PUDDING

Charcoal drawing by Lucia Penick

HUMMINGBIRDS AND THE GREAT BEYOND

Once we'd gathered our wits, we consulted a hummingbird guidebook and called the American Birding Association headquarters in Colorado to find out if what we saw was some kind of ritual display. As we told the very helpful lady named Susan who answered our call, there were no other hummingbirds around to impress, he had just finished feeding and was not performing for food, the weather was mild, and nothing else was happening to disturb our new feathered friend. Susan told us that hummingbirds are the only birds able to fly forward, backwards, sideways, upside down, straight up, straight down, and hover in place, because they can rotate their wings in a circle, but she herself had never heard of the display we saw. After researching the archives there, Susan called back and confirmed there were no reports or knowledge of an infinity flight pattern/ritual or anything close to it.

So we were left to draw our own conclusions about this strange incident. Three possible explanations came readily to mind: (1) it was instinctive behavior; (2) it was learned behavior; or (3) it was purely accidental. But there are serious problems with all three, as you'll see.

We humans are fascinated by hummingbirds. Lucky for us, they spend much of their time around flowers and feeders at our eye level. We constantly study, observe, photograph, and film them in action, more than any other bird. As a result, there's not much if anything we don't know about the life of hummingbirds, including their habits and idiosyncrasies. Instinctive behavior in birds and animals consists of habitual, repetitive actions that are common to *all* members of a species, so it is behavior that's observed very, very often, especially in a species as thoroughly studied as hummingbirds are. Therefore, if the particular infinity flight pattern in question was an *instinctive* habit or ritual of hummingbirds, like a mating dance, surely it would have been well known and well documented long before Julie and I observed it. The fact that it was never previously reported tends to rule out some kind of instinctive behavior.

Then perhaps it was *learned* behavior. Although hummingbird brains are smaller than a pea, they are incredibly powerful. If we measure intelligence by comparing brain size to body size (hummingbirds weigh less than a nickel), they are the most intelligent of all animals, including humans. Their awesome intelligence has been the subject of extensive research. Among many other unusual traits, hummingbirds are capable of "vocal learning," which is the ability

LEECHES, LOVERS, BEARS, AND CHOCOLATE PUDDING

to learn complex songs by imitation rather than instinct. Is it therefore possible for them to learn a particular flight pattern in the same way, by imitating it? This seems plausible—except for one thing. Where would a hummingbird find an infinity sign to imitate? It's not something that exists in nature but is a written symbol created and used exclusively by humans. No matter how extraordinarily bright our hummingbird was, he could not have learned information that was not available to him.

Maybe it was nothing more than a nice accident that this hummingbird just happened to fly a symbolic route without knowing what he was doing, like the proverbial monkey typing away mindlessly until he eventually types The Gettysburg Address accidentally. If our friend had made only *one* revolution in the *rough* shape of an infinity sign, it's certainly possible that it was purely *accidental*. But he made eight complete revolutions. They were all perfect infinity signs. And each one was identical to the others in terms of size, shape, speed, location in space, and his body alignment in relation to the ground. The odds of this hummingbird duplicating the same "accident" several times over are infinitesimal at best. The sheer precision of his performance clearly indicates that it was intentional, not accidental.

So if the set of perfect infinity patterns performed that morning was not the product of instinctive, learned, or accidental behavior, what was it? To answer that, we have to enter the "twilight zone" of speculation, but our physical world has always been filled with mysterious events that defy rational explanation (thank goodness) and this appears to be another one.

Julie and I are prepared to assume our hummingbird *knew* he was flying the infinity pattern several times over, but again, how could he know that if he could not have learned it? One possible solution is that *this particular bird* was born with knowledge of the infinity sign (as distinguished from an instinct innate to *all* hummingbirds). That raises the question of reincarnation. Some nearby native cultures believe that hummingbirds are in fact dead ancestors. Perhaps John Wallis, the English mathematician who introduced the infinity symbol in 1655, was reincarnated as a hummingbird and wanted to show off his handiwork (or show us who he really was in a bird's body). If this sounds a little facetious, it's because I'm skeptical of reincarnation theory despite several smart friends who subscribe to it.

HUMMINGBIRDS AND THE GREAT BEYOND

There's also a more practical objection to reincarnation as an explanation. Since hummingbirds are extremely territorial about sources of food and our two hummingbird feeders were visited frequently every day during the five months they were up, this particular hummingbird undoubtedly spent a lot of time around our feeders and we spent a good bit of time observing him. Therefore, he had ample opportunity to show off or signal us on numerous other occasions, as one might expect him to do if he was a reincarnated human with knowledge of the infinity symbol, but he displayed that infinity pattern to us only that one time.

The only other possibility involves someone or something "speaking" to us through the hummingbird. As we watched him face us and hover at eye level only four feet away, fly a perfect and seamless infinity pattern eight times, and then hover again while looking squarely at us, Julie and I both had the distinct (and eerie) feeling that he was sending a *message—to us*. Which of courses raises these immediate questions: (1) What was the message? (2) Who or what sent it? (3) Why us?

Because the infinity sign is such a specific, universal, and well-known symbol, it obviously contained the message or at least the major part of it. Infinity refers to something without end or limits. Space? Possibly, but I suspect science will eventually discover that space is physically finite just as it is temporally. If we eliminate space, that leaves us with something supernatural rather than natural—especially if we assume the messenger was part of the message. In many native cultures of the Western Hemisphere (hummingbirds are extinct in the rest of the world), they are endowed with potent religious and spiritual significance. A good example is the widespread belief that hummingbirds are messengers "between worlds" or of the gods. As mentioned above, some cultures think hummingbirds are dead ancestors back from the afterlife. In this light, our hummingbird is also a symbol just like the route it flew. The two symbols taken together suggest something spiritual, something infinite and eternal. If that was the message, it could be interpreted to mean an eternal afterlife or a supernatural reality that exists alongside our natural one.

However, as appealing as that interpretation is, it conflicts with my own metaphysical ideas. Even though I believe in a transcendent God that co-exists with us and an afterlife for everyone, this God of mine is non-traditional in many

LEECHES, LOVERS, BEARS, AND CHOCOLATE PUDDING

ways but primarily in that he is completely *inactive* in our Universe. (Why a hands-off God and what kind of afterlife are explained in my book, *Beyond Faith: Our Role in Transforming God*.) Unfortunately, I cannot reconcile my personal beliefs with the idea of a message from the afterlife or the supernatural reality in general, although I can't rule it out either and it's sorely tempting to make an exception this one time. (In what is probably nothing more than an interesting coincidence, the hummingbird delivered his "message" about the same time that I started writing the book.)

That doesn't leave us much to explain the incident in question. Maybe the "message" was just the mystery of it, the same kind of generic message or signal that has been received in many different forms by countless people ever since we existed. Despite my metaphysical views, I firmly (and happily) believe that the Universe, including our own planet, is chock full of mysteries that will always defy scientific explanation, as awesome and essential as science is. It may even turn out that our own natural world is not *altogether* natural because it somehow overlaps the supernatural world in certain respects.

In the meantime, we'll continue to enjoy and ponder our still-vivid memory of the fine-feathered messenger who visited us years ago. It would be nice to see him—or whoever impersonated him—again, but sadly enough, North American hummingbirds rarely live longer than five years, so we'll have to wait until the next life. There, of course, we would hope, if not expect, to find out who sent the message and what it was.

* * * * *

After I posted this story on a public internet blog, someone else posted the following story about a similar hummingbird encounter and messages from the "other side":

> *I was relaxing in my yard when I suddenly saw a hummingbird. In the 23 years I've lived in this house, I have never once seen a hummingbird! I was awestruck by its beauty and its quickness. It did appear to be on a mission. It hovered briefly, but once it was sure it got my attention, it quickly took off skyward. Ten seconds later the phone rang. It was the family of my close friend of over 50 years telling me that he had passed*

HUMMINGBIRDS AND THE GREAT BEYOND

away suddenly the night before. I'll be forever grateful for the message of excitement and joy the hummingbird sent through the spirit of my friend: that he was indeed on an important mission and in quite a hurry to fly off to a heavenly place, where there was a joyful reunion awaiting. A place where we would all meet once again. It was a supernatural experience and it will always symbolize my friend Frank and his heaven-bound soul.

JUST JULIE

If you take the best of Florence Nightingale, Amelia Earhart, Maria Montessori, Carol Burnett, and Joan of Arc and mix it all together, what do you get? You get Julia St. Clair Lake Penick, born 12/20/42 in Augusta, Georgia, my wife and best friend for almost 50 years now. Julie aka Boo aka Sweetpea is an educator, adventurer, writer, saint, comic, earth-mother, and hero, all rolled together into one petite but extraordinary package.

In the course of a full and busy life, Julie often found herself in very funny, very dangerous, or downright bizarre situations. How she got into and then out of those situations is now the stuff of legend in our family, so it's time to introduce this amazing woman to the rest of the world.

The Decider

One reason our marriage has lasted so long is because early on we adopted a strict division of responsibility between us. It was Julie's brainchild. With her precise sense of timing, she presented the idea to me at a particularly euphoric moment during our original two-day honeymoon in Biloxi, Mississippi, when I was somewhat distracted by more mundane possibilities. Here's how she achieved her coup:

"Bill, dear, I have a good idea. Want to hear it?"

"Of course, my love. Anything you say."

"Since you're now the man of the family, I think you should make all the BIG decisions and I'll make the LITTLE ones so you don't have to bother with them."

"Why, Julie, that's a splendid idea. You are so smart and considerate."

Julie was the picture of innocence, so I suspected nothing and committed myself wholeheartedly to this wonderful plan. However, a couple of hours later, it dawned on me that one small detail was missing.

"Julie, dearest, how will we know whether a decision is BIG or LITTLE?"

LEECHES, LOVERS, BEARS, AND CHOCOLATE PUDDING

"Oh, Bill, didn't I tell you? That's a LITTLE decision."

That was the moment, after exactly one day of marriage, that I realized I was no match for my very sweet, angelic, devilishly clever wife, so I did the manly thing and capitulated then and there, which has resulted in a uniquely harmonious marriage.

But just to make sure I never forgot the message, Julie etched it in my memory a few years later by giving me a tee-shirt with this question on the front: "If a man speaks in the forest, and there is no woman there to hear him, is he still wrong?" With Julie watching warily to see if I had any fingers crossed, I of course answered the question "correctly" and was rewarded that night with a wonderful dinner. (I shudder to think what my punishment would have been had I answered it "incorrectly.") At least she didn't make me put my answer in writing, but she did expect me to wear my tee-shirt out in public once a month. You can imagine the kind of feedback I got from friends and strangers alike. One hundred percent of the women answered the question with a resounding "yes." Although a little more quietly, 95% of the men answered the same way, especially if accompanied by their wife, girlfriend, sister, mother, or daughter—the other 5% of heretics were unmarried.

"Just Little White Lies"

I should have been more alert on our honeymoon because of three things that happened during our courtship. Actually, they were just three "little white lies," the term Julie used to blithely distinguish them from real lies. I of course fell for all three of them, emanating as they did from this lovely, innocent, and irresistible creature who was becoming the center of my life. I was ready to believe anything she said—only after plighting my troth for life did I learn to spot that telltale twinkle in Julie's eye whenever another "little white lie" was in the works.

L. W. L. No. 1: Knowing that I duck-hunted, Julie told me, with a perfectly straight face, that she was the Annie Oakley of duck hunters. The resulting hunt on a cold December day with two mutual friends was a disaster in every way. As soon as we got into the duck blind and handed Julie/Annie a loaded shotgun that she started waving around while everyone else dove for cover, it was pretty obvious she knew nothing about guns. Unlike Dick Cheney, she didn't shoot anyone accidentally, but it was a close thing. On the way home, Julie managed to (1) single-handedly sink our boat in 10 feet of very cold water; and (2) stay perfectly dry herself while the rest of us went down with the ship. How she pulled off this amazing circus feat is described in another story entitled "Down with the Ship, Said He—Hell No, Said She."

L. W. L. No. 2: Julie also assured me that she had hiked and camped all over the country since early childhood, so I thought it would be different and romantic to spend part of our real honeymoon camped beside an alpine lake in the Colorado Rockies. Well, it was certainly different but definitely not romantic. Unbeknownst to me until disaster struck, Julie had filled my backpack, not hers, with cosmetics in glass bottles that froze and burst during our two-day hike up the mountain and made a mess of my spare clothes, not hers. She made another kind of mess after popping several packs of Feen-a-mint anti-constipation gum that kicked-in big time during our first night in a tent, which was not conducive to sleep or sex.

When we finally reached our destination at 12,500 feet during a summer snowstorm and my benumbed and bedraggled wife angrily told me she wanted an immediate divorce from "such a deranged [expletives deleted] idiot" who liked "all this [expletives deleted] camping crap," I realized three things: (1) my sweet and innocent wife was quite proficiently profane, (2) she'd snookered me again, this time into believing she was a wilderness pro, and (3) this was going to be a completely celibate honeymoon. But then it got even worse.

We were soon joined in our very remote location by an older man with a large pistol that he'd recently used to murder his wife. That was the last straw for Julie. If she could've borrowed the man's gun, she no doubt would have followed his example and terminated her own unwanted spouse for getting her into this miserable situation. The next three days with our new friend were a bit surreal and positively sexless, but we survived to spend the second phase of our honeymoon in Las Vegas, where my blackjack-crazed wife lost all of our drive-home money except for $19 hidden from her in my shoe. As you can imagine, the five-day drive back to New Orleans was rather bleak—and entirely chaste. For further information about how not to plan a honeymoon, read "The Best of All Possible Honeymoons? Not Quite!"

LEECHES, LOVERS, BEARS, AND CHOCOLATE PUDDING

However, to give Julie the credit she deserves, she did not divorce me (nor I her for the Las Vegas part) and she became an avid and skilled woodsperson who backpacked all over the Rockies with me and the children.

L. W. L. No. 3: This was the big one, the one that sealed my fate. It was the "slight exaggeration" (another Julie euphemism) that inspired me to make an immediate proposal of marriage, which was quickly accepted. Things turned out very nicely indeed, except for the unpleasant fact that I had to work for a living instead of clipping coupons and spending Julie's allegedly vast fortune as I'd dreamed of doing.

By the spring of 1964, Julie and I were falling in love but marriage was at best a long way off. I still had two and a half years of law school to finish before we could even think about getting married. But a single telephone call changed everything.

The subject was a big spring dance at the University of Virginia, where I was in law school. Cad that I was, I'd mentioned the dance to Julie as well as another young woman I'd dated in Charlottesville. Having put myself in an uncomfortable bind, as I frequently did, I called Julie in New Orleans to talk her out of coming because of the "huge" expenses she would incur. Well, she deftly turned the tables on me, as she frequently did with amazing grace. I wish I had recorded her end of that conversation, because it was a spontaneous masterpiece. It went like this: "Oh, Bill, you have nothing to worry about. My parents have tons of AT&T stock and have given me a lot of it, so I'll just sell a few shares." (Emphasis added) What my opportunistic brain heard was this: "My family is LOADED, so don't sweat the small stuff." Julie + $$$$$$ = my pot of gold at the end of the rainbow. And it all fit: her family lived in a big house on Audubon Park and Julie wore nice clothes. I already knew she was someone special but this new information elevated her in my greedy eyes to the status of a princess (with keys to the royal treasury).

After assuring Julie of my undying devotion, I politely canceled my other date and started re-thinking my future by adding a rich wife to the equation. In order to avoid certain adverse tax consequences of marrying Julie, I raised the issue in a small tax seminar I was taking with a young, open-minded instructor and six other students who were all friends. After congratulating me on my good luck, they all advised me to "close the deal" by marrying Julie as soon as possible. They also collaborated with me in composing the world's first committee-drafted love letter in which I (a) told Julie she was the one for me; and (b) advised her about saving taxes on all her stock after we got hitched. Since the letter mentioned marriage for the first time ever and contained all that tax gibberish, Julie asked her beloved father, a truly wonderful man, to look at it. His reaction to the letter was very predictable: he laughed his head off and said "Doots [his nickname for Julie], the fellow thinks you're loaded!"

He of course was right, but his observation does raise an important ethical question. Now that Julie knew I had jumped to the wrong conclusion, don't you agree, dear reader, that the only honorable thing for her to do was to save me from myself and come clean about the fabricated fortune? Maybe it is shameful of me to talk about honor when I was ready to two-time Julie, but you have to admit that a lifetime commitment to sacred wedlock is much more serious than one stupid dance. In any event, Julie for once in her life did not do the honorable thing. Actually she did just the opposite and took unfair advantage of my ignorance by pressing me for a specific wedding date. I was in checkmate, yet again.

Why, you ask with the benefit of hindsight, didn't I get more information before taking the plunge? That may be a reasonable question in 2014, when money, sex, and everything else are fair game by the second date, but it was a far different world back in 1964. Money especially was a taboo topic of conversation. It would have been considered very indelicate of me to ask Julie for the sordid details of her alleged wealth. Even worse, she may have suspected that my sudden interest in her financial status was pretty perverse, heaven forbid, and I certainly didn't want to blow the game at this point. Furthermore, I trusted Julie and still do—aside from a few "little white lies" here and there, she's the most honest person I've ever known.

Our headlong rush into matrimony was almost derailed by an untimely "bug." After our official betrothal, Julie joined me and a good friend, Steve Chaplin, in New York City to see the 1964 World's Fair (considering the times, Julie was in a separate hotel room). Anticipating that I would soon be rolling in dough, I blew my budget buying an engagement ring at the famous Diamond Exchange. We were going to a party that night at a friend of Steve's, so I had the "bright" idea, surely with encouragement from Steve who's always getting me

LEECHES, LOVERS, BEARS, AND CHOCOLATE PUDDING

into trouble, of hiding the ring in an ice cube to put in Julie's drink. You guessed it: another plan of mine that went awry. It was all copacetic until Julie took her drink out on the veranda, some 30-odd stories up in the air. When she finally spotted the ring, she mistook it for an insect and was about to dump her drink over the railing before I literally tackled her.

Still blissfully ignorant about the real size of Julie's dowry, I officially plighted my troth that summer, only three months after the fateful phone call. I did become a bit suspicious when I didn't receive a substantial signing bonus upon tying the knot, but thought it would certainly come on my birthday a few weeks later. Alas, instead of a big birthday check, I got the bad news. With that impeccable timing of hers, Julie finally confessed that her fortune consisted of exactly eight shares of AT&T stock that her parents gave her annually as birthday presents, minus the 13 shares she'd already sold. Worse still, her parents had no AT&T stock but did have a mortgage. You can imagine the shock as I watched my dreams of leisure and luxury go up in smoke. All because of that blasted spring dance! In addition to the loss of my imagined millions, I blame it for a $375 ticket I got on the way to Washington, D. C., to pick up Julie for the dance, when my car spun out of control on a slick highway and passed a parked police car while going backwards.

But now I thank my lucky stars every day for Julie's Little White Lie No. 3. Without that gentle push, I probably would have postponed our marriage for another two-plus years until I'd finished law school and found a job. Julie may have changed her mind during the wait, which would have altered my life in ways too awful to contemplate: no Casey, Ginger, or Will, no seven wonderful grandchildren, and no 49 years and counting of fabulous romance and adventure with the love of my life. So let's hear it for little white lies—or at least the "good" kind that Julie employed so masterfully.

Janet's Gang

Julie's little-white-lie expertise is undoubtedly a product of her charter membership in the legendary Janet's Gang. It consisted of seemingly sweet and normal 9- to12-year-old girls who are now prominent, law-abiding citizens but back in the early 1950s struck fear in the hearts of all the good, decent folks on

JUST JULIE

Walnut Street near Audubon Park. Janet, the alleged ringleader according to Julie, came from a family of 10 children and a free-range monkey named "Blessed Heart." Since a monkey can execute certain nefarious assignments that little tomboys cannot, we can assume that Blessed Heart was a valuable if heedless asset of the Gang's.

Julie has always claimed she was just a follower, but that hackneyed defense doesn't ring altogether true in this case. Having been led astray so often by Julie's charms and blandishments, I can assure you she is more than capable of leading such a dangerous organization and getting away with it. This is not meant to impugn Janet's reputation, since playing second fiddle to Julie, like I've always done, is still a big deal. And Janet, when I finally did meet her, denied that she was the chief gangsterette (after first denying there was any such gang), although she refused to name the real leader. We'll never know for sure because of the Gang's blood-oath of secrecy. But based on my half century of close contact with Julie, I'm sure she was part of the inner circle or held some key position like "enforcer."

And what, pray tell, did the Gang do to earn such a reputation? Unfortunately, the worst of it will never see the light of day because of that blood-oath, but we do know that "For Sale" signs suddenly started appearing all over the neighborhood and real estate prices plummeted. Those poor homeowners who could not afford to flee installed barbed wire and burglar bars. And once the deadline for criminal prosecution had passed, little drips and drabs of top-secret information began to emerge because former gang members, including Julie, couldn't resist the temptation of boasting about their lesser but still impressive exploits.

They routinely antagonized the golfers on the old Audubon Park course by stealing or hiding their golf balls, taking or moving the flags that marked the holes, hiding up in the oak trees and throwing acorns at the golfers, running across the course, and filling in the holes. When neighbors left town on vacation,

LEECHES, LOVERS, BEARS, AND CHOCOLATE PUDDING

the gangsterettes sometimes invaded their houses and, like Zorro, moved pictures around or re-hung them upside down. They never stole anything, except for a few old anatomy books with those "lewd" pictures that were part of every pre-teen's education. Like a coven of young witches, they sometimes convened at night in their nightgowns, with poor Blessed Heart in tow, and spooked many a traumatized couple who were parked in Audubon Park "watching the submarine races" that were so popular back then. However, the most terrorized group in the neighborhood consisted of the members' younger brothers who wanted to join this all-female gang of hoodlums. Although no bodies have been uncovered yet, most of those male siblings eventually developed PTSD (post-traumatic stress disorder) and had trouble relating to women later in life, so go figure. From the few known clues and the criminal mentality of the gang members, we can only wonder how they escaped the FBI's "Most Wanted" list and concealed their dark legacy this long.

Julie was saved from a life of crime when she (1) discovered boys as romantic objects; and (2) realized she could make an honest living. *Gone with the Wind* was probably the catalyst in both cases. Julie has always adored the book and movie both and has revisited them many times over the years. But none of her teenage friends liked how the story ended, so my enterprising wife came up with the bright idea of composing different endings and selling them to other students at McGehee's School for a quarter each. It was the Apple of its day. Every two or three weeks, Julie would produce a new ending, which sold out in minutes. Even some teachers bought them. All of those honestly earned quarters were quickly spent, of course, but thankfully they inspired Julie to go straight (except for those little white lies of hers). If only Julie had been selected to write the sequel to *Gone with the Wind* (the actual sequel crashed and burned), it no doubt would have been a bestseller and belatedly fulfilled her promise to me of an immense dowry.

Needless to say, I heard nothing about Janet's Gang or Julie's role until long after we were married and had children. So far, thank goodness, there's no conclusive evidence Julie passed her criminal gene on to our kids, although we've had a few scares (see, for instance, the story entitled "The Parents-Are-Out-Of-Town Party"). Unfortunately, when it comes to those little white lies, all of our children have rejected my policy of Absolute Truth (as displayed in these stories) and have instead adopted their mother's policy of relative truth. Surrounded and outgunned in my own family, I'm a lost cause but I'm hoping that some sympathetic reader will show me how to save the grandchildren from this crooked path before it's too late.

The Comedienne

The three children fortunately did inherit Julie's irrepressible sense of humor. It's irrepressible because it has even survived her advanced Alzheimer's. Just yesterday, at dinner, Julie leaned in close, batted her eyelashes up at me in a seductive way, and said in a husky voice "Come to me, my darling." Our tablemate almost fell out of her chair laughing. A month earlier, Julie started humming an obscure song I had been thinking about that morning, so I told her about the coincidence and asked her if she thought our minds were linked. After a slight pause and a quizzical look, she said, "What I think is you're crazy" and then laughed at her own joke. On another occasion, during some friends' visit, when I asked Julie what she thought about being married to me for 49 years, she said it was "a little long," so I asked jokingly if she was trying to tell me something and she gave me an emphatic "Yeah!" while laughing and nodding her head vigorously.

At dinner one night in Nursing Care at Lambeth House, when another resident and friend accidentally bumped me with her wheelchair, I said to her, "That's okay—you can push me around as much as you like." Julie, who didn't see the bump and thought I was talking to her, got a big smile on her face and said to me, "Really, Bill? Boy, do I love you!"

As a kind of enjoyable therapy for Julie, we usually spend an hour every afternoon singing old songs, since she loves to sing and still has a lovely voice. During a recent session, I was thumbing through our book of lyrics and saw the title of "Somebody Stole My Gal," which I read out loud because it has special significance for her (see below). Julie, who was looking the other way, thought I was stating a fact and responded thus in a half-worried, half-joking voice: "No, Bill, your girl is right here next to you." She eventually started expressing herself mostly in song with made-up tunes and lyrics. Julie was singing along in her wheelchair on Mother's Day, 2014, when I picked up a large box of flowers from the kids at the front desk, laid it in her lap, and asked her if she would hold it. Her reply, in song, was "You gotta be crazy!"

In December of 2009, three years *after* Julie was diagnosed with Alzheimer's, we were sitting in a New Orleans restaurant with all of our children and then-five grandkids, fortunately with the adults and kids at opposite ends of a long table. One of our offspring (whose name I will not disclose, but any of them could have done it) brought up the subject of a recent study that compared penis sizes of urban versus rural men. It allegedly concluded that men who live in the country are better endowed than men who live in a city. Without missing a beat, Julie announced to the family that "We're moving, Bill." It was so quick and clever that the rest of us were momentarily stunned before erupting in laughter. Word of her joke traveled so far that even now, years later, my motley male friends still tease me about moving to the country.

Julie's had a wonderful sense of humor as long as I've known her. A classic example occurred early in our marriage during one of those torrential rainstorms that periodically flood our city at or below sea level. Worried about her being home sick, I left work early and drove about four miles through flooded streets past abandoned Cadillacs and Lincolns before my 18-year-old VW Bug finally stalled. Since our house was not far, I took off my shoes and socks, rolled up my pants, grabbed my briefcase, and started walking in knee-deep water—hoping I didn't encounter an uncovered manhole. By the time I got home, I was a pretty sorry-looking specimen. Instead of the hero's welcome I so richly deserved, Julie greeted her wet and bedraggled husband with a whoop of laughter and "Did you have a hard day at the office, dear?"

Perhaps Julie's most famous off-color contribution to the family was the song "Somebody Stole My Pants" that she taught our children when they were still quite young. Based on the tune and lyrics of that same "Somebody Stole My Gal," it goes like this:

    Somebody stole my pants.
    They took 'em at a dance.
    Somebody came and took them away.
    I didn't even know they were leavin'.
    The pants that I love so.
    I'll catch a cold I know.

JUST JULIE

Gee, I feel so queer
Just standin' here
In my brassiere.
I'm so broken-hearted now;
Somebody stole my pants.

As you can imagine, the song spread like wildfire among the pre-teen set and Julie became something of a revered guru to young girls all over New Orleans. Casey and Ginger have, in turn, carried on the tradition with their own children (Will's kids are still too young). Ginger's daughter, Olivia, who's a member of the Colorado Children's Choir at age eight, loves the song and sings it constantly, so maybe it will make the Hit Parade one day.

Julie's sense of humor also includes the semi-sinister, which is not altogether surprising in light of her Janet's Gang background. But, strange as it may seem, it was only on April Fools' Day that her dark side took over my sweet wife's mind. I still remember her chasing little Ginger around the house brandishing a syringe that she said contained lice. It was of course empty and needle-less but our daughter didn't know that and ran for her life. (Casey, the older sister, probably helped plan that particular ambush.) While one of the kids (I cannot remember which one) was eating dinner at the kitchen counter and Julie pointed to an alleged roach in his/her soup, the poor victim pushed back so violently that he/she broke the stool and banged his/her head on the wall.

Ginger was also the target of Julie's most outrageous April Fools' joke. Shortly before Ginger's wedding, she and Julie went out shopping in Atlanta, where she was then living. I was to meet them in the hotel lobby. At the appointed hour, to my utter surprise, my previously-glowing daughter rushed in crying and threw her arms around me. "I'm so, so sorry, Dad. I had no idea," she sobbed. I was clueless until I saw Julie looking like she just ate the canary and suddenly realized it was that day again when she becomes Mr. Hyde. Ginger too understood the situation as soon as I reminded her of the date. Apparently my unrepentant wife had somehow convinced her that I was on the verge of a nervous breakdown from excessive work, was scheduled to enter a rest home for an extended period of time, and would therefore have to miss Ginger's wedding, which was all very sad, but the good news was that her brother Will would walk her down the aisle in my place! Not only did it take something of an evil genius

LEECHES, LOVERS, BEARS, AND CHOCOLATE PUDDING

to think up a story like that, but it also took an Oscar-worthy performance to sell such a tall tale to our very smart daughter. Now perhaps you can understand a little better why I fell so easily for those "little white lies."

Try as we did to turn the tables on Julie, the kids and I were never able to fool her, except on one glorious occasion. But it took a "perfect storm" of converging conditions for Julie to let down her guard. For some odd reason, she chose April 1 to stop smoking "cold turkey." She was already in a serious stage of withdrawal by that afternoon when she had to pick up Will at school. While running across St. Charles Avenue, she tripped and fell on the streetcar track, which was the tipping point. According to Will, who was waiting for her on the corner with a friend, Julie started sobbing, screaming, and pounding the ground with her fists. When the friend asked him if that wasn't his mother, Will answered "No, she's just a friend of the family." That may sound rather ungallant of him, but after all he was only 13 at the time and the mother he had disavowed did exactly the same thing to me.[*]

By 6:00 that evening, Julie was a basket case. We were sitting at the kitchen counter drinking wine to soothe her frayed nerves when the phone rang and Julie answered. It was Casey calling from Kenyon College in Ohio, where she was a freshman. And it was clearly bad news, from all indications. Julie's verbal responses of "You did what!" and "Oh, no!" got progressively more frantic. Just when she appeared ready to rip the phone off the wall again,[†] she thrust it at me with a "You talk to her!" I could hear Julie slamming drawers all over the house searching in vain for a stray cigarette she hadn't thrown away. In the meantime, I learned what Casey had told Julie: at a recent fraternity party, she had too much to drink and had informed the college dean he was a jackass,

---

[*]Julie disavowed me in Taos, New Mexico, when we were just learning to ski back in 1967. I foolishly entered a Nastar slalom race even though I was still a beginner—big mistake! The course was much longer and steeper than I expected. The other racers looked to me like Olympic champions and the assembled onlookers responded enthusiastically. Well, all that changed when my turn came. After hitting the first four poles (out of 40 or so) and falling down each time, I quit the race. Apparently the shocked spectators near Julie were colorfully outspoken about my pitiful performance, so when I skied over to her for some much-needed TLC, she turned around and skied away to hide the fact she even knew me! She didn't stop for me until the Nastar crowd could not see us anymore.
[†]Julie did that once before, on Christmas Eve, while talking to her mother.

etc. (which is something Casey might very well do), had been expelled from school, and wanted Julie to pick her up at the airport the next morning. It was a classic April Fools' trick that even Julie came to applaud after regaining her sanity a few days later.

I was the victim of Julie's notorious sense of humor one Halloween many years ago, when our first grandchild Emma was only three years old. It happened in Atlanta, where Casey (Emma's mom) and Ginger lived at the time. I was playing with Emma when Julie, oh so innocently, asked her what kind of costumes she wanted Pops (me) and Nana (Julie) to wear on Halloween night. Without a moment's hesitation (which set off my internal alarm bells), Emma gave her answer: she wanted Nana to dress up as a cat and Pops as a princess! Before I had a chance to protest, everyone else in the room jumped up and voiced their approval of Emma's choices. Julie of course was the loudest. It was all a set-up organized by my loving wife. The timing and certainty of Emma's answer along with Julie's gigantic grin clearly proved beyond doubt that Emma had been carefully rehearsed, obviously by the usual suspect. So my fate was sealed—but I had no idea how unkind Fate could be until later.

Within minutes, the girls rushed out to a thrift shop and got me the slinkiest, tightest, shiniest red dress imaginable, with lots of sequins, no less. (See photo and notice Julie's very guilty smile.) They all had a ball getting me into it and then applying the makeup and jewelry. Things got worse when the trick-or-treating started in the very last place I wanted to "come out" in: a redneck suburb of Atlanta. If looks could kill, I would have died a hundred deaths. I don't remember even one homeowner laughing at my outfit. Disgust was the principal reaction, but there were some that were outright hostile, like "get that thing out of my neighborhood or else …," i. e., before I call the police or get my gun. I understood the message soon enough and started hiding behind trees. But I somehow survived and Emma had a special Halloween. And dear Julie laughed about her "husband the drag queen" for months.

LEECHES, LOVERS, BEARS, AND CHOCOLATE PUDDING

Automotive Misadventures

As most mothers of our generation know, driving carpool to and from school is the ultimate test of anger management. To her credit, in the course of carpooling dozens of nasty, whiny, relentless children (including our own) thousands of miles over some 20 years, Julie never once ejected, flattened, or even spanked any of her young reprobates, although what she thought about doing is another matter. Compared to that unblemished record, her driving lapses, like wrecking her mother's brand-spanking new Oldsmobile on Christmas day and nailing an innocent little canoe in our driveway, are relatively minor—except for a few bizarre incidents that "could only happen to Julie."

The first occurred several years ago while we were in California driving to Yosemite National Park (and while Ginger and Will and their 400 guests were destroying our house in New Orleans during the infamous "parents-are-out-of-town party"). Julie was driving on a lonely, winding two-lane highway when it circled right around a blind turn but we went straight, crossed the oncoming lane and left the road at a good rate of speed, and then crashed sideways through a barbed-wire fence before coming to a stop. However, we counted ourselves very lucky (not yet knowing what was going on in New Orleans at that moment) because we missed a large 18-wheeler in the oncoming lane by 15 seconds and did not roll over while sliding sideways across a boulder-strewn field. Although we weren't hurt, our rental car was in bad shape. The barbs on the fence left deep gouges across the hood and top. Far worse was that dreadful hissing sound from two of the tires that had been punctured, but our luck held. Before the tires went flat, we just managed to find a nearby town and, better yet, an open gas station with two matching tires, even though it was a Sunday and the Fourth of July. Those funny stripes all across the car did attract some quizzical looks later in San Francisco, but on the other hand, they made it much easier to find the car in a big parking lot and did not cost us a dime because of the rental insurance we bought, for once.

Which leaves the still-unanswered question of why the car left the road. Julie has always insisted that a green-colored snake flew in her open window and distracted her, although we had the car for another week and never did find the beast. However, as a lawyer who believes that life on Earth is subject to the often-spooky whims of purely random chance, I must admit that the absence of any tangible evidence does not prove anything because a flying snake that suddenly appears out of nowhere could, by definition, disappear the same way.

We now turn from mythical creatures of Julie's vivid imagination to real live critters. In the spring of 2005, before Hurricane Katrina, Julie's beloved Honda became so infested by vicious little gnats that it was uninhabitable (just like our previous Chevy wagon, "The Great White Whale," that was overrun by hordes of fat roaches feasting on our then-young kids' crumbs; after no luck with aerosol bombs and pest control operators, we negotiated a time-share compromise with the roaches, who ruled the roost undisturbed at night but left us alone during the daytime). We tried everything on the gnats in Julie's Honda, without success. Finally, to my dismay, Julie asked her good friend Murray if she had any ideas. Julie and Murray are both lovely, incredible individuals, but run for cover whenever they put their heads together on some harebrained scheme, like accidentally dying their hair bright green as teenagers with some kind of Mongolian beetle juice. What they did to the poor Honda was no exception, unfortunately. To kill the gnats, they scattered several boxes of mothballs throughout the car and then closed it up tight for three days!

Well, the results were indeed spectacular. At night, Julie's car glowed with an eerie light and even seemed to vibrate a little. I thought it might explode. A small mushroom cloud was in fact released when we finally mustered enough nerve to open up the car again. The gnats of course were gone, vaporized no doubt, but at a terrible cost. The Honda was the epicenter of a Dead Zone—like Chernobyl, no living thing, not even stink bugs, dared come within 50 feet of it (which did at least keep the neighborhood dogs from soiling our lawn). The mailman threw our mail from the street. The neighbors shunned us. It literally took an Act of God to undo what the two ladies had wrought: those noxious fumes and Julie's beloved Honda both came to a violent end under five feet of Katrina floodwater.

The next automotive calamity occurred in Ireland when Julie used her ample charms (not on me) to redeem herself after locking the only key in our rental car. Why she had the key is still a mystery, because she had lasted a mere 15 minutes behind the wheel before refusing ever again to drive where left is right, the roads have no lines or shoulders, the road signs are unreadable, the frequent roundabouts are lawless, no one else knows how to drive, and the sheep are everywhere.

Anyway, because it was safer than driving, we hiked a good bit in Ireland and even climbed its tallest peak, Carrauntoohil. On the day in question, our destination was a well-known trail with a nice pub located conveniently at the trailhead. After parking and using the pub's bathrooms, Julie must have gone back to get something in the car when she accidentally locked the keys inside. She was frantic, poor thing, but I admittedly was less than sympathetic. And I had little confidence in Julie's "I'll show you" assertion that she'd take care of the problem. While I started on my first of three pints at the bar to allegedly "figure out what to do," she disappeared outside and went to work. Only later did I learn that she stood by the car and played "a damsel in distress" to perfection, crying woefully and wringing her hands. Soon she had attracted a crowd of about a dozen local lads inspired to help this sweet, pretty, and seemingly alone (she probably removed her wedding ring) lass, so they proceeded to eventually dismantle one of the car doors. That's when I, halfway through my second pint, made the mistake of looking outside and seeing (1) the car door in pieces on the ground and (2) my happy wife surrounded by a bunch of proud and smitten-looking Irishmen. I immediately ordered a third pint.

By the time I finished my last beer and went outside, the reassembled door was back on the car and Julie was bestowing thanks and flirting shamelessly with each of her gallant saviors. The sudden appearance of her husband was of course most unwelcome by everyone, especially Julie. But after I apologized and she eventually pardoned me, we enjoyed a beautiful hike together and then wet our whistles with a couple of pints at the pub. Apparently it was a tourist destination, because we watched with amusement as a busload of American tourists were herded inside, stood by the bar drinking beer and taking pictures for exactly 20 minutes, and were then herded out again for their next stop. What a pity, especially in Ireland, which is unique as it is because of the wonderful people who live there.

Julie is also the hero of the next story and I, alas, am the villain again. My dirty deed this time was nothing more than persuading Julie to take my car in for a brake tag inspection, which doesn't sound so bad, does it? Well, in all

JUST JULIE

fairness, I should probably give you a little more information. My car (as opposed to Julie's) was a true rattle-trap: one of the original VW Bugs that was a mere 16 years old and had been through one of our many floods before Katrina. In the last year, the reverse gear had stopped working most of the time, the windows often fell down into the door, the lights were erratic at best, and the car sounded like a tank. Perhaps I should have mentioned those problems to Julie, but then she would have never agreed to my request. So we exchanged cars and I went off to work, with fingers crossed and a guilty conscience.

Julie wisely enlisted our daughter Casey to go with her to the brake tag station. The inspector was an older gentleman who unfortunately had a very soft voice, which became another problem because Julie's been totally deaf in her left ear since a waterskiing accident at age 16. As a result, she couldn't hear the instructions from the inspector on her left side, so Casey had to climb halfway through her window, pivot to face the inspector, and then relay his instructions to Julie's good right ear through the window. And the old car, right on cue, chose to ignore his directions and proceed in her own way, stopping to rest every few feet, to the inspector's mounting frustration (since it was almost closing time), Julie's mounting stress (cursing [expletives deleted] about her "no-good husband's no-good car"), and Casey's total amusement ("What a hoot!"). Well, the inspector finally ended his and Julie's agony by issuing a brake tag even before all the testing was completed. Once again, Julie (with an assist from Casey) had managed to work a minor miracle that would have been impossible for me, but I still got what I deserved that evening when she "sentenced" me to the usual 30 days of laundry duty. I was lucky it wasn't worse.

(It's truly shameful how humans abuse their cars, often in needless and bizarre ways. During a weekend canoe trip with friends on Black Creek in Mississippi, we watched a teenager try to impress his girlfriend by driving an open, military-style jeep across the wide, shallow river. He didn't make it. The poor jeep stalled in about four feet of water midway across. As we paddled quietly by, the very wet and unhappy passenger was colorfully expressing her outrage at her soon to be ex-boyfriend.)

LEECHES, LOVERS, BEARS, AND CHOCOLATE PUDDING

Sleepwalking And Celebrities

There is a connection of sorts between the two, but it is subtle and may require your full attention. Let's start with sleepwalking. That's something that Julie did frequently as a child, but of course no one warned me. I discovered it one night after Julie had gone to bed and I was downstairs in our living room working with an expert witness in preparation for trial the next day, when Julie came *hopping*, like a kangaroo in a negligee, through the living room and into the kitchen. Her eyes were open but she was obviously sound asleep. Luckily, my witness didn't call for a paddy wagon. According to her later explanation, Julie dreamed I was meeting downstairs with Henry Kissinger (a celebrity, in case you didn't notice) and did not want to disturb us, so she thought about something Henry and I wouldn't notice and came up with a kangaroo! Actually, her imitation of a kangaroo was almost believable, except for the negligee.

I was better prepared for Julie's nocturnal expeditions after that. And I already knew she had very vivid dreams because, unlike me, she'd always remember them when she woke up and talk to me about them.[‡] A good example is the dream that she and I were camping out in the mountains and asleep in a tent when Nature called her and she did what she always did in that situation: I woke up to see Julie squatting beside our bed in midstream and sound asleep. The spot cleaned up easily enough but poor Mama dog, with her sensitive nose, sniffed Julie's "mark" for days and looked seriously worried about the prospect of some canine competitor in the household. In a sequel, Julie dreamed she was in a hotel but could not find a bathroom, so she apparently sleepwalked out of our bedroom, closed the door behind her, and then returned to knock on the door, which woke me up. When I opened the bedroom door, my sound-asleep wife said "Excuse me, sir. Is there a bathroom on this floor?" The rug escaped that time. And while vacationing in a rental house in Orange Beach, Alabama, I woke up just in time to catch Julie going down the front steps for a neighborhood stroll

---

[‡] I remembered just *one* dream in 73 years of dreaming. In that dream, I was all decked out in tails and getting ready to perform Brahms' Second Piano Concerto as soloist with the New York Philharmonic at Carnegie Hall. As I walked onstage to a thunderous ovation, it suddenly occurred to me that I (a) didn't know the first thing about playing a piano; and (b) could not read music. I was in the middle of explaining that to my shocked fans when I fortunately woke up.

in a flimsy nightgown, again sound asleep. Life with Julie is always an adventure, day and night.

Although she never revealed any of the lurid details to me, Julie often dreamed of the three great heartthrobs in her life, Paul Newman, Paul McCartney, and the young John Travolta of Urban Cowboy fame. Despite golden opportunities with both Pauls, her love was unrequited in all three cases. Julie's encounter with Mr. McCartney was much more intimate than the one with Mr. Newman, which I'll therefore save for later.

We met the McCartneys at an invitation-only reception before an exhibition of Linda's fine photography (of The Beatles primarily) at Joshua Pailet's gallery in the French Quarter. After going through an informal receiving line, I headed straight back to the bar, thinking Julie was right behind me. Well, she had better things to do. Instead of sticking with me, she and Paul Baby had drifted off to a quiet corner and allegedly talked alone for a full hour about raising children (presumably not together, but one never knows), according to Julie's suspiciously evasive account. She claimed Paul Dear "wanted her advice" about raising his 16-year-old daughter Chelsea who was then out roaming the Quarter with a chaperone (and is now a successful fashion designer). Although Julie was very nonchalant about her little tete-a-tete with Sir Paul, she's never whistled so much in her whole life.

Julie also made a real impression, mostly physical, on the actor Walter Matthau. It's common knowledge that the ladies' bathrooms in the Broadway theaters are packed to the gills during intermissions. On this one occasion, Julie barely got there in time and then raced back to her seat before the lights went out. As she turned a corner at breakneck speed, she slammed into Walter and almost knocked him down. Julie was quite embarrassed but her victim was extremely gracious, despite his painful ribs. And much earlier, when she was a teenager working a summer job as a secretary, she met the New Orleans singer Fats Domino and even took some dictation from him.

By way of a sneak preview of what's coming in the next section, I'll tell you a little something about Julie and bathtubs. They have always played a bigger role than normal in Julie's life because she thinks of them as not only places to bathe but also (a) to sleep; and (b) to meet celebrities. It was in a bathtub that she, at a tender age, befriended a charming young man (definitely not me) who did in fact become quite famous and powerful later. I mention that little tidbit for the sole purpose of proving the connection between sleepwalking, celebrities, and bathtubs, so the details of that particular tryst are not important.

The Bravest Person I Know

Julie's courage in confronting her Alzheimer's is extraordinary, but that's the way she's always been throughout the 50 years I've known her. She's brave in her own quiet, humble way, just doing what has to be done, regardless of the risks or pressures, and then moving on as if it was nothing. Never once has Julie ever bragged about her heroics. Here are a few examples of that wonderful courage, with the caveat that there are undoubtedly many others I can't remember in my dotage.

It probably all started at around age five, when Julie ate her first raw oyster at Manale's Restaurant to please her beloved father. This may not sound like a big deal in a city where raw oysters are ubiquitous, but try to imagine how scary it must have been for such a little girl to actually swallow one of those slimy things. Later in life, she dealt just as bravely with even slimier things, like leeches, which must be vilest of all creatures. Again, just imagine dozens of them crawling up your legs and sucking your blood, then pulling them out of your skin one by one with your fingers and getting back into the leech-infested water. Julie did that over and over again for hours, without a complaint, during our canoe trip in Quetico, Canada (see story entitled "Leeches, Lovers, Bears, and Chocolate Pudding"). After that, it was probably a cinch for her to help me clean ducks I'd shot hunting, even though that required her to cut open their bellies, reach inside with her bare hands, and rip out their still-warm hearts, livers, and other internal organs, which she did without any qualms.

There are many other examples more perilous than oysters, leeches, and ducks. Flying and heights always made Julie very uneasy, so you'd think she would stay far away from skydiving, hot-air ballooning, mountain climbing, and high ski lifts. Nope. In every case, her fears were trumped by her love of adventure and willingness to try anything new. Although the skydiving was simulated, it was still pretty darn scary to jump into a void and float on a column of air. Julie did that in December of 2010, four full years after her Alzheimer's was diagnosed. That was also the year we and two friends took our first ride in a hot-air balloon and soared without engine, wings, or steering wheel high over New England (followed by a sumptuous celebration with champagne). And our canoe trip in Quetico involved flying on a small seaplane (with canoe strapped to the pontoons) to a remote lake in the Canadian woods.

Julie jumped at any chance to hike the mountains of Colorado, New England, and Europe, which sometimes required her to (a) ascend and descend a steep rock-face on her hands and knees (Ireland and New Hampshire); (b) traverse narrow ridges on slippery snow or loose scree (Colorado); (c) jump from boulder to boulder going up and down at 14,000 feet (Colorado); and (d) walk on glaciers and trails right next to long drop-offs (Switzerland). The narrow, dusty trails going into and out of the Grand Canyon were also quite intimidating. Even worse for Julie were those first few rides in open chairlifts up ski mountains, especially when they stopped in mid-air over deep ravines (Buttermilk at Aspen) and dangled there ominously in the wind, but she overcame her initial fears and continued to ski even with Alzheimer's.

Julie loved almost everything about the Great Outdoors and accepted the attendant risks without hesitation. Whether it was (a) being trapped uphill by a rain-swollen river high up in the Rocky Mountains; or (b) canoeing over waterfalls on the Chattooga River of *Deliverance* fame; or (c) running pell-mell off of high mountaintops and ridges to escape lightning; or (d) spending three days of our honeymoon in the Rockies with an armed wife-killer, Julie never flinched or wavered. (For more details, see story entitled "Out and About in the Great Outdoors.")

On two outdoor occasions, she proved her willingness to risk her own life to save our children and even me. We started taking our kids backpacking into the Colorado Rockies in the Bicentennial Year of 1976 when they were 5, 7, and 10 years old. During one such trip a few years later, our little gas-filled stove suddenly erupted in flames. I was some distance away, but all three kids were standing near the stove and might have been hurt badly if it exploded, so my intrepid, quick-thinking wife grabbed the flaming object with her bare hands and heaved it far away, like the brave soldiers who save their buddies from live grenades.

LEECHES, LOVERS, BEARS, AND CHOCOLATE PUDDING

And while Julie and I were canoeing a flooded Mulberry River in the Ozarks of Arkansas with friends, we literally wrapped our aluminum canoe around a tree on a submerged island in the middle of the river. When I tried to cross a deeper channel to shore, I was swept downstream by the very strong current and got tangled up in a willow grove, where I almost drowned. Julie watched this and was just about to jump into the treacherous water to come save me when I caught hold of a tree and pulled myself ashore. If she had done that, she probably would have drowned herself, but I have no doubt she was willing to risk her own life to save mine. The same thing happened to her when she started across the channel, but this time our friends reeled her in like a fish with the help of a rope tied around her waist. (Again, see "Out and About in the Great Outdoors" for more detail.)

Julie's encounter with the black bear in Canada is only the beginning of her bear history. *Night of the Grizzlies* (1969) is the true account of two young women camping in Wyoming who were attacked and killed by grizzly bears while asleep in their respective tents. Unfortunately, Julie started it when I was away, so she wound up sleeping in the bathtub because the book was so terrifying to someone who had already spent the night in a tent in dark woods with wild bears around and she felt safer in the tub for some odd reason.[§]

Casey, then 7, found her asleep in the tub the next morning. After hearing Julie describe it, the book sounded much too scary for me to read. But I did reassure her that there were *absolutely* no grizzly bears in Colorado (as opposed to the smaller, nicer black bears that I knew were no match for her) because they had all been driven north into Wyoming, Montana, and Canada.

Well, I turned out to be wrong, not for the first or last time. Just days after that 1976 backpacking trip with the kids in Colorado, we read about a hunter who had been jumped and mauled by a grizzly bear before killing it only 50 miles or so from where we'd just been camping. Thinking the newspaper was wrong about the type of bear, I called the nearest ranger station out there and was informed it was definitely a grizzly. (The poor hunter, pictured in the paper

---

[§] Julie spent another night in a motel bathtub while traveling with a good friend whose loud snoring drove Julie to seek a quieter spot in the bathroom. Not surprisingly, her sleepy friend almost flipped out when she went to the bathroom in the middle of the night and saw the body in the tub. Apparently Julie sleeps quite soundly in bathtubs.

with bandages from head to toe, had been charged with killing an "endangered species," but the charges were later dropped after a public outcry.) Between the book she read and the chance there might be other grizzlies in the Colorado mountains (none have been reported since then), I was sure Julie would balk at any further camping there, especially with the kids, but I was wrong again. Rock that she is, Julie never hesitated to go back to Colorado and camp in remote mountain sites, which we did for another 20 years.

Julie's amazing courage was not limited to her outdoor exploits. When Casey was 10, she fell off her bike and fractured her skull. To make a bad situation even worse, in the car with Julie on the way to Ochsner Hospital, Casey went totally blind from her injury (she later recovered her sight). Although Julie was never good with directions, she proved her mettle that day by driving Casey across town to the ER under immense pressure and may well have saved our daughter's life.

There are many other examples of Julie's fortitude but I'll just mention three. She dropped out of college after two years to help with her very sick father. Sometime later, with three young kids at home and a teaching job, Julie returned to college part-time, worked hard, and graduated *cum laude* from Tulane University in 1996 at age 54, a proud moment for the entire family. She was just

LEECHES, LOVERS, BEARS, AND CHOCOLATE PUDDING

as undaunted by the overt hostility we often encountered in St. Tammany Parish, a KKK stronghold, when we took inner-city kids in the TEEP program over to Covington to experience the rivers and woods every summer for 30 years, starting when our own children were still babies. And finally, it took a lot of guts (or whatever) for Julie to *start* a Play-Doh war with several grandchildren during a family reunion at a Colorado ranch. She lost that war but somehow survived, although our rental house was the big loser.

But it's the way Julie has confronted her Alzheimer's that really shows how strong she is. She knew exactly what the diagnosis meant for her. She knew from that dreadful day in 2006 that she would gradually lose her ability to remember anything, to process sensory information, to communicate normally, to control her bodily functions, to read and do all the other things she loved, and to enjoy her family and friends. Julie knew she would eventually become isolated from the rest of the world in her own mental cage until she dies from her untreatable condition. And yet I've never heard Julie complain even once about how unfair it is. Instead, she has lived her life to the fullest extent possible for her under the circumstances. She continued to travel, hike, ski, exercise, and socialize for as long as she could after her diagnosis. She continued to care deeply about family and friends and anyone in the world who is suffering. Even after becoming a nursing care patient in 2011, Julie has remained generally upbeat, affectionate, cooperative, and happy, even funny at times. The

JUST JULIE

last eight years are, to me at least, the ultimate proof of just how amazingly brave she is.

However, in order to be honest with you readers, I must reluctantly confess that Julie did in fact lose her nerve on one occasion, just one, in the last half century. It happened at the Clark Art Institute in Williamstown, Massachusetts. As we were walking down a long hallway, who should come walking from the other end right towards us but Paul Newman, the real love of Julie's life, and his wife Joanne Woodward. No one else was around, so I initially worried that Julie might throw herself on Paul and profess her undying devotion. What she did instead was to panic, no doubt triggered by the depth of her feelings, and turn quickly aside to gaze with feigned interest at a large Greek statue of a strapping male nude whose private parts happened to be directly in front of Julie's unseeing eyes. The Newmans passed by with very slight smiles on their remarkable faces. Julie kicked herself for years after missing that golden opportunity.

* * *

I want to leave you with a positive picture of my beloved Julie, so come with me to the stunning town of Telluride, Colorado, where the two of us went to ski one winter many years ago. The action took place near closing time in a nice bar with only a couple of other patrons left. After a good day of skiing and two large bottles each of Chimay Ale from Belgium (plus the altitude), we were feeling absolutely no pain. Then, out of the blue, my usually shy wife took off her shoes, put a rose between her teeth, climbed up on our table, and proceeded to dance to the jukebox music and the applause of the employees and patrons both. Ever since, that image of Julie dancing on the tabletop always reminds me of the innocent and authentic *complexity* of the woman I love as much now as the day we married almost 50 years ago.

THE MYSTERIOUS CHARM BRACELETS

Why "mysterious"? Because *two* gold bracelets full of charms simply vanished from the exact same spot in our house at the same time and then *one* of them turned up out of the blue in another spot a year later. We'll have more on that little mystery later, but first a word about the idea of an anniversary charm bracelet(s).

If you've read any other of the many tales about our family misadventures, you may remember that our first year of marriage was filled with mishaps and mayhem. Within two weeks of tying the knot, Julie and I had accidentally trashed two Uptown houses that absent friends had so generously lent to us for a week each. That reign of terror was followed by three nights alone on top of a Colorado mountain with an armed stranger who allegedly had just killed his wife, and then two nights in Las Vegas that bankrupted us for the next two years. After that, we lived underground in an airless apartment in Charlottesville and Julie taught nursery school with an Amazon woman who killed her husband with a poison mushroom and often sent Julie home with a squirrel or two she had caught and killed for dinner (we buried them properly). I'm sure there are many other similar memories from that first year that I've simply repressed. It was that kind of year.

So what better way to celebrate the fact that we survived it than a charm bracelet to remind us of the highlights, good or bad? And if that first year was any indication of what was awaiting us, a charm bracelet would provide a record of the "slings and arrows of outrageous fortune" that were sure to find us in the future. As luck would have it, after such a tumultuous year, our first wedding anniversary happened to occur during a wonderful and relatively peaceful trip to Europe, so a charm celebrating that happy occasion was the obvious choice. That's how the annual ritual got started, even though Julie wore very little jewelry generally.

Since the chosen charm remained a secret from Julie and the children until it was unveiled on the anniversary date of July 9, the kids always engaged in a lot of guessing games, attempted bribery, and other forms of collusion to find out ahead of time. Every year of our marriage seemed just as eventful as the previous one (unlike my fairly routine life before Julie happily changed it all for the better), so the kids rarely guessed right. Of course it didn't make their task any easier that I enjoyed fooling them by picking very unusual charms. It was and still is fun for everyone in the family.

By 1997, there were two bracelets and a total of 32 charms. Then they all vanished into thin air, without any possible explanation. Or so it seemed. With the benefit of a little hindsight, I discovered the villain and it was me. This is what I remembered doing: As a precaution before leaving the house empty during a vacation trip out of town (we had no safe), I hid *both* bracelets in the toe of *one* old boot that no burglar would steal and then promptly forgot about it. Shortly after we came home, I had another harebrained idea of donating old clothing and stuff that we no longer used to the Salvation Army, including those old boots. And that's where the charm bracelets wound up, unbeknownst to us until we started looking for them weeks later. Mystery solved! Or so it seemed.

Hoping against hope that some honest soul at the Salvation Army had found the bracelets and turned them in, we raced out to the thrift store but there was no sign of the lost bracelets. Then we made the rounds of almost all the pawn shops in New Orleans (which was an interesting experience, as you can imagine), thinking that someone may have hocked the bracelets, but again, nothing turned up. Thus it was that some lucky employee or customer of the Salvation Army Thrift Store had wound up with about $6,000 worth of 14-karat gold jewelry inside a $5 boot. Or so it seemed. Our insurance claim for the amount listed in our policy was duly paid, which brought that unhappy chapter of our lives to an end. Or so it seemed....

...Until one day a year or so later, when *one* of the missing bracelets magically reappeared. We found it in some rarely opened desk drawer. But the other bracelet was never found, despite ransacking the house looking for it after finding the first one. That itself was puzzling because we *always* kept the two bracelets together, except when I took one into the jeweler to attach a new charm to it, but the jeweler confirmed that had not happened during the period in question. So finding one bracelet at home without the other was an even deeper mystery—and I was not the villain this time. I still think about this 22 years later

THE MYSTERIOUS CHARM BRACELETS

but have never come up with any kind of possible explanation, other than some guardian angel gone rogue.

Julie and I refunded half of the insurance proceeds to a baffled insurer. And before finding the one bracelet, we had worked with our friend Ken at the jewelry store to replace all of the missing bracelets and charms, but in a few cases, we had to substitute a new charm for the original if it was no longer produced. And now we have two bracelets (the found original and the replacement) representing the same years of our marriage.

As of July 9, 2019, our anniversary collection consists of four bracelets and 68 charms, including the one original bracelet with 11 charms that we found after losing it. And we have a safe to put them in and keep us from "donating" them unwittingly to the Salvation Army. Here they are, year by year, starting from our wedding date of July 9, 1964, plus a little outside history to illustrate the times:

Year 1 (7/64 to 7/65)

The first charm was a Swiss **fondue bowl** because Julie and I celebrated our first wedding anniversary while traveling in Europe where we discovered the pleasures of fondue. (That charm was replaced in 1997 by a replica of the **Eiffel Tower**.) Also, Julie got pregnant (which was first diagnosed as sciatica) and promptly demolished four very big (three scoops each!) hot fudge sundaes after a dinner out. The sad news was that her beloved father died. I graduated from the University of Virginia Law School. We accidentally trashed two houses borrowed from absent friends and then fled to Colorado and Las Vegas for a disastrous belated honeymoon.

In other news of that period, the U. S. initiated military action in Vietnam after the alleged Gulf of Tonkin incident. Martin Luther King led the legendary civil rights march in Selma, Alabama. Johnson defeated Goldwater in the presidential election. A first-class stamp cost 5 cents. *My Fair Lady* won the Oscar for Best Picture.

LEECHES, LOVERS, BEARS, AND CHOCOLATE PUDDING

Year 2 (7/65 to 7/66)

The anniversary charm was a **pair of baby shoes** to celebrate the birth of our daughter Katherine Carnel (Casey) Penick. We moved into an apartment on Walmsley Avenue in New Orleans and I attended Tulane University Law School for one year. Hurricane Betsy hit New Orleans and left us without power for about two weeks (fortunately before Casey was born).

During that same year, the Watts riots occurred in Los Angeles. Medicare came into being. Israel won the Six-Day War against Egypt, Syria, and Jordan. The Best Picture was *The Sound of Music*.

Year 3 (7/66 to 7/67)

I was admitted to the practice of law in Louisiana, so the charm was a miniature **scales of justice**. I began practicing as an associate in the New Orleans firm of Lemle & Kelleher. We moved into a shotgun house on Audubon Street.

Thurgood Marshall became the first African American Justice on the Supreme Court. The birth control pill was introduced to the public. The Oscar went to *A Man for All Seasons*.

Year 4 (7/67 to 7/68)

The charm was a **bicycle** to celebrate the Easter picture in our local newspaper of Casey riding behind Julie in a baby seat in Audubon Park. Julie became pregnant again. This was also the year that our dog Mitchell ate my boss' wife's coat while they were visiting us as our guests.

Martin Luther King and Robert Kennedy were assassinated. North Vietnam launched the Tet Offensive which changed the tide of the Vietnam War. The infamous My Lai Massacre occurred. The first human heart was transplanted. The cost of a stamp rose to 6 cents. *In the Heat of the Night* was voted the Best Picture.

THE MYSTERIOUS CHARM BRACELETS

Year 5 (7/68 to 7/69)

The charm was a **stork** to celebrate the birth of our daughter Virginia King (Ginger) Penick. Our other daughter, Casey, started going to school. We purchased a weekend home in Covington ("Piccadilly") on the Bogue Falaya River and started taking 9-to-11-year-old campers from the TEEP summer program there for the weekend.

Russia invaded Czechoslovakia in response to the Prague Spring under the liberal President Dubcek. The first nuclear non-proliferation treaty was signed. Nixon defeated Humphrey for President. The Best Picture was *Oliver!*

Year 6 (7/69 to 7/70)

The charm of a **ballerina** was dedicated to young Casey's funny and historic debut as a ballerina: after all of her dancing partners had left the stage as instructed, Casey walked to the front by herself looking for us and picking her nose. It was a truly special moment that brought the house down. I became a partner at Lemle & Kelleher.

Neil Armstrong became the first person to set foot on the moon. Four students were killed during anti-Vietnam War demonstrations at Kent State University. Ted Kennedy left the scene of his automobile accident at Chappaquidick while his passenger drowned. *Midnight Cowboy* won the Best Picture Oscar.

Year 7 (7/70 to 7/71)

Our son William Sydnor (Will) Penick, Jr. was born, so the charm was a **football**. We also moved into a new house on Bellaire Drive.

The Pentagon Papers were published. The Supreme Court approved the busing of students to achieve racial balance in schools. Stamp prices rose to 8 cents. The Best Picture was *Patton*.

LEECHES, LOVERS, BEARS, AND CHOCOLATE PUDDING

Year 8 (7/71 to 7/72)

The charm this year was a miniature **dog** because the wonderful mutt Mama joined our family. Our daughter Ginger started school.

President Nixon visited China. The weekly show *All in the Family* debuted on television. Republican operatives were caught trying to bug the Democratic National Committee headquarters at Watergate. The Oscar went to *The French Connection*.

Year 9 (7/72 to 7/73)

The charm was an **abacus** to celebrate the fact that Julie passed her required math course at UNO.

The U. S. ended its military operations in Vietnam. Eleven Israeli athletes were assassinated by Islamic terrorists at the Summer Olympics in Munich. The first space station was launched. Nixon was re-elected over McGovern. *The Godfather* won the Oscar.

Year 10 (7/73 to 7/74)

Julie and I took our first real ski trip to Taos, New Mexico, so the charm was a tiny **set of skis**.

Vice-President Agnew resigned in disgrace. President Nixon fired the special prosecutor investigating the Watergate matter (the "Saturday Night Massacre"). The Supreme Court legalized abortion in Roe vs. Wade. Israel won Yom Kippur War over Egypt and Syria. The heiress Patty Hearst was kidnapped. The price of a stamp rose to 10 cents. *The Sting* was selected Best Picture.

Year 11 (7/74 to 7/75)

The charm was a **shovel** to commemorate our first backyard vegetable garden, which was a limited success. Our son Will started school.

THE MYSTERIOUS CHARM BRACELETS

President Nixon resigned after the House of Representatives impeached him and Vice-President Ford became President. North Vietnam took control of South Vietnam. The Best Picture award went to *The Godfather, Part II*.

Year 12 (7/75 to 7/76)

This was the year that Julie began her long career teaching at the Jewish Community Center kindergarten, so to commemorate that auspicious event, she received a miniature **blackboard** as her charm.

Carter defeated Ford in the presidential election. Israeli commandos freed the hostages held by Islamic terrorists at the Entebbe Airport in Uganda. The cost of a stamp rose to 13 cents. *One Flew Over the Cuckoo's Nest* was voted the Best Picture.

Year 13 (7/76 to 7/77)

The charm was a **covered wagon** to celebrate our bicentennial trip to Colorado in a very crowded car with all three kids (then 10, 7, and 5) for their first backpacking adventure in the Rockies (although it would be hard to forget that particular odyssey, with its customary ups-and-downs).

That was also the year of our first landing on Mars. Deng Ziaoping came to power in China and started to reform its economy. *Rocky* won the Oscar for Best Picture.

Year 14 (7/77 to 7/78)

All five of us wound up sleeping in one bedroom for a couple of weeks during a renovation of the house, so the choice of an **open sardine can** as the anniversary charm was a fitting reminder.

Elvis Presley died. The first test-tube baby was born. A stamp cost 15 cents. The Oscar was won by *Annie Hall*.

LEECHES, LOVERS, BEARS, AND CHOCOLATE PUDDING

Year 15 (7/78 to 7/79)

Because Julie started jogging seriously, her charm that year was a **roadrunner**.

A potentially catastrophic accident occurred at the Three Mile Island nuclear power plant in Pennsylvania. Israel and Egypt signed a peace treaty at Camp David with President Carter presiding. Members of Jim Jones' cult committed mass suicide in Guyana. Margaret Thatcher became Prime Minister of Britain. Pope John Paul II was elected. *The Deer Hunter* was voted Best Picture.

Year 16 (7/79 to 7/80)

During the course of a driving vacation to pick up Casey at the Nantahala Outdoor Center (where she learned to kayak very well), we panned for gold on one occasion, so the charm was a **gold panner**.

The U. S. Embassy in Tehran, Iran, was seized by followers of Ayatollah Khomeini and the staff held for several months. Russia invaded Afghanistan. The 24-hour news channel CNN started. The Oscar went to *Kramer vs. Kramer*.

Year 17 (7/80 to 7/81)

The charm was a **pair of dice** to celebrate our purchase of a condo in Breckenridge, Colorado. That particular choice of charm was sadly prophetic, because the collapse in oil prices cut the market price of our condo in half only six months after we bought it.

Reagan won the presidency over Carter. AIDS was first identified. The first personal computer was introduced. Stamp prices jumped to 18 cents. The Best Picture was *Ordinary People*.

Year 18 (7/81 to 7/82)

Julie and I enjoyed a picture-perfect week of backpacking around Lake El Dorado in the Rockies and saw an eagle, which is why her charm that year was an **eagle**.

THE MYSTERIOUS CHARM BRACELETS

Sandra Day O'Connor became the first woman on the Supreme Court. President Sadat of Egypt was assassinated. The cost of stamps rose again, to 20 cents. *Chariots of Fire* won the Oscar.

Year 19 (7/82 to 7/83)

The charm was a **gavel** because Julie this year got involved in several community projects and on a couple of boards.
 Princess Grace (formerly the actress Grace Kelly) died in an automobile accident. CDs were introduced to eventually replace vinyl records. *Gandhi* was voted Best Picture.

Year 20 (7/83 to 7/84)

On Christmas Day, our three kids blindfolded and "kidnapped" Julie and me and then abandoned us in a large room with champagne and snacks at the wonderful old Cornstalk Hotel in the French Quarter, so the charm was a **Christmas stocking** to honor that special occasion. (That charm was replaced by a **Christmas tree** in 1997.) We ate pizza for Christmas dinner because most restaurants were closed and wound up watching the new movie *Dune*, which Ginger and Will were also watching, unbeknownst to us, but they knew we were there because they recognized Julie's cough. This was also the year that Casey went off to Kenyon College in Ohio as a freshman.
 U. S. invaded tiny Grenada. Two hundred and thirty-seven Marines were killed in their Beirut barracks by a terrorist bomb. A commercial jetliner that strayed over Russian territory by mistake was shot down by a Soviet fighter plane. The Oscar went to *Terms of Endearment*.

Year 21 (7/84 to 7/85)

To celebrate our first trip to New York City with all of the children, the charm was a replica of the **Statue of Liberty**.
 Reagan won a second term over Mondale. Gorbachev became the Soviet leader and started initiating reforms. Islamic terrorists hijacked a commercial

LEECHES, LOVERS, BEARS, AND CHOCOLATE PUDDING

airliner and a large cruise ship. The New Orleans World's Fair took place. The price of a stamp went up 22 cents. *Amadeus* won for Best Picture.

Year 22 (7/85 to 7/86)

The charm was a **bowling ball** because Julie and I started taking our kids' dates and friends out to bowl as a way of getting to know them better in a relaxed setting. (In 1997 it was replaced by a **set of bowling pins**.)

There was a catastrophic accident at a nuclear power plant in Chernobyl, then in the Soviet Union, now Ukraine. The space shuttle *Challenger* exploded. The United States bombed Libya. The Oscar went to *Out of Africa*.

Year 23 (7/86 to 7/87)

The original charm of a **pill jar** was to commemorate the sad fact that all of us were sick at one time or the other throughout most of the year. (That charm was lost in 1997 and was replaced by a **druggist's mortar and pestle**.) With Will's departure for The Gunnery in Connecticut, Julie and I had an empty house for the first time.

The secret Iran-Contra arms operations were revealed. Robert Bork's nomination to the Supreme Court was rejected by the Senate. *Platoon* was selected Best Picture.

Year 24 (7/87 to 7/88)

Julie and I took up golf as a later-in-life hobby, so the charm was a **golf bag and clubs**. This was also the year of Ginger and Will's infamous Parents-Are-Out-Of-Town Party with 400 "guests."

The United States military in the Persian Gulf shot down an Iranian commercial airliner by mistake. The dangers of global warming became a major topic in the news and in Congress. Stamp prices were raised to 25 cents. The Oscar was awarded to *The Last Emperor*.

THE MYSTERIOUS CHARM BRACELETS

Year 25 (7/88 to 7/89)

The charm was a **bottle of champagne in a bucket** to celebrate our 25th anniversary.

    The senior Bush was elected president over Dukakis. Chinese students took over Tiananmen Square in Beijing in a rally for democracy and thousands were killed by government forces. *Rain Man* won the Oscar.

Year 26 (7/89 to 7/90)

A **trophy cup** was the charm to honor Will's winning of The Gunnery Cup at his graduation.

    It was quite a year: The Berlin Wall came down. The Soviet Union's domination of eastern European countries was ended. The internet was established. The United States invaded Panama. Nelson Mandela was released from jail in South Africa. The Exxon Valdez oil tanker ruptured off the coast of Alaska. The Best Picture was *Driving Miss Daisy*.

Year 27 (7/90 to 7/91)

The **graduation cap** charm commemorated Ginger's graduation from Washington College.

    Iraq invaded Kuwait and in turn a coalition led by the United States invaded Iraq in the First Gulf War. East and West Germany were reunited under a democratic government. Margaret Thatcher resigned as prime minister of Great Britain. The cost of a stamp rose to 29 cents. *Dances with Wolves* was the choice as Best Picture.

Year 28 (7/91 to 7/92)

A **bride and groom** charm represented Casey's marriage to Keith Hayes. (It was later replaced by a **wedding cake**.)

    The Soviet Union broke up. Boris Yeltsin became the first elected president of Russia. The Cold War ended after 46 years. Anita Hill accused

LEECHES, LOVERS, BEARS, AND CHOCOLATE PUDDING

Clarence Thomas of sexual harassment during his Supreme Court confirmation hearing. *The Silence of the Lambs* won the Oscar.

Year 29 (7/92 to 7/93)

Julie cut her beautiful and legendary long hair short, so what else could the charm be but a pair of miniature **scissors**?

Clinton defeated the incumbent president, Bush. The North American Free Trade Agreement (NAFTA) was signed. The World Trade Center was bombed by Islamic terrorists. Federal agents raided the compound of the Branch Davidian religious cult in Waco, Texas. The Best Picture was *Unforgiven*.

Year 30 (7/93 to 7/94)

Julie received two anniversary charms this year. One was a **chapel** to commemorate Ginger's marriage to John Inmon. The other was a **diploma** representative of Will's graduation from Carnegie-Mellon University.

The European Union was created. The terrible genocidal massacre occurred in Rwanda. Nelson Mandela was elected the first black president of South Africa. O. J. Simpson was arrested for the murder of his wife. The Oscar went to *Schindler's List*.

Year 31 (7/94 to 7/95)

The charm was a **lamb** because of our first trip to sheep-covered Ireland.

The Federal Building in Oklahoma City was bombed by a homegrown, right-wing terrorist, killing 168 people, including many children. The price of stamps was increased to 32 cents. *Forrest Gump* was chosen Best Picture.

Year 32 (7/95 to 7/96)

The charm was a **lamp of knowledge** to honor Julie's graduation *cum laude* from Tulane University at age 53, which all three of our proud children attended.

THE MYSTERIOUS CHARM BRACELETS

Dolly the sheep was cloned successfully. O. J. Simpson was acquitted by a jury of killing his wife. Israel's agreement to transfer the West Bank to Palestine was undone by Prime Minister Rabin's assassination shortly thereafter by an Israeli student. Peace finally came to Bosnia and Croatia. The Oscar was won by *Braveheart*.

<u>Year 33 (7/96 to 7/97)</u>

A **doe and fawn** was the charm to celebrate the birth of our first grandchild, Emma Marie Hayes (her middle name was my mother's name).

The incumbent president, Clinton, defeated Dole. The city of Hong Kong was returned to China by Great Britain. *The English Patient* was voted Best Picture.

<u>Year 34 (7/97 to 7/98)</u>

Will and I ran the New York City Marathon that year, but an **ambulance** was picked as the charm because I, while training for the marathon, got lost in Manhattan's Central Park and Julie, who suspected I was injured, was trying to get two officers in a police car to look for me when I finally showed up (and got a friendly talking-to by her new buddies).

President Clinton was charged in the Monica Lewinsky sex scandal. The Good Friday Accords ended years of violence between Catholics and Protestants in Northern Ireland. Most members of the European Union adopted a single currency, the euro. The Oscar went to *Titanic*.

<u>Year 35 (7/98 to 7/99)</u>

Julie earned a **sheepdog** as her charm after letting some sheep loose during a hike in Norway and laughing hysterically at my comical impersonation of a sheepdog running after the sheep.

The House of Representatives impeached President Clinton for lying about the Lewinsky matter but the Senate acquitted him. Two students attacked Columbine High School in Colorado and killed several students and teachers. Serbia started a war against Kosovo and NATO bombed the Serbian capital. Stamp prices rose to 33 cents. *Shakespeare in Love* was selected as Best Picture.

LEECHES, LOVERS, BEARS, AND CHOCOLATE PUDDING

Year 36 (7/99 to 7/00)

Julie and I took a harrowing boat ride from the west coast of Ireland to the remote island of Skellig Michael, which was filled with puffins (and rock huts dating back to the sixth century), so the charm was a **puffin**.

The human genome was deciphered. A supersonic Concorde jetliner crashed in Paris. The Oscar was awarded to *American Beauty*.

Year 37 (7/00 to 7/01)

The charm was a **baseball glove** to celebrate the birth of our grandson Ethan Sawyer Hayes. (It should have been a kayak or lacrosse stick.)

The junior Bush defeated Gore in the presidential election after the Supreme Court stopped the recounting of votes in Florida. The American naval vessel *Cole* was bombed by Al Qaeda terrorists in Yemen. Stamp prices were raised again, to 34 cents. *Gladiator* won the Oscar.

Year 38 (7/01 to 7/02)

To mark the 9/11 terrorist attacks on the World Trade Center and the Pentagon, Julie's charm was a **New York City firefighter's helmet**. We visited the site the following year and were especially moved by all of the pictures, postcards, notes, poems, and other remembrances on the picket fence around the nearby church that survived.

In response to the 9/11 attacks, the United States military attacked Al Qaeda and the Taliban in Afghanistan. Scandals and bankruptcies involving major American companies like Enron came to light. The cost of a stamp went up to 37 cents. *A Beautiful Mind* was named Best Picture.

THE MYSTERIOUS CHARM BRACELETS

Year 39 (7/02 to 7/03)

Julie's charm was a little **go-cart racer** to celebrate the birth of our grandson Aubrey James Inmon. (It should have been a rocket ship.)

The United States and Great Britain invaded and occupied Iraq in the Second Gulf War. A space probe confirmed that the Universe is 13.7 billion years old and consists of some unknown "dark" energy and matter. The space shuttle *Columbia* exploded. Boston's Cardinal Bernard Law resigned as a result of covering up the sex scandal within the Catholic Church. The Oscar went to *Chicago*.

Year 40 (7/03 to 7/04)

When Will married the lovely Sienna Oosterhouse, the obvious choice for an anniversary charm was a **swan**.

Iraq's former ruler Saddam Hussein was captured. Massachusetts became the first state to legalize gay marriage. The Best Picture was *The Lord of the Rings: The Return of the King*.

Year 41 (7/04 to 7/05)

After a wonderful walking trip through the Cotswolds in England, Julie received **St. George and the Dragon** as her charm.

The incumbent president, Bush, defeated Kerry. Israel ended its occupation of the Gaza Strip after 38 years. Angela Merkel became the first female chancellor of Germany. *Million Dollar Baby* won the Oscar.

Year 42 (7/05 to 7/06)

Another year of two charms: The first was a **koala bear** to celebrate the birth of our granddaughter Olivia St. Clair Inmon. The second charm, **Noah's Ark**, marked the flooding of New Orleans by Hurricane Katrina. Fortunately, we were in Williamstown at the time, but we did have five feet of dirty water in our house and lost just about everything on the first floor. We eventually sold the house as is to a neighbor and lived in Williamstown full time until the spring of 2008.

North Korea tested a nuclear device for the first time. A space probe spotted apparent water geysers on one of Saturn's moons. Thirty-nine cents was the new price of a stamp. The Best Picture was *Crash*.

Year 43 (7/06 to 7/07)

The charm was a **sunflower** to commemorate a wonderful trip to Tuscany in Italy. Sadly, it was in December of 2006 that Julie's Alzheimer's was diagnosed and she was started on a couple of drug trials at The Memory Clinic in Bennington, Vermont.

Pluto was dropped as a planet. Nancy Pelosi became the first female Speaker of the House. American and United Nations scientists concluded that global warming is caused by human activity. The cost of a stamp went up to 41 cents. *The Departed* won the Oscar.

Year 44 (7/07 to 7/08)

To celebrate the birth of our granddaughter Lucia Clothilde Penick, the charm selected was a **crown**.

A major economic meltdown in the United States (and all over the world) triggered massive government spending to contain the crisis. Fidel Castro stepped down as the ruler of Cuba after 49 years. In less than a year, stamp prices rose again, to 42 cents. *No Country for Old Men* was selected as the Best Picture.

Year 45 (7/08 to 7/09)

Julie and I had moved into Lambeth House of New Orleans only a few months before President Obama's inauguration in January of 2009 and still did not know a lot of the employees and fellow residents. After hearing his inaugural address that morning, we were sitting in the dining room to order lunch when the head waitress, Vanessa, asked us what we wanted to drink (meaning coffee, tea, or juice, since Lambeth House did not have a liquor license). I jokingly ordered

THE MYSTERIOUS CHARM BRACELETS

champagne to celebrate our new president. Vanessa smiled but didn't say a word, turned around and went back to the kitchen, and came out again with two glasses of champagne on a serving tray for us. When I asked where the champagne came from, she smiled again and said, "Never mind." I can only assume that Vanessa, who is African American, and the rest of the kitchen staff were also celebrating our first African American president. The looks on the faces of the other residents present made this a very special and comical moment for us, commemorated by little **champagne glasses** as the charm. We each had a second glass of champagne before finishing lunch.

(This amazing story did not end there. By the time President Obama was re-elected in 2012, Julie had moved out of Independent Living into Nursing Care. On the morning after his reelection, Vanessa surprised us by appearing in Julie's room with two glasses of champagne on a tray. The fact that she remembered what happened four years earlier and then went to the trouble of repeating this wonderful gesture was very moving for both of us. And then, because some or all of our kids were in town, she invited all of us into the kitchen before the dining room opened for dinner for glasses of champagne to celebrate the occasion, which was memorable.)

Obama became the first African American president after defeating McCain. Because of the ongoing recession, unemployment hit 8.1%. The new president opened trade with and travel to Cuba. Bernie Madoff pleaded guilty to a massive Ponzi scheme. A crippled commercial airliner landed safely in the middle of the Hudson River. Stamps now cost 44 cents. The Best Picture was *Slumdog Millionaire*.

Year 46 (7/09 to 7/10)

Some of the family tried simulated skydiving in Denver that year, which took place on the second level of a three-story tower with a huge ground-floor fan blowing air through the net that served as the second-story floor. Even with her Alzheimer's and mild fear of heights, my intrepid wife insisted on trying it. Her charm of course was a **skydiver**.

Obamacare passed Congress. A space probe found evidence of water on the moon. An oil rig off the Louisiana coast caught fire, killing and injuring a number of workers and releasing massive amounts of oil into the Gulf of Mexico. The Supreme Court ruled that the government cannot limit corporate spending on political campaigns. The unemployment rate hit 10%. The Oscar went to *The Hurt Locker*.

Year 47 (7/10 to 7/11)

The charm was a **rocking horse** to celebrate the birth of our granddaughter Pilar Julia Penick.

American troops killed Osama bin Laden in Pakistan. The Arab Spring began. An earthquake in Japan created a nuclear meltdown at the Fukushima Power Station. *The King's Speech* was voted Best Picture.

Year 48 (7/11 to 7/12)

All of the kids and grandkids visited New Orleans for Julie's December birthday and Christmas, so the charm was a **Christmas tree**. There was a memorable dinner of the whole family at Manale's Restaurant during that occasion.

Obama was re-elected over Romney. Hurricane Sandy devastated the East Coast. Obamacare was upheld by the Supreme Court. The price of a stamp was increased to 45 cents. The Best Picture was *The Artist*.

Year 49 (7/12 to 7/13)

The charm of a **ladybug** celebrated the birth of our granddaughter Isabel Marie Penick.

Pope Francis became the first Latin American pontiff. Twenty young children and a teacher were killed in a shooting at Sandy Hook School in Connecticut. Terrorists killed four Americans at our embassy in Benghazi, Libya. The Taliban shot and wounded a 14-year-old girl in Pakistan for championing the education of girls. Several people were killed or wounded by a bombing at the Boston Marathon. Stamps go up to 46 cents. *Argo* won the Oscar.

THE MYSTERIOUS CHARM BRACELETS

Year 50 (7/13 to 7/14)

The charm was a pair of **lovebirds** to commemorate our 50th wedding anniversary.

The civil war in Ukraine began and Russia annexed Crimea. ISIS forcefully occupied vast stretches of territory in Syria and Iraq. The price of a stamp jumped to 49 cents. *12 Years a Slave* was chosen as the Best Picture.

Year 51 (7/14 to 7/15)

The charm of a **heart** was chosen to celebrate our family: three generations of love from ages 2 to 74.

The Supreme Court approved gay marriage nationwide. A refugee crisis developed in Europe around people fleeing Africa and the Middle East. A white supremacist killed several worshippers at a historic black church in South Carolina. The Oscar was awarded to *Birdman (or the Unexpected Virtue of Ignorance)*.

Year 52 (7/15 to 7/16)

To mark my first attempt at driving a dogsled in Lapland, Finland, the charm was a **dogsled**.

In a major surprise, Great Britain voted in a national referendum to leave the European Union. *Spotlight* won the Oscar.

Year 53 (7/16 to 7/17)

The charm was an **elephant** to commemorate my bathing with three elephants in a river on a trip to Nepal.

Trump upset H. Clinton, with some help from Russia and the FBI Director, James Comey, who was then fired by Trump. An attempted coup in Turkey failed. The Best Picture was *Moonlight*.

LEECHES, LOVERS, BEARS, AND CHOCOLATE PUDDING

Year 54 (7/17 to 7/18)

Because of the "compassionate sea lion" that checked on my wellbeing while I was snorkeling with our grandson Aubrey in the Galapagos Islands, the charm this year was a **sea lion**.

Trump withdrew the United States from the Iran Nuclear Pact. The "Me Too" movement against sexual abuse of females went global. Stamp costs were raised to 50 cents. *The Shape of Water* was selected as the Best Picture.

Year 55 (7/18 to 7/19)

Will and I finished writing a play called "Endings" after two or three years of collaborating, so the charm chosen was a **set of tragedy/comedy masks**.

The Democratic Party won a majority in the House of Representatives and opened several investigations of President Trump. Special Counsel Mueller's report contained substantial evidence of Russian interference in the 2016 presidential election and of President Trump's efforts to obstruct the investigation. A Saudi journalist working for the Washington Post was assassinated in Turkey on apparent orders of the Saudi royal family. Great Britain failed to negotiate an exit deal for leaving the European Union. Brett Kavanaugh's nomination to the Supreme Court was approved by the Senate despite testimony of sexual abuse in his past. Stamp prices jumped to 55 cents. The Oscar went to *Green Book*.

A VIEW FROM THE PASTURE

"Some Englishman once said that marriage is a long dull meal with the pudding served first." So claimed one of the characters in Julian Barnes' *The Sense of an Ending*, which won the prestigious Man Booker Prize in 2011. As good as the book is, that particular statement certainly does not describe the long, happy, and *exciting* marriage that Julie and I enjoyed. Our retirement in 1997 was the "pudding," with cherries and whipped cream on top. There have been a few blips since then, like the 9/11/01 attack that grounded us for a time, giving up the TEEP summer picnics in Covington that we hosted for 30-plus years, Hurricane Katrina that destroyed our home base in 2005, and Julie's Alzheimer's diagnosis in 2006 that changed our long-term plans and ultimately ended her life in 2020, but overall we made good use of the last two-plus decades, as a few examples will demonstrate:

New friends, including elephants, sea lions, huskies, and hummingbirds "up close and personal," plus rhinos, reindeer, ibexes, sharks, crocodiles, monkeys, giant tortoises, sea turtles, yaks, water buffalo, moose, deer, elk, eagles, albatrosses, owls, flamingos, bats, sheep (lots of them), wolves, bears, foxes, coyotes, lightening-bugs, blue-footed boobies, and a few other interesting critters, including some of the human kind, like the new and rediscovered old friends in Williamstown, Massachusetts, and here at Lambeth House in New Orleans;

New adventures, including paragliding, dogsledding (or "mushing" to the aficionados), snorkeling, ziplining, skydiving (simulated), ice-swimming, rock-climbing, canoeing, sea kayaking, cross-country skiing, a hurricane, three New England winters, one marathon, and 2 and $8/9$ "fourteeners" in Colorado;

New destinations, including Nepal, the Galapagos Islands, Finland, the Yukon River, the Alps, Denmark and Norway, England, Ireland, Scotland, Switzerland, Italy, France, Prague, Budapest, and Vienna; and

New creations, including *seven* wonderful grandchildren, a second home, a book, a play, a short biography, a legal memoir, and a number of family stories.

LEECHES, LOVERS, BEARS, AND CHOCOLATE PUDDING

Travels With Julie

Another reason why Julie and I retired relatively early in 1997 is that we had not traveled outside the U.S. since our belated-honeymoon trip to Europe in 1965 (see story entitled "The Perks of Pregnancy") and our Canadian canoeing adventure in 1967 (see story entitled "Leeches, Lovers, Bears, and Chocolate Pudding"), some 30 years before. And it's a good thing we did because Julie's terrible diagnosis in 2006 prematurely closed our window of opportunity to finally see the world together. In addition, we chose not to fly for two years after the 9/11 attack and then canceled a planned trip to Italy's Cinque Terre because of a travel advisory. But we made pretty good use of the shortened time we did have.

IRELAND:

Julie loved the Irish people and they of course loved her. Especially the Irish men, including the dozen or so lads who worked for over an hour taking apart our rental car to extract the key that this pretty and abandoned damsel-in-distress (Julie, at her best) had locked inside, while I waited in a nearby pub drinking beer (see "Automotive Misadventures" chapter of the story entitled "Just Julie").

Our love affair with Ireland definitely did not begin auspiciously. After arriving at Shannon Airport on the western side of the island and picking up our rental car with all the reversed controls, we couldn't find an airport exit and therefore drove around in circles for 15 or 20 minutes. Eventually we spotted a gathering of some kind well off the road and drove there to get directions out of the airport. Well, as you may have already guessed, it was a small and decrepit Roma colony. Our car was soon surrounded by mothers holding undernourished babies and begging for money to buy them food. Out of both compassion and fear, Julie and I quickly handed over all of our Irish money, but we did get good directions and finally escaped the airport loop.

And that's when the fun really started. Driving a stick-shift car in Ireland on the wrong (left) side of the road was an absolute nightmare. Everything was backwards, like a mirror image. The gearshift was on my left and the three floor pedals were reversed. Other cars passed us on the right instead of left. Except for the major highways, the roads (which were always two-way) were barely wide enough for two small passing cars, much less for large trucks or buses, and rarely had any shoulder to escape onto because of all the stone walls built right up to the roadway, so driving was a constant game of chicken. There were no centerlines and no rules of the road, as far as I could tell. And the country roads were like obstacle courses, littered with stray sheep, bikers, or people just talking. The usual road signs were entirely missing from those county roads we used most of the time. Instead, there were tall wooden poles with 20–30 hand-painted signs pointing in all possible directions to a nearby town or B&B or pub or whatever, which was all very democratic but totally confusing to us. My intrepid wife, who chased wild bears and climbed high mountains, gave up driving in Ireland forever after just 15 minutes at the wheel.

With a lot of luck and prayer, we did manage to reach our first destination, a beautiful lodge on the west coast where we stayed for three luxurious days of little or no driving. And, with the owner's help, we made contact with a legendary fly-fisherman who was willing to take us out in his boat to fish for salmon. It turned out that our guide was an Englishman who had married an Irish woman and moved to Ireland. He was delightful. Julie and I had a wonderful outing with him even though we did not catch any fish. He told us about going out one day on the same lake and hooking a salmon that was too big to land with the lightweight tackle he was using, so he had to follow it around the lake in his boat to keep it from breaking the line. A friend on shore saw the situation and came out in his own boat to help. When our guide finally brought the fish close into the boat for his helper to net, they saw that it probably weighed about 30 pounds, a really huge salmon, and the helper got so excited that he accidentally knocked the fish off the hook while trying to net it. Julie and I communicated with our new friend for a couple of years after that and sent him some New Orleans chicory coffee, which he loved, but then found out he had died from the cancer he had while out fishing with us.

Although we stayed a couple of days in Dublin during our first trip and took in all of its tourist sites, we spent most of our time on the western coastal area which is more Celtic and probably more authentic. When in Ireland, do as the Irish do, so we hit a different pub every night and met some incredibly warm

LEECHES, LOVERS, BEARS, AND CHOCOLATE PUDDING

and wonderful folks, not to mention all the free "pints" we got as visiting Americans. We also got invited to two wedding receptions, which we enjoyed immensely. The pubs are the social center of all the small towns and cities we visited. At night, the locals bring their babies, children, grandchildren, pets, and even some farm animals. I remember a nice conversation with a young American woman who had married an Irish lad and moved from New York City to a small Irish city. She felt totally safe but was still lonely in her new homeland. In Killarney, we found a great restaurant and got to know the owner, who told us about his 10-year effort to restore a castle, and a visit to his restaurant by Justice Sandra Day O'Connor of the U.S. Supreme Court, who entertained him with some risqué jokes.

The Gallarus Oratory in County Kerry on the west coast is one of the most amazing structures we've ever seen anywhere. As I recall, it is an early Christian "church" that was built in the sixth century. It's shaped like the inverted curved hull of a large boat maybe 40–50 feet long and constructed entirely of stones about a foot or two wide. What's truly amazing is that no mortar of any kind was used to bind the stones together. They were just wedged together in such a way as to remain in place for some 1,500 years, despite powerful Atlantic storms. It is a true engineering marvel from the so-called "dark ages." And we even had a bonus. Standing right outside the oratory, we watched a lone sheepdog round up about 100 sheep spread out all over a grassy hillside and direct them through a small gate, all in less than a minute!

Skellig Michael is the very top of a sharp peak that juts out of the Atlantic Ocean some eight miles west of the Irish coast. We got there in a small, open fishing boat. Even though it was a "calm" day, the troughs between the waves were a good 15 feet deep, so we prayed again just as we did while driving (maybe that's why the Irish are so religious). Despite her history of seasickness, my courageous wife did fine, but the two other tourists on the boat got very sick. Our little boat was high-tech compared to the open rafts used by the Irish monks to get back and forth from Skellig Michael after settling it in the sixth century! Their little community, which lasted about 800 years, lived in tiny mud-and-rock shelters called "beehive huts" and subsisted mainly on puffin eggs as well as some fish and a few vegetables. They survived not only the fearsome North Atlantic weather but also the occasional visits of Viking marauders. The monks

A VIEW FROM THE PASTURE

must have been very dedicated and very tough to live in that kind of environment and cross the ocean on rafts. The "beehive huts" were barely big enough to fit an adult in the fetal position. Since the entire island was sloped at a steep angle of 60–70 degrees, the only flat areas had to be carved out of the rocky sides. But the puffins were plentiful and friendly. For us, it was a truly grand experience, including the roller-coaster ride out and back.

Charcoal drawing by Lucia Penick

LEECHES, LOVERS, BEARS, AND CHOCOLATE PUDDING

On our second trip to Ireland, we rented a house on the Ring of Kerry peninsula overlooking Dingle Bay (where the movie *Ryan's Daughter* was filmed) and had our own rabbit in the backyard to enjoy. When I called the rental agent about getting a key from her, she just laughed and said to look under the rock by the front door. You gotta love the Irish! Nearby was Carrantuohill, the tallest mountain in Ireland even though it was only 3,500 feet high as I recall, but still we couldn't pass up the chance to put another notch in our mountaineering belts. So we packed a lunch and planned to be home by mid-afternoon at the latest. Well, it may not be a towering mountain but the climb was really difficult, including steep sections we navigated on all fours. There was a huge cross at the top, which almost inspired us to pray for divine intervention or at least a helicopter to take us down. Anyway, we got back to the house at 9:00 PM, totally beat and thoroughly humbled.

SCOTLAND:

We also attempted to climb the highest mountain in Scotland, called Ben Nevis, about 4,000 feet high, but were foiled about two thirds of the way up by a heavy summer snowstorm. And we went to Loch Ness looking for "Nessie," the Monster, but she declined to make an appearance despite our blandishments. But there was still a lot to see. We started in old Edinburgh, which was colorful and enjoyable, although we were somewhat distracted by the fact that all or most of the locals had unusual faces that were round and flat (as did many of the Hungarians we saw later in Budapest). We found the Scottish countryside to be much more interesting, especially the lakes, or "lochs" as the Scots call them. The northern half of the country is quite rugged and beautiful but sparsely populated, which explains the two-way highways with only a single (and cost-

A VIEW FROM THE PASTURE

efficient) driving lane. On a detour to the picturesque Isle of Skye off the west coast, we discovered an old hotel with a golf course, of sorts. The fairways seemed to meander in and out of forests and, even worse, they all crossed each other, so Julie and I spent most of the time either looking for the right green or dodging behind trees to avoid crossing shots by other golfers. It probably would have taken us a whole day to finish a full 18 holes, assuming we survived.

ENGLAND:

On our first trip to England after retiring, we skipped London because Julie and I had seen a lot of it back in 1965. This time we concentrated on Bath, Oxford, and a self-guided walking tour through the enchanting Cotswolds. It was a wonderful experience for both of us, but sadly enough, it was our last foreign trip together before the tragedy of losing our beloved house in New Orleans to Hurricane Katrina three months later and the much greater tragedy of Julie's Alzheimer's diagnosis the following year of 2006.

Bath is a lovely, historic town that is famous for its elegant Roman baths and other well-preserved structures. In addition to all of that, we made good friends of the couple that ran the B&B where we stayed. I remember a very lively dinner out with them and a very sad parting when we had to leave. We corresponded with them for three or so years after that and exchanged a number of books. Our next stop was Oxford, where we toured the famous university and learned a new English word. In one of the local museums, a sign instructed us to "see an invigilator" if we needed to use a bathroom. Well, we didn't know whether an "invigilator" was human or something else entirely and we didn't want to look like stupid Americans, so we bit the bullet and didn't ask. (We

LEECHES, LOVERS, BEARS, AND CHOCOLATE PUDDING

found out later that this strange word refers to an exam monitor. There's a picture of the sign in our Williamstown house.) Oxford is also where Julie first exhibited some bizarre behavior that I realized later was a result of her Alzheimer's. Of two or three incidents on this trip, the only one I can remember now occurred while we were crossing a wide and busy street. Julie walked very slowly while looking around, like she was in a daze and unaware of the oncoming traffic, but fortunately snapped out of it when I grabbed her hand and pulled her along. Although the other incidents were relatively minor as I recall, this was the beginning of a distressing pattern that became clearer over the next year and a half.

However, the rest of our trip, consisting of nine days walking by ourselves from lodge to lodge throughout the Cotswolds, was absolutely delightful. Our first night at a B&B in a small town was memorable because of the story related by the owner, who had been a British officer in the first Gulf War of 1991 against Saddam Hussein. The end of that war came when the Allied forces completely encircled about 200,000 helpless soldiers of the Iraqi Army, "sitting ducks" just waiting to be annihilated. Our host recalled that he and the other Allied troops were ready to fire as soon as President George H. W. Bush gave the order. Instead, Bush ordered the fighting stopped and the Iraqi soldiers spared. According to our host, who was a career soldier until he retired because of a medical disability, what Bush did was the greatest display of statesmanship in his lifetime.

Except for one day of rest in the middle, Julie and I walked leisurely for about six or seven hours daily through beautiful, gently rolling landscapes dotted with sheep farms and iconic little English towns with classic names like Moreton-in-Marsh, Stow-on-the-Wold, and Shiptop-under-Wychwood. Our route, selected by the Country Walkers service, often took us right through sheep enclosures where Julie could admire the little guys. And we also saw dozens of wild pheasants in the wooded areas. Lunch always consisted of sandwiches at one of the ubiquitous pubs. We carried only small daypacks with rain gear and water because Country Walker transported our suitcases by car to the next B&B it had reserved for us. One of the B&Bs was owned and operated by an artist who had been in New Orleans to visit our friend Joshua Pailet, a fellow artist (photography) and gallery owner. Many of the homes and buildings were 400–500 years old.

Two years later, in 2007, we took our then 10-year-old granddaughter Emma to Oxford on an intergenerational Road Scholar trip designed for 9-to-11-year-old "Harry Potter" fans. Emma had literally consumed all eight of the "Harry Potter" books, including the last one of 800-plus pages in a day and a half! There were about 15 other kids with the same interest in fantasy stories. Oxford University was the perfect venue because one of its great dining halls was featured in the "Harry Potter" movies and many famous fantasy writers taught there, including J. R. R. Tolkien, author of *The Hobbit* and *The Lord of the Rings*. There were lectures by contemporary writers, live play performances, visits to nearby museums and castles, various English games from long ago, and a final dinner in the great university dining hall with an actor dressed up as the "Harry Potter" character he played in the movies. Emma was enthralled and we were too. Hats off to Road Scholar for making the trip so interesting for kids and elders alike.

During an afternoon off to explore Oxford on our own, we stopped in a shop that supposedly had the best hot chocolate in town. Unfortunately, I don't know if that reputation is true or not. After getting our hot chocolate in tall elegant glasses and sitting down, Emma and Julie left for the bathroom. Emma had also ordered a plate of cookies, which I found irresistible during their absence. But in the excitement of retrieving the cookie and pulling off the perfect crime, I created enough evidence to convict me three times over, by knocking my glass of hot chocolate directly into myself. I had the hot, sticky stuff from the top of my head to my crotch. My glasses were covered and wiping them with a napkin only made it worse. As luck would have it, this is also when the girls emerged. I couldn't see anything but I did hear Emma shouting to Julie that "Pops looks like the Gingerbread Man." They were both laughing too hard to be of any help, so I had to blindly find my own way into the bathroom and get some water to wash with. My shirt was soaked. My pants looked like the victim of a dysfunctional sphincter muscle. But I did get my glasses cleaned and returned to the table where the girls were enjoying their drinks and cookies while giggling over my appearance. When the nice waitress brought me a new hot chocolate, I begged her to remove it as quickly as possible. On the bus ride home with our

LEECHES, LOVERS, BEARS, AND CHOCOLATE PUDDING

30 or so fellow travelers, I was of course the star and the butt of numerous jokes, many that questioned my potty training as a child.

NORWAY AND DENMARK:

After spending a couple of days in lovely Copenhagen, home of a wonderful Roman museum, we took an overnight boat with a nonstop casino to Oslo, the capital of Norway. Julie and I both loved Oslo. Our second day there happened to be Norway's National Day (celebrating its independence from Sweden), lucky for us. The main boulevard running by the royal palace was filled with marching bands and with thousands of friendly, beautiful, mostly blonde natives in traditional attire. We even saw the king come out on his balcony. It was a real treat to be a part of that. In the process, we discovered that Norway has the best ice cream in the world, in terms of taste and thickness (it doesn't melt!). As a true aficionado of ice cream, Julie found her heaven and insisted, wherever we were in Norway, we take an ice cream break every afternoon at 3:00 PM sharp, which we did.

Our favorite destination in Oslo was the Vigeland Sculpture Park. Opened in 1949, it contains the artist's entire output of over 200 sculptures, some of them very complex renderings that contain numerous human figures. *The Angry Boy*, a well-known image of a little boy stomping his foot during a temper tantrum, reminded us of a few similar scenes in our own household. The artist himself designed the park, a gift from the city, and filled it with streams and bridges and gardens that made the whole thing an extraordinary experience for both of us. We spent two full days there.

Oslo was also the home to another artist, the surrealistic painter Edvard Munch, whose best-known work is the autobiographical *The Scream*. Early one morning, Julie and I went to the museum dedicated to his works and found it virtually empty except for some unmanned cameras on tripods. We spent about 15 minutes all alone looking at and trying to understand *The Scream*. About a week or so later in a motel in central Norway, we turned on the TV and there we were, gazing at *The Scream* in the Munch Museum. We were the stars of an English-language travel show about "cultural tourists" in Europe. Our brief moment in the sun, but I must admit we did not look very "enlightened" or

A VIEW FROM THE PASTURE

"cultural" at that early hour of the morning (looking at the video of the show we got later). At least we didn't do anything uncouth on camera—or maybe the TV producer just cut those parts.*

From Oslo we took a train to Bergen on the Atlantic coast, where the sun set at midnight. Late one night, we took a funicular to the top of a mountain overlooking Bergen and enjoyed a brilliant sunset with a glass of wine. Then, at about 12:30 AM, we started down the mountain on a paved and lighted pathway through dense forests. Halfway down, someone or something started playing "Greensleeves" on a flute, which was both beautiful and eerie. It sounded like a live performance, but we didn't see any sign of human life, so we concluded it had to be a friendly and very musical Norwegian troll. Whatever it was, the whole night was truly magical.

We boarded a local passenger ship in Bergen and sailed up the west coast to Tromsö above the Artic Circle. On the way up, we enjoyed great views of the magnificent fjords with their blue-green waters. The ship stopped in a few interesting towns and let us off to roam on our own for three to four hours. In one of those towns, we stumbled upon a rare Norwegian bowling alley and stopped to roll a game, since Julie and I were recreational bowlers at home, with our own balls, no less. Whether bowling would fit our image as "cultural tourists" is a good question. As we crossed the Arctic Circle, passengers doing so for the first time were invited to mark the event by kneeling before the ship captain and have him pour a ladle of freezing ocean water down their backs. I chickened out but Julie, being Julie, volunteered and was formally inducted into the Arctic Adventure Club or whatever it is. Her reward was a certificate and a warm glass of aquavit, the national liqueur.

On the way back to Oslo, we stopped in a small town with a famous Russian (wooden) "stave" church from the 11th century with its typical dome boards tied together at the top. Sitting right next to a gorgeous waterfall, it was quite a sight. But the best thing about that stop was our dinner that night.

---

* Julie and I "starred" in another TV show a few years later. During her treatment at the Alzheimer's clinic in Bennington, Vermont, the clinic director arranged for us to be interviewed on camera at our Williamstown house for a health series produced by an Albany, New York, TV station. He also arranged to feature us in a story about "Living with Alzheimer's" that appeared in USA Today in November of 2008.

LEECHES, LOVERS, BEARS, AND CHOCOLATE PUDDING

Unbeknownst to us, the hotel chef was a legend who got fed up with the big city (Oslo) and fled here to the center of the country. His specialty was reindeer, which I ordered over Julie's passionate protest. It was superb. Finally, Julie's curiosity got the better of her and she had a taste, which overcame her scruples about eating "Rudolph and friends." After ordering and eating her own plate of reindeer, she started feeling guilty and made me swear my holiest oath that I would never tell our children, grandchildren, or fellow kindergarten teachers back home.

We spent the next idyllic week in a rented house overlooking a fjord 1,500 feet below us. Unfortunately, we dealt directly with the owner, a sheep farmer, who was probably the only Norwegian who did not speak English. (Even the kid at the bowling alley spoke English and two other foreign languages!) He was very nice, as were all of his fellow citizens, but as a result of the language barrier, Julie and I never figured out how to operate his new-fangled washing machine right out of a science fiction novel, so we reverted to hand washing. However, that was nothing compared to the comfortable house and the incredible scenery. In addition to hiking and picnicking all over the mountains bordering the fjord, we tried another mountain a couple of hours away, which is where I had to catch three fast and malevolent sheep on foot after Julie let them out of a pen (see the story entitled "The Dark, Dark Side of Sheep"). The day after that fiasco, since I was exhausted from the two-hour chase, we decided to picnic on a small beach on the fjord. It was of course too cold to swim, but we set out to get our feet wet until we looked down and saw that the crystal-clear water was filled with jellyfish, of all things, just like those stinging critters in our own Gulf of Mexico.

ITALY:

Between the people and the history, this was probably our favorite destination. Julie loved the young children especially and the good parental care. We went to Italy three times after retirement, twice by ourselves and once with two of Julie's old friends. We also canceled a trip to Cinque Terre a year after the 9/11/01 attack because of a terrorist warning.

A VIEW FROM THE PASTURE

As I recall, we split the first trip between Rome and Florence and points in between. Among the many awe-inspiring historical and artistic treasures we enjoyed, Michelangelo's statue of *David* and the Roman Coliseum stand out in our memories. It was a wonderful trip in every respect but relatively uneventful compared to our various adventures and mishaps in Ireland, England, and Norway.

On our second trip, we rented a virtual suite in a 15th-century manor just outside the old walled city of Montalcino in the heart of Tuscany for two weeks. The manor house was still owned by the same family that built it and started making Brunello wine, one of Italy's finest, 600 years ago. We were surrounded by fields of very fat, very ripe grapes that were in fact harvested on the day we left. The family was quite friendly, especially the young son who visited us every morning, to Julie's delight. And we got a personal tour of the wine cellar that was part of the original construction but still used today.

We explored all over Tuscany in our rental car, including Montalcino itself, with its beautiful old churches, busy public squares, and cobblestone streets barely wide enough for a medieval ox cart, which I discovered the hard way. On our first drive through Montalcino, the streets (without any sidewalks) got gradually narrower until the car (without side-view mirrors) almost scraped the buildings on either side. It felt like a claustrophobic horror house. Then we came to a tiny circle that was a dead-end, where we almost decided to just abandon the car and walk home. To turn around, I had to back the car very carefully into a tiny opening that happened to be the top of a long stairway, so one little mistake would have wiped out a number of good citizens in the busy square below. Happily enough, we made it and learned our lesson about not driving in Montalcino. But we did spend several delightful evenings sitting in that same square before dinner, enjoying a glass of Brunello wine and watching bunches of cute little children playing.

After Julie's Alzheimer's was diagnosed in 2006, we returned to Italy with her old friends from McGehee's School, Sandy Reese and Carol Finley. Through a connection of Carol's, we enjoyed a personal tour of the Vatican with two young American priests, who were delightful and very informative. Among other advantages, we had 15 minutes or so alone with our guides in the Sistine Chapel, which is usually filled to the brim with tourists. Carol and Sandy also went to an early-morning service (Julie and I decided to sleep in) in a small Vatican courtyard that was conducted by Pope Benedict himself.

From Rome, we took a very crowded train (which was hard on Julie, but she rose to the occasion, as always) to the beautiful seaside town of Sorrento near Naples and Mount Vesuvius, the famous volcano that erupted in 79 AD and destroyed the Roman cities of Pompeii and Herculaneum. Although our walks along the hilly coast were glorious, the day we spent at the well-preserved ruins of Pompeii was the high point. As pointed out by our excellent guide, the engineering ingenuity of the ancient Romans in building streets, aqueducts, drainage facilities, houses, and sports arenas in this once-bustling city was evident everywhere. And to go along with the many bars, there were several brothels with painted depictions on each door of the particular services offered within. Apparently the Romans did not leave very much to chance, except for the nearby volcano, which by the way is still active.

SWITZERLAND:

Julie and I spent the first week in the recreational, auto-free town of Saas-Fee ringed by the Alps. There were hiking trails galore, so we hiked all over the place, sometimes on glaciers and often through little mountainside villages. Up high, we encountered two beautiful and friendly Alpine ibexes with two curved horns on their heads. The scenery of course was spectacular. At night, dinner in the lodge was always followed by an informal floorshow featuring our German hosts making jokes and doing pantomime, etc.

Our next stop, Lauterbrunnen, is set in a long, beautiful valley contained within high vertical rock walls on each side that are punctuated by a series of waterfalls. At one end of the valley lie the three famous mountains, the Eiger (known for its North Face), the Jungfrau, and the Mönch; at the other end is the medieval town of Interlaken on the land bridge between two lovely lakes. We walked all over the valley, from one to the other. We went down into an ice cave and up to the resort town of Grindelwald that looks over the valley walls. And we rode up to the top of the Jungfrau on a train in a circular tunnel through the middle of this 14,000-foot mountain, an incredible engineering feat. When we boarded the train at the bottom, it was a sunny summer day, but at the summit, it was very cold and snowing heavily. There was even a dogsledding concession, which would suggest the top of the Jungfrau is cold and snowy throughout the summer. On our long walk back to the lodge, we first heard and then saw a small avalanche, an alarming experience even though it was some distance away.

PRAGUE, BUDAPEST, AND VIENNA:

The Untours travel company arranged for us to stay for one week each in very well-vetted apartments in all three of these cities. In Vienna, for example, our apartment contained hundreds of fine, old books and some wonderful pieces of art. It was owned by an older female physician, who was leaving on vacation when we arrived, spoke perfect English, and was incredibly delightful.

Our first stop, Prague, was beautiful, busy, and spotless. Julie and I were both impressed by how handsome, cultured, and friendly the local inhabitants were. As part of the Untours package, we were treated to a fairly intimate evening of chamber music by the world-famous Talich Quartet. On a darker note, we visited the former Theresienstadt concentration camp maintained by the Nazis during World War II, where thousands of Jews and other Czechs died. That was a terribly sad and moving experience in stark contrast to the happy, bustling atmosphere of Prague.

Despite its prime location on both sides of the Danube River, Budapest was disappointing. Most of the historic buildings had been reconstructed and the locals were generally unfriendly and unattractive. There were of course exceptions. One was the goulash, which was delicious. After turning up her nose at such a pedestrian dish, Julie finally decided to take a small taste of my dish and wound up gobbling down the rest of my meal with relish. We also took a very nice boat ride up the Danube with an interesting guide, who told us the Hungarians were closely related to the Turks.

The definite high point of Budapest for us was the largest synagogue in all of Europe, built in the mid-19th century. The Nazis did not destroy it but instead used it as a showplace to fool the world into thinking they were treating the Jews humanely. Adolph Eichmann, the architect of the Holocaust, apparently had an office in the synagogue, which is a grotesque irony. Behind the synagogue is a large, fascinating garden dedicated to the many Holocaust victims from Hungary and to Raoul Wallenberg, the Swedish diplomat who saved thousands of Hungarian Jews by providing them with passports and visas. (Wallenberg disappeared when Russian troops liberated Budapest and he probably died somewhere in Siberia.) In the garden are sculpted trees with leaves bearing the names and serial numbers of local Jews who died in the Holocaust. It was a celebration of life and courage in a most meaningful way.

Vienna was a welcome change, although it had its own reminders of the Holocaust. In particular was a statue of an older Jewish man on his hands and knees cleaning a city sidewalk with a toothbrush, as happened often during the Nazi occupation. But the city itself is beautiful and very easy to navigate (we took buses everywhere without any problem). Many of its famous museums are clustered together around some lovely open spaces. Our favorite of the museums was the Leopold, which features the paintings of two local artists, Klimt and Schiele, including the latter's large and wonderful canvas of a Catholic cardinal at the moment of being caught in the act of embracing a nun. Vienna is also the home of the "sacher torte," created in 1832 by Mr. Sacher for Prince Metternich and now touted as the most famous cake in the world. Several hotels and restaurants proudly and loudly claimed the honor of producing the very first "sacher torte," so of course we had to try as many as we could manage—they all tasted great. We also saw the famous Lipizzaner Horses perform with absolutely incredible precision. And Vienna being the music capital of the world, we did attend one opera (the tickets were half-price because we literally could only see half the stage) and one concert of the Vienna Philharmonic.[†]

PARIS:

In 2007, Julie and I hooked up again with her high school friends Sandy and Carol for a week in Paris. Although the two of us had been there in 1965, we did not come away from that occasion with any vivid impressions or memories of the city or environs, probably because of Julie's pregnancy and the Parisians' superiority complex (see other story "The Perks of Pregnancy"). And since our two colleagues had never been there, we started from scratch and visited just about all of the famous sites, including the Louvre, d'Orsay (our favorite), and Picasso Museums, plus Napoleon's Tomb and the Pantheon (which was fascinating). However, what I remember best about that trip was a boat ride along the Seine at night with dinner and music. The city, of course, was beautiful from that vantage point—and we didn't have to deal with any of the local inhabitants.

CANADA:

Our most interesting post-retirement trip to Canada involved a long ride on the famous Trans-Canadian Railroad that runs from Toronto to Vancouver on the west coast. Unfortunately, although planned several months before, the trip happened to fall just two weeks after the 9/11 attacks of 2001. Since we were already in Williamstown when the attacks occurred and had made arrangements

---

[†] Julie and I heard the Vienna Philharmonic again in New York City. While living in Williamstown, MA, for three years after Hurricane Katrina, we often took a nice two-and-a-half-hour train ride along the Hudson River to NYC to see a play or concert or meet friends for a short visit. During one year, we heard five of the greatest orchestras in Europe and Russia perform in Carnegie Hall (the Berlin with Simon Rattle conducting, the Concertgebouw, the Vienna, plus the St. Petersburg and the Kirov under Valeri Gergiev).

LEECHES, LOVERS, BEARS, AND CHOCOLATE PUDDING

to stop in the Canadian Rockies for a few days, pick up a new Isuzu Trooper SUV in Seattle, and visit two of the children in California and Colorado on the drive home, Julie and I decided not to cancel the trip. It turned out to be the right decision, although there were some bittersweet moments.

We had our own roomette on the train, with a pull-down bed, our own bathroom, and even swivel chairs as I remember. Until we got close to the Rockies, the scenery was colorful but not spectacular. It was the people, some good, some bad, who really caught our attention. On the one hand, all of the Canadians on board and at the stops could not have been more attentive or generous, simply because we were Americans and therefore victims of the recent attacks. In addition to lots of sympathy, we got free food, free drinks, and free medical care in the form of a vaccination that Americans were advised to get. At the opposite extreme was a large group of Texans who could not have been more obnoxious. Unlike anyone else on board, they partied loudly and continuously all over the train, as if 9/11 had never happened. We were ashamed of our countrymen.

The other thing we noticed was the total absence of any security on the train or at the various stations along the way. Passengers of all types left backpacks unattended on the train while they got off at station stops. As hypersensitive as we were after all the images of burning buildings and trapped people, Julie and I just knew there was a bomb in each of those backpacks. Then we started remembering the pictures of our train crossing over dramatic mile-high trestle bridges west of the Rockies and thinking that's when those backpacks would explode. Once you get an idea like that in your head, it's impossible to deal with it rationally, which led us to make a terrible decision: we canceled our train tickets from Jasper to Vancouver and replaced them with bus tickets. More on that later.

The plan was to stop in Jasper, a resort town in the middle of the Canadian Rockies, for four days before heading on to the west coast. That was a good decision. We stayed at the renowned Chateau Lake Louise at the head of one of the most beautiful lakes in the world. From there, we took day hikes and glacier walks around Lake Moraine (with the bluest water we'd ever seen) and other nearby sites. Aside from the incredible scenery, the area is also noted for its grizzly bears. There were warning signs everywhere, even in the small town of Banff, because the grizzlies are not shy about going into town looking for food and are quite good at figuring out how to get into allegedly bear-proof garbage cans that require seven different steps to open them. It took us a full 15 minutes to just read the directions.

Although the often-photographed glacier at the other end of Lake Louise had melted down to half its normal size, Julie and I planned to hike the trail that goes all the way around the lake but hesitated when we saw the warning sign about grizzly bears at the head of the trail. As we were pondering what to do, up walked an overweight, out-of-shape, perfumed English couple in Hawaiian shirts and loose-fitting sandals who asked if they might join us. As I found out later, Julie's immediate reaction was the same as mine: if we did encounter a hungry grizzly, the two of us in hiking boots could run much faster than the Brits and would be back at the lodge before the bear finished dining on them, so we gleefully (and shamefully) accepted them as hiking partners and guarantors of our own safety. We did not run across any grizzlies and our new friends were good company, so it turned out to be a nice hike. Back at the lodge, when a park ranger noticed that we were wearing "bear bells" to avoid surprising any nearby bruin, he pointed out with a big smile that the bears consider them to be "dinner bells."

After a wonderful four days in the mountains, we headed on to Vancouver at the end of the line—and that's when our good luck ran out. The first bus, which was dirty and crowded, lasted about two hours before it broke down in the middle of nowhere. Then it took about three hours to get another bus to us. That one lasted no more than an hour before it too quit. The third bus arrived about three and a half hours later and looked just as decrepit as the first two, but it somehow made it all the way to Vancouver (all of which for some reason reminded me of my own halting efforts to advance a golf ball down a fairway). By the time we reached our hotel at 3:00 AM, both of us were hungry, angry, and exhausted but glad that all the bad luck was behind us. Or so we thought. Since there were no bellhops at that time of night, we had to lug our suitcases up an elevator and down a long hallway to our room. So close, but then our electronic key failed to work. After considering different ways of breaking the door down, we hauled our luggage back to the first-floor lobby to get another key and then up again to our God-forsaken room, only to discover this key didn't

LEECHES, LOVERS, BEARS, AND CHOCOLATE PUDDING

work any better than the first one. And of course in those primitive times, we didn't have cellphones to call the front desk. Julie absolutely refused to lug our bags down and up again, so I reluctantly left her there by herself and rushed down to the lobby once again. This time the clerk came with me and made sure we got in the room, where we crashed in our clothes and slept 12 hours. Although we were glad nothing bad happened, it didn't help our moods to learn that "our" train arrived safe and sound in Vancouver, right on time.

The rest of the trip was fine, thankfully enough. Vancouver was fascinating. We took a ferry to Seattle, where we picked up our new car after signing just one document! After visiting old friends there, we drove by Mount Ranier and through the devastating and widespread wreckage left by the eruption of Mount St. Helens before stopping for a couple of days of hiking at Mount Hood. Then we meandered down the road along the beautiful Oregon coast. Our last stop in that state was a night at the Out 'n'About Treesort in Cave Junction, which was memorable. It was a real tree-house motel in the middle of a dense forest. There were 16 separate units of different sizes, levels, and designs, including one for children only about three feet off the ground with three-foot high doors. Apparently the Treesort was the brainchild of a tree architect and unreconstructed hippy from the 1960s who designed each unit himself. When he started the project, the local authorities refused him a permit to run a motel, so he cleverly got around that by charging nothing for the "room" itself but $75 for an Out 'n'About tee-shirt. He eventually got his permit. Julie and I chose the highest unit, which was built all the way around a huge spruce some 30 feet off the ground. To get there, we had to climb two ladders and cross two swinging bridges, but it was definitely worth it. There was a very efficient pulley system to haul up the luggage. Inside were a space heater, a single toilet, a comfortable bed, and lots of blankets. The only "windows" were 360 degrees of canvas roll-downs. The night was full of intriguing sounds, including the howling of wolves not that far away. It was definitely "a night to remember."

Our next stop was the Redwoods National Park in northern California, which was extraordinary. Then down the coast highway to San Francisco, where we spent a couple of days before driving on to Los Angeles to visit our son, Will, who had moved there from New York the year before the 9/11 attacks. From there we drove east to Santa Fe, one of our very favorite cities, and finally up to

A VIEW FROM THE PASTURE

Denver to see our daughter Ginger and her family before heading home to New Orleans. Except for a few glitches here and there (and a few bad decisions along the way), it was a fantastic trip.

Since our house in Williamstown, Massachusetts, was only three hours from the Canadian border by car, Julie and I also made several short trips to our northern neighbor. We visited the very interesting city of Quebec on two occasions after meandering leisurely through Vermont or New Hampshire. The famous Chateau Frontenac Hotel, which is also a historic landmark, was our home both times. Walking through the old section of Quebec was a special treat. On one of those trips, we drove downriver some distance along the St. Lawrence River and found some interesting sites, including an immense cathedral out in the middle of nowhere, a swinging bridge over a large waterfall, and a lovely Stations of the Cross on the side of a hill.

Nova Scotia was another place of interest for both of us, so we set out twice to see it but actually reached it only once. On the first attempt, which took us through Maine into Canada, we got as far as Moncton, New Brunswick, before our travel plans were interrupted, ironically, by the remnants of a hurricane that had originated in the Gulf of Mexico and then followed us up the east coast of the U.S. all the way to Canada. It was still a dangerous storm after such a long run that the roads into Nova Scotia were closed. We had no choice but to hunker down for three days in a Moncton hotel. Luckily, we at least were able to enjoy the World Series on TV and had no problem finding a table in the dining room.

Our second attempt was more successful. We drove with our friends Dick and Carol Paul and their two dogs, Mulligan and Kelly, in their SUV. Since Dick wound up driving the whole way, Julie and I in the back seat enjoyed having the dogs close by, and they did too because of the surreptitious snacks they loved. Dick and Mulligan, a beautiful golden retriever, had as close a human-canine relationship as I've ever seen. That made it much easier for Dick when he and Mully were trapped in a Halifax hotel elevator for three hours. On the other hand, it happened on Sunday, when those with the emergency elevator keys were nowhere to be found, which is why it took so long to free the captives. From Halifax, we took the coast road counterclockwise all the way around the virtual island, without incident and with lots of beautiful scenery. Interestingly, while

LEECHES, LOVERS, BEARS, AND CHOCOLATE PUDDING

all the names along the southern coast were English, the northern coast was almost exclusively French and the origin of the French-Cajun population of Louisiana.

NEW ENGLAND AND NEW YORK CITY:

Every year from our retirement in 1997 to August of 2005, Julie and I spent much of each summer and part of the fall in Williamstown. After Hurricane Katrina essentially destroyed our home of 34 years in that August of 2005 until we moved into Lambeth House of New Orleans in the spring of 2008, we lived in Williamstown year-round. And for two years after that, in 2008 and 2009, we spent a couple of summer months at our Massachusetts house. During those 12 years (1997–2009), we had ample opportunity to explore much of the Northeast and New York City in particular where Will was living until he moved out West in 2000.

Sometimes we drove into New York City but more often took the very comfortable Amtrak train from Rensselaer, New York, right across the Hudson River from Albany, to Penn Station in the Big Apple. It was a very scenic ride of exactly two and a half hours along the east bank of the river. On almost every trip, we'd enjoy a play, concert, or opera and at least one dinner at a fine restaurant, including Windows on the World at the very top of a World Trade tower that was later destroyed in the 9/11/01 attack. On one special occasion in NYC with an old college friend from Philadelphia and his lovely wife, we saw two great plays, enjoyed several terrific meals, and had a wonderful weekend. (We still see a good bit of each other because they retired to Baton Rouge, LA, just an hour away from New Orleans.) On the bad side, Julie and I probably did agree just once to go with Will to watch his beloved New York Yankees play at Yankee Stadium, but any such unpleasant occasion has been mercifully erased from my memory. (I will root for any team against the Damn Yankees.) However, despite all the sights and sounds of New York City, it was the site of the 9/11 attack two years later that left us with the most vivid and meaningful memories. The World Trade Center was of course gone by that time but there was the immense empty hole in the ground that spoke volumes and, even more dramatic, the little church nearby that was miraculously untouched by all the

A VIEW FROM THE PASTURE

destruction just two blocks away. Its white fences were literally covered with personal letters to the victims of the attack, family photos, flower bouquets, and other forms of remembrance and grief. The emotional impact was overwhelming for both of us. We walked back uptown in silence, holding hands and remembering the horrific TV images of death and destruction on that day of infamy.

In addition to the 9/11 attack, we also happened to be in Williamstown when Hurricane Katrina devastated our home in New Orleans in 2005 and when we learned that Julie had Alzheimer's in 2006. As heartbreaking as those events were, we both loved our time together in New England, primarily because of all the wonderful friends there. Many of them were friends of mine from college who never left Williamstown or returned later, but many others were good folks we met after starting our summers there. That included, ironically enough, two couples from New Orleans who had been displaced by Hurricane Katrina and wound up in Williamstown. And another couple consisting of a National Book Award winner and a renowned history professor at Williams College, who endeared themselves to us forever by inviting Julie and me to their home for an intimate New Year's Eve dinner shortly after we returned from seeing what Katrina had done to our house in New Orleans. There was a similar outreach by wonderful friends after Julie's diagnosis. In addition to hosting our own children and many good friends from the South at our Williamstown house on numerous occasions, we visited other old friends in Boston, Pittsburgh, New Jersey, Lake George, NY, and other places all over the Northeast.

I've spoken to you generally about the goodness of the people we encountered in New England but here's a specific example that I'll never forget. The leading lady was a 10-year-old girl from a middle-income family in Williamstown. After seeing on TV what Hurricane Katrina had done to New Orleans, she decided she wanted to do something to help all the victims living there. Within a few days after the storm, she had organized a town-wide bake-sale with some of her classmates and talked a local bank into matching whatever they raised. To everyone's utter surprise, especially the bank president's, the bake-sale cleared some $4,000, which also says a lot about the folks in and around Williamstown. The fact that a 10-year-old kid, in just a few days, could raise $8,000 to help needy strangers in a faraway place was astounding to us and everyone we talked to. Julie and I wound up meeting her and taking her whole family out to dinner. When she's a bit older, I sincerely hope that young lady runs for some high public office.

Besides the friends and generally nice people, there was much else to like about New England. Williams College, founded in 1793 with the grand sum of $5,000, is just as interesting for an alumnus like me as it was 60 years ago. Williamstown was selected as the site of the Clark Art Museum in the 1950s because it was close enough to the population centers of New York City and Boston but far enough away to be relatively safe from the threat of a nuclear attack, a reality once again as I write this on March 6, 2022, during Russia's invasion of Ukraine. In any event, the Clark has become one of the main cultural attractions of many in the "Berkshires" of western Massachusetts. Others include the Tanglewood Music Center, Jacobs Pillow Dance Center, Norman Rockwell Museum, Williamstown Theatre Festival and two other great summer playhouses nearby, and the restored homes of Herman Melville, Emily Dickinson, Edith Wharton, and several other famous figures. The Baseball Hall of Fame in Cooperstown, New York, is just two hours away. Julie and I also enjoyed wonderful county fairs and food festivals throughout New England and the adjacent Adirondacks area, although we did find their versions of Cajun food, like a red beans and rice dish with three beans floating in water, to be somewhat lacking. We hiked in the woods and mountains all around Williamstown, including Mount Greylock, the highest point in Massachusetts, and Pine Cobble on the Appalachian Trail, with its plentiful blueberries and a view of our house. During our three winters there after Katrina, we skied several times at resorts in southern Vermont. For Julie and me, that whole area was an ongoing banquet.

MEXICO AND CENTRAL AMERICA:

The very last trip that Julie and I took together was a week-long cruise from New Orleans down the east coast of Mexico to Belize with our very dear friends Judy and Fred Hotstream in 2009, I believe. The vessel was immense, with room enough for 4,000 or so passengers, multiple restaurants, and at least one large swimming pool. The major attraction for us on board was the nightly karaoke session in a local bar that the two girls thoroughly and loudly enjoyed. The ship stopped in several ports that allowed us to go ashore for a few hours to visit Mayan ruins and some beautiful natural scenes. My favorite stop was an offshore marine center where, with the help of a guide, I took a "ride" on a very swift porpoise, which was thrilling. Unfortunately, the others were not feeling well and could only watch while I hung on for dear life. Although a little bittersweet, the trip was fun for all of us.

Travels Without Julie

Aside from visiting our three children in North Carolina, Colorado, and California, I stopped traveling altogether after Julie entered Nursing Care at Lambeth House in 2011. It was not until 2015 that I started traveling again, by myself, on trips offered by touring companies like Road Scholar and Country Walkers. During the next five years, I hiked the so-called "circuit" around Mont Blanc through France, Italy, and

LEECHES, LOVERS, BEARS, AND CHOCOLATE PUDDING

Switzerland, spent nine days in Finnish Lapland, canoed the Yukon River in western Canada, hiked the Himalayas and bathed with elephants in Nepal, and explored the Galapagos Islands with my grandson Aubrey. Each one of those trips is described elsewhere in this book. That's also true of the 2018 dogsledding adventure in Alaska's Denali National Park with two of our children, Casey and Will. I totally enjoyed all of those trips but definitely missed the humor, wisdom, joy, and love of my lifetime companion—and still do.

So let me start in 2019 with my Road Scholar hiking trip in the Bavarian Alps between Munich, Germany, and Salzburg, Austria. Our guides, a young couple, were great fun, the scenery was spectacular, and the meals were awesome, but it was the group itself that made the trip something special for me. Almost everyone was both funny and interesting. By the second night, a "hardcore" of us had discovered the wonders of a little after-dinner schnapps, a German liqueur. It became a nightly ritual to retire to the bar and review the day's events with a touch of schnapps to aid our memories. As our group grew, so did the quantity of schnapps. By the end of the trip, we were all fast friends—really. Despite the delays caused by the pandemic, we're still in touch about booking another trip together, specifically a hiking trip in the Lake District of England. And just five months ago while I was still in Williamstown, I spent two very enjoyable days at the Trapp Family Lodge in northern Vermont with two "hard-core" members who had come up from Texas to see the New England fall colors. Unfortunately, the lodge did not have any schnapps, to our great surprise and disappointment.

Before leaving the Bavarian Alps trip, I want to tell you about an occasion that still makes me smile. Midway through our journey, we were offered the option of paragliding, which involves riding the mountain air currents at 5,000 or so feet above ground while seated in a lawn chair hanging from a large, elongated parachute that is somehow "steered" with two simple wands by a "pilot" seated in another lawn chair right behind you. On paper, it sounds absolutely terrifying if not insane. In actuality, it's safe and exhilarating. I knew that because I had paraglided once before in Chamonix, France, before hiking the Mont Blanc Circuit. On this trip, four of us decided to try it but a fifth just could not make up her mind. She was very shy and had barely spoken a word during the first three days of the trip. And she was terrified of the whole idea but nevertheless dying to try it. Eventually, the four of us talked her into doing it and I'm so glad we did. She loved it! We all took off at about the same time, so I could hear her far above me telling her pilot to go even higher. After we all landed, she couldn't stop talking about the whole experience. What it did for her self-confidence generally was amazing. She joined the schnapps group and started mingling actively with everybody on the trip. She really found her stride, thanks to the paragliding.

Later that same year, 2019, I went back to Italy with my dear friend from TEEP, Alvin Edinburgh. Since it was his first time in Europe, it was fun for me just watching his reactions to all the incredible sights and experiences in Rome, Florence, and Venice. Surprisingly enough, the food was only so-so, including one gigantic steak in a beautiful outdoor restaurant with live music in Tuscany that was so bad I couldn't cut it, much less eat it. The size of our tour group was two or three times larger than the groups on my Road Scholar and Country Walkers trips, so it was difficult to really know anyone very well, but Alvin and I did make friends with a nice couple from Baltimore and spent a whole day getting lost in Venice with them.

There was one more short trip, to Jackson Hole, Wyoming, in February of 2020, before the pandemic changed everything. Julie died in early January, but I decided not to cancel the trip because I hoped it would help me deal with her loss just to get out of town, as it did, and because Julie and I had spent some time there many years before. Over the course of just four days, we dogsledded, cross-country skied, snowshoed, and visited a national elk preserve. We stayed outdoors and busy, which is just what I needed. The only other person in the group who I remember was an older woman who announced that it was her 44th Road Scholar trip. She participated in all the outdoor activities and was quite remarkable generally.

The coronavirus arrived in New Orleans less than a month later. Along with many others at Lambeth House, I got it on March 11 and spent two and a half weeks isolated in my room, although my symptoms were not as bad as some. There was of course no traveling for the rest of that year, but I did make plans for 2021, including a family reunion in Hawaii, a cruise from the tip of South America to Antarctica (to include a "camping out" night in sleeping bag and individual tent on the Antarctic mainland and a possible "polar plunge" into the frigid waters wearing only a bathing suit, if I didn't chicken out at the last minute), and hiking trips in Iceland, the Lake District of England, and Patagonia in southern Chile. All of them were canceled and rebooked for 2022.

Unfortunately, the first four months of that year were disastrous. In January, the Antarctica trip was canceled at the last minute because of Covid in our port of embarkation. I had already flown to Atlanta and checked my bags on to Buenos Aires, Argentina, when I got the word. Since that was my fourth foiled attempt to reach the South Pole with three different companies, I concluded I was not meant to go there and scratched it off my wish list. Then in early April after a week of good skiing in Breckenridge, Colorado, with son-in-law John and grandson Aubrey (who is a skiing fanatic), I tore the ACL ligament in my right knee in melting snow on the very last run of the trip, no more than three minutes from our condo. Back in New Orleans, my regular orthopedist told me that I was too old (81) for ACL surgery, but I found another surgeon who took me on despite my age and did a great job. Casey came down for the surgery and stayed for a week, sleeping on the couch, which probably saved my sanity. Three months later, when I was on track for a complete recovery, the surgeon proudly announced that I was now his oldest ACL surgery patient by seven years.

Four months after that operation, I enjoyed a wonderful family reunion and surprise birthday celebration on the island of Kauai in Hawaii. One of the highlights was a long boat ride halfway around the island, escorted by a school of playful dolphins, to a cove where we snorkeled in crystal-clear water numerous colorful denizens of the deep. There were also rowdy dinners with lots of mai tais and margaritas. And an interesting trip to a cultural center. On the last day, the group presented me with a birthday cake and a series of photos of each family member holding a card with a painted letter that spelled "Happy Birthday."

In October of 2022, I went with a Country Walkers group (including two old friends from the 2019 Bavarian Alps trip) to Patagonia for a week of moderate hiking to test my knee, which worked fine. Spanning the southern portion of both Chile and Argentina, Patagonia's incredible vastness makes the open spaces in the American West look like backyards. It is filled with stunning mountains, endless grasslands, gigantic glaciers, colorful wildlife—and very few people. On one hike, we watched a puma (cougar) stalk, on her belly, a feeding guanaco (small llama) that barely escaped at the last minute. We also walked on 100-foot-deep glaciers and gazed on an amazing array of water birds up close.

My new lady friend, Mathilde, and I were scheduled to hike the Lake District of England in June of 2023 but had to cancel that trip after she fell and broke her hip while hiking in Colorado two months earlier. For the same reason, I also canceled a hiking trip in Switzerland "from the Jungfrau to the Matterhorn." The two of us have booked trips next year to Greece and Switzerland and have our fingers crossed.

PREPARING FOR THE IDITAROD (IN MY DREAMS)

All breeds of domestic dogs are of course descended from wolves, but huskies certainly seem closer to their wild progenitors than poodles or chihuahuas do. In addition to their general appearance, huskies are very comfortable in extreme terrains and temperatures that would destroy most other kinds of dogs. But what sets them apart for me is their extraordinary eyes of blue or brown or one of each that "glow" in the dark like a wolf's eyes. Despite this wild side, huskies are very friendly, intelligent, and trainable. But they also love nothing better than speed and have perfected all sorts of devious ways of reducing their loads so they can run even faster, as I first saw and then learned for myself the hard way.

Lapland (Finland)

In the period of 2016–2018, I had the pleasure of driving dogsleds pulled by huskies on three different occasions. My introduction to mushing (the aficionado's name for dogsledding) occurred in the northern part of Finland above the Arctic Circle that is called Lapland. I actually heard the dogs before I saw them. On the morning of our scheduled sledding adventure, our small group of American travelers woke up to the melodious sound of about 100 huskies howling expectantly. It was loud enough to be next door even though our canine chorus was two miles away. We found out later that huskies are bred and trained to run (with loads) and therefore express their excitement vocally whenever the sleds and harnesses come out. Interestingly, all of the huskies I met in Finland and later in North America always mushed mutely (obviously to save breath), contrary to some literary images of huskies howling happily as they ran.

The sleds were designed for one driver, who stood on the thin wooden runners and held on to the waist-high crossbar, and one passenger, who sat on the canvas seat in front of the driver and hoped for the best (sometimes vainly, as I'll get to shortly) because he had no control whatsoever over the operation of the sled. The driver had a bit more control over his fate, but not much. He did not have any kind of steering wheel but did have a primitive brake consisting of

LEECHES, LOVERS, BEARS, AND CHOCOLATE PUDDING

a metal blade he could press down into the snow with one foot while balancing on the other. Except for that, the six dogs pulling the sled controlled its speed and direction. To help them pull their load uphill, the driver sometimes had to lighten the load by running behind the sled while pushing on the crossbar. The acrobatics and timing of getting both feet back on the narrow runners of a moving sled at the crest of a hill just before the dogs started racing downhill were always a little dicey, to say the least. If you botched it, like I did a few times, you'd find yourself in a semi-horizontal predicament, holding onto the crossbar for dear life with your helpless feet splayed out behind you, while the unrestrained dogs ran at top speed until they stopped behind another team.

Since the huskies knew the route to take through the forest, we were only instructed to keep our sleds in line and never pass the sled ahead of us. We all managed to do that until we came to a sharp, tilted turn at the bottom of a hill, which required a lot of braking to survive intact. My passenger and I made it, barely, and mushed another 200 feet or so when one of the sleds behind us came flying by at breakneck speed. It took us a moment to realize the sled had neither a driver nor passenger, so without all that weight to pull, the dogs were running for all they were worth and having a ball. One of the guides on a snowmobile finally ran them down after a good chase. We found out later that the driver had taken that dangerous turn too fast and caused the sled to tip enough to eject both of its occupants. Neither one was hurt because they landed on soft snow, but unfortunately for the driver, his passenger was his wife, who gave him a big piece of her mind.

The trip was sensational in every way. I dined in Helsinki the first night with a delightful Finnish couple I met through a mutual friend in New Orleans. Our group of Road Scholars headed north the next day into a true winter wonderland. The drama started quickly as we were boarding an icebreaker vessel to take us out into the well-frozen Baltic Sea to swim, when the ship shifted mysteriously and almost pulled the gangplank loose while I was on it. After breaking through a mile of three-foot thick ice, we all donned dry-suits and swam, i.e., floated, in the open water behind the icebreaker. We visited a reindeer farm and then a real, working hotel constructed entirely out of ice and decorated with beautiful ice carvings and sculptures. For anyone brave enough to spend the night in sub-zero temperatures on beds of ice in one of the 12 bedrooms, there

PREPARING FOR THE IDITAROD

were plenty of heavy blankets and animal skins. On another day, after snowshoeing with the group in a pristine white forest, I found a small bowling alley (250 miles north of the Arctic Circle!) and tried my luck, but the balls never rolled straight, no doubt because of the nearby North Pole's magnetic effect.

On our one free day, everyone else opted to snowmobile or snowshoe while I unwisely elected to try some cross-country skiing, even though my only previous attempt in Colorado years before was a complete fiasco. To make matters worse, the rental skis did not come with any instructions, so I was all on my own. The public cross-country trails were filled with graceful Finns of all ages who probably learned to ski before they could walk and made it look like ballet in the snow. And then there was me, flailing and lurching wildly before the inevitable crash. The locals were very sympathetic and sometimes helped me up, but they usually gave me a very wide berth, for obvious reasons. I did slightly better after a two-beer lunch, but it was still sensationally ugly. Since I'm fairly comfortable on downhill skis, my abject failure on cross-country skis was probably due in part to the same magnetic forces that ruined my Finnish bowling debut. Or maybe it was those nefarious Russians. After all, I was closer to Russia than Sarah Palin ever was. That could also explain why the Northern Lights did not show up the whole time we were in the perfect place to see them. Yep, it all sounds like a classic Russian plot. Take note, Mr. Mueller.

Northern Minnesota

About a year later, I took my 16-year-old grandson, Ethan, to northern Minnesota near the Canadian border for two days of mushing. The sleds there were designed for two drivers standing side-by-side on a metal plate instead of the sled runners, which made our job easier but not as much fun. In addition, the dogs could not run as fast as they would normally because the snow was relatively soft and thin due to unusually warm temperatures. On the other hand, that also exposed more rocks and roots that made the trails somewhat more hazardous, as we saw for ourselves. The oldest member of our small group was an 85-year-old veteran (nine years older than me) who had a sled all to himself for some reason. As his sled was traveling at a good clip, it struck something unseen in the snow that stopped it on a dime. As a result, the elder driver was literally catapulted over the crossbar and landed directly on the top of his head. Expecting a broken neck or worse, I was very surprised and relieved when he stood up, dusted off the snow, and got back on his sled. The only injuries suffered by our group were a few scratches from overhanging tree branches on the trails.

Ethan and I did suffer some emotional trauma when I challenged him to a contest to see who could stand barefoot in the snow the longest. No, I had not been drinking—I was inspired by the story of an everyday American who had learned from an Indian guru in only one week how to stand barefoot in snow for a full hour! Well, Ethan and I lasted all of 25 seconds, to the great amusement of our fellow guests watching through the windows of our cabin.

Unfortunately, I was due for a bit more embarrassment before I could get out of town. Given their well-deserved reputation as heavy-duty haulers, huskies are surprisingly small and rarely exceed 60 pounds. So when the guides showed us how to hand-walk a husky between its house and sled by lifting his chest harness and making him walk only on his hind legs, that seemed unnecessary and uncomfortable to me. Well, once again, I learned the hard way just why the guides did that. After a good day of mushing, I unhooked our lead dog from the sled and started walking her as instructed back to her house. She was one of the smaller dogs and probably weighed 40 pounds or less. Since I weighed 175 pounds, I was sure I could control her if I let her walk on all four legs. As soon as her front paws hit the ground, she took off and literally pulled me right off my feet. Stretched out horizontally on the ground while holding frantically on to her harness, I was helpless. She hauled me 30 feet or so before Ethan came to my rescue. Being dragged ignominiously by a wee dog through snow and mud like a ragdoll is a humbling experience. It also proves that old saw about big things coming in small packages, just as my brave but petite wife did when she took on that massive bear in Canada.

Denali (Alaska)

The next stop was Denali National Park in central Alaska a year later in March of 2018. I found a good dogsledding service through a friend's son who had moved from New Orleans to the town of Talkeetna just outside the park (one extreme to the other) and even climbed the mighty Denali (Mount McKinley)

PREPARING FOR THE IDITAROD

itself, the tallest mountain in North America at 20,310 feet. After some understandable hesitation, Casey, Ginger, and Will all agreed to go with me, obviously to keep an eye on their certifiably-insane father (who appreciated their concern), but Ginger unfortunately got sick at the last minute and had to cancel. Her place was taken by Casey's partner Stacey, who fit right in and knew as much about movies as did the screenwriter Will. We had two guides and a total of 40 dogs between the six of us.

After a training day, we headed west out of Healy on the park boundary for four days on the so-called trail, which was undetectable to me under all the snow but not to the guides or dogs. Each member of my team had his or her own team of six huskies for the whole trip. Mine were Daphne, Otto, Sophia, Polly, Pirate (who had different colored eyes and was my favorite), and Panda. They were surprisingly shy at first, but by the end of the trip, they were my good buddies, despite trying to kill me, as I'll explain later. They showed their affection in the mornings when they first saw me by jumping up and enclosing me tightly (and I do mean tightly) with their front legs. My team worked very well together, unlike some of the other dogs that had to be transferred from one team to another. And it was clearly the fastest team of dogs out there because it kept overtaking the lead guide's sled that I followed throughout the trip.

That blazing speed was great fun on the open straightaways but a mixed bag for me whenever the trail twisted and turned through trees or bushes. I found that out early one morning when I was still half-asleep and the fully rested dogs were anxious to run. The guides had warned us the night before about a very sharp turn just outside our camp, so I have no excuses. Within seconds of starting out, my dogs took that turn at top speed. I knew it was coming but just forgot to use the foot brake. The result was rather spectacular, from what the others told me: the dogs took a hard left and I took a hard right (I could have used a good seatbelt) in a classic demonstration of centrifugal force. I didn't just fall off the sled—I was launched into the air, remained airborne for what seemed like a lifetime, and finally crashed to the ground at Stacey's feet. Unfortunately, no one was videoing my little circus act. Fortunately, nothing was broken, which would have been a serious problem out in the middle of nowhere, so a much wiser me got back on the sled after the guides returned it. My canine friends did not look

LEECHES, LOVERS, BEARS, AND CHOCOLATE PUDDING

very remorseful. In fact, they looked downright smug about unloading me so quickly and surely were plotting to do it again.

Which they did two more times that same day! Okay, okay—I know what you're thinking. Just remember that dogsledding is trickier than it looks. (And don't forget those pesky Russians just over the horizon. No telling what they did to my poor dogs.) But back to mushing, which is especially tricky going downhill through thick woods before crossing a frozen river, as we did many times. The dogs knew where the shifting trail was, but I did not and could not just follow the guide's lead because he was often out of sight around a bend of trees. So if,

when, and how hard to apply the foot brake for a sharp turn I couldn't see was always a crap shoot. On two such occasions, I guessed wrong and wound up flying off the sled like that first time, to the amusement of Will, who followed me in our line of mushers. After my third calamity, the little rascal told me with a straight face that I was perfecting the art of falling off a sled because each of my exits was better than the last one. It made me feel much better to know that Will and the girls had also fallen off their sleds at least once, but I was the undisputed champion.

PREPARING FOR THE IDITAROD

Once again I failed to see the Northern Lights, but the stars on clear nights were truly spectacular, out in the middle of a huge, gorgeous nowhere. Since we had no electricity or running water for all four days, I had ample opportunities to enjoy the night skies (as well as the fresh, forest-scented air) on my many nocturnal jaunts to the outhouses. Because the nighttime temperatures usually hit 20 below zero (compared to positive 10–15 degrees during the daytime), I couldn't just run outside in my PJ's, but the sights, sounds, and smells made up for having to don boots and jackets. Our lodging on the trail consisted of small ranger cabins that sometimes had, at most, an old decrepit couch or bed, but we usually slept on the floor in sleeping bags. There was always a propane stove for cooking the unidentifiable one-pot meals (which were surprisingly good and filling) and a wood-burning stove for heat. Drinking, cooking, and cleaning water came from melted snow. A few of the older dogs picked by the guides were allowed to sleep inside with us, while the others slept outside in the snow. It was spartan but warm and cozy. And our two very competent guides were fun, which made for memorable evenings.

I would guess that we mushed an average of 20 miles a day, less when it snowed and more when it didn't. Even when we sledded in snow, the only part of us that got cold was the area around our nose and mouth that was not covered by our balaclavas or goggles. The physical effort required to drive the sleds also helped to keep us warm. We were fortunate that our first day out was crystal clear and afforded us a distant look at Denali's peak, which is usually covered in clouds. Aside from the infrequent ranger cabins, we were surrounded for four glorious days by nothing but Mother Nature at her best, consisting of vast, snow-covered landscapes of mountains, forests, steppes, and rivers.

The only thing missing from this tableau was wildlife. Since it was only March and the winter had been a harsh one, the grizzly bears in the area were probably still hibernating. But moose don't hibernate and are far more dangerous than grizzlies, which generally steer clear of the huskies, unlike moose. Any wild animal that weighs 1,000–1,500 pounds and is equipped with lethal antlers and hooves would be dangerous, but moose in addition are short-tempered, unpredictable, territorial, and fearless. In preparing for the trip, I read the book *Winterdance* (by Gary Paulsen) about the author's experiences in running his first Iditarod across Alaska, not far from where we were and at the same time of year. In the scene I remember best, a moose charged out of a nearby forest and attacked another driver's lead dog for no reason at all. Even though the driver shot him five times at close range with a high-powered pistol, the assailant finished off his canine victim and still managed to get back to the forest before dying. So when we stopped one day for lunch in a place called Moose Alley that was a narrow opening through a thicket of close-in trees and bushes, I lost my appetite. I imagined there was an angry moose hiding behind every tree and bush, just itching to jump out and pulverize us all. The dogs were firmly anchored to the ground (as they always were when we left our sleds) and we had no weapon as far as I knew, so we were sitting ducks. And as much as I needed to go to the bathroom just then, I was not about to enter that forbidding forest filled with bloodthirsty beasts. But the imagined army of marauding moose never materialized, thank goodness, and we went on our merry way.

By the way, if you have no plans to dogsled through moose country anytime soon, I would definitely recommend that book *Winterdance* to you. The Iditarod, of course, is a classic test of human and canine endurance: a grueling 8–15-day race by dogsled across 1,150 miles of the toughest terrain in Alaska. One funny example from the author's amazing journey with his 16 huskies was the sight of four buffaloes racing down a hill at full speed onto a frozen lake and sliding happily on the ice. They obviously enjoyed it because they did the same thing over and over again. We usually don't think of wild animals doing something just for the fun of it, but we still have a lot to learn about them. Unfortunately, our group did not encounter any free-spirited or other kind of buffaloes on this trip. Maybe next time. Or when I get around to running the Iditarod.

Jackson Hole, Wyoming

My last mushing trip was somewhat anticlimactic because we only rode on the sleds while professional guides drove them. It was a short Road Scholar trip in February, 2020, that I'd booked many months before and then almost canceled after Julie died in early January, but eventually decided to attend in hopes that it would help me deal with my loss, as it did. And the timing turned out to be perfect: two weeks after the trip, the Covid pandemic hit Lambeth House like a

PREPARING FOR THE IDITAROD

hurricane and infected dozens of residents, including me. Unlike many others, I survived, but did not travel outside the country for over two years because of the pandemic.

Our four winter days in Jackson Hole were quite active, even though most of the group were in their 70s or 80s (I was 79). During the usual introductions, one participant said this was her 44th Road Scholar trip (it was my fifth). We spent most of the time outdoors either snowshoeing, cross-country skiing, dogsledding, or watching thousands of elk at a national preserve. My dogsledding guide allowed me to stand next to him on one of the sled runners behind the sled basket, so I at least was doing something active, other than driving the sled. And, I am proud to say, this was my only mushing experience that did not involve at least one fall off the speeding sled. There is some kind of lesson in that for me, if I ever have the chance to go mushing again, but I don't want to jump to conclusions.

THE COMPASSIONATE SEA LION

It was another remarkable encounter with the animal kingdom. Although it lasted only a few seconds like the hummingbird encounter, the memory is just as indelible. The setting this time was a Road Scholar trip to the Galapagos Islands with our then-14-year-old grandson Aubrey. The particular scene was underwater in a quiet cove filled with wild but playful sea lions. The messenger was one of those graceful creatures. And the message? In view of the fact that this encounter could have easily cost me my hand or even my life but did not, I'm sure there was some kind of message.

With three other guests, Aubrey and I spent a week on a small boat visiting several of the famous islands on the equator 600 miles west of Ecuador in the Pacific Ocean. As bleak and isolated as they were, the islands were teeming with life, including countless sea lions of all ages on the white- and red-sand beaches, on the ancient volcanic rocks, and in the crystal-clear blue and green water. Although we snorkeled almost every day (with sharks, manta rays, sea turtles, penguins, and exotic fish), we didn't meet the sea lions underwater until midway through the trip. On that unforgettable occasion, our guide took us to a small, protected cove that was a playground for the resident sea lions and a true wonderland for us.

After visiting the area in sea kayaks and watching the sea lions play with our rope lines in the water, we returned later to swim with them. I had on flippers, a snorkel mask, and a full-length wetsuit. Only my hands were uncovered. There were six of us, including our native guide, and about 15 of them. As soon as we left our little "panga" raft and got in the water, which was probably 30 feet deep and clear as glass, the sea lions went crazy, in a good sense. They had some new playmates. They swam in and out of our group, showing off their incredible speed and agility in water by dipping, diving, twisting, turning, and performing other acrobatic feats for us. It was a once-in-a-lifetime show. Although they would sometimes swim close enough to brush us with their flippers, none of it was ever threatening. They were just playing with their new friends. By getting in the water with them, we became one with them.

LEECHES, LOVERS, BEARS, AND CHOCOLATE PUDDING

Aubrey and the other guests were experienced snorkelers who were able to dive and twist with the sea lions. I, on the other hand, was snorkeling for the first time in all of my 77 years and therefore was not the most robust of dance partners. After 15 or so minutes of frenetic activity, I got tired and paddled off the dance floor to rest a little by floating quietly in my buoyant wetsuit on top of the water with my head down and arms outstretched. That's when the comely messenger arrived, just as quietly, in contrast to all the other sea lions which were still doing their dazzling tricks. I watched as she (an assumption, based on her exquisite gentleness) left her playmates and swam slowly up to my extended and uncovered right hand. Then she put her nose right up against it, while gazing at me. A couple of seconds later, I looked away briefly, to see if Aubrey was watching. When I looked back, most of my right hand was in the sea lion's mouth. If I hadn't seen it, I would not have known, because I felt absolutely no pain or pressure of any kind on my hand, but reacting instinctively, I did withdraw it. Instead of trying to hold on to my hand by clamping down, the sea lion actually opened her mouth and looked at me for a second before swimming slowly away and joining in the play of her colleagues.

When I later described the incident to our trip leader, he had never heard of anything like that happening in all of the 26 years he'd been guiding groups and swimming with the sea lions. He was also quite astonished that I still had a hand and all five fingers because sea lions, which have very sharp teeth and very strong jaws for catching fish to eat, have been known to attack humans on rare occasions. Some later research confirmed that troubling fact. In one shocking case, a sea lion jumped out of the water and pulled a young girl off a pier—fortunately, she was rescued but suffered numerous bites.

With that new information, I realized how much danger I had been in and how lucky I was to survive without a scratch. If the sea lion had clamped her

THE COMPASSIONATE SEA LION

teeth together, I would have lost most of my dominant hand. She might then have attacked me in other ways or dragged me underwater and drowned me. And if she had bitten off my hand, there would have been a large amount of blood, which could have attracted some of the numerous sharks in the area. That would also have endangered Aubrey and his other companions, who probably would have been coming nearer to rescue me. To do that would have required them to call over the "panga" raft, somehow get me into it, meet up with the main vessel, get me aboard that, and then find a hospital possibly miles away. The chances are good that I would have bled to death before all of that happened. Even now, years later, I still shudder to think of what might have happened to me and Aubrey and so many others if the sea lion had just closed her mouth on my hand.

But she didn't. Why then did she grab my hand in the same powerful jaws she used to crush fish and defend herself? Perhaps she thought it might be something edible. After all, since my arm was covered to the wrist by the black wetsuit, she may have assumed the hand was not attached to me. If so, she probably would have nibbled on it a little to see how it tasted. But she didn't bite down or even nibble, which is proof enough for me that eating my hand was not her objective.

Nor do I think it was simple curiosity on her part. As soon as we humans entered the water, the excited sea lions immediately started cavorting all around us in a remarkable display of friendship. By the time of my encounter, they had been swimming among us for a good, long time and probably knew as much about us as they needed to. This particular sea lion must have known I had been part of the group playing with them. And before taking my hand in her mouth, she touched it gently with her nose, as if to smell it, but in light of how things turned out, her gesture could have been her way of kissing my hand.

So why did this remarkable creature smell or kiss my hand and then take it into her mouth? In hindsight, it surely was at the very least an act of friendship but probably much more than that. As strange as it might sound, I think she may have thought I was hurt and came over to check. Remember that I had been actively swimming, twisting, and moving in the water, like everyone else, right up to the time I decided to rest on the sidelines. Thus, while all the other human playmates were still swimming around in the water with the sea lions, I alone suddenly stopped moving and became relatively stationary. Several seconds

LEECHES, LOVERS, BEARS, AND CHOCOLATE PUDDING

later, my friend left the ongoing party and came over to me. Instead of approaching me from behind, below, or the side, she came from the front, at eye level where I could see her coming. And unlike the sea lions' high speeds during our underwater dance, she came on very slowly, presumably not to frighten me. When I did not move my hand after she put her nose against it, she then took it in her mouth in the most gentle way possible, like a nurse holding a patient's hand. I did not feel her sharp teeth or even the slightest pressure on my hand. And when I moved to withdraw my hand, she didn't try to hold on to it but actually opened her mouth to make it easier for me. Then she swam quietly away as if she was satisfied I was okay, instead of bolting away if she'd been disappointed or frightened. It all adds up, in my mind anyway.

Which raises this obvious question: Does a sea lion have the mental and emotional capacity to (a) recognize that a totally different kind of creature may be hurt; and (b) respond to that situation in a helpful way? If we assume that all sea lions function at approximately the same mental and emotional level, the answer to this question is probably no, based on our present state of knowledge. But is that a fair assumption? Think of the great variations of intelligence and emotion in the human race. Science is beginning to discover milder degrees of similar variations in many of the "higher" forms of animals, birds, and fish. Perhaps my friend was just more perceptive and caring than her fellow sea lions. After all, she was the only one of them to leave the great fun they were all having and come over to me. It may well be that most sea lions are not capable of what we call compassion, but that does not rule out the possibility or even probability that this particular sea lion was.

Unfortunately, I can never prove why my amphibious friend left her merry band of colleagues and came over to see me. On the other hand, I do know what she did and how she did it, all the way from the way she approached me in such an unthreatening manner to the way she held my hand in her mouth so gently. That tells me that our meeting was intentional, not accidental. She had a purpose in doing what she did. And part of her purpose must have been to connect or communicate with me, a wholly different kind of animal, in the only way she knew how. It's not the specific content of her message that's important but her elegant effort to tell me something. That effort was the message. And that's why this unusual encounter was such a spiritual moment in my life.

TRIALS AND TRIBULATIONS

There is enough excitement and glory in trial work to offset the abundant tedium and frustration of practicing any kind of law. Here are a few examples of that from my own 31 years of practice with a large New Orleans defense firm. The cases described were unusual or noteworthy for one reason or another. Since they represent just a small percentage of the cases I handled and/or tried, I've simply forgotten about many that would have otherwise made this list. And of those included here, I can remember the important facts but not the names of some, so bear with me. With two or three exceptions as noted, I served as the lead attorney for our client(s).

Before and during trials, I no doubt was even more difficult to live with than I usually was, so I'll be forever grateful to my awesome wife, Julie, for sticking with me instead of walking out or just dispatching me. With her usual patience, common sense, empathy, understanding, and sense of humor, Julie got me through the constant highs and lows that come with trying cases. She was always there for me with an encouraging word, a missing insight, or just a timely back rub. And since she was a wonderful "sounding board" who saved me from trying a lot of bad ideas, she definitely deserves to share some of the so-called glory with me from the cases won. Not surprisingly, with her big heart, Julie usually took the victim's side in personal injury cases.

Neumeyer:

This is by far the longest trial I ever handled. I was in court for *12* hours a day from 8:00 AM to 8:00 PM, *six* days a week including Saturdays, for *seven* continuous weeks! We ate lunch and dinner in court, consisting of po'boys that were thoroughly picked over by the jurors (12 regulars plus four alternates) and the judge's staff before the half-demolished leftovers finally got around to the lawyers (I never liked po'boys after that). But it was worse for the jurors who received a most ungenerous stipend of $14 a day for their service and wound up losing jobs and vacations because of the long time away from work. (It was

LEECHES, LOVERS, BEARS, AND CHOCOLATE PUDDING

probably an angry juror hoping for a mistrial who called in three bomb scares that temporarily cleared the whole courthouse during this trial.)

Why was the trial so long? One theory is that the plaintiffs' attorney, besides loving to hear himself talk, was being paid by the hour in addition to a percentage of any monetary recovery, because his clients were well-off real estate developers, so he dragged the trial out as long as possible. As a result, I went "missing" from home for the full seven weeks. To get to the courthouse across the River in Gretna, I had to leave before the kids got up for school. When I got home well after 9:00 PM, the kids were already asleep, or I had to start preparing immediately for the next day of trial.

Sundays were usually spent at my office downtown or meeting with witnesses. It was so bad that Will at one point asked Julie, "Does Dad still lives here?"

The plaintiffs were represented by the legendary Fred Gisevius, the dean of plaintiffs' attorneys in this area. As an ex-boxer, he was still in excellent physical shape and always light on his feet in a courtroom with a captive audience. There were rumors, however, that Fred at age 68 or so (younger than my present age!) was "over the hill," but he quickly and emphatically proved otherwise by making a two-hour opening statement to the jury without using a single note. Everyone in the courtroom was spellbound. It was the best courtroom performance I've ever witnessed. To make matters even worse for the defendants, the trial judge was terrified by the size of the case itself and by Gisevius, who consequently got away with murder throughout the trial. Bill Christovich, a real prince and outstanding trial lawyer, represented one doctor in this medical malpractice case and I represented two.

The plaintiffs claimed that the defendants over a year and a half caused their young son to develop a serious and permanent seizure disorder and then failed to diagnose or treat it. Medical experts from Mayo and Johns Hopkins testified in support of the plaintiffs' claims. Bill and I called several local experts, but we also worked hard to condense our defense to one week, compared to the six weeks Gisevius took, and that probably made more of a difference to the long-suffering jury than all of our experts and legal skills. After deliberating several hours, the jury came back in at 2:00 AM with a verdict in favor of all

TRIALS AND TRIBULATIONS

three defendants. To his credit, Fred was quite gracious and complimentary after the trial.

Going back to the office after crashing for a day was a very mixed bag. Returning as the "dragon slayer" was fun, but that moment of fame barely lasted the proverbial 15 minutes, which I couldn't even enjoy because of the 100-plus other cases that I had ignored for seven weeks and needed immediate attention, like right now. After many days without stopping for lunch, I achieved a certain degree of control, only to lose it again when the next trial came up. Feast or famine: such is the life of a trial lawyer.

Shields (I think):

This was a humdinger in every way: characters, issues, intrigue, betrayal, slander, contempt of court, etc. Plus a three-week jury trial in Covington, followed by bizarre post-trial motions and appeals. It was a trying and traumatic experience for everyone involved, including the judge and jury!

The plaintiffs' attorney had been the star trial lawyer at Lemle & Kelleher when I arrived there in 1966 and my mentor for six years until he left to start another firm, which he left in turn to become a personal injury lawyer for victims. He was indeed a brilliant trial lawyer but he could be somewhat unpredictable at times, as demonstrated in this case. I'll call him "Jeff."

My client, Dr. X, was even more of a character than my opponent. He was a general practitioner who also performed relatively simple surgery, which is how he wound up in this malpractice case. After removing Mrs. Shields' gall bladder, he discovered that her liver could no longer drain into the intestine because of a three-inch gap in the common bile duct that connected the two, a true life-threatening emergency in every sense. The plaintiffs claimed Dr. X had negligently cut out the missing duct when he removed the patient's gall bladder. We claimed the subject duct ran through her gall bladder instead of outside of it, a very rare anatomical anomaly, and Dr. X had unknowingly removed part of it when he removed the gall bladder. Interestingly, the missing three-inch piece of duct was never found.

What happened after Dr. X discovered the problem is a bit fantastic and would be laughable if the consequences to Mrs. Shields (the family's

LEECHES, LOVERS, BEARS, AND CHOCOLATE PUDDING

breadwinner because her husband was disabled) had not been so tragic. After realizing the duct was too short to suture together, Dr. X phoned a local general surgeon for help, quickly. When the surgeon took one look at the surgical mess, he exclaimed "Holy Shit!" and immediately left the operating room to call another surgeon in New Orleans. While he was doing that, Dr. X was in the hospital library thumbing through books for some kind of solution, leaving the poor patient with an open belly on the operating table in the care of an anesthesiology assistant. Eventually, on advice from his colleague, the local surgeon attached the liver-end of the duct to a synthetic tube that drained the liver to a bag outside Mrs. Shields' body and then sent her by ambulance to New Orleans. By the time of the trial three years later, Mrs. Shields had undergone 15 additional operations to repair or replace the drainage tube and treat serious infections. Dr. X had $2 million of malpractice insurance and a big bank account of his own from various real estate ventures, so his exposure to a very sizeable judgment was very real.

Perhaps I should mention at this point that Dr. X, sometime in the past, had gotten into an argument with the trial judge and threatened to punch him out (something I found out about halfway through the trial), which probably explains why Jeff spent almost every recess laughing with the judge in the privacy of his chambers while I cooled my heels outside. This cozy relationship between lawyer and judge was to change dramatically at the end of the trial, so read on.

One of my expert witnesses was a general surgeon from Nebraska who had published a short article about encountering the same kind of anatomical anatomy we were claiming to be the problem in this case. He was an old turkey hunter who had never testified in court before but was all fired up to win the case for me. I was a little apprehensive when I first met him and therefore prepared him for court very carefully, which turned out to be a total waste of time. My "warrior" expert was a complete disaster, if not worse. Jeff absolutely destroyed him on cross-examination.

We finished all the testimony on a Friday afternoon of the third week and showed up Monday morning to make closing arguments to the jury. Then all hell broke loose. The judge convened a meeting of the attorneys to tell me that the case had apparently been settled over the weekend, which I knew nothing about. Apparently Jeff, unbeknownst to me, had called the insurance company's claims manager, whom he knew from his days at Lemle & Kelleher, and negotiated a settlement of the claim for $1 million. I was not only stunned but angry that this was done behind my back. When I called the insurer to confirm the settlement, I was instructed to get Dr. X's consent to it, but he strongly objected to any settlement and wanted the jury to decide the case. So there I was, caught in a whirlwind between Dr. X. and his insurer and the judge, who was anxious to finish the case one way or the other. To convince his insurer not to settle, Dr. X even agreed to pay any judgment against him in excess of $1 million out of his own pocket despite his policy limits of $2 million.

When I informed Jeff and the judge that the insurer had withdrawn its offer, Jeff argued long and loud that the settlement was a done deal and legally binding on the insurer, but the judge correctly ruled it was not binding because it was not in writing or made in open court. By this time, my well-prepared closing argument was pretty much forgotten in all of the turmoil, but I managed somehow to make some sense to the jury. Jeff, in his closing, made a fatal mistake (which reminds me of Hillary Clinton's "basket of deplorables" remark that may have cost her the 2016 election). To connect with a particular juror, he tried to make a joke about his own expanding waistline and the juror's, by name, who did not laugh. A few hours later, that juror cast the deciding vote in a 9–3 verdict in favor of Dr. X (at least nine votes out of 12 are required for a verdict).

Shortly thereafter, Jeff filed a written motion to compel the trial judge to enforce the alleged $1 million "settlement." Among other things, he asserted in very colorful language that his former buddy, the judge, had "colluded" with me and Dr. X to cheat the plaintiffs out of the settlement money, which was absurd in light of how the judge felt about Dr. X after the threat to punch him and how he favored Jeff's side of the case during trial. The motion was emphatically denied, but Jeff persisted with that argument on appeal and even became more outrageous with his allegations of unethical misconduct. He also informed me that he would only communicate with me in writing from then on. (And when Dr. X advised me that his agreement to waive $1 million of insurance coverage was binding only in the trial court and not on appeal, which was ridiculous, that was the final straw—I started wondering whether I was going to lose my mind like everyone else in the case.)

LEECHES, LOVERS, BEARS, AND CHOCOLATE PUDDING

In response to his slanderous accusations against the trial judge and me, the Court of Appeals in Baton Rouge issued a scathing written opinion condemning Jeff's conduct in the strongest language I've ever heard from any court. But we still had to orally argue the merits of Jeff's motion and appeal, not once but twice, which suggested the appellate court was having trouble making up its mind. In the end, it split: two of the judges voted to affirm the jury's verdict and the trial judge's ruling on Jeff's "settlement" motion, while the third judge voted to reverse the verdict and enter judgment for the plaintiffs. Jeff then asked the Louisiana Supreme Court to review the case but it declined to do so by a vote of 4–3, suggesting that three justices on the court probably would have reversed the jury and/or trial judge.

So I won the case by the narrowest of margins on all three judicial levels: 9–3 in the trial court, 2–1 in the appellate court, and 4–3 in the Supreme Court. If that one juror had voted the other way, there would have been a "hung jury" and another full trial by a different jury. If that had happened, Dr. X and his insurer could have easily lost $5–10 million or more in damages considering the extent of Mrs. Shields' injuries and suffering. We dodged the bullet by the hair on my chinny-chin-chin, but a win is a win—although this one was bittersweet because of everything the Shields suffered through no fault of their own.

(Jeff was my opponent in only one subsequent case. We communicated entirely in writing. The defendant doctor, an OB, failed to diagnose the patient's false pregnancy that she carried all the way to term before finding out there was no baby and never had been. It was a clear case of malpractice because the OB had diagnosed the "pregnancy" without doing a basic pregnancy test, so we wound up settling before any trial for a nominal sum.)

Gulf South Machine:

I represented the plaintiff business in this products liability case that was tried before a federal court jury for three weeks. My client was owned and operated by three brothers named Holak who were all born behind the Iron Curtain and then moved to Ponchatoula, Louisiana. I frankly don't remember how we got connected initially, but it turned out to be a long and satisfying relationship.

TRIALS AND TRIBULATIONS

The defendant was Kearney & Trecker, a large machine tool manufacturer in Milwaukee. It was represented by its national trial counsel out of Omaha, named Malcolm somebody. What I do recall vividly about him was that he was a first-class jerk. Besides being arrogant and very nasty, he considered my foreign-born clients to be sub-human, despite the fact that they spoke perfect English and were good, hard-working citizens in every way. As a result of Malcolm's attitude, the case was infused with a high level of personal animosity. A compromise settlement was never discussed. It was a do-or-die war from the outset.

Gulf South Machine was in the business of fabricating metal parts, like bathroom fixtures, for large national companies. It claimed that a highly complex, automated machine purchased from Kearney & Trecker was defective and had malfunctioned over a long period of time, thereby causing hundreds of thousands of dollars in direct costs and serious damage to its entire business. The defendant claimed that its machine was not defective and Gulf South Machine had caused its own problems.

I was lucky enough to find a former Kearney & Trecker engineer who had done some work on the machine in question before being fired. Not surprisingly, he was very cooperative and helpful in building our case. The trial involved a lot of records, expert witnesses, and heated cross-examination. The jury wound up awarding $750,000 in damages to my client (a big judgment in those days), including $200,000 of attorneys' fees as a punitive measure, no doubt in response to my opponent's questionable behavior in court. The Holaks were ecstatic, not only about the money that allegedly saved their business but also about "beating the shit" out of dear Malcolm.

Interestingly, the trial judge (who was later found with $30,000 of cash, i.e., bribe money, in his desk and sent up the river) offered the attorneys the opportunity of talking to the jurors after the case was over. Malcolm declined and left in a huff, but the Holaks and I took the jurors across the street for drinks and spent over an hour with them. I was frankly blown away by the amount of very complex engineering and financial information they had understood during the trial. They also offered some interesting observations about the individual attorneys and parties. One example I remember well is the fact that the primary Holak brother came to court the first day with brightly and obviously dyed blonde hair, which had made me worry about the jury's reaction, but they turned out to like him despite his topside.

Incensed by his loss to the "Bolsheviks," Malcolm became more outrageous on appeal. He refused to cooperate with me in the most mundane of matters and even resisted the appellate court at times. As a consequence, he was twice held in contempt of court and ordered to pay me additional attorneys' fees. And his appeal was denied on the merits, so his unhappy client had to pay out the full judgment, plus legal interest and punitive damages in the form of attorneys' fees. I never heard from Malcolm again and suspect that he is now chasing down immigrants for the Trump administration.

Payne:

I had the misfortune of representing a doctor (through his insurer) in this malpractice case who made Malcolm in the previous case look like a saint. On top of that, the injury in this case was the worst I've ever seen and the so-called medical care was also the worst I've ever known (and I've seen some gross medical malpractice in my career). It was a case that was easily worth $10–20 million in compensatory damages (and much more in punitive damages if they had been allowed under Louisiana law). We wound up settling for $100,000, which is a somewhat painful memory, as I'll explain.

The plaintiff was a 13-year-old African American who was brought to a local emergency room in obvious shock from what turned out to be meningococcemia, a virulent form of meningitis. Unfortunately for him, my client was on duty that day. What he should have done for this patient was to immediately put him on a drip and restore his blood pressure. What he did was…NOTHING! For several hours the poor patient just lay there, getting worse and worse. The clueless doctor finally called a pediatrician at another hospital for advice and was told to send the patient to him by ambulance IMMEDIATELY before he died. It took the ER doctor another two hours to accomplish that, even though the pediatrician called him back several times to hurry things up. When the pediatrician finally got the patient, he realized that most of his blood had been automatically shunted away from his extremities to save his trunk and brain. Therefore, to save the patient's life, the pediatrician and a team of surgeons had to amputate all four of his limbs. The patient did survive, which in this case may not have been a blessing.

Meeting with the pediatrician was much easier than meeting with my own client. The former told me this was the worst case of gross malpractice he could imagine and was more than willing to testify to that in court. The guilty doctor would not even meet with me at first and thought the whole case was nonsense! When I finally did get in to see him, he was not only defensive and uncooperative but obviously felt no sympathy or remorse. It turned out that he had once been suspended from practicing medicine because of a drug addiction and had spent his career as a journeyman ER doctor who didn't stay long in any one hospital. (Another defense attorney and friend told me that he went to my client's house to discuss some other case and found the doctor naked and passed out on his bed, so he left very quickly.) Then, out of the blue, the defendant doctor suddenly died, which saved me the trouble of doing it myself.

But the case proceeded against his insurer and I wound up taking the plaintiff's deposition. That was a very sad experience. But also inspiring, because he was fairly upbeat for a teenage boy without any arms or legs. He was behind in school but trying to keep up with the encouragement of his sainted mother, who was present at the deposition. It was pretty clear, however, that he probably would have wound up working in some form of manual labor, which now of course was no longer an option for him, so he was going to need a lot of custodial care for the rest of his life. I often think of him many years after the case ended and hope he's doing as well as possible under the horrendous circumstances.

A few years before this case was filed, the Louisiana Legislature had passed a law capping the damages payable by a physician or his insurer in a malpractice case at $100,000. By paying that amount in settlement, a defendant admitted liability and entitled the victim to recover up to another $400,000, depending on the extent of his loss, from a state-operated fund to which the doctors and insurers had to contribute in order to qualify for the $100,000 cap. In addition, the fund would pay any and all future medical and custodial expenses necessitated by the admitted malpractice, which would certainly apply to this patient's situation.

LEECHES, LOVERS, BEARS, AND CHOCOLATE PUDDING

When this suit was filed, the constitutionality of the $100,000 cap had not yet been tested in the Louisiana Supreme Court. Although the insurer and I realized we could not possibly defend the case successfully and were therefore ready to put up our $100,000, we didn't want to test the damage cap in a case of such blatant malpractice and horrific injuries, so we bided our time. When the Court did uphold the cap in another case, we put up our $100,000 and got out as fast as we could.

It was a great result from the insurer's standpoint, but my heart was definitely not in it. As an advocate representing a client's interests in an adversarial system, my primary duty to my client sometimes conflicted with my own personal sense of fundamental fairness, as it certainly did in this awful case. By saying that, I don't mean to suggest that the insurer or I did anything unethical or even questionable by invoking the statutory cap. On the other hand, it still disgusts me that the insured doctor got away with something worse than murder and never had to face the music for what he did, at least not in this world. True justice was definitely not achieved in this case.

???????:

This was another tragic case involving an unimaginable injury. I represented Monsanto, the defendant. The plaintiff, a contractor doing work at the Luling plant across the Mississippi River, was leaving in his pickup truck when it was struck by a train at a crossing on Monsanto's property. The force of the collision was so great that the plaintiff was catapulted out of the truck window and landed on a stack of rail ties some 20–30 feet away. He suffered severe brain damage that left him in a permanent vegetative state. He was also paralyzed from the neck down. When I took his wife's deposition, he was living at home with her and their two young teenage children. With the poor man sitting motionless and oblivious in a wheelchair nearby, it was obvious that his family was devoted to him and was suffering terribly.

The crossing and the road over it were both owned and maintained by Monsanto. The train tracks were owned, operated, and used by an independent railroad company that was not sued. Monsanto's road intersected with a public highway with a red traffic light at the intersection, which was only three car lengths away from the crossing. On the day in question, there were three cars stopped on Monsanto's road for the light. The plaintiff's truck was the fourth vehicle in the line leaving the plant. According to the witnesses, the truck stopped right on the tracks, behind the car in front. Other than a sign, there were no warning bars or signals at the crossing.

All of the witnesses stopped in cars in front and back of the plaintiff's truck heard the warning horn of an approaching train and could see it coming from their left side because the tracks were perfectly straight at that point. None of them noticed anything to indicate that the plaintiff was aware of the train, such as trying to move his truck off the tracks. When the driver directly in front of him realized his danger, she quickly pulled her car out of line and onto the shoulder to give him room enough to drive his truck forward and off the tracks, but he apparently made no effort to do so or to get out of the truck, even when the driver behind him honked his horn frantically. Why he did nothing to escape the oncoming train will always remain a mystery. Perhaps he had a seizure, stroke, or heart attack, but we'll never know.

The suit claimed that Monsanto was liable for maintaining an unsafe and defective crossing that should have had crossing arms and warning lights that activated when a train was coming, especially since the crossing was on a busy road and so close to the red light at the highway intersection. The plaintiff's attorney, a very successful veteran, had track-crossing safety experts to support his contentions. We had experts to counter them. And we had the plaintiff's own apparent negligence. But considering the extent of the plaintiff's injuries and the dismal situation of his loving family, a jury would have been hard-pressed to deny them some monetary relief, no matter how strong a defense we mounted. In addition, Monsanto was a gigantic company that could afford to pay a big judgment, which is always a problem for a deep-pocket company like Monsanto in a trial by jury. If a jury was really moved to help the plaintiff and punish Monsanto, it could have easily awarded damages in the $20–25 million range and an appellate court would not have touched it. So, after two meetings with Monsanto's general counsel in St. Louis, we settled the case before trial for $2.4 million, a personal record.

LEECHES, LOVERS, BEARS, AND CHOCOLATE PUDDING

Couto:

I set another record in this case: losing the largest ever damage award in a Louisiana medical malpractice case up to that time. My client, the defendant's insurer, was ordered to pay the grand sum of $140,000 for two deaths, which seems a piddling amount now (2017) but was considered a "runaway" jury verdict then (1972). The damages awarded by judges and jurors in such cases after that grew exponentially and eventually moved the state Legislature to enact the damage cap that applied in the Payne case, but for the moment, I held the dubious record for losing the most money in a malpractice trial.

It was the first big case I handled on my own and it turned out to be baptism by fire: a three-week-long jury trial with several complex medical issues and a total of 10 expert witnesses. The loss of a young mother and her unborn child on one side and a large insurance company with high limits on the other gave the plaintiff, the grieving husband, a decided emotional advantage with the jury. And in the middle of trial, Dr. X, the insured physician, settled with the plaintiff for any personal excess exposure of his, leaving his insurer (and me) to take the heat—as we did (in Louisiana, unlike all but one other state, a liability insurer could be included in a suit as a named defendant and identified as such to the jury, so the judgment here was against St. Paul Insurance Company).

In addition to the record amount of damages, I made history in another way during this trial and made a little "good law" in the process. Because one of my primary expert witnesses was scheduled to be out of the country while the case was tried, I took his video-taped deposition, which at the time was a new technology that I thought would impress the jury more than just hearing his deposition read. But when I offered it during the trial, the plaintiff's attorney objected that the video component would unduly enhance the weight of the witness' testimony and thus prejudice his client. The trial judge sustained the objection but would permit me to just read the deposition to the jury in the traditional way. Instead of doing that, I decided to file an emergency appeal of the ruling, initially in the Court of Appeals, which affirmed, and then in the Louisiana Supreme Court, which reversed and allowed me to show the video-taped deposition to the jury for the first time ever in this state. It was so novel way back then that it even made the newspapers. But it resulted in some long work days for me, because I had to research and brief the video issue at the same time that the general trial was going on.

My appeal of the jury's verdict on liability was based on two arguments. First, that the trial judge, over my objection, had unwittingly signaled the jury that Dr. X had admitted his liability by settling with the plaintiff during trial. He didn't mention the settlement but he did tell the jury that Dr. X had been voluntarily dismissed from the suit "for reasons you [the jury] should not worry about" and the trial would continue only against his insurer, which was more than enough to pique the jurors' curiosity and lead at least some of them to guess why Dr. X had been dismissed. Since most laymen like the jurors think that a settlement is an admission of liability by the settling defendant, the judge's statement undermined our defense and tainted the jury's verdict.

Most of my brief dealt with the second argument that the weight of the evidence did not support the jury's finding that Dr. X had negligently caused the two deaths. It took a lot of time and space to wade through three weeks of recorded trial testimony, including all the expert opinions, and then organize that into a written argument. The result was a truly misnamed "brief" of 134 typed pages, the longest I ever wrote, by far. And it got a good laugh out of my opponent, Larry "Cadillac" Smith, already a big name among plaintiffs' attorneys, who kidded me about writing a brief much too long for any appellate judge to read. Well, I got in a little kidding of my own when his brief came in at a mere 132 pages.

A three-judge panel of the Court of Appeals, including as I recall Jim Garrison of the infamous Jack Kennedy assassination probe when he was the District Attorney, gave us additional time to argue the case orally. They eventually agreed with my first argument about judicial error and granted me a new trial, a daunting prospect even though that's what I had requested. Then something really surprising happened. Just as I would have done in his place, Larry applied to the Louisiana Supreme Court for a writ of review, expecting it to either reinstate the jury verdict or affirm the Court of Appeals. It did neither. Without a hearing and in the space of one short paragraph, it granted Larry's application but, instead of a brand-new trial in the district court, it ordered the Court of Appeals to decide the issue of malpractice from the long trial transcript and our original appellate briefs. From poor Larry's point of view, that was the worst possible result because he knew he'd fare better with a new jury than the appellate court which had questioned the first jury's finding of fault in its original opinion. And his misgivings turned out to be prescient. The Court of Appeals ruled the jury was wrong and dismissed the case, a happy but totally unexpected outcome. A jury's finding of fact is usually untouchable on appeal if it's supported by any evidence and here there was ample evidence, including five expert opinions, that Dr. X had committed malpractice. To get around that, the appellate court just disregarded the jury's verdict in toto because of the trial judge's prejudicial comments.

And that's how I lost the record and shed the dreaded albatross.* With the benefit of hindsight and some hard-earned wisdom, I probably should have quit the practice of law then and there while I was still ahead and relatively sane. But, if nothing else, lawyers are stubborn, including this one.

????????:

Larry Smith and I were adversaries in only one other malpractice case, but before I get to that one, let me tell you briefly about another case where we circuitously wound up on the same side. It occurred before Couto, when I was still an associate in the firm, but it was so long ago that I cannot remember how the defendants lined up. Larry sued either Methodist Hospital or the attending physician on behalf of an injured patient. That defendant, whichever one it was, then sued the other health care provider to reimburse any damages it had to pay the plaintiff. That turned out to be an unorthodox and unwise move on the part of the original defendant because it placed itself in the middle of a two-front war. Representing the third-party (or second) defendant was my senior partner, Martin Hunley, the acknowledged dean of medical malpractice defense attorneys, with me assisting him. As one of his experts, Larry had engaged a Pittsburgh pathologist, Dr. Cyril Wecht, who had gained some notoriety as the first doctor to challenge the conclusions of the official Jack Kennedy

---

* In the Galapagos Islands this summer (2017) with our 14-year-old grandson, I saw several of the famous birds for the first time. They were very sweet-looking and affectionate with each other, contrary to the negative connotation they've evoked ever since "The Rime of the Ancient Mariner" was published.

assassination investigation. Martin and I argued, along with Larry, that the original defendant was the only party at fault and that's exactly what the jury found. I later wound up representing Methodist Hospital in all of its malpractice cases for many years until I retired, and I still play golf weekly with its former general counsel.

As for the other case in which Larry and I were adversaries, I was a bit more seasoned by then, luckily for me, because it turned out to be a very challenging and hard-fought trial. The suit alleged that my client, Dr. X, had negligently failed to diagnose and treat a young boy's spinal meningitis that left him with a severe and permanent disability. When he arrived in court for the opening day of trial, Dr. X was a nervous wreck because someone had left a dead fish on his doorstep that morning, which he took to be an old Mafia warning that he was a marked man. He didn't even make it through one full day of trial before he started complaining of chest pains, so I sent him home and he never felt well enough to return. I had to try the case without him and read his pre-trial discovery deposition to the jury in place of his live testimony. The trial judge also barred me from introducing an important piece of evidence. And, as I recall, the ubiquitous Dr. Wecht showed up again as one of Larry's expert witnesses.

After a very contentious week of trial, the jury came back with a verdict in favor of Dr. X and the Court of Appeals affirmed. Dr. X, an older religious man, was so ecstatic that he wrote a letter of praise to one of the firm's founding fathers, Harry Kelleher, comparing me to Jesus because "Mr. Penick can walk on water." Although I certainly appreciated his very kind words, I thought it was a bit unfair to Jesus to mention him in the same breath with any lawyer, much less me. Unfortunately, Mr. Kelleher was so taken with the letter that he read it to the whole firm at its next meeting. The ribbing I got lasted a good six months.

????????:

This was another lengthy jury trial in a malpractice case involving frightful injuries. The plaintiff, a young woman who attempted but failed to commit suicide by shooting herself right between the eyes with a .22 caliber pistol, sued a psychiatrist, a psychologist, and a psychiatric hospital. I represented the psychiatrist, Dr. X. It was alleged that the defendants had been negligent in

LEECHES, LOVERS, BEARS, AND CHOCOLATE PUDDING

giving her a weekend pass from the hospital when they should have known she was suicidal. My experts, who were national authorities on the subject of suicide, actually agreed with her that Dr. X had been negligent in one way but disagreed that it was a proximate cause of her attempted suicide, which of course made our defense a little dicey to say the least.

The facts were certainly bizarre. The plaintiff had been hospitalized for severe depression and suicidal tendencies. After spending some time there, she requested a weekend pass to visit her boyfriend. Dr. X, her attending physician, saw her on Wednesday and tentatively approved her request, subject to another scheduled evaluation on Friday before she was released. Unfortunately, Dr. X was late for his Friday appointment because he stopped to attend a friend's party on his way into New Orleans from Covington. By the time he did reach the hospital, the patient had already been released for the weekend.

Apparently the plaintiff's relationship with her boyfriend was known by her health care providers to be sometimes volatile, which raised the question of why she was ever released from the hospital into his care. Their weekend started off well enough until they got into a heated argument Saturday night. On cross-examination, the boyfriend, i.e., bum (much too kind a word for him), admitted their argument ensued after his confession that he had recently contracted genital herpes, obviously from another sexual partner, and may have infected the plaintiff when she unknowingly slept with him the night before. Because of his unbelievable villainy, I vividly remember losing some of my professional objectivity at that point and attacking him personally in a way I never did before or after. Unfortunately, his despicable behavior did not end with the Saturday night argument. Although he knew his emotionally fragile girlfriend was terribly upset over the herpes matter, he left her alone on Sunday morning to go out and get donuts, for God's sake, with a loaded pistol on the premises, which she found and used while he was away. I wish she had used it on him instead of herself or at least sued him instead of the defendants.

In any event, the poor plaintiff suffered very severe brain damage. At the time of trial, she was living with and dependent on her elderly parents but would eventually require full-time custodial care.

Whatever his reasons, the plaintiff's attorney (a friend of mine) never brought his client to court during the trial. But I did, because I feared the jury would conclude from all the medical testimony about the extent of her injury that she was a mindless zombie and I knew from her discovery deposition before trial that she wasn't. Despite the brain damage, she looked and sounded better than she was and still had a pretty good memory of her childhood. So I subpoenaed her and called her to the stand as my witness. It was certainly unorthodox and quite risky to do that, but it worked out just as I hoped. She was the picture of a pretty, outwardly-healthy young woman. Her forehead wound had been repaired cosmetically. To make sure she did not get upset or tired on the stand, I questioned her very gently (unlike her no-good boyfriend) for no more than 10 minutes about her childhood only and she did fine (and even looked like she enjoyed it). Her testimony was totally inconsequential of course, but it was important for the jury to see her for themselves and that may have helped us on the question of damages awarded.

My two suicide experts, from St. Louis and Baltimore as I recall, were both critical of Dr. X for missing his scheduled appointment with the patient on Friday before she left on her weekend pass. On the other hand, they testified he would have been justified in approving her pass even if he had seen her that Friday, although the hospital record reflected some questions about her stability between Wednesday and Friday. On my direct examination of them, I beat around the bush in every possible way about the issue of Dr. X's malpractice in hopes that my opponent would not notice, but he did and they testified my client had been guilty of malpractice as the attending psychiatrist. Between plaintiff's expert witnesses and my own, we had little chance of winning on the malpractice issue anyway, which left only the issue of proximate cause.

Midway through the trial, the attorneys for my two co-defendants settled out of the case and left me to defend it alone. The jury, however, still had to apportion any fault between the three original defendants. It found all three were liable and awarded the plaintiff damages of about $1 million, which could have been a lot worse. More importantly, it assigned most of the fault to the other two defendants, so Dr. X's insurer had to pay a very small percentage of the award, something under $100,000 as I recall. My client was happy with the result and did not appeal.

LEECHES, LOVERS, BEARS, AND CHOCOLATE PUDDING

?????????:

I represented the same psychiatrist, Dr. X, in another malpractice case and won a jury verdict for him in one of the rural parishes, but I don't remember any of the facts. In a third case against Dr. X, he had a different insurer and defense counsel. I represented the other defendant, a Covington hospital. The plaintiff's husband committed suicide soon after being released from or turned away by my client (my recollection is fuzzy). What I do remember is that the plaintiff, the victim's wife, knew he had left their house with a pistol but she finished putting on her makeup before starting out to look for him, even though she had good reason to believe he might be suicidal. That 15-minute delay turned out to be fatal because he shot himself just minutes before she found him. Despite a friendly warning from Dr. X's counsel about the risk of challenging a grieving widow, I chose to cross-examine her about the delay in acting and then argued to the jury that plaintiff's own negligence superseded any negligence on the part of either defendant. And that apparently convinced the jury. They found that both defendants were guilty of negligence but it was not the proximate cause of the husband's death, presumably because of his wife's intervening fault. The verdict in our favor was affirmed on appeal.

?????????:

I defended three or four other cases against psychiatrists who were accused of having improper and damaging sexual relations with their patients, but one in particular stands out in my memory because it was so egregious and sad.

The patient was the young and beautiful wife of a surgeon who was a colleague and friend of the defendant psychiatrist, another Dr. X. When his wife developed severe postpartum depression after the birth of their second child, her husband recommended she see Dr. X. The doctor-patient relationship eventually evolved into a torrid but volatile love affair that was on-again, off-again several times. Even after her husband found out and Dr. X then moved to Missouri, the plaintiff went back and forth between the two men. In her deposition, she testified that she found Dr. X to be irresistible primarily because of his voice, which reminded me of the movie *A Fish Called Wanda*, but unfortunately the movie had a much happier ending than this real-life tragedy. While her case was still pending, the plaintiff killed herself on the third try by running out onto a busy highway.

Since Dr. X's conduct was utterly indefensible and the damage to plaintiff's family was immeasurable, Dr. X and his insurer admitted liability and settled the case out of court by paying the $100,000 maximum set by the statutory cap previously mentioned.

Blum (I think):

This was the case that caused Julie to finally stop eating raw oysters, which she had consumed in abundance with spiritual ecstasy from the age of five when her beloved father taught her to do so. I, on the other hand, hated the critters and had tried vainly for years to stop Julie from the time it became known that raw oysters sometimes caused serious, life-threatening infections. As they say, a picture is worth a thousand words, thanks to this case, as I'll explain later.

The young and active patient underwent a fairly routine knee operation at Methodist Hospital without incident, but the next day he started running a fever and exhibiting other signs of a very serious infection. Although the operative site looked good, it was assumed the infection had started there. The patient was administered increasingly heavy doses of strong antibiotics but kept getting worse and worse. Over the next two months, he developed unstoppable gangrene in both of his arms and legs. To make it even worse if that's possible, he was conscious the whole time and able to see what was happening to his body, in addition to the excruciating pain.

During that time, his wife had engaged an attorney who took serial photographs of the physical devastation from day to day. When the patient finally died in the hospital, his infection had never been identified despite numerous cultures.

His wife filed suit against Methodist, whom I represented, and several doctors represented by other counsel. She was represented by my old friend and adversary from the previous case involving the young woman who shot herself with a .22 caliber pistol. He chose in this case to waive his right to trial by jury. In the course of her discovery deposition before trial, I learned that the Blums had gone out to dinner the night before his scheduled surgery and he had eaten something like three dozen raw oysters, which is what provided us with a defense. Up to that point, we had been trying to defend against what everyone thought was a hospital-based infection, a tough sell in most cases. After the deposition, we could argue that the patient contracted his infection from eating the raw oysters and brought it with him into Methodist the next day, unbeknownst to anyone because it took 24 hours for the infection to manifest itself. It was still going to be a tough case to defend for the hospital because the type of infection had never been identified by culture, but I found an LSU doctor who was an expert on the oyster-borne infection called "vibrio vulnificus" and he concluded from all of the clinical information in the hospital records that this was the very thing that killed the patient. After a three-week trial, the judge ruled in favor of all defendants on the basis of my expert's testimony primarily.

Back to Julie for a moment. I got copies of the photos showing the patient's physical deterioration from his infection and brought them home for Julie to see. They did the trick, not surprisingly, because they were really gruesome. She swore to never eat another raw oyster after that and never did.

Saran:

Tony Saran, the plaintiff, was a burly Greek immigrant who had created a very successful business of painting offshore rigs and other structures in the Gulf of Mexico. He contracted with my client, Marathon Oil Company, to paint one of its large and complex rigs with certain specified Glidden paint. When the job turned into a nightmare and Saran was fired, he sued both Marathon and Glidden for breach of contract and defective paint that ruined his business reputation and caused him to lose millions of dollars. He was represented by Sam LeBlanc, an excellent trial attorney in another large New Orleans defense firm who once ran unsuccessfully for mayor and later joined the Peace Corps at age 65 with his wife.

We tried the case to a federal court jury for over three weeks. During a settlement discussion midway through the trial, Sam told me that his client had designed and patented a special knife that he would include in any agreement. It was an intriguing knife with a wickedly curved blade that looked like a very efficient way of cutting someone's throat. I was tempted (not that I've ever wanted to cut anyone's throat, with the possible exception of the defendant doctor I represented in the Payne case) but the price was too high, so we finished the trial. The judge, who had always been a loose cannon, was so impressed by plaintiff's evidence that he exclaimed in front of the jury at one point that the Glidden paint used on this job was "the worst paint I've ever heard about." His highly prejudicial comment certainly did not help Glidden's defense that its paint was not defective.

At the end of the testimony, I believed that Sam had presented a pretty strong case against Marathon on the issue of liability, so I made a decision that was probably unwise in retrospect. In addition to arguing that Marathon was not liable for any damages in my closing statement to the jury, I made the alternative argument that any damages should not exceed such-and-such a figure if they did find my client to be liable. Unfortunately, that sounded like an admission of liability no matter how much I stressed it was not. The jury awarded damages to Saran against both defendants in an amount twice the figure I had suggested, but that was reduced by half on appeal, so the ultimate result was not that bad. However, I never made an alternative argument like that in any other case and have sometime wondered if Marathon might have walked had I not done so in that case. And I really did want one of Tony Saran's knives, for display only, of course.

???????? and ????????:

Since we're talking about cases I lost, let me tell you about the two I lost to a plaintiff's attorney named A. D. Freeman. In the first, six different doctors, including a surgeon, a gastroenterologist, an internist, a GP, and two others I can't recall, failed to diagnose the patient's appendicitis until she was very sick and scared. All six were insured by the same company and were accused of the same malpractice, so I represented all of them. The surgeon had died by the time of trial, but the other five were in court the whole time, writing countless notes for me to read. In its unknowable wisdom, the jury found that only the deceased surgeon was guilty of malpractice, even though he missed the exact same boat as the other defendants who were not liable.

LEECHES, LOVERS, BEARS, AND CHOCOLATE PUDDING

In the second case, I represented Baptist Hospital, the sole defendant. The patient was an elderly but spry woman who broke her hip from a fall while trying to climb out of bed over the side rails. She had succeeded in getting out of her bed so many times, despite warnings and precautions, that the nurses had dubbed her "Houdini."

That turned out to be the decisive factor in the eventual outcome. Although the jury returned a verdict in favor of Baptist, the trial judge took the rare step of overturning it and awarding damages to "Houdini," which was affirmed on appeal. (After the jury's verdict but before it was overturned, the hospital thanked me with a very nice vase that I still have.)

?????????? X 10:

For several years, I handled all of the workmen's compensation and personal injury litigation for Kaiser Aluminum's plant in Chalmette, just south of New Orleans. Two of the workmen's compensation claims were filed by employees who were burned when they walked across one of the molten aluminum "pots" in the ground to save time and had a foot break through the hard crust on top. Of the many other suits, maybe seven or eight went to trial. There were only two judges in Chalmette at the time: one who was very pro-plaintiff and anti-Kaiser; the other who was just the reverse. I therefore knew as soon as a case was allotted to one judge or the other whether we were going to win or lose, regardless of the merits of each case, which did have the beneficial effect of encouraging settlements out of court.

In one Kaiser case involving a serious heart attack, I was working late with a medical expert in our living room preparing him for trial the next day. Julie had gone to bed but suddenly came hopping quietly past us in a nightgown on her way to the kitchen. She was sleepwalking, as she did on several other occasions. I learned the next day that she thought she was a kangaroo and I was downstairs meeting with Henry Kissinger on important business that she didn't want to interrupt, but she as a kangaroo needed something very badly in the kitchen. I lost the case, as expected, but enjoyed Julie's impersonation of a kangaroo.

TRIALS AND TRIBULATIONS

My opponent in many of the Kaiser cases was the "colorful" Rick Tonry, a lawyer, playboy, and short-lived politician in St. Bernard Parish. He was a true character in every sense. His initial ambition was to be a Jesuit priest. While at the seminary, he taught English at Jesuit High School in New Orleans, but shortly before taking his vows, he changed his mind and became a lawyer instead (an example of "going from one extreme to the other"?).

After practicing law for a while, Rick ran for a vacant seat in the U. S. House of Representatives against a young New Orleans lawyer named Bob Livingston, who I knew as a member of the same high school fraternity. Although Rick was declared the winner of that election, he never served a day in Washington. Just because several thousand dead and buried voters in St. Bernard Parish somehow managed to cast ballots for him (a time-honored tradition in Louisiana called "ringing the bell"), the House canceled the results and called a new election, which Bob won, the start of a long and distinguished career that ended sadly right before he was to succeed Newt Gingrich as Speaker of the House. Rick served time for vote fraud and then resumed his legal practice until he was convicted again, this time for bribing an Indian chief to get the tribe's casino business. Although he was guilty as sin, as he privately admitted, he beat the rap on appeal (as his own attorney) by finding an obscure statute that excluded "heads of state" from the federal bribery laws and arguing successfully that his Indian chief was a "head of state," to the undisguised frustration of the judges on the appeal court.

Rick and I met as opposing lawyers between his two convictions. After several cases together, we became friends. He was bright, charming, eccentric, and hilarious.

Julie and I were always invited to his legendary New Year's Eve parties in Chalmette but regretfully never went. We did wind up at dinner with Rick at a mutual friend's house where Julie was completely charmed by him. When he told the story of being escorted (over his objection) in handcuffs to his mother's funeral by prison guards, Julie wept at the outrage. A few years later, we were out to dinner with Julie's mother and stepfather, who were classic New Orleans Uptowners and thought Rick was a true devil, when in walks the devil himself and rushes over to greet his "old friends." Julie of course (being Julie) jumped up to give him a big hug, to my in-laws' utter shock and gaping mouths. Rick

LEECHES, LOVERS, BEARS, AND CHOCOLATE PUDDING

was savvy enough to understand the situation and bad enough to milk it for all it was worth by telling my squirming in-laws in his most charming way how much he'd heard about them from Julie and me. "Theater of the absurd" at its best! Julie and I laughed about that for a long time.

The last time I saw Rick was in 1997. As luck would have it, I was called to serve jury duty just weeks after I'd retired (the first time) from practicing law that year. My first stop as a prospective juror was Judge Yada McGee's courtroom where I had tried my last (or so I thought) jury trial just a month before. The judge recognized me when I entered the courtroom with about 30 other prospective jurors and actually laughed good-naturedly at my role reversal. She then read the names of several doctors who would appear at the scheduled trial (which happened to be a medical malpractice case) as either parties or witnesses and asked if any of the prospective jurors knew any of them. Because I knew every doctor listed, Judge McGee, with a smile and wave, excused me from that jury panel. It was the next day that I ran into my old buddy Rick in another courtroom where he represented the plaintiff in a personal injury case. I was one of the first 12 prospective jurors picked randomly but one of the attorneys used a peremptory challenge to excuse me "without cause." I didn't know which attorney had done that because it's all done at the judge's bench outside of anyone else's hearing. However, I found out the next day from the judge's clerk that Rick had excused me because "Penick knows too damn much about me."

Before leaving the Chalmette scene, let me tell you briefly about one other case I tried down there. It was a malpractice case against the local hospital and a doctor. A friend of mine from another firm represented the hospital and I represented the doctor. In the course of questioning the 30 or 40 prospective jurors about possible biases, my friend asked them if anyone had any preconceived opinions about the defendant hospital. One man raised his hand and announced in a very loud voice that "I wouldn't take my dog to that hospital." He was of course excused from the jury panel but the damage was already done and, not surprisingly, the jury found the hospital liable (but not my doctor). Before the jury retired to deliberate, we attorneys expected the judge to follow protocol and resolve our disputes over the law charges he would then read

TRIALS AND TRIBULATIONS

to the jury, but he declined to do so and gave us an hour to work it out between ourselves, which was the first and last time I ever saw that happen.

?????????:

Since I just made reference to it in passing, this is a good time to discuss my last (plus one) jury trial, the one before Judge Yada McGee—and tell you something about her. She was one of my favorite judges, not because of any extraordinary intelligence but because she was very brave and very fair. A good example of that occurred in another malpractice case defended by one of our associates, Susan Northrop. The plaintiff and her attorney were black; Susan and the defendant doctor were white. Judge McGee was black. During the jury selection process, plaintiff's counsel used his peremptory challenges to remove all the prospective jurors who were white without having to state his reason for doing so, although it must have been pretty obvious. The result was an all-black jury. To make a record for appeal, Susan moved for a mistrial on grounds her opponent had discriminated against prospective white jurors. To Susan's surprise, Judge McGee granted her motion and dismissed the jury after giving the plaintiff's lawyer a severe tongue-lashing (on the record, no less). She did the right thing, but it still took lots of courage for a black elected judge to do that to a prominent black lawyer who was politically active in the local black community.

    She demonstrated the same courage and sense of fairness in my case, a malpractice claim against Methodist Hospital, my client, for allegedly injuring the plaintiff's newborn baby. Unfortunately, the plaintiff was represented by a real jerk who had no qualms about bending the truth. He had a well-qualified expert from Johns Hopkins to testify against Methodist but he did everything possible to deny my unmistakable right to depose his expert before trial. As the trial approached, I filed a motion to exclude his expert from testifying. Even though she knew he had no case without his expert, Judge McGee again did the right thing and granted my motion, which the Court of Appeals then reversed but ordered the jerk to produce his Baltimore expert for deposition before trial at his own expense, which was a touch of justice. In the middle of the trial, we settled the claim, a wise move as I found out later from the jurors (with the judge's permission) that they were prepared to find for the plaintiff.

(There was a heavy rain and resulting flood in New Orleans a few weeks before that trial started. In trying to drive home from my office downtown, I got stuck in a massive, four-directional traffic jam on a major flooded avenue and had to spend the night in my car along with hundreds of other stranded motorists. Luckily, Julie was out of town, but unluckily, the car stopped just in front of mine was occupied by none other than the jerk in the case above, whom I was barely speaking to at the time. When I drifted off to sleep in the car, I actually dreamed about having one of those James Bond cars with machine guns on the front. No such luck, of course, but wishful thinking can sometimes be most enjoyable.)

Dubuclet:

My official retirement in 1997 was short-lived because of this case. It was an extremely complicated and difficult malpractice case that I had taken over from one of my partners two or three years before and then passed on to another partner to handle after I retired. The plaintiffs were represented by Fred Gisevius, whom you met earlier in connection with the seven-week Neumeyer trial. In this case, the statutory cap on damages did not apply and the insurer we represented had lost the records to prove its policy limits, which exposed it to an unlimited judgment. The severity of the injury made that a very big problem because a huge damage award was definitely not out of the question.

While I was just starting to enjoy my retirement, the attorney then handling the case came to my house and asked me to try the case with him, which I reluctantly agreed to do even though the trial was only three months away and I had a lot of catching up to do on details I'd forgotten. The trial was expected to last three or four weeks, not that unusual for Gisevius. I made the opening statement to the jury and then cross-examined one of the plaintiff's key medical experts on the second day of trial, at which point Gisevius substantially reduced his settlement demand to a figure that our client accepted, to my sheer delight. Whereupon I retired, once again, tired but happy to my blissful state of leisure and never again darkened the door of a courtroom anywhere.

TRIALS AND TRIBULATIONS

???????? and **Isom**:

When these two cases were tried, I was still an associate at the firm and assisted senior partners at trial. In the first one, our client was represented by Carl Schumacher. The plaintiff operated a large chicken hatchery in Covington and sued a pharmaceutical company on grounds that its chicken vitamins were defective and caused his hens to lay soft-shelled eggs that were unmarketable, resulting in substantial financial losses that almost put him out of business. In answer to one of Carl's questions on cross-examination, he in all seriousness claimed to know exactly how the vitamins harmed his hens because "the chickens told me so." To his credit, Carl was quite gentle with the elderly plaintiff, who steadfastly defended his uncanny ability to communicate with chickens but wound up losing the case. (After personal encounters with a hummingbird and a sea lion who were apparently trying to communicate something to Julie and/or me, I now wonder whether chickens can communicate too.)

In Isom, Martin Hunley and I represented a charming but inept neurosurgeon, Dr. X, who had literally mutilated the plaintiff's back while trying to release a pinched nerve, which is a fairly routine procedure. After making his incision, Dr. X became totally lost in pursuing his target but did not give up (as he should have). Over the next *eight hours*, he cut and removed tissue all over the patient's lower back looking in vain for the subject nerve. Only when he realized he had slashed his way to the patient's left hip, about 12 inches away from his target on the right side of the spinal cord, did Dr. X finally stop. By that time, unfortunately, Isom's lower back was permanently ruined.

It was as clear a case of medical malpractice as I've ever seen and it was compounded at trial by an equally clear case of legal malpractice, a double whammy for the poor innocent plaintiff. Isom's attorney was as inept as Dr. X. He was a family friend who had obviously never before tried any kind of case, much less a complex malpractice case with serious injuries in front of a jury. Though he did have a legitimate expert to testify about Dr. X's negligence, the witness never got a chance to do so because the plaintiff's attorney never asked him the right questions. Oh, the lawyer tried time and time again to find the right question, but all of them were subject to some objection that the court granted. It finally got so bad that the presiding judge called a meeting of the lawyers in his chambers and essentially told Isom's attorney how to ask the key question about Dr. X's alleged negligence. Despite three or four of those meetings, the lawyer never could get the important question right, so the jury never knew the expert witness believed Dr. X was grossly negligent and consequently returned a defense verdict in less than 15 minutes.

My contribution to this undeserved victory was finding another neurosurgeon willing (most reluctantly) to testify for us and borrowing a full-length human skeleton to illustrate the experts' testimony at trial. After one of those meetings in the judge's chambers while Dr. X was on the witness stand, we all emerged to find him surrounded by interested jurors as he pointed out something on the skeleton. Not surprisingly, Isom's lawyer did not object or move for a mistrial, as he should have.

I ran into Isom himself a year or so later in a blood bank where he worked as a technician. He was not bitter but he knew full well that his lawyer's incompetence had lost the case, although he also tried to make excuses for the old gentleman. That conversation was certainly sad but it was also uplifting to see that Isom was facing his undeserved disability with such grace and forgiveness. Nevertheless, I will always remember this case as one in which a good man who deserved better was cruelly victimized by our medical and legal systems both.

??????? and ???????:

In two of the several other cases I handled for Monsanto, I was partly responsible for another miscarriage of justice in the first but then got my comeuppance in the second.

After an accidental release of some toxic gas at its Luling plant, Monsanto was sued in federal court by a handful of nearby residents who claimed sickness and injury from the gas. They also filed the suit as a class action on behalf of hundreds of other alleged victims, which is often used by plaintiffs' attorneys to augment their own fees by increasing the scope of a case. Since class actions are dangerous and expensive cases for a company to defend and bad for its public relations regardless of outcome, I initially filed a motion with the presiding judge to dismiss the class action aspect of the case on some kind of legal grounds I don't recall now. I knew, however, that it would be a tough motion to win unless I had a secret weapon, which turned out to be the associate lawyer helping me on the case. Not only was she extremely smart, more importantly she was extremely pregnant with twins and that's why she was the perfect choice to argue the motion orally to the judge. My plan was perhaps a bit shameful but it was obviously brilliant, even if I say so myself, and it worked like a charm. The young woman could barely reach the podium and even sounded a little out of breath. Just as I hoped, the judge was a nervous wreck about an imminent delivery and granted our motion halfway through her argument in order to spare himself and his courtroom. As good as her oral argument was, I'm not sure the judge heard a word of it before ruling in our favor. With that aspect of the case out of the way, we were later able to settle the few remaining claims on good terms. (Several years later, the subject judge was impeached by Congress for corruption, unrelated to this case.)

Two or three years after that case, the gods of justice got their revenge in another federal court case against Monsanto for some kind of injury. It was a tough case to begin with, as I remember, but then my key witness cratered on the stand, so I was quite pessimistic about winning at that point. But my hopes revived during my closing argument to the jury of six women (the number agreed to by the parties) because they smiled and nodded and seemed to be hanging on every word. Well, it took them all of 28 minutes to come back with a big judgment against my client. I didn't get a single vote from my duplicitous "friends" on the jury. There is an important lesson here, but as the father of two daughters, I'll keep my mouth shut.

??????? and ???????:

Trial attorneys often get unexpected reactions from judges as well as jurors. Here are two examples of that, in cases before the same New Orleans district judge. The first involved a malpractice claim against a plastic surgeon who had since moved to California and refused to come back for the trial. When the judge made some unnecessary and prejudicial comments in front of the jury about my

LEECHES, LOVERS, BEARS, AND CHOCOLATE PUDDING

client's absence, I objected and moved for a mistrial, which triggered a most unusual reaction from the judge. He literally exploded in rage at me, right in front of the jury, and then stormed off into his chambers, slamming the door behind him for good measure. He returned to the bench a few minutes later and quite gleefully denied my motion, which turned out to be a blessing in disguise because the jury subsequently found in my client's favor.

In a later case before the same judge (without a jury), the trial happened to fall on the same day as some big horse race at our local track where the judge spent most of his time when not working. It was obvious from the outset that the judge had his mind on other things and wanted to end the trial as soon as possible. When the opposing lawyer rested his case and before I started mine, the judge essentially invited me to make a motion for a directed verdict dismissing the case. I had not planned to make such a motion because the plaintiff had presented enough solid evidence to defeat such a motion, but I couldn't ignore the judge's invitation and therefore made the motion, which he quickly granted before dashing off the bench, presumably on his way to the track. And that was the end of the case, just like that. I always told our kids growing up that "timing is everything" and this case proves the truth of that. It also proves the old adage about "not looking a gift horse in the mouth." Okay, okay—I'll move on now.

????????:

My good friend Harry Carter represented the plaintiff in this very bizarre malpractice case. The doctor I defended, Dr. X, apparently had a clitoris fetish. Whenever he performed a vaginal hysterectomy or other procedure, he "gratuitously" snipped all or most of the patient's clitoris, without informing (or charging) the patient or getting her consent. He allegedly removed the clitoris for hygienic reasons, but in this case (and probably many others), he caused the patient severe pain and ruined her sex life.

Dr. X's conduct was unethical and unwarranted on many different levels. Harry had a number of medical experts who were eager to testify against my "quack" of a client and put him out of business. Despite an extensive search, I could not find an expert witness to defend him, so his insurer happily settled with

TRIALS AND TRIBULATIONS

Harry. That was the right thing to do, but it certainly would have been an interesting case to try.

????????:

The central issue in this malpractice case was the definition of "death" in Louisiana, which then had no statute or case law on the subject.

While playing in his father's auto-repair shop, a young boy was crushed by a car that fell off of a mechanical lift and was rushed to the nearest hospital with grievous injuries. It was Sunday. The doctor I represented was driving past the hospital on his day off when he responded to an emergency page from the hospital for any doctor in the vicinity and then spent the next 24 hours working tirelessly in an unfamiliar hospital to save the boy's life. After placing him on a heart-lung machine and trying to revive him medically, the defendant doctor and others determined from several electrical studies that the patient was brain-dead. They so informed the parents and asked them if they would consent to using their son's undamaged organs for transplant purposes, which they did. The patient was then taken off of the heart-lung machine and, after his heart stopped beating on its own, his organs were harvested. Afterwards, his parents alleged in their suit against the doctor and hospital that they had been misinformed that their child was "dead" as opposed to "brain-dead" and would never have consented to anything if they'd known he was still "alive." Thus the question was whether he was alive or dead before his removal from the heart-lung machine.

The preeminent physician in New Orleans at that time was Dr. Alton Ochsner, who founded the renowned Ochsner Medical Center back in 1941 (I believe) and was the first doctor in the country to identify smoking as a major cause of cancer. Dr. Ochsner and my father had been friends and fellow surgeons at Ochsner before my father died in 1963. In fact, they were the two doctors who surgically separated Siamese twins successfully for the first time. Since I knew Dr. Ochsner through my father, I asked him to look at the case and, if necessary, to testify as an expert witness. He kindly agreed and concluded that the injured boy was already "dead" when his parents gave their consent to take his organs. Soon after I had taken Dr. Ochsner's deposition to use at trial, the plaintiffs accepted a nominal sum in settlement from the hospital, represented by other counsel, and voluntarily dismissed their claim against my doctor without any payment.

????????:

What I remember best about this case is that the Boston Red Sox were in the World Series. Unfortunately, the decisive seventh game of the 1986 Series happened to fall on the night before the lawyers were to give their closing arguments to the jury, a terrible coincidence.

But let me back up and tell you a little about the case itself, which was tried in a Baton Rouge state court. The plaintiff fell through some kind of defective flooring and injured his back. He sued the company that manufactured or designed the flooring material, which I represented. The case had been tried once before and ended with a hung jury. The client was represented at that trial by one of my junior partners in the firm. It then decided, in all of its infinite wisdom, to bring in a more senior attorney, me, for the second trial. Bad call, as it turned out. My opponent was a very fine trial attorney named John de Gravelles, who is now a federal judge. Lest I forget, he was also an avid baseball fan like me, which is an important fact.

After three days of testimony, I went back to my motel room in Baton Rouge to prepare my closing argument to the jury. It was a close case, so I needed to make a good argument. But I also needed to watch just a wee bit of the final Series game on TV. Well, my good intentions didn't stand a chance. Three hours lost watching the Red Sox lose again (so I had to wait another 18 years before they won their first World Series since 1918). I cobbled together something of a closing argument in the short time left but was a very tired and emotionally-drained puppy the next morning when I arrived in court. Then I looked at John and realized he was in worse shape than I was. He of course had done the same thing I did. We both stumbled through our closing arguments and then together bemoaned the Red Sox' "Curse of the Babe" while the jury deliberated. They must have taken pity on us in our weakened conditions because they split the baby (or whatever) by finding my client liable but awarding the plaintiff only half the amount he was entitled to. Neither party appealed, but I got a lot of

TRIALS AND TRIBULATIONS

ribbing from my junior partner who had tried the case the first time around and almost won it. He must have been a New York Yankees fan.

????????:

The accident and injury involved in this case were really unbelievable. Warning to faint-hearted readers: it is impossible to describe them in delicate terms.

It all happened on an offshore oil rig but was not covered by maritime law for some obscure reason, so I got to defend the case and take my first and only helicopter ride (very noisy). On one side of the platform, the poor plaintiff was bending over with his legs spread apart to lift up a heavy bag of drilling mud. On the other side, a large industrial machine was reeling in a heavy metal cable (called a "wireline") used to move tools up and down the drilling hole. The accident occurred when the cable suddenly snapped as a result of the extreme tension on it. The upper end of the broken cable flew across the rig at high speed, somehow snaked between the victim's parted legs without touching either one, and reached the end of its length at the exact point in space occupied by his testicles, where it snapped with immense force like the end of a popping towel. He did not see it coming because his back was turned but his blissful ignorance ended quite abruptly. Given the fact that so many different variables occurred at the same precise instant, the odds of all that happening as it did were at least one in a trillion.

The trauma caused the plaintiff's testicles to swell up to the size of large grapefruits (he had photos), not to mention the incredible pain. His testicles remained grossly swollen and inflamed for many months (I remember the medical term was "epididymitis"), during which time he had absolutely no sex life for obvious reasons. Some of my more irreverent colleagues at Lemle & Kelleher suggested that my client, the rig operator, file a counterclaim against him to recover damages for all the money he could make off of weirdos wanting to see his enlarged testicles. Instead, we eventually settled his claim.

****

LEECHES, LOVERS, BEARS, AND CHOCOLATE PUDDING

Here are brief summaries of a few other noteworthy cases and situations I was involved in:

1. While celebrating in the immediate aftermath of a favorable jury verdict, my clients, two female gynecologists, after two rounds of drinks, offered to remove my appendix for free as a thank you for defending them successfully. All I had to do was come by their office anytime and they would snip it out, just like that. My good old sixth sense told me to decline their invitation, whatever it was, and hold on to my appendix, which is still with me.

2. The plaintiff in this malpractice case claimed that the surgeon was picking his teeth with a toothpick when he accidentally dropped it into her open abdominal cavity and then couldn't find it, so it's still lodged somewhere in her belly. The case eventually was dismissed.

3. My first-ever jury trial involved two large men who were quarreling when the defendant bashed the plaintiff over the head with a four-foot length of 4x4. Amazingly, the victim survived. I lost, but the damages awarded were reasonable.

4. Speaking of fearsome weapons, my mother-in-law's housekeeper, Odelise, used a brick in a pillowcase to crack open a hated neighbor's head. Pascal Calogero, who later became Chief Justice of the Louisiana Supreme Court and is now a fellow resident at Lambeth House, filed suit for the victim and I defended Odelise—for free, of course. On the morning of trial, Pascal and I were desperate to settle the case instead of spending a day or two in court, so he waived his fee and Odelise put up $900, which did the trick.

5. While still an associate, I assisted Allen Fontenot in defending a serious products liability case. Upon meeting the company engineer who designed the allegedly defective part, he jammed his metallic briefcase

TRIALS AND TRIBULATIONS

into my stomach by way of greeting and almost knocked me over, which made me wonder how we could possibly defend this guy in court. Far worse was the fact that our client, a large automotive company, in response to plaintiff's official request, produced a key design drawing that had been altered "after the fact." Allen and I only learned about this later when opposing counsel showed us a copy of the original drawing that he had somehow acquired. The company wisely settled soon after that bombshell. (I also remember three medical malpractice cases, not mine, in which a defendant doctor changed his then-handwritten records after the fact and then lied about it under oath, only to be caught later.)

6. Every trial lawyer has a "killer instinct" that is sometimes overt, sometimes covert. Mine was the latter and pretty mild compared to others I've seen. But every now and then a witness, such as the boyfriend in the attempted suicide case, brought out the worst in me. In my first jury trial in federal court, I represented an employee who had been consistently mistreated and then wrongfully fired by the employer-defendant, who was just a mean SOB through and through. So I went after him on cross-examination until he finally exclaimed in front of the jury, "You're trying to make me look like an ogre," at which point I ended my cross-examination. He said it much better than I could have and the jury nailed him for it.

7. In my second year of practice, I assisted Martin Hunley again in a medical malpractice suit filed by Jim Garrison, the then-popular District Attorney of Orleans Parish before he got involved in the Jack Kennedy/Clay Shaw assassination probe, on behalf of himself as the injured victim of a back operation that went awry. We strenuously contested the defendant's alleged liability, to no avail. In his final argument to the Orleans Parish jury, Garrison asked for damages of precisely $168,732, consisting of $100,000 for his pain and suffering and $68,732 of medical expenses, which is exactly what the unanimous jury gave him after deliberating just 30 minutes. Celebrity does have its advantages.

8. In by far the easiest malpractice case I ever tried, the dermatologist I defended thought I was a miracle worker and rewarded me with two cases of incredibly fine wine, one after winning in the trial court and another after winning on appeal, even though the plaintiff had no case to begin with.

9. Lady Luck is the heroine here. John Schwegmann, who opened several novel and successful supermarkets in the New Orleans area, filed an antitrust suit against all of the major distilleries for alleged price-fixing and asked for hundreds of millions of dollars in damages. It meant huge fees for the lawyers lucky enough to represent the defendants. Soon after the suit was filed, while I was still an associate at Lemle & Kelleher, I received a call out of the blue from a well-placed attorney in New York. In looking for someone in New Orleans to represent his client, Bacardi, in the suit, he had read in Martindale-Hubbell, a national directory of lawyers, that I had attended Williams College and the University of Virginia Law School, just as he had. And that's how Lemle & Kelleher wound up representing Bacardi (and two other defendants) in a suit that generated substantial fees for the firm. Although I did not handle the case, I probably should have gotten some kind of bonus for bringing in a big client but don't recall if I did.

10. The New Orleans Blood Bank was sued numerous times by patients who contracted hepatitis from blood transfusions. The plaintiffs always lost because they had to prove the Blood Bank had been negligent and they could not do it, since there was no way at that time to test donated blood for hepatitis. As a result, those kinds of cases dried up, until I got down to my very last case for the Blood Bank, which we won in the trial and appellate courts and then lost in the Louisiana Supreme Court. And besides just losing, we made "bad law" from the viewpoint of Louisiana blood banks, which the Court ruled could be held liable without proof of negligence. It reminds me of those major league pitchers who no-hit the

TRIALS AND TRIBULATIONS

other team until its very last batter hits a home run to win the game. No justice in baseball or law.

11. Trial work does have a few perks. In two products liability cases against large corporate clients, I did get to travel expenses-paid to Wales and Germany to interview or depose witnesses. Otherwise, it was Chalmette or Baton Rouge or Ponchatoula or other such tourist destinations in Louisiana. That may be a slight exaggeration, since I did go to Las Vegas (to depose an overworked minister) and Green Bay (home of a fire protection company as well as the Packers) and a few other desirable places, now that I think about it more.

12. Another travel perk involved legal seminars in other cities, but the only one I remember is the first one I ever attended, in Atlanta, with Julie, who I think was pregnant. We stayed in the brand-new Hyatt Regency Hotel with its then-revolutionary interior lobby of 21 stories. The hotel messed up our reservation for a regular room and therefore put us in the magnificent Presidential Suite on the top floor, where we were visited by a very decent cat burglar in the middle of the night, unbeknownst to us until the police woke us up the next morning at 6:00 AM. Apparently the cat burglar was a real pro and champion climber. He entered all or most of the rooms on the top 10 floors through unlocked doors to a small outside balcony, obviously with some inside help. Julie and I didn't find anything missing, including the cash in our pockets, but did find my briefcase outside on the balcony. The disappointed burglar must have expected to find plenty of money, jewelry, and other goodies in the Presidential Suite but instead found a couple of penniless, pregnant youngsters not worth his trouble. I'm glad to report that the burglar was never caught.

13. As an active trial lawyer in Louisiana courts, I prepared myself for just about anything—except for real-time sexual assault in open court. Which of course is exactly what happened. I was not simply an observer but the actual victim. Unfortunately, my assailant was anything but a sex object.

LEECHES, LOVERS, BEARS, AND CHOCOLATE PUDDING

That honor belongs to the one-and-only Rick Tonry, my adversary and friend from Chalmette with a long and colorful history, as previously described.

The shocking event occurred in the stately courtroom of the Fourth Circuit Court of Appeals in New Orleans. Rick and I were there to argue my appeal of an adverse judgment in a personal injury case. Because ours was the last one on the docket that day, the only other people left in the courtroom were the three appellate judges, their clerk, and a court reporter, all of whom were seated at some distance in *front* of Rick and me. The two of us sat at a table in chairs on either side of the podium used to address the court. There was only a foot between the podium and each chair.

As counsel for the appellant, I stood first and took my place behind the podium. About two minutes into my oral argument, just as I was about to make an important point, I felt a soft tap on my right buttock but managed to continue with my argument. A few minutes later came three harder taps on my derriere. This time, I pretended to look down at my notes and stole a quick peek at my nearby adversary. Despite his most innocent look, the subtle but unmistakable grin on his face told me everything I needed to know. None of the three sitting judges had a clue about Rick's assault because they could not see what happened behind the podium. Since Rick also knew that, I expected another diversionary attack but nothing happened for several minutes and I started to relax. Then, as I reached the climax of my argument, Rick grabbed my right cheek and gave it a good squeeze. I pretended to cough in order to stop myself from yelping and/or laughing.

After I had somehow finished my argument and Rick had taken my place at the podium, I was sorely tempted to take revenge on his ample backside but figured I'd be the one to get caught. He did buy me a beer and halfway apologized after we left the courthouse.

TRIALS AND TRIBULATIONS

****

You brave readers who've made it this far will be happy to know that you might have had another 20-30 pages to go if my memory was working better. In recalling the cases recounted here, I had flashes of recall about many other interesting matters but couldn't come up with more than that. For example, I remember there was some kind of really bizarre incident in litigation against a south Louisiana sugar mill that I represented, but that's as far as I have gotten so far. Thus the bad news for you readers is that there may be an addendum to this little memoir of sorts if my old memory should revive. In the meantime, thanks for reading this much.

ACKNOWLEDGEMENT

The author wishes to thank three very special people for their indispensable contributions to this project:

Sue Marchal, a true tech wizard who bravely steered her clueless client through all the treacherous traps of online publishing and essentially made this book happen;

Gina Rathbone, my editor across the ocean in Wales, who carefully corrected countless mistakes of mine and thereby made my ancient relics much more presentable and readable; and

Lucia Penick, my lovely granddaughter and accomplished artist by age 14, who created the beautiful charcoal drawing of a bear with pot on the back cover, in addition to other wonderful drawings to the text.

Printed in the USA
CPSIA information can be obtained
at www.ICGtesting.com
CBHW080935061024
15322CB00065B/968